HARRIMAN TRAILS

A Guide and History

THIRD EDITION

HARRIMAN TRAILS

A Guide and History

Willam J. Myles and Daniel Chazin

2010
NEW YORK-NEW JERSEY TRAIL CONFERENCE

Library of Congress Cataloging-in-Publication Data

Myles, William J., 1913-
  Harriman trails : a guide and history / by William J. Myles and Daniel Chazin. -- 3rd
ed.
      p. cm.
  Includes index.
  ISBN 978-1-880775-66-0
  1. Hiking--New York (State)--Harriman State Park--Guidebooks. 2. Hiking--New York
(State)--Bear Mountain State Park--Guidebooks. 3. Trails--New York (State)--Harriman
State Park--Guidebooks. 4. Trails--New York (State)--Bear Mountain State Park--
Guidebooks. 5. Harriman State Park (N.Y.)--Guidebooks. 6. Bear Mountain State Park
(N.Y.)--Guidebooks. I. Chazin, Daniel D. II. Title.
  GV199.42.N652H375 2010
  917.47'3--dc22
                                    2010047486

Published by
New York-New Jersey Trail Conference
156 Ramapo Valley Road
Mahwah, New Jersey 07430-1199

Book and cover design: Nora Porter
Cover photo: *Autumn Reflections, Silvermine Lake* by Nick Zungoli

TABLE OF CONTENTS

THE REVOLUTIONARY TRAILS

THE WOODS ROADS

THE MINES IN BEAR MOUNTAIN/HARRIMAN PARK

THE STORY OF BEAR MOUNTAIN

THE LAKES IN BEAR MOUNTAIN/HARRIMAN PARK

THE ROADS IN AND AROUND THE PARK

THE UNMARKED TRAILS

THE HISTORICAL TRAILS

THE STONE ROADS

DOODLETOWN AND IONA ISLAND 265

THE DUNDERBERG SPIRAL RAILWAY 285

Preface

For many years, the Trail Conference was very interested in publishing a guide to Harriman trails. Several manuscripts were submitted, but they did not measure up to the standard to which we aspired. Then, about 1990, I was told that Bill Myles had been writing a trail guide to Harriman and was interested in having the Trail Conference publish it. I was provided with a copy and thought very highly of it. We finally had the guide that we were looking for!

Serving as the editor of this work was an interesting experience. I will never forget the day that I received a phone call from Bill, asking whether he could come to see me. At the time, he was in his upper 70s, and I was usually the one to drive to meet with him in his West Orange home. I was surprised that he would be driving all the way to Teaneck just to meet with me.

Bill came into my home, sat down, and showed me a passage that I had edited. He asked, with some annoyance: "You see, I wrote 'go down.' Why did you change that to 'descend'?" I think that Bill taught me an important lesson about editing—a good editor finds a way to improve the style while retaining the words of the author. And the reader will notice quite a few places in the book where it still says "go down"!

Writing this book was truly a labor of love for Bill, who never learned how to type. He wrote out the entire book by hand—and then recopied it by hand when he made various changes. For a period of two years or so, I corresponded regularly with Bill. Needless to say, he did not have a computer, so all of our correspondence was via U.S. Mail. Bill carefully answered all of my questions, and the result was a more accurate book.

When the second edition of the book was published in 1999, Bill was still around to provide advice. But, unfortunately, he passed away in 2006, so I must accept sole responsibility for the changes and updates made for this edition.

It is a real tribute to Bill that the publication of the first edition of this book led to the Park authorizing the Trail Conference to mark and maintain a number of trails that were previously unmarked and/or unmaintained. Trails in this category include the Buck Trail, Dean Trail (now part of the Menomine Trail), Green Trail (now part of the Arden-Surebridge

Trail), Parker Cabin Hollow Trail and Stony Brook Trail.

The major structural change that has been incorporated into this edition is the reorganization of the unmarked trails chapters. In the first two editions, the unmarked trails were divided into two chapters ("The Unmarked Trails" and "More Unmarked Trails"), but the only distinction between the two chapters was that the trail descriptions for the "Unmarked Trails" were more detailed. For this edition, we have reorganized the unmarked trails into three categories: Woods Roads, Unmarked Trails and Historical Trails. The Woods Roads are wide routes that can, for the most part, be followed without undue difficulty by an average hiker equipped with map and compass. The Unmarked Trails are more difficult to follow, and even an experienced hiker will probably not be able to trace the entire route of the Historical Trails. I would like to thank John Timm for hiking all of the unmarked trails (including the Historical Trails) and carefully rewriting the descriptions for this edition, as well as assisting in the categorization of these trails.

The first two editions of this book included a number of historical photographs. Many of these photos were provided by the Palisades Interstate Park Commission (PIPC). Thanks to the assistance of Susan Smith and Peter Olivia of PIPC, I was able to visit their Iona Island archives, where I found nearly all of the photos credited to PIPC that appeared in the first two editions of the book (in some cases, I found better photos of the same subject). All these photos are included in this edition.

Unfortunately, however, we have not been able to find original copies of most of the other historical photos that appeared in the first two editions of the book. If copies of additional historical photos can be located, we would be glad to consider using them for future editions.

I would like to thank John Mack, Dave Sutter and Ike Siskind for their valuable comments. I would also like to thank Elizabeth "Perk" Stalter for her careful review of the Doodletown section of the book, as well as for her making available the photo of John Stalter that appears on page 176. Jeremy Apgar produced the beautiful map of Doodletown that appears on page 271. Sarah Savage served as project manager. Finally, I want to thank Nora Porter for her outstanding efforts in designing and laying out the book, and Chip Porter for his work on the photographs.

—Daniel Chazin
November 2010

Preface to the First Edition

Writing this book has been a labor of love. It was inspired by reading the first (1923) edition of the *New York Walk Book*, written by Raymond Torrey and Frank Place. They combined a great enthusiasm for trails in the New York metropolitan area with an impressive ability to describe what they saw. Another, lesser, inspiration was Bill Hoeferlin's *Harriman Park Trail Guide* (1944). This handy little booklet gave trail distances and a list of scenic attractions, from Agony Grind to Witness Oak.

Through the years, as I hiked in Harriman Park, I became interested in stories about the trails, and of places I saw along the way. At last, I gave in to my friends' suggestions and decided to write a book. This, now, is the result: a detailed description of 225 miles of 43 marked trails, as well as 103 miles of 56 unmarked trails. Wherever possible, I have related the history of the trail—who made it, and how it changed through the years.

The trail descriptions are not intended to make it unnecessary to use a map and compass. Anyone hiking the trails in Harriman Park—especially the unmarked trails—should take along a compass and a map of the Park, and know how to use them. Throughout the book, references are made to Maps #3 and #4 of the New York-New Jersey Trail Conference, which cover the Harriman-Bear Mountain Trails.

In the course of writing this book, the author has had the help of many people. It was always a pleasant experience to become acquainted with these people, who willingly shared their knowledge. Most helpful was Jack Focht, Director of the Trailside Museum. Week after week, Jack carried down from the Park headquarters attic the correspondence files of Major Welch from 1912 to 1939. Thanks are also due to former PIPC Executive Director Nash Castro, who helped in many ways and made available the minutes of Commission meetings from 1909 to 1990, and to Bob Binnewies, the present Executive Director. Tim Sullivan, Chief Ranger, shared his closet-full of maps, and answered numerous questions about Park history.

The story of Doodletown was reconstructed with the help of Denzel Livingston and his wife Grace. Recently, Grace has been a part-time switchboard operator at Park headquarters. Also helpful was ex-Doodletown resident Elizabeth Stalter.

At the other end of the Park, in Sloatsburg, the author became acquainted with Marvel Becraft Babcook, Fred Waldron and Clarence Conklin. They all were interested, and willingly shared their memories. Meyer Kukle helped in many ways, especially with interviewing knowledgeable old-timers.

Mention must be made of the author's friends who helped to scout many faint trails that deserve to be remembered: Erwin Conrad, Jay Kadampanattu and David Sutter—all of the Union County Hiking Club. In addition, several friends—including George Neffinger, Frank Oliver, Tim Sullivan and James Ransom—took the time to review the manuscript and made many helpful suggestions.

Thanks are also due to the volunteers who typed the manuscript into the computer: Carole Coe, Mimi Davisson, Francine Foley, Michael Golub, Mark Gorbics, Patricia E. Guempel, Howard J. Dash, Kenneth King, Linda R. Kline, William G. Koellner, Donald J. Little, Bob Miller, Bill Pruehsner and Robert Spellman.

Finally, I want to thank our editor, Dan Chazin, for correcting many inconsistencies in my text and for providing precise measurements of the trails.

—Bill Myles
November 1991

Preface to the Second Edition

Since the first edition of this book was published in 1992, a number of changes have taken place to the trails in Harriman/Bear Mountain Park. The Appalachian and Arden-Surebridge Trails near Island Pond have been rerouted, the White Bar Trail has been extended to the Johnsontown Road circle, the new Menomine Trail has been blazed to provide access for hikers from the Silvermine parking area, and the Diamond Mountain and Tower Trails have been combined into a single trail. All of these changes, and many others, have been incorporated into this second edition of my book. Additional historical information has also been added, and several mistakes have been corrected.

I would like to thank my editor, Dan Chazin, for his work in producing this second edition. Also, I want to thank Andy Smith, a ranger with the Park, for the information he provided regarding his family and the Pittsboro Trail, and Elizabeth "Perk" Stalter, author of a book on Doodletown, for much valuable information on the history of Doodletown. I am grateful to my friend Jay Winslow who produced, for this edition, beautiful black-and-white prints from original color slides. Finally, I want to thank Kay Bresee of the Appalachian Trail Conference who spent many hours making the necessary changes and corrections for this edition of the book.

—Bill Myles
July 1999

Anthony Wayne Trail

Length: 2.8 miles • Blazes: white

Miles

0.0   Leave PG Trail at Turkey Hill Lake.

0.3   Cross Woodbury town line.

0.5   Turn right on old woods road.

0.55 Turn left off road.

0.6   Cross brook and old Route 6.

0.7   Cross new Route 6.

1.05 Cross Seven Lakes Drive.

1.2   Cross 1779 Trail.

1.75 Cross Palisades Interstate Parkway.

1.9   Enter gate on left and go uphill on bike trail.

2.1   Go left on Beechy Bottom East Road.

2.45 Go left on older road.

2.5   Turn right, rejoining Beechy Bottom East Road.

2.55 Turn right, uphill.

2.8   End at Timp-Torne Trail.

The Anthony Wayne Trail (AW) starts on the Popolopen Gorge Trail (red square on white) at the southwest end of Turkey Hill Lake. The lake—a reservoir which feeds Queensboro Lake—was built in 1933-34 by a unit of the Civilian Conservation Corps. The trail follows a woods road that goes south through a valley, with Summer Hill on the left, toward Route 6 (Long Mountain Parkway).

The route that the Anthony Wayne Trail has followed so far was once known as the Curtis Hollow Trail. That was before Turkey Hill Lake was made, when the trail went north through Curtis Hollow (now the lake) and across West Point land to the Forest of Dean Road. The old trail can still be seen, faintly, on the hillside at the northwest end of the lake.

At 0.5 mile, AW turns right, leaving the road. Then, in 200 feet, it turns right onto an old woods road (which was Long Mountain Road until 1919 and made into a fire trail in 1946; it is no longer maintained by the Park). It follows the road for 75 feet, then turns left to cross a brook and a once-paved road (Route 6 from 1919 to 1967; widened in 1936). To the left is Brooks Place, a Park maintenance yard. Located on the site of a picnic/car camping area that was built about 1920, it is named for the Brooks family, who once lived nearby (see p. 308).

AW crosses present-day Route 6 at 0.7 mile. On the far side and down the bank to the left, it crosses a little stream and joins an old road (the 1946 fire trail). This is a region of wild grapes, wild roses and, unfortunately, piles of rubbish. The Anthony Wayne Trail then crosses Seven Lakes Drive at an abandoned comfort station. Behind the comfort station, a trail starts west to Cranberry Mine.

In another 0.15 mile, AW crosses the route that General Anthony Wayne is thought to have taken in 1779 (now designated as the 1779 Trail). At 1.75 miles, it crosses the Palisades Interstate Parkway on an overpass and reaches the Anthony Wayne Recreation Area. This great playground, which gave its name to the trail, was first opened in June 1955. The trail was marked in 1960 by the Tramp and Trail Club.

AW now goes left through a gate and up toward West Mountain on a gravel road, blazed with blue-on-white plastic markers as the Horn Hill Bike Trail. It then turns left onto Beechy Bottom East Road, which it follows for 0.35 mile (the large water pipe along this trail comes from the water plant at Queensboro Dam). Just beyond, the Fawn Trail (red F on white) begins to the right. At 2.55 miles, AW turns right, uphill, and climbs the foot of West Mountain, to end at the Timp-Torne Trail (blue), 2.8 miles from the start.

Appalachian Trail

Length: 18.9 miles (Bear Mountain Bridge to Route 17) · *Blazes: white*

Miles

0.0 Bear Mountain Bridge (toll booth at west end).

0.4 Tunnel under Route 9W.

0.75 Junction of paved paths behind Bear Mountain Inn.

0.85 Park service road leaves, left.

1.05 Cross wooden bridge.

1.95 Turn right onto Scenic Drive.

2.75 Summit of Bear Mountain; Perkins Tower.

3.45 Join abandoned section of Scenic Drive.

3.8 Cross Perkins Drive.

4.35 Cross Seven Lakes Drive.

4.6 Fawn Trail begins, right.

4.8 Turn right, off bridle path.

5.05 West Mountain; view east.

5.15 Timp-Torne Trail joins.

5.25 View west.

5.8 View west.

5.95 T-T leaves, left.

6.5 Cross Beechy Bottom East Road.

6.7 Cross Horn Hill Bike Trail.

6.8 Cross wooden bridge over Beechy Bottom Brook.

6.85 Turn sharp right; R-D Trail joins from left.

7.05 Cross Palisades Interstate Parkway.

7.2 Cross Beechy Bottom West Road.

7.35 Cross 1779 Trail.

7.85 Black Mountain; views to south and east.

8.25 View of Silvermine Lake.

8.35 Cross Silvermine Ski Road.

9.25 William Brien Memorial Shelter; Menomine Trail crosses.

10.05 R-D leaves, left; Bockey Swamp Trail crosses.

11.25 Cross Seven Lakes Drive.

12.15 Stevens Mountain.

12.7 Cross old road; R-D joins from left.

13.4 Cross Arden Valley Road.

13.45 Lake Tiorati Trail begins, left.

13.9 Fireplace, right.

14.5 Hurst Trail, left, to shelter.

14.6 R-D leaves, left.

15.1 Left on Surebridge Mine Road.

15.2 Leave road.

15.95 Long Path (aqua) crosses.

16.35 Island Pond Mountain.

16.6 Lemon Squeezer.

16.7 A-SB joins briefly.

16.85 Briefly join "Crooked Road."

17.05 View of Island Pond to left.

17.15 Cross stone spillway.

17.25 Cross gravel road leading to Island Pond.

17.3 Turn left onto Island Pond Road.

17.4 Turn right, uphill.

17.8 Summit of Green Pond Mountain.

18.35 Cross upper branch of Old Arden Road.

18.45 Turn right onto lower branch of Old Arden Road; A-SB begins, left.

18.5 Turn left onto Arden Valley Road.

18.7 Cross New York State Thruway.

18.9 Route 17.

From the tollgate at the west end of the Bear Mountain Bridge, the Appalachian Trail (AT) turns left through a gate into the area of the Trailside Museum and Zoo. (If the gate is locked—after about 4:30 p.m.—follow the blue-blazed trail to the right that rejoins the AT at the Route 9W underpass.) Along the path is a nine-foot-high statue of Walt Whitman. It was made by sculptor Jo Davidson for the 1939 World's Fair, and in 1940 it was given to the Palisades Interstate Park by W. Averell Harriman. Further along is a redoubt of old Fort Clinton, seized by the British on October 6, 1777. At 0.4 mile, the trail goes through an underpass beneath Route 9W, then follows a paved path around the south end of Hessian Lake. At 0.75 mile, it reaches a junction of paved paths behind the Bear Mountain

Inn. Here the Major Welch (red ring on white) and Suffern-Bear Mountain (S-BM) (yellow) Trails begin.

From the junction, the AT climbs up a park service road. At 0.85 mile, the park service road turns sharply left, while the AT continues ahead on a new route opened on National Trails Day in 2010. It climbs steeply on a series of over 700 hand-hewn granite steps, supported in places by stone crib walls. At 1.05 miles, the trail crosses a 28-foot-long wooden bridge and soon reaches a beautiful viewpoint over Iona Island and the Hudson River. After passing a seasonal waterfall, the AT continues to climb more gradually, reaching an area known as the "pine flats" at 1.85 miles. Here, the trail turns right, rejoining the previous AT route, and climbs to the Scenic Drive. At 1.95 miles, the AT turns right and follows the Scenic Drive for 0.3 mile, with more views from the road.

The AT turns left at 2.25 miles, leaving the Scenic Drive, and continues uphill, crossing the Scenic Drive twice more before reaching the 1,305-foot summit of Bear Mountain at 2.75 miles. The stone tower on the summit is a memorial to George W. Perkins, Sr., first president of the Palisades Interstate Park Commission (from 1900 to 1920). Here also, fixed on a stone just below the summit, is a plaque in honor of Joseph Bartha, Trails Committee Chairman of the NY-NJ Trail Conference from 1940 to 1955. The Major Welch Trail ends at the Perkins Tower. The AT heads west from the summit and, at 2.95 miles, it turns left and reaches a series of panoramic viewpoints to the west and south.

Stone steps on new AT route up Bear Mountain

7

After descending a stone staircase between large boulders at 3.45 miles, the AT continues along the abandoned section of the Scenic Drive (once called the Bear Mountain Bypass) to cross the Perkins Drive. It descends to cross the Seven Lakes Drive at 4.35 miles and briefly joins old Doodletown Road, which also carries the 1777W Trail. At 4.6 miles, the Fawn Trail (red F on white) departs right, to go over a low shoulder of West Mountain. The AT soon starts steeply up the mountain and reaches a viewpoint to the east at 5.05 miles. In another 500 feet, the Timp-Torne Trail (T-T) (blue) joins from the right. The joint trail passes another viewpoint to the east, then crosses to the western side of the ridge, with a number of striking views. The Anthony Wayne Recreation Area is in the valley to the west. At 5.95 miles, T-T departs to the left, while the AT begins its descent.

The first section of the Appalachian Trail was marked in 1922 through Harriman Park from the Elk Pen at Arden to Tiorati Circle. The entire trail from Arden to the Bear Mountain Bridge was officially opened on Sunday, October 7, 1923. The Bridge itself was opened on Thanksgiving Day, November 27, 1924. The new Appalachian Trail came across it, and for 0.5 mile followed the old Queensboro Trail high above Popolopen Creek. It then started steeply up Bear Mountain. This part of the trail was cut off in 1927 by the Popolopen Drive, and a new route was marked to the left of the road. The steep way up the north side of Bear Mountain was used as the route of the AT until 1931. Then, at the request of Major Welch, the AT was marked from the south end of Hessian Lake up past the ski chute to the firetower on the mountaintop. The firetower was replaced in 1934 by the Perkins Memorial Tower, and the older tower was rebuilt on Diamond Mountain in 1935. The old AT route up Bear Mountain was still maintained as an alternate approach to the AT, and it later became the Major Welch Trail. In 1939, the AT blazes were changed from yellow to white, to match the color used south of the Delaware River (the AT in Connecticut was blue until 1949).

During the following years, the route up Bear Mountain was moved several times to avoid eroded sections. In 1976, the route down the west side was changed, to eliminate a dangerous sandy slope. It was rerouted down Perkins Drive to the point where the earlier trail had crossed. That older route, down to Seven Lakes Drive and up to West Mountain, had been joint with the Timp-Torne Trail, first blazed in 1921. T-T was rerouted away from Bear Mountain in 1960. In 1988-89, the trail from the ski jump up the east side of Bear Mountain was rerouted once more to avoid an eroded route and add new views. The relocated trail followed a paved road (the Scenic Drive) for 0.3 mile.

By 2000, the AT route up the east face of Bear Mountain had become eroded and unattractive. Especially in view of the heavy use of this section of the AT by day visitors to the Bear Mountain Inn, the Trail Conference decided that it should be relocated to an entirely new route. The most attractive route required traversing an area of jumbled boulders to the northwest of the existing AT. To build a new trail through this area, the Trail Conference recruited professional trail builders to lead the construction effort and train hundreds of volunteers.

Construction of the new route up the east face of Bear Mountain began in 2006 and was completed in the spring of 2010. By the time this relocation was completed and opened on National Trails Day in 2010, more than 700 individuals had volunteered over 25,000 hours of their time to construct this section of the AT. Construction of the stone steps and crib walls required the same kind of masonry skills that were utilized by the Civilian Conservation Corps in the 1930s to build roads, walls and buildings in Harriman-Bear Mountain State Parks. Funding for the project was provided by the Trail Conference, the National Park Service, the Appalachian Trail Conservancy, the New York State Office of Parks, Recreation and Historic Preservation, and the Palisades Interstate Park Commission.

The new route of the AT on the west face of Bear Mountain, from the summit to Perkins Drive, was opened in September 2010. This relocation, which incorporates a short section of the former route of the Major Welch Trail, eliminated a half-mile roadwalk along a section of the Perkins Drive that is open to traffic. It is anticipated that a mile-long loop of the AT north of the summit, of which the eastern half will be handicapped-accessible, will be completed by December 2010, and that the remainder of the Bear Mountain Trails Project, including a new AT route on the east face of the mountain from the Scenic Drive to the summit, will be completed in 2012.

After going down off West Mountain, the AT at 6.5 miles reaches Beechy Bottom East Road, an old woods road that was improved in 1933 by the Civilian Conservation Corps. Until 1997, the AT turned left and followed the grassy Beechy Bottom East Road for 0.1 mile, but now it crosses the road and parallels it on a footpath. It then drops down to cross the Horn Hill Bike Trail and, at 6.8 miles, it crosses Beechy Bottom Brook on a wooden bridge. The AT then goes up and turns sharply right as the Ramapo-Dunderberg Trail (R-D) (red dot on white) joins from the left. At

7.05 miles, the joint trail goes across the Palisades Interstate Parkway. Immediately afterward, a faint old road, the old Beechy Bottom West Road, is crossed. Soon the 1779 Trail crosses, and AT/R-D goes up and over a low ridge. It then begins a steep climb to the 1,200-foot summit of Black Mountain, from which there are good views to the south and east. The line between Orange and Rockland Counties crosses the trail here and runs northeast to Bear Mountain and the bridge. AT/R-D then descends and, after passing a panoramic viewpoint over Silvermine Lake, it crosses a wide gravel path, the Silvermine Road, at 8.35 miles. This fire road was built in 1934 by the Temporary Emergency Relief Administration. AT/R-D then climbs gently to the level top of Letterrock Mountain, and at 9.25 miles reaches the William Brien Memorial Shelter. In front of the shelter, a blue-blazed side trail goes to a spring-fed well nearby, and the Menomine Trail (yellow) crosses. To the right, the Menomine Trail goes down to the Silvermine parking area on Seven Lakes Drive in 1.35 miles; to the left, it leads in 0.85 mile to the Red Cross Trail.

This shelter is named after William Brien, the first president of the New York Ramblers. In 1954, he bequeathed $4,000 for a shelter, which was built in 1957 at Island Pond. Because of vandalism, that shelter was demolished in 1973 and the name transferred to the former Letterrock Shelter, which was built in 1933 (*N.Y. Post*, 6/23/33).

At 10.05 miles, AT/R-D comes down to the foot of Goshen Mountain, where the unmarked Bockey Swamp Trail crosses. To the right, the Bockey Swamp Trail follows the little brook down towards Silvermine Lake. The R-D departs to the left and begins to climb Goshen Mountain, while the AT goes right on a woods road. AT soon turns right, leaving this road. It goes down to another woods road, which it follows for a short distance, reaching the Seven Lakes Drive at 11.25 miles. The trail crosses the Drive, then a region with two brooks, and goes up Stevens Mountain. It then turns south, following an old woods road, known as the Youmans Trail. After leaving this road, the AT crosses a descending dirt road (the original Arden Valley Road). Here, the R-D comes in from the left and rejoins the AT. Then, at 13.4 miles, the AT/R-D crosses the present-day paved Arden Valley Road on Fingerboard Mountain. A short distance beyond, the Lake Tiorati Trail (blue) begins to the left. It leads downhill 0.3 mile to Tiorati Circle, where there is a convenient parking area and restroom facilities.

DANIEL CHAZIN

Silvermine Lake from viewpoint on the AT

The original route of the AT was over Goshen Mountain, joint with R-D. It came down west to cross an old woods road, where it parted from R-D, and continued over two knolls to the Seven Lakes Drive, 100 yards north of Tiorati Circle. It then climbed up to the Fingerboard Fire Tower (built 1922) and turned south to the R-D (*N.Y. Post*, 1/4/24). In November 1931, the AT was di- verted through a tent camp on the knoll northeast of Tiorati Circle, and then went jointly with R-D up Arden Valley Road (*N.Y. Post*, 11/13/31). In 1934, the AT was made to coincide with R-D from Goshen Mountain to Tiorati Brook Road, which it followed for 0.35 mile to Tiorati Circle. The present route up Stevens Mountain was devised in 1978 by Chief Ranger Tim Sullivan.

Proceeding now along the ridge of Fingerboard Mountain, AT/R-D passes a telephone line and two water tanks. The concrete water tank to the left was built in 1927 to supply water to the facilities at Lake Tiorati and the camps at Lake Cohasset. It was replaced in 2006 by the green circular tank to the right. At 13.9 miles, a half-mile from Arden Valley Road, the trail comes to a stone fireplace. Here was the beginning of the Fingerboard-Storm King Trail (FB-SK), which was blazed north to Storm King Mountain in 1922 by J. Ashton Allis and Raymond H. Torrey.

At 14.5 miles, the blue Hurst Trail begins to the left. It passes the Fingerboard Shelter (built 1928) and goes down to the Seven Lakes Drive.

Going through the Lemon Squeezer

In another 500 feet, R-D continues straight ahead, while the AT turns right and begins to descend. After 0.5 mile, the AT reaches Surebridge Mine Road, where it turns sharp left, passing the shafts of the Greenwood Mine to the left of the trail. During the Civil War, the ore from this mine was brought to the Greenwood Furnace at Arden. At 15.2 miles, the AT crosses Surebridge Brook and climbs the 1,240-foot Surebridge Mountain. It then goes down to cross a brook. At 15.95 miles, the Long Path (aqua) crosses. The AT continues up the northeast side of 1,303-foot Island Pond Mountain. At the summit, the remains of Edward Harriman's summer shelter are visible. When the new AT was described by Raymond Torrey in 1924 (*N.Y. Post*, 1/4/24), he mentioned a wooden fire tower on the summit of Island Pond Mountain.

Now the AT goes downhill to the Lemon Squeezer, a narrow passage formed when a great piece of rock broke off the side of the cliff. A blue-blazed side trail bypasses the steepest part of the descent.

Coming out of the crevice, at 16.7 miles, the AT briefly joins the Arden-Surebridge Trail, which comes in from the left, and soon departs to the left. After going over a little rise, the AT turns right, at 16.85 miles, onto the Crooked Road, an old miners' road which once marked the boundary of Harriman Park. The AT passes the north end of Island Pond, then turns left and ascends a hill, which affords a view of Island Pond to the south. Now descending, the trail passes, to the left, the rusted remains of a rotary gravel classifier, and then crosses a stone spillway, which carries water from the pond to Echo Lake in the Harriman estate (see pp. 299-300). After crossing a gravel road (built in 1963) that leads to Island Pond, the AT, at 17.3 miles, turns left onto Island Pond Road. In another 450 feet, the trail leaves the road to the right and begins its climb of Green Pond Mountain, reaching the summit at 17.8 miles.

At 18.35 miles, the AT crosses the upper branch of the Old Arden Road (built in 1894, and also known as "Harriman's level road"), then turns right on the lower branch of the road (the Arden-Surebridge Trail starts here). The AT bears left and joins paved Arden Valley Road at 18.5 miles, and soon passes the entrance to the hikers' parking area known as the Elk Pen. The AT now crosses a bridge over the New York Thruway, the Ramapo River and the Metro-North/Norfolk Southern Railway (formerly Conrail; previously the Erie Railroad), arriving at Route 17 at 18.9 miles. Agony Grind is just ahead.

The AT originally followed the northern shore of Island Pond, went over Green Pond Mountain and continued down to the Elk Pen. This pretty route gave great views to the south across Island Pond. However, after a fishermen's access road was built from Arden Valley Road to the lake in 1963, the area at the north end of the lake became littered and unsightly. To avoid that messy place, the trail was rerouted in 1980 around the southern end of the lake. However, conditions at the northern end of the lake subsequently improved, and the reroute around the southern end, which lengthened the trail and eliminated all views of the lake, was unpopular with hikers. In 1993, the original route along the northern end of the lake was restored (except that the AT now runs a short distance inland, rather than along the shore of the lake). Another relocation, which restored the original route over Green Pond Mountain, was completed in 1994.

Until 1947, Island Pond Mountain was called Echo Mountain. It has two 1,300-foot summits, connected across a half-mile by a saddle about 200 feet lower. There was confusion about names in this region until the Trail Conference decided that the northern summit, overlooking Echo Lake, was Echo Mountain. The southern summit was named Island Pond Mountain, and the ridge west of Island Pond became Green Pond Mountain (Trail Conference Minutes, 2/5/47).

The first section of the Appalachian Trail was blazed in 1922 from Route 17 over Green Pond Mountain, across the north end of Island Pond to the Crooked Road, and through

PALISADES INTERSTATE PARK COMMISSION

Arden Valley Road ford at the Ramapo River

the Lemon Squeezer. There it joined the A-SB up to the old firetower. The entire trail through the Park, from Arden to Bear Mountain, was officially opened on Sunday, October 7, 1923.

In those days, there were about 60 elk in a great enclosure between Southfields and Arden, known as the Elk Range. They had been brought from Yellowstone Park in December 1919. They did not thrive, and their number gradually decreased until 1942, when the remainder of the herd was sold to a dealer from Hoosick Falls (Commission Minutes, 12/10/42, pp. 355-57).

How to cross the Ramapo River at Arden was a problem for the trail blazers. Arden Valley Road was a 16-foot-wide gravel road that came down to the old iron furnace at Arden, nearly a mile north of the present AT crossing. Prior to 1929, hikers on the AT had to cross the Ramapo

River at the Arden railroad station and take the Old Arden Road to the Elk Pen—a detour of 1.25 miles. In 1929, a footbridge was built over the Ramapo River at the Elk Range by Raymond Adolph, Park Forester, and in 1934, the Park opened a new paved Arden Valley Road from the Elk Range to Lake Cohasset. From Route 17, the new road went 0.2 mile north down to the river level, where it went under the railroad tracks through an underpass. The Ramapo River went through the underpass, too, and met Arden Brook. The river bottom there was paved with concrete so that cars could ford the river. Stepping stones were provided for walkers. Naturally, hikers on the AT cut up over the bank to cross Route 17. The present bridge, which carries Arden Valley Road over the Thruway, the railroad and the river, was built in 1954.

Arden-Surebridge Trail

Length: 6.25 miles • Blazes: red triangle on white

Miles

0.0	Begin where dirt road from Elk Pen joins Arden Road.
0.03	AT leaves to left.
0.35	Turn left, leaving Arden Road.
0.5	Cross stream.
0.8	Turn left at gully and ascend steeply.
0.9	Turn right at top of steep climb.
1.0	Viewpoint to northwest.
1.25	Turn right onto Island Pond Road.
1.3	Cross outlet of Island Pond.
1.45	Bear right; road ahead leads to Island Pond.
1.5	Turn left, leaving Island Pond Road.
1.85	Turn left and descend.
3.05	Turn left onto Crooked Road.
3.2	Cross stream.
3.25	Turn right, leaving Crooked Road.
3.45	Briefly join AT at base of Lemon Squeezer.
3.7	LP joins from left; White Bar Trail starts to right.
3.75	Bottle Cap Trail starts; turn right.
4.0	Lichen Trail starts to right.
4.45	Turn right on Surebridge Mine Road.
4.55	"Times Square": R-D crosses; LP departs to right.
5.0	Cross brook; Dunning Trail starts to right.
5.1	Go right, leaving fire road.
6.0	Red Cross Trail starts to left.
6.25	Trail ends at Lake Skannatati.

To reach the start of the Arden-Surebridge Trail (A-SB), take Arden Valley Road east for 0.3 mile from Route 17, and park in the Elk Pen parking area. You will see a dirt road leading east across the meadow; follow this road for 0.1 mile until you reach the Arden Road (also known as

"Harriman's level road") at the other side of the meadow. Here, a triple blaze on a tree marks the start of the A-SB Trail. Turn right and follow the Arden Road southward. The Appalachian Trail (AT) leaves to the left in 150 feet, but A-SB continues ahead on the road. At 0.35 mile, A-SB turns left, leaving the road, and begins to climb gradually up Green Pond Mountain. After descending a little and crossing a gully at 0.75 mile, the trail turns left and climbs steeply up the mountain, following the route of the former Green Trail. At 0.9 mile, near the top, it turns right and follows a ledge, then bears left and climbs to reach a viewpoint to the northwest from a rock to the left of the trail. After a relatively level stretch, A-SB turns right at 1.25 miles onto Island Pond Road.

A-SB crosses the outlet of the pond and then bears right at a road junction. (The road straight ahead leads to an abandoned ranger cabin at the south end of Island Pond.) Shortly after this junction, A-SB turns left at 1.5 miles, leaving the road, and goes around the south and east sides of Island Pond, passing through gullies and over knobs. After going down a long hill, the trail turns left, at 3.05 miles, onto the "Crooked Road," an old miners' road which once marked the boundary of Harriman State Park. A-SB crosses a stream and soon turns right, leaving the road, and climbs to the base of the Lemon Squeezer, where it briefly joins the AT.

A-SB does not go up through the Lemon Squeezer, but instead turns right, goes south along a rocky hillside, and soon joins a woods road. At 3.7 miles, at a large boulder, the Long Path (aqua) joins from the left. Immediately afterward, the White Bar Trail starts to the right, while the joint A-SB/LP turns left, passes the end of a swamp, and starts to climb. In another 300 feet, the A-SB/LP turns right, while the Bottle Cap Trail (see pp. 25-26) continues straight ahead.

A-SB/LP now begins to climb more steeply. At 4.0 miles, after A-SB/LP passes a swamp on the left, the Lichen Trail (blue "L" on white) starts to the right. After passing through laurels and rhododendrons, the A-SB/LP descends a ledge, climbs briefly, goes down through a hemlock grove, and emerges on the Surebridge Mine Road. The section of A-SB from the Bottle Cap Trail up to the hemlock grove was named the "Lost Road" in 1921 by J. Ashton Allis (*N.Y. Post*, 11/11/21).

A-SB/LP turns right (east) on the Surebridge Mine Road and in about 500 feet reaches a junction known as "Times Square," marked by a stone fireplace beside a large boulder. Here, the Ramapo-Dunderberg Trail (red

DANIEL CHAZIN

Lakes Skannatati and Kanawauke from the A-SB Trail

dot on white) crosses, and in another 75 feet the Long Path departs to the right. A-SB continues along the road and begins to descend. At 5.0 miles, it reaches a brook where the Dunning Trail (yellow) starts to the right. On the other side of the brook, there is a large mine opening to the left of the trail. After passing three smaller mine openings, A-SB bears right, leaving the wide path, and drops down a bank. It soon passes several stone foundations to the left. After going by the edge of Pine Swamp, the trail goes up Pine Swamp Mountain. There are limited views from the summit, but on the way down A-SB passes an excellent viewpoint over Lakes Skannatati and Kanawauke. At 6.0 miles, the Red Cross Trail begins to the left. A-SB then descends steeply and, at 6.25 miles, ends at the parking area for Lake Skannatati. Here the Long Path comes in from the right, crosses Seven Lakes Drive and continues over a shoulder of Rockhouse Mountain.

The Arden-Surebridge Trail was first blazed during the summer of 1921 by J. Ashton Allis. He was a leader of the Fresh Air Club and the AMC and was a founder of the new Palisades Park Trail Conference. In preparation for his AMC hike the following weekend, he marked the route as a short-cut from Arden station to the R-D Trail on Hogencamp Mountain. It is shown as the "Allis Short Trail" on a map in the *N.Y. Post* (10/14/21). By December 1922, it had been extended by members of the Green Mountain Club from the R-D Trail to Camp Thendara on Lake

Tiorati, and was marked with white wooden arrows and red metal triangles inscribed "A-SB."

From the Erie Station at Arden (located about 0.7 mile north of the present-day Arden Valley Road), the trail crossed Arden Brook at the Harriman Dairy bottling house and went up the wooden steps beside the old Greenwood Furnace. From the upper terrace, it followed the Echo Lake Road, which proceeded to the east on the south side of Arden Brook. At a fork, the trail turned right and went through the chicken farm and pastures. Then, at another fork, it turned left onto an old grass-grown road that led to the west side of Island Pond. After leaving the grassy road, A-SB went over a rise, crossed the outlet brook from Island Pond, and climbed to the top of Island Pond Mountain (then known as Echo Mountain).

It was there, on Echo Mountain, that the new Appalachian Trail, built in 1922, met the A-SB which J. Ashton Allis had built in 1921. Both trails followed the same route down through the Lemon Squeezer, which had been discovered and named by Allis. From the Lemon Squeezer to "Times Square," A-SB followed the same route that it still does today.

From "Times Square" to Lake Tiorati the trail was just a footpath in 1922. It was widened by the Park in 1936 as a fire road, from the Hurst Trail up to Pine Swamp Mine (Dunning Trail). In 1966, it was widened further, up to the Surebridge Mine Road (which also was widened to

Lake Cohasset).

In 1924, because of a hunting incident, Roland Harriman closed the Echo Lake Road to hikers. They then used the Harriman Level Road south to the Elk Range. This route, too, was closed in 1953 when the new Thruway sliced into the hillside. After that, hikers went south from the Arden station along the west side of the Erie tracks, joining the original Arden Valley Road where it came down to the river level (see p. 14). They followed that old road up to the new entrance road and the bridge that was built across the Thruway in 1954. That route, too, was abandoned after rail service to Arden ceased about 1970.

In June 1978, A-SB was rerouted south over Pine Swamp Mountain. This change was made in order to divert the trail away from the entrance to Camp Thendara on the Seven Lakes Drive, near Lake Tiorati, where there had been parking problems and complaints of vandalism.

In the spring of 1995, the western end of A-SB was relocated. This reroute eliminated the roadwalk on Arden Valley Road and the steep climb up Island Pond Mountain, which was often icy in the winter. From its start near the Elk Pen, A-SB now follows a route around the southern end of Island Pond which was used by the AT from 1980 to 1993. However, A-SB uses the route of the old Green Trail to climb Green Pond Mountain, shortening the old AT route by nearly half a mile.

Beech Trail

Length: 3.85 miles • Blazes: blue

Miles

0.0   Start on LP near St. John's Church.

0.6   Cross Route 106.

0.75 Town line.

1.2   Rockhouse Mountain Trail, left.

1.6   Cemetery.

2.05 Hasenclever Fire Road.

2.8   Tiorati Brook Road.

2.95 Cross Tiorati Brook and go left from road.

3.85 End at Red Cross Trail.

The Beech Trail begins at its intersection with the Long Path, 0.55 mile north of Lake Welch Drive. To reach this point, park at St. John's Church and proceed along St. John's Road a short distance to Lake Welch Drive. Follow the aqua blazes of the Long Path to the north, proceeding up Polebrook Mountain through an area of old farms and cellar holes. After descending from an old farm field and crossing a small swampy area, you will find the blue blazes of the Beech Trail, which begins on the right. The trail goes northeast on a woods road (the old Green Swamp Trail). Near the start of this woods road is the foundation of a cabin, the home of Martin and Maybelle Youmans until 1928. The Beech Trail passes Green Swamp on the right and impressive boulders and cliffs on the left. At 0.6 mile, it crosses Route 106 and continues northeast on another woods road (the old Rockhouse Mountain Trail). The town line between Haverstraw (to the south) and Stony Point (to the north) is crossed at 0.75 mile.

At 1.2 miles, the Rockhouse Mountain Trail goes off to the left (the junction is marked by a cairn), while the Beech Trail continues straight ahead. It reaches an old cemetery at 1.6 miles. (You will note Youmans' grave on one side of a stone wall, and several Jones graves on the other side.) A bit further along, the trail passes an old farm where there are remains of stone foundations and a root cellar. (From the farm, a rather vague road goes down easterly to a swampy area. It crosses a brook and climbs up to the Hasenclever Road which once led to the village of Sandyfield, now covered by Lake Welch.)

Continuing to the northeast, at 2.05 miles the Beech Trail crosses the Hasenclever Road. It follows the shoulder of Nat House Mountain, and then descends along a pretty brook, a tributary of Tiorati Brook, passing a fine cascade at 2.5 miles which the trail blazers named "Arthur's Falls." Tiorati Brook Road is reached at 2.8 miles. Here, to the left, there is a large filled area where parking is permitted (in winter, Tiorati Brook Road is closed, so this parking lot cannot be used). The trail turns right onto Tiorati Brook Road and crosses a bridge over a tributary of Tiorati Brook. It re-enters the woods and follows the brook for 0.15 mile, then rejoins the road and crosses a bridge over Tiorati Brook. Immediately after crossing the brook, the Beech Trail turns left and heads up a flank of Flaggy Meadow Mountain through open woods, following an old woods road. It ends at the Red Cross Trail, 3.85 miles from the beginning. From this point, Tiorati Brook Road is 0.75 mile to the left on the Red Cross Trail.

Cemetery on the Beech Trail

This is one of the newer trails, blazed in 1972 after discussion by the Trail Conference (Trail Conference Minutes, 10/4/72). The work was done by members of Westchester Trails Association, who named the trail in honor of Art Beach. At that time, Art Beach was the representative of the Trail Conference to the Park administration. Due to a Park policy against naming trails for living persons, the name was spelled Beech (the 1984 Park map spells it Beach). It was during the construction of this trail that the device of using offset double blazes to show the direction in which the trail turns was invented.

The little cemetery on the trail has caused much speculation. Fifty acres on the south side of the stone wall were the farm of John Rose, which was acquired by the Park through condemnation in 1930. The grave is that of Timothy Youmans, who died on April 7, 1865 while serving in Company K of the 56th New York regiment. (The Civil War ended on April 9, 1865.) Samson Youmans, who served in that same Company, died in 1897 and was buried in St. John's Cemetery.

Twenty acres on the other side of the stone wall, including the farm with the root cellar, were owned until July 11, 1928 by Isaiah Charleston. He bought the farm in 1902 from William and Rebecca Jones. The graves are those of John R. Jones (1817-1896); his wife, Highlyann Babcock (1821-1886); and their little son Hiram Jones (1856-1859). Also buried there is John Strickland, who married Ruth Youmans (she died in 1897).

On the other side of the Cedar Ponds Road (Hasenclever Road), about where Lake Welch Drive is now, was the 25-acre farm of John R. Jones, Jr. His father's grave is the one on our trail.

Blue Disc Trail

Length: 2.8 miles · Blazes: blue dot on white

Miles

0.0	Johnsontown Road Circle.
0.15	Left, onto woods road.
0.45	Kakiat Trail joins briefly.
0.75	Top of "Almost Perpendicular."
1.35	Gas line crosses.
1.5	Cross woods road and stream.
1.65	Elbow Brush.
2.0	T-MI Trail crosses.
2.05	Claudius Smith Rock.
2.8	End at Tri-Trail Corner.

The Blue Disc Trail formerly started from Seven Lakes Drive in Sloatsburg (at the second entrance to Johnsontown Road), but it now begins just west of the circle at the end of Johnsontown Road, where parking is available.

From 100 feet west of the bridge over the stream just west of the circle, the trail follows a paved road (the route of a gas pipeline) which goes up to a station of the Columbia Gas Transmission Co. This pipeline, which later again crosses our trail, was built in 1949 and widened in 2007. It goes across the Park in a southeast direction, from north of Tuxedo to Wesley Hills, and transports gas from Pittsburgh to Piermont, N.Y.

At the gas pipeline station, the Blue Disc Trail turns left and soon joins a woods road (until 1991, the blazes followed the gas pipeline road for another 0.15 mile to join the Kakiat Trail). After 0.3 mile on the woods road, the Kakiat Trail (white) joins briefly, and Blue Disc starts a steep climb to the top of "Almost Perpendicular," a name given to the cliff in the early years by the Fresh Air Club (*N.Y. Post*, 4/21/36). At first, the trail goes up an eroded road. Leaving that about halfway up the cliff, the trail continues to the top, where there is a good view to the south. After another 0.6 mile, the trail crosses the gas pipeline. Here, the faint Fox Trail goes off to the right and descends to Spring Brook in the valley below.

In another 0.15 mile, Blue Disc crosses a woods road and a stream and begins to run along the foot of a ledge. A bit further, below the ledge, the trail is blazed through a crevice known as "Elbow Brush." The trail begins to parallel a stream and then runs along a swamp. At 2.0 miles, Blue Disc crosses the Tuxedo-Mt. Ivy Trail (T-MI) and climbs to the top of Claudius Smith Rock (see p. 136). The Blue Disc Trail continues north. It descends over slabs of bare rock, then climbs Big Pine Hill, with a 360° view. Blue Disc now descends steadily, for much of the way over bare, sloping rocks that are often slippery in winter. The White Cross Trail (which begins from the T-MI Trail, 250 feet to the right of the Blue Disc crossing, and can be used as an alternate route) is less slippery. At the foot of the hill, Blue Disc crosses a natural rock dam (that retains the water in Black Ash Swamp) and ends at Tri-Trail Corner, 2.8 miles from the Johnsontown Road Circle, where it meets the Ramapo-Dunderberg (red dot on white) and Victory (blue V on white) Trails.

In the '20s and early '30s, the Tuxedo Trail went from Tuxedo to the Reeves Farm on Johnsontown Road, approximately following the route of the present-day Kakiat/Blue Disc trails. Hikers liked to climb the cliff which had been named "Almost Perpendicular." From the cliff top, a trail marked with green cairns went to Claudius Smith Rock. In 1931, the New York Mountain Club scheduled a hike on the Green Cairn Trail (*N.Y.*

DANIEL CHAZIN

View from the top of Claudius Smith Rock

Post, 1/9/31). Then, in the spring of 1932, Paul H. Schubert of Ridgewood (Queens) blazed a trail (marked with red discs with white centers) from Sloatsburg to the R-D Trail at the foot of Black Ash Mountain, using the Green Cairn Trail for part of the route.

Schubert had come from Germany in 1891 and worked as a printer for the *New York Staats-Zeitung*. A member of the Paterson Ramblers, the Woodland Trail Walkers, the Wanderbirds, and the NY/NJ Trail Conference, he also blazed the Trail of the Raccoon Hills. He died on October 8, 1961 at the age of 84 (*Walking News*, Dec. 1961).

From Sloatsburg, Schubert's Red Disc Trail went directly up Sleater Hill and continued along the ridge on the property of Miss Julia Siedler of Montclair, N.J. to Almost Perpendicular. That cliff and the land to the north, up to Black Ash Mountain, were the property of Tuxedo Park Association. At various times, both Miss Siedler and the Association closed their lands to ensure that these trails did not become public thoroughfares.

The Red Disc Trail went up the cliff with the help of a leaning dead tree on which Schubert had nailed slats as a ladder. A rope at the top helped climbers up the last stretch, where a sign read "Danger." By March 1938, the tree had fallen down, so he relocated the approach about 0.2 mile to the west, using a steep road toward Daters Mine. Just before the mine, the trail reached a level region and then turned right onto an old road that is part of the present route (which was chosen in 1970). After 1938, the blaze on this trail was changed to a half-and-half red/white disc, and the C.C.N.Y. Hiking Club took over the trail. In 1940, Miss Siedler closed the portion of the trail which was on her property, so it was rerouted to come up from Johnsontown Road. Then, in October 1943, the blazes were replaced by blue metal discs supplied by Alexander Jessup.

North of Almost Perpendicular, the trail goes over Pound Mountain. About 0.15 mile from the cliff, a side trail went left to a large rock, called Bonora's Rock. In 1928, John Bonora of 99 Varet Street, Brooklyn, a young member of the Paterson Ramblers Club, built a cabin against this rock. It had windows, a fireplace, double deck bunks, and a spring nearby. Known as Rockneath, it was a favored stopping place for those who knew the way.

Bottle Cap Trail

Length: 1.9 miles · Blazes: bottle caps

Miles

0.0	Start from A-SB/LP.
0.05	Double caps; go up right.
0.4	Reach crest of ridge.
0.55	Descend steeply.
0.7	Cross brook and Surebridge Mine Road.
0.95	Cross R-D Trail.
1.25	Go up left from stream.
1.3	Go along hill, overlooking swamp.
1.5	Cross brook and ascend.
1.75	Top of hill.
1.9	End at fire road (old A-SB).

The Bottle Cap Trail, although marked, is not a Conference trail. Its origin has not been recorded, but it seems likely that the trail was made back in the 1930s when members of the Green Mountain Club wanted an alternate route from the railroad station at Arden. The trail was marked with bottle caps nailed to the trees. The caps were renewed about 1945 by GMC members, and again in 1985 by the "Wednesday Hikers" led by Frank Haines. The latter group also marked the trail with many cairns.

The trail starts at a junction with the Arden-Surebridge Trail/Long Path (A-SB/LP) near the foot of Surebridge Mountain, 300 feet east of the end of the White Bar Trail. Here, A-SB/LP turns right, while the Bottle Cap Trail proceeds uphill along a broad path made by bulldozers during the 1988 fire season. In 350 feet, it turns right, leaving the bulldozer path, and continues up Surebridge Mountain.

After reaching the ridge of Surebridge Mountain at 0.4 mile, the Bottle Cap Trail continues north, along the ridge, for 0.15 mile. It then curves to the right and drops down several steep places. At 0.7 mile, it joins a bulldozer track which comes in from the left, crosses the brook which drains Surebridge Swamp, and crosses the Surebridge Mine Road. The trail then continues on an old mine road (the Surebridge Mine is in the trees to the right). It goes up a hill and, at 0.95 mile, crosses the Ramapo-Dunderberg Trail.

From here, the Bottle Cap Trail descends a gully, crosses a little brook, and follows along the north side of the brook for about 0.15 mile. It then veers left, away from the brook, and traverses the hillside overlooking a large swamp. It descends to another stream (the inlet of the swamp), which it soon crosses, and then proceeds uphill. At 1.75 miles, it reaches the top of a hill and descends to end at a fire road (the former route of the A-SB Trail) at 1.9 miles. From here, the hiker should turn left on the fire road and, in 60 feet, bear right on an old road which leads downhill for 400 feet to Seven Lakes Drive, opposite the entrance to Camp Thendara.

Breakneck Mountain Trail

Length: 1.5 miles · Blazes: white

Miles

0.0 Start on T-MI Trail.

0.15 West Pointing Rock.

0.8 Trail comes out on open rocks.

1.2 Turn left and descend.

1.45 Unmarked trail, left, leads down to Breakneck Pond.

1.5 End at S-BM Trail.

The Breakneck Mountain Trail starts from the Tuxedo-Mt. Ivy Trail (red dash on white), about 400 feet north of Pine Meadow Road East. It proceeds to the northeast along the ridge of Breakneck Mountain, passing (at 0.15 mile) "West Pointing Rock," a 10x14-foot boulder, with a sharp projection on its west side. At 0.8 mile, the trail comes out on open rocks, with a limited seasonal view over Breakneck Pond. It turns right and descends, then continues in a northeast direction. At 1.0 mile, the trail again crosses open rocks, and at 1.2 miles, it turns left and goes down. It proceeds through a hollow and then turns left and ascends. An unmarked

West Pointing Rock

PETER OLIVIA

trail that leads steeply down to Breakneck Pond goes off to the left at 1.45 miles, and the Breakneck Mountain Trail ends at the Suffern-Bear Mountain Trail (yellow), 1.5 miles from the start.

The Breakneck Mountain Trail was first blazed in the fall and winter of 1927 at the suggestion of Major Welch, General Manager of the Park (*N.Y.Post*, 9/2/27). It was built to connect the T-MI Trail with the S-BM Trail. Breakneck Mountain itself (known among local people as Knapp Mountain) had been acquired by the Park from Emma Louisa Knapp on June 27, 1917. Breakneck Pond had been the property of Rockland Finishing Company of Haverstraw (*N.Y. Times*, 4/8/28), while Cranberry Mountain, on the west side of the lake, belonged to William Huffman. Both of these properties were acquired by the Park in 1928.

In January 1924, George F. Parmelee of the Fresh Air Club cleared a trail along the east side of Breakneck Pond. There were no camps then, and the lake shore was quite wild. The trail ran from the old earth dam at the north end of the pond (built about 1890) through the laurels beyond the south end, and terminated at the woods road which carried the T-MI Trail across the north end of Big Green Swamp. (This road continued northwest to a junction with the Cranberry Mountain Trail and is now known as Pine Meadow Road.) The old trail through the laurels can still be followed by curious hikers.

Brooks Lake Trail

Length: 1.0 mile • Blazes: red square on white

Miles

0.0 Begin at parking area in town park and head south (clockwise).

0.3 Turn right; Timp-Torne Trail joins briefly.

0.6 Cross stream on rocks at northwest corner of lake.

0.9 Emerge onto grassy field at town park; pass pavilion on right.

1.0 End at parking area in town park.

This short loop trail, blazed in 2004, circles Brooks Lake. It begins at a town park, just west of Firefighters Memorial Drive in the village of Fort Montgomery, where parking is available. Followed in a clockwise direction, the trail heads south on a wide fire road for 125 feet, then turns left and continues on a narrower gravel road.

After making a short but rather steep descent, the Brooks Lake Trail turns right at 0.3 mile, joining the Timp-Torne Trail (blue). The two trails run together for only 100 feet, crossing a wet area on a boardwalk, after which the Timp-Torne Trail leaves to the left, while the Brooks Lake Trail bears right and heads north along the west side of the lake.

At the northwest corner of the lake, at 0.6 mile, the trail crosses a stream on rocks. In another 125 feet, there is a view over the lake from a rock to the right. After briefly paralleling and then crossing an old stone-wall-lined woods road, the trail emerges onto a grassy field at 0.9 mile. It passes a wooden pavilion to the right, with beautiful views over the lake, and descends to end, 1.0 mile from the start, at the parking area.

The Brooks Lake Trail was established in 2004 at the suggestion of local residents. The construction was financed with a grant from the New York Recreational Trails program.

Buck Trail

Length: 1.6 miles • Blazes: yellow (left branch, yellow with black stripe)

Miles

0.0   Start at Seven Hills Trail.

0.35   Begin to descend from crest of rise.

0.7   Trail widens to woods road.

0.95   Little Doe Trail begins, left.

1.15   Trail divides:

Right branch:

1.4   Cross inlet of Breakneck Pond.

1.6   End at Pine Meadow Road West.

Left branch:

1.4   Begin to descend from crest of rise.

1.6   End at Pine Meadow Road.

To reach the start of the Buck Trail, take the Seven Hills Trail (blue on white) up Conklin Mountain from the Lake Sebago hikers' parking area on Seven Lakes Drive. At 0.35 mile, near the crest of the rise, the Buck Trail begins to the left.

The Buck Trail climbs to just below the summit of Conklin Mountain and continues along the crest of the ridge, with views to the north when there are no leaves on the trees. At 0.35 mile, the trail begins a gentle but steady descent, and at 0.7 mile, the trail widens to a woods road and begins to pass through dense stands of mountain laurel. The unmarked Little Doe Trail begins to the left at 0.95 mile (it is nearly invisible here), and at 1.15 miles, the trail divides.

The right branch of the trail continues to follow the woods road through laurel, crossing the inlet stream of Breakneck Pond at 1.4 miles and ending at Pine Meadow Road West (just before the junction of Pine Meadow Road West and Pine Meadow Road East) at 1.6 miles. The left branch of the trail (marked with yellow blazes with a black stripe) proceeds ahead on a footpath, passing old stone walls, and descends to end at Pine Meadow Road, 1.6 miles from the start.

The Buck Trail appears on the 1920 Park trail map. It was then known as the Breakneck Pond Trail. In 1921, the Boy Scouts' White Bar Trail came up Diamond Creek and followed the Buck Trail over Conklin Mountain. At the north end of the mountain, the scouts followed a woods road (now Pine Meadow Road) down to the Cranberry Mountain Trail, and continued up to Big Hill on the Old Turnpike. The names Buck and Little Doe were first used in 1943 on Bill Hoeferlin's Map No. 5. The Buck Trail was an unofficial, unmarked trail until 2007, when it was officially adopted by the Trail Conference and blazed yellow.

Just northeast of the cairn that marks the junction of the Buck Trail with the Seven Hills Trail, a four-acre parcel was owned from 1885 to 1910 by Enoch Conklin and his sons Roger and Elias. There is no evidence that they ever lived there.

North of the fork in the trail at 1.15 miles, many stone walls and the cellar hole of an old farmhouse are still visible. This 17-acre parcel was given in 1850 by Jonas Wood to Andrews Hill, who had married Susan Wood in 1833. That couple may have built the house beside the trail. In 1855, they bought a larger farm on the ridge west of Stony Brook, and in 1862 they sold the 17 acres to Joseph W. Conklin. Joseph sold it three years later to James R. Johnson of Johnsontown.

Conklin Mountain was probably named after Timothy Conklin. His 412 acres, from Stony Brook up to the ridgetop, were bought at auction on December 17, 1850 by Matthew Waldron (1824-1903).

From the mountain ridge down to Seven Lakes Drive, the land through which the Little Doe Trail goes was the property of the Asylum of the Sisters of Saint Dominic (Blauvelt, N.Y.). They had received it as a gift in 1914. To the northeast of this property, the land on both sides of Pine Meadow Road, from the lake edge to the mountain ridge, was home to the Waldron family until 1916.

Conklins Crossing Trail

Length: 0.6 mile • *Blazes: white*

This trail is a short-cut between the Suffern-Bear Mountain (S-BM) and Pine Meadow Trails. It starts from the Pine Meadow Trail (red square on white) at the east end of Pine Meadow Lake, about 0.1 mile from the site of Conklin's Cabin, and crosses a rocky gully. On the right, an unmarked trail leads around the south side of the lake. The trail ends, 0.6 mile from the start, at the S-BM Trail (yellow) on the Ramapo Rampart (a name coined by Frank Place). A very large boulder, known as "The Egg," is 0.15 mile to the left on the S-BM Trail, and another 0.2 mile further is the Stone Memorial Shelter.

Prior to 1935, when Ramsey Conklin and his family were still living at Pine Meadow, this trail started at their farm and crossed over the Rampart. It continued down into the valley, and followed Sky Meadow Road to Route 202 at Wesley Chapel (now Wesley Hills). In 1942, the owner of the land at the upper end of Sky Meadow Road closed the trail to hikers. The section down from the S-BM Trail was abandoned, as was another trail to Horse Stable Rock. From Pine Meadow to S-BM, the trail was maintained by Jim Stankard of the Westchester Trails Association from 1962 to 1973. As late as 1973, the abandoned section could still be followed. (Since then, it has become overgrown.)

Cornell Mine Trail

Length: 1.75 miles • Blazes: blue

Miles

0.0   Start at Bridle Path.
0.3   Reach Route 9W.
0.9   Cross old dirt road.
1.75 End at R-D Trail.

The Cornell Mine Trail begins on the Doodletown Bridle Path/1777E Trail, 0.5 mile south of the South Parking Area at Bear Mountain. It descends to the abandoned Doodletown Road and follows it to Route 9W, just north of where Doodletown Brook goes under the highway. From this point (elevation 20 feet) the trail climbs nearly 1,000 feet in the next 1.45 miles. It crosses the Route 9W bridge over the brook, then turns right, re-enters the woods and follows the brook uphill, using the route of the Iona Island Aqueduct for a short distance. On the way, there are views of the reservoir and water treatment plant built in 1974 to serve Iona Island, which had been acquired by the Park in 1965.

At 0.9 mile, the trail crosses an old dirt road. In another 0.45 mile, after briefly following a second dirt road, the trail begins to go steeply uphill along a ravine. Small mine openings may be seen on the way up. The Cornell Mine Trail ends at the Ramapo-Dunderberg Trail (red dot on white), 1.75 miles from the start, where another small mine opening is visible. On the hillside west of that point there are two larger horizontal shaft openings.

Bill Hoeferlin's Hikers Region Map #16 of August 1943 shows the original route of the Cornell Mine Trail. It began where the old (1809) Dunderberg Road crossed Timp Brook (this point has been covered by the reservoir which was built in 1974). The trail climbed towards Bald Mountain, where it crossed a little brook on the 400-foot contour. The present-day route, which comes up somewhat to the east of the older route, joins the latter at the brook, and continues up the ravine, following approximately the original line.

At its meeting of December 1,

1971, the Trail Conference decided to make a new Cornell Mine Trail starting from the Bear Mountain Inn. By the end of February 1972, the new route had been cleared and blazed by the AMC. The steep route up the ravine, which had become badly eroded, was relocated in part by the West Hudson Trail Crew during 1998 and 1999. In 2010, the northern part of the trail, from the Bear Mountain Inn to the fork where the Cornell Mine Trail departs from the Bridle Path, was deblazed (this trail section is still blazed as the 1777E Trail).

The present Cornell Mine Trail goes up through a parcel of land on the side of Bald Mountain which was acquired by Thomas A. Edison in 1890. His 194-acre lot started at the old Dunderberg Road and went to the 1,080-foot level (the knob which the R-D Trail crosses, east of its junction with the Cornell Mine Trail). Edison's property line crossed the Cornell Mine Trail at the 810-foot level, so his land did not include the larger mine openings near the top of the mountain. (The history of these mine openings is given in our discussion of the Cornell Mine, pp. 361-63.)

The land on the north side of Bald Mountain was part of a grant made on October 30, 1749 by King George II to four children of Richard Bradley, who was the Attorney General of New York. In 1849, it was bought by Caleb June of Doodletown from three Sheldon brothers for $48.88. Thereafter, it was known as the Sheldon Lot.

In 1885, the parcel was sold by Andrew June to Thomas Nelson of Brooklyn, who sold it five years later to Thomas Edison.

At that time, Edison was deeply involved in a project to concentrate iron ore with magnets. He had extensive works in Ogdensburg, New Jersey, and another in Putnam County, New York. There is little evidence of mining activity on Edison's property. At the 610-foot level, there is a large trench near the trail. Another test hole is at the 810-foot level, the upper edge of the parcel.

In 1891, Edison transferred title to the Bald Mountain lot to his New York Concentrating Works, but he abandoned all of his iron projects soon afterwards, because the price of iron had dropped after the opening of the Mesabi Range mines in Minnesota in 1892. Edison sold his lot to the Park in 1928.

Diamond Mountain-Tower Trail

Length: 0.8 mile · *Blazes: yellow*

Miles

West Branch (former Diamond Mtn. Trail)

0.0 Start from Pine Meadow Trail.

0.25 End at Seven Hills/Hillburn-Torne-Sebago Trail.

East Branch (former Tower Trail)

0.0 Start from Pine Meadow Trail.

0.02 Pass septic tank.

0.25 Climb over ledges, with views.

0.5 Site of former fire tower.

0.55 End at Seven Hills Trail.

The Diamond Mountain-Tower Trail starts uphill from the Pine Meadow Trail (red square on white) about 250 feet west of where the latter crosses Christie Brook, 0.15 mile west of Pine Meadow Road. One branch of the trail (the former Tower Trail) goes off to the right, while the other branch (the former Diamond Mountain Trail) turns left.

The west (left) branch of the trail climbs steeply up Diamond Mountain. After crossing open ledges, it ends, 0.25 mile from the start, at the Seven Hills/Hillburn-Torne-Sebago Trail. There is a good view at this point toward New York City.

The east (right) branch of trail goes up on a wide path. In another 100 feet, it passes a large concrete septic tank, built in 1934 to collect the sewage from the camps that were to be built on the four new lakes. The camps were not built, and the sewage system was never used. Upstream from the tank is an incomplete dam that was intended to create Lake Oonotookwa ("place of cattails") on Christie Brook.

The trail then turns left and goes steeply up over ledges, reaching one at 0.25 mile with a good view of Lake Wanoksink and Pine Meadow Lake. At 0.5 mile, the trail passes the site of the fire tower which was removed in 1986. Just beyond, the Diamond Mountain-Tower Trail ends at the Seven Hills Trail (blue on white).

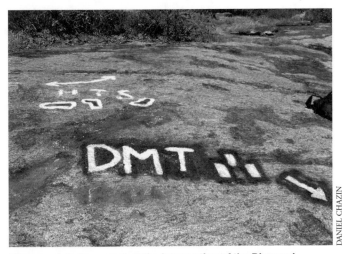

DANIEL CHAZIN

Blazes painted on a rock at the intersection of the Diamond Mountain-Tower and HTS Trails

On April 14, 1937, Raymond Torrey wrote to Major Welch: "Someone has made a new trail from the firetower on Diamond Mountain down to Christie Brook without asking anyone . . . . It is a handy short trail. I think we have enough trails." The new trail, known as the Tower Trail, was marked with a red T. Years later it was learned that it had been made by Kurt Stettner, a member of the Wanderlusters Club. His trail actually ended at the Stone Giants (Ga-Nus-Quah), 0.4 mile down the Pine Meadow Trail. In 1944, the color was changed to yellow, and in 1974 a black

T was added at the beginning and end. Stettner died in February 1945 (Trail Committee Minutes, 3/21/45). In 1981, the trail was made to start from the Pine Meadow Trail near the old CCC ruin.

The Diamond Mountain Trail was first marked about 1939, but the name of its builder is not recorded. Until 1993, it was blazed white. In 1993, it was consolidated with the Tower Trail, and the joint trail—now officially known as the Diamond Mountain-Tower Trail—was reblazed yellow.

Dunning Trail

Length: 3.75 miles · Blazes: yellow

Miles

0.0   Start from Nurian Trail.

0.15 Overhanging rock at edge of Green Pond.

0.4   Cross Nurian Trail.

0.45 Left on Island Pond Road.

0.55 Boston Mine.

1.1   Left on White Bar Trail.

1.35 Right on Crooked Road.

1.7   Cross R-D Trail.

2.1   Bowling Rocks.

2.25 Abandoned Dunning Trail leaves, left.

2.65 Crooked Road leaves, right.

2.85 Hogencamp Mine, up on left.

3.05 LP comes in from left.

3.1   LP leaves, right.

3.6   Pine Swamp Mine, left.

3.75 End at A-SB Trail.

This beautiful trail starts from the Nurian Trail (white) where the latter reaches the hilltop from the Valley of Boulders. Dunning proceeds south over a little rise, then goes left along the rocky edge of Green Pond, passing under an overhanging rock. It parallels the Nurian Trail which, at places, is only a few yards away. Although it provides a sheltered route in cold, windy weather, it is rather slippery when there is ice on the rocks. The Nurian Trail soon comes in from the left and, in 75 feet, leaves to the right. At 0.45 mile, Dunning reaches Island Pond Road. It turns left on this road for a short distance, and then turns right and passes by the Boston Mine. This mine, which was last worked in 1880, is a large cut in the hillside, with a water-filled shaft. The ore was sent to the Clove Furnace at Arden (see pp. 359-60).

Dunning goes over the hill to the right of the mine (it went to the left until 1972) and continues eastward. At 1.1 miles from the start, Dunning turns left and joins the White Bar Trail. Both trails run together for 0.25 mile. Dunning then turns abruptly to the right and soon starts uphill, following the old "Crooked Road." On the ridge of Black Rock Mountain, 1.7 miles from the start, the Ramapo-Dunderberg Trail (R-D) (red on white) crosses. (The Bald Rocks Shelter is 0.15 mile to the south on the R-D Trail.) From here, Dunning proceeds downhill and eastward, crossing a little stream and then a bare, rocky area. The boulders that dot the bare rock gave rise to the name "Bowling Rocks."

About 0.15 mile downhill from Bowling Rocks, the original route of the Dunning Trail goes left into the laurels. This path, now unmarked, leads in 0.3 mile to the Long Path. Dunning continues downhill, following the Crooked Road. At 2.65 miles, the Crooked Road turns sharply down right, while Dunning continues straight ahead. (The Crooked Road, a lovely old grassy road, descends 0.5 mile to Little Long Pond, passing through the abandoned Girl Scout Camp Quid Nunc, which means "what now?")

In another 0.2 mile, the trail passes the extensive cuts of the Hogencamp Mine on the hillside to the left. A short distance beyond, as the trail passes a swamp on the right, the tailings from another shaft of the Hogencamp Mine can be seen on the left. This mine was worked from 1865 to

Green Pond

1885, when the Clove Furnace was finally shut down (see pp. 366-67).

At 3.05 miles, the Long Path (aqua) joins from the left. It runs jointly with Dunning for a short distance, and then departs to the right and goes to Lake Skannatati. Dunning continues to the northeast on fairly level ground. It runs along the west side of Pine Swamp and passes the Pine Swamp Mine to the left (see pp. 369-70). A high pile of tailings can be seen from the trail, and a 25-foot cut—which leads into an interesting passageway tunnelled into the hillside—is visible if one climbs up beyond the pile of tailings. Soon afterward, the Dunning Trail ends at the Arden-Surebridge Trail (red triangle on white), 3.75 miles from the start.

In 1934, Dr. James M. Dunning, chairman of the AMC Trails Committee, personally maintained the AT from the Bear Mountain Bridge to the Connecticut line. In April 1933, he proposed a new trail, to be a short-cut to the R-D Trail for hikers from Southfields. The proposal was endorsed by Major Welch, General Manager of the Park. Dunning, Ridsdale Ellis and other AMC members cut the new trail from Nurian's trail to the Crooked Road and thence to the R-D on the ridge. By June 1933, the red-blazed trail was complete. Unfortunately, Dunning had used Nurian's route from Stahahe Dam to Island Pond Road, and this led to a historic dispute. Kerson Nurian would not tolerate the new red markers, and he painted them out. Dunning then started his trail on the top of the ridge and relocated it along nearby Green Pond, and the dispute subsided.

The Dunning Trail was blazed red until 1943, when Joseph Bartha repainted it yellow and extended it from the R-D Trail past Hogencamp and Pine Swamp Mines to end at the A-SB Trail. In 1979, the Dunning Trail was rerouted to avoid passing an open cut of the Hogencamp Mine at the edge of the trail (the Long Path now uses that route, however).

Fawn Trail

Length: 1.0 mile · Blazes: red F on white

Miles

0.0 Begin on AT, 0.25 mile from Seven Lakes Drive.

0.1 County line.

0.75 Cross Timp-Torne Trail.

1.0 End at Beechy Bottom East Road.

The Fawn Trail provides an easy route from the Appalachian Trail (AT) (white) and Doodletown Road to the Anthony Wayne Recreation Area on the other side of West Mountain. It is a fairly level trail, and in June it passes through masses of laurels in bloom.

The Fawn Trail begins on the AT, 0.25 mile south of Seven Lakes Drive, and heads west. At 0.75 mile, on a low ridge, it crosses the Timp-Torne Trail (blue). At 1.0 mile, it ends at the Beechy Bottom East Road, the route of the Anthony Wayne Trail (white). To the left, the Anthony Wayne Trail goes downhill to the Anthony Wayne Recreation Area.

The Fawn Trail was shown on the first Park trail map (1920). It started from the junction of Doodletown Road with Seven Lakes Drive. That Drive, built in 1913, used an already existing road (built in 1809) from Queensboro through Doodletown to Jones Point. Later, the AT was built (1922) and then a Bridle Path (1935).

In 1971, the Tramp and Trail Club asked permission from the Conference to mark and maintain the Fawn Trail, from the old fireplace on the AT to the Timp-Torne Trail. They marked it orange. In later years it was marked by the Park with red plaques as a ski trail, but in 1984 it was reinstated as a Conference Trail and reblazed red by Dick Warner. In 1987, Paul Leikin marked it with red F on pink blazes. Subsequently, the blazes were changed to red F on white, and the western end of the trail was slightly relocated to the north so that it now ends at a junction with the Anthony Wayne Trail.

During the 1988 forest fire season, bulldozers were used to make a fire lane which included parts of the Fawn Trail. In the intervening 20 years, the bulldozer scars have largely faded away.

Hillburn-Torne-Sebago Trail

Length: 5.2 miles · Blazes: orange

Miles

0.0	Start at T-MI Trail.
0.1	Turn left, uphill; Stony Brook Trail begins, right.
0.2	Cross Diamond Creek.
0.6	Join Seven Hills Trail.
0.85	Diamond Mountain-Tower Trail leaves, left.
0.9	Seven Hills Trail leaves, left.
1.8	Cross Pine Meadow Brook.
1.85	Briefly join Pine Meadow Trail.
2.25	Briefly join Seven Hills Trail.
2.65	Cross gas pipeline.
3.05	Raccoon Brook Hills Trail crosses.
3.3	Top of "Russian Bear."
4.15	Join Seven Hills Trail.
4.35	Turn left, off Seven Hills Trail.
4.65	Top of Ramapo Torne.
5.2	End at Seven Hills Trail.

When the Hillburn-Torne-Sebago Trail (HTS) was first blazed, it went from Lake Sebago dam, over Ramapo Torne, and down to Route 17 (now Route 59) in Hillburn, a distance of 5.9 miles. This accounts for the name of this trail, which now begins on the Tuxedo-Mt. Ivy Trail, goes over the Ramapo Torne, and ends at the Seven Hills Trail.

To reach the start of the HTS Trail, leave Seven Lakes Drive just north of the dam at the south end of Lake Sebago and follow the red-dash-on-white blazes of the Tuxedo-Mt. Ivy Trail, heading south. In 0.15 mile, HTS begins on the right. It runs along Stony Brook for 400 feet and then turns left, uphill. Here, the Stony Brook Trail (yellow) begins to the right. After crossing Diamond Creek, a tributary of Stony Brook, HTS goes steeply up Diamond Mountain. On the way up, there are several limited viewpoints over Lake Sebago. At the top of the ridge, the Seven Hills Trail (blue on white) joins from the left, and both trails continue southwest along the crest of the ridge. The Diamond Mountain-Tower Trail (yellow) goes off to the left at 0.85 mile, after which HTS reaches an excellent viewpoint at the summit of the mountain. Soon afterwards, the Seven Hills Trail diverges left, while HTS turns right and descends over Halfway Mountain. At 1.8 miles, HTS reaches Pine Meadow Brook.

This point on the brook, where the water tumbles down over boulders, is called the Cascade of Slid, a name given by Frank Place. HTS turns left onto the Kakiat Trail (white), which follows the north side of the brook. A few yards upstream, HTS turns right and crosses the brook on a wooden bridge (which occasionally is washed away). The trail climbs up from the brook, turns left briefly on the Pine Meadow Trail (red square on white), and then goes right, up Chipmunk Mountain. At 2.25 miles, the Seven Hills Trail (blue on white) joins from the left, then soon departs again to the right. HTS climbs to the hilltop and crosses the pipeline of the Columbia Gas Transmission Company, built in 1949 and widened in 2007. Downhill to the right, the gas line (which is walkable) crosses the Pine Meadow Trail 0.5 mile from Reeves Meadow.

At 3.05 miles, the Raccoon Brook Hills Trail (black on white) crosses, and at 3.3 miles HTS arrives at the top of a cliff. Here stood the "Russian Bear"—a rock formation which fell down in 2004. From here, there is a good view of the Torne Valley and the Ramapo Rampart beyond, with the Ramapo Torne visible to the southwest. The trail then descends, climbs again, crosses a hollow and then climbs the opposite slope to meet the Seven Hills Trail once more at 4.15 miles. After running together for 0.2 mile, Seven Hills bears down to the right, while HTS turns left and continues gently upward, reaching the top of Ramapo Torne at 4.65 miles, with views over Torne Valley and Ramapo Valley (traversed by the New York Thruway).

HTS now begins a steep descent, first on a footpath, then on a woods road, passing several viewpoints on the way down. It ends, 5.2 miles from its start, at a junction with the Seven Hills Trail. (To the left, it is 1.6 miles along the Seven Hills and Pine Meadow Trails to the Reeves Meadow Visitor Center on Seven Lakes Drive.)

HTS was first blazed in 1928 by Kerson Nurian. Nurian made the trail without asking permission of the landowner, of the Park or of the Trail Conference. He started the trail on Route 17 (now Route 59) in Hillburn,

DANIEL CHAZIN

View from the Ramapo Torne

0.3 mile north of the Hillburn Erie R.R. station (where a brook crosses the road). It went up over the side of Hillburn Mountain, then down across Torne Valley (where the Orange and Rockland Power substation is now) on an old route first blazed in 1922 by J. Ashton Allis. There was no landfill there then. The trail then climbed steeply to the top of Ramapo Torne.

Going north from the Torne, HTS used the older (1922) route of the Seven Hills Trail (white blazes) for 0.2 mile, then turned right toward Little Torne (later named Russian Bear). It was Dr. Myrtle Lothrop Massey of the Interstate Hiking Club who, in 1929, saw on the cliff the profile of a performing bear (*N.Y. Post*, 1/10/30). Dr. Massey often invented fanciful names for rock formations, but this is the only one still remembered. She died on September 30, 1945, at the age of 69.

In 1931, Paul Schubert of the Paterson Ramblers marked the Trail of Raccoon Hills. His trail, which started from the Ramapo Torne and followed the route of HTS for some distance, was marked with a red half disc with a white center. In the fall of 1936, Jack Spivack of the New York Ramblers extended the Seven Hills Trail to Suffern. Going south from the Torne, he used the route first marked by Allis, and his extension joined the S-BM Trail just south of the Kitchen Stairs. Spivack also reblazed the entire Seven Hills Trail, using blue blazes instead of white.

In 1937, there were three sets of blazes leading north from the Torne, and hikers became aware of the

"Great Ramapo Trail War" (*N.Y. Post*, 12/3/37). One day, Schubert found that his Raccoon Hills blazes had been painted black. Spivack's Seven Hills extension to Suffern was painted black, too, while the blue blazes north from the Torne were painted yellow. A sign was put up at the junction of the Seven Hills extension and S-BM which read: "Tie-trail to HTS." The extension itself was reblazed with a T. In January 1938, Torrey discovered that the "painter-outer" was Kerson Nurian. He was single-handedly eliminating the joint markings (although he himself, ten years earlier, had used a portion of the Seven Hills Trail for his HTS Trail). Because all these trails were on private land, neither the Trail Conference nor the Park had jurisdiction over them.

Schubert angrily removed his blazes north from the Torne, and started his trail from Torne View instead. Spivack repainted his Seven Hills blue blazes, and after Nurian's identity became known, the Trail War subsided. In 1933, Nurian had a dispute with Jim Dunning (see p. 39), and he would have another dispute with the Conference in 1948 about the Triangle Trail (see pp. 133-34). Nurian maintained the HTS Trail until 1939, when he turned it over to Charles Wolfman.

In 1940, the trails south of Pine Meadow Brook were officially closed to hikers by the landowner, the Ramapo Land Company (Pierson Estate). It was only after 1963, when the Park acquired a large parcel of Pierson land (including the Torne), that these trails were restored to their present length. Since the land immediately south of the Torne remains in private ownership, the trails in this area have not been reopened, and for many years HTS terminated at the Torne.

Until 2003, HTS continued across the T-MI Trail and turned left on Woodtown Road, ending at the Lake Sebago dam. This short portion of the trail was considered to be unnecessary, since the T-MI Trail provides a shorter route to Seven Lakes Drive at the dam, and it was abandoned in 2003, shortening HTS by 0.15 mile.

For many years, an unofficial trail, known as the "Old Red" Trail, climbed the northwest side of the Ramapo Torne. Known to many hikers, it provided the opportunity to make the climb of the Torne into a loop. In 2007, at the request of the Trail Conference, the park authorized this trail, and it was blazed as an 0.5-mile extension of the HTS Trail, which now ends at the Seven Hills Trail.

Hurst Trail

Length: 0.5 mile · Blazes: blue

The Hurst Trail starts from Seven Lakes Drive near the south end of Lake Tiorati, about 0.1 mile north of the entrance to Camp Thendara. At the edge of the road there is a cable barrier across the trail (the barrier closes the fire road which also starts at this point). The Hurst Trail follows the fire road for 125 feet, then goes up to the right. After passing under telephone wires, it bends left and climbs Fingerboard Mountain. It passes to the left of the Fingerboard Shelter and shortly afterward ends at the Ramapo-Dunderberg/Appalachian Trail.

The Hurst Trail was first blazed in November 1922 by Haven C. Hurst, a member of the Green Mountain and Sierra Clubs. After his accidental drowning in the Hudson River off 119th Street on June 5, 1923, the trail became known as the Hurst Memorial Trail (*N.Y. Post*, 6/15/23). When first made, the Hurst Trail crossed the R-D/AT on the ridge of Fingerboard Mountain about 125 yards north of the shelter, on the north side of a knob. This point is a few hundred feet north of the present end of the trail. From here, the trail went west and northwest down the slope. Passing around the north end of a swamp (where the Long Path meets it today), it joined the Surebridge Mine Road, which it followed out to Upper Cohasset Lake.

The Hurst Trail was a favorite way to Paradise Rock, on a rocky hilltop overlooking Upper Cohasset Lake. A short bushwhack uphill from the trail where it followed the road around the swamp led to the rock. Traces (a trash basket and water pipes) can still be found there of a shelter which was built about 1937, with private funds, for the use of the girls' camps on the Cohasset Lakes below.

Before 1949, the Hurst Trail was blazed with a black H on a white square. The trail was then regarded as unauthorized. In 1949, the blazes were changed to blue, and on October 5, 1955 the Conference voted it an official trail. By this time, the trail appears to have been abandoned west of AT/R-D. The first Conference Map #4 (1975) shows the Hurst Trail ending at AT/R-D.

Kakiat Trail

Length: 7.4 miles • Blazes: white (at junctions, a black "K" on white)

Miles

0.0   Tuxedo (Grove Drive).

0.25   Level off on abandoned telephone line.

0.5   Descend steeply to cross stream.

1.0   County line crosses.

1.2   Orange Trail to Dater Mtn. Nature County Park begins, right.

1.35   Path goes up left towards Daters Mine.

1.5   Blue Disc Trail joins briefly.

1.8   Gas pipeline crosses.

2.05   Cross Spring Brook.

2.2   Briefly join White Bar Trail.

2.3   Cross Seven Lakes Drive.

2.6   Hilltop.

3.05   Bridge over Stony Brook; Stony Brook Trail joins.

3.15   Bridge over Pine Meadow Brook; leave Stony Brook Trail.

3.4   Cascade of Slid; HTS Trail crosses.

3.75   Seven Hills Trail joins.

3.8   Cross Pine Meadow Brook.

4.1   Raccoon Brook Hills Trail starts.

4.6   RBH Trail loop crosses.

4.85   Torne Valley Road crosses.

5.0   Cross Torne Brook.

6.0   S-BM Trail crosses.

6.4   Power line service road; Mountain Trail begins to right; Kakiat turns left.

6.65   Gas line crosses.

7.15   Turn right, near river.

7.4   Trail ends; parking area is 0.1 mile to left.

The Kakiat Trail starts in Tuxedo. To reach the trailhead, follow the Ramapo-Dunderberg Trail (R-D) (red dot on white) from the railroad station a bit north along the tracks and turn right onto East Village Road.

After going under the Thruway, turn left on Grove Drive until the R-D turns right, into the woods, at a concrete catch-basin where the road bears left. The Kakiat Trail begins here, going up to the right on a woods road. The trail climbs to a shoulder of Pine Hill, then bears right and levels off on a woods road—the route of an abandoned telephone line. At 0.5 mile, it goes steeply down to cross a stream. Soon it joins a woods road which curves to the east, around the foot of Dater Mountain, passing massive stone blocks that have fallen from the cliffs to the left. A small concrete monument to the right at 1.0 mile marks the boundary between Orange and Rockland counties. Then, at 1.2 miles, the Orange Trail goes off to the right, leading into Dater Mountain Nature County Park.

At 1.35 miles, as Kakiat bends sharply to the right, a path goes up left toward Daters Mine. This once was the start of the Blue Disc Trail (see p. 24). Now, however, Blue Disc joins briefly at 1.5 miles. In another 0.3 mile, Kakiat crosses a gas pipeline and goes down to cross Spring Brook on stepping stones. At 2.2 miles, Kakiat briefly joins the White Bar Trail, which follows abandoned Johnsontown Road, and, in another 500 feet, it crosses Seven Lakes Drive. Kakiat climbs a bank into the woods again and goes uphill on a woods road, then down through an evergreen grove past an old farm site. At 3.05 miles, Kakiat crosses Stony Brook on a wooden bridge. It turns left, joining the Stony Brook Trail (yellow) and, after 500 feet, leaves the Stony Brook Trail and crosses to the north side of Pine Meadow Brook on another wooden bridge.

The hemlock grove and cellar hole on the hillside above Stony Brook are the site of a farm known as "the old Bentley place." In 1855, Henry C. Wanamaker sold the 75-acre farm on the ridge to John and Cornelia Becraft. At the same time, he sold the adjacent 62 acres along Johnsontown Road to Jacob Waldron, retaining a right of way to the ridge farm. That right of way is now the route of our Kakiat Trail. John and Cornelia immediately sold 50 acres on the ridge to Andrews and Susan Hill. In 1864, the Hills sold the place to Joel Becraft. Joel kept it until 1904, when he was 75 years old. Then he sold the ridge farm to Fred and Sarah Bentley of Tuxedo Park. Bentley sold the farm in 1906 to Robert Prentice of New York City, but continued to use it for a number of years. Prentice sold the farm to the Park in 1916. In 1919, the old farmhouse was demolished and the evergreens planted.

Although they lived in Tuxedo Park, Fred and Sarah Bentley were not rich people. They arrived in New York City from England in 1888. Their friend Pierre Lorillard met them at the boat, and made them welcome at his new country place, Tuxedo Park. Fred Bentley became the head gardener at Tuxedo, and developed quite a good business working for the well-to-do residents there. Lorillard gave him the use of a farm, east of the river, where the Italian Village was later built. Bentley had twelve teams of horses for his gardening/hauling business, and to get more hay for his horses he bought the Becraft farm above Stony Brook. He died in 1934.

The Kakiat Trail originally started where Pine Meadow Brook joined Stony Brook. There it met the then unmarked Stony Brook Trail. In October 1935, Frank Place and Park Ranger William Gee extended the trail from Stony Brook to Tuxedo. They used the older Tuxedo Trail (Hikers Region Map #5, 1935) which went to Tuxedo from Robert Reeves' farm on

Johnsontown Road. To avoid crossing Reeves' land, they built a bridge over Stony Brook. By March 1936, the new bridge had been washed away, but it was rebuilt a month later. It has been washed away and rebuilt many times since then.

After crossing Johnsontown Road and going around Dater Mountain, the new extension headed north and downhill towards Tuxedo. It joined a woods road along the Ramapo River that led to the Italian Village and the footbridge over the river. When the Thruway was built in 1954, the Kakiat Trail went down along the Thruway fence to the Village. The residents of the Village objected to the trail and, in December 1974, Art Paul of the Tramp and Trail Club relocated the Kakiat Trail to follow an abandoned power line on the hillside and then go down to Grove Drive.

The trail goes over boulders up along the north side of Pine Meadow Brook. At 3.4 miles, it passes the Cascade of Slid. This cascade is quite impressive during the spring. Here, the Hillburn-Torne-Sebago Trail (orange) comes down from Halfway Mountain and crosses the brook on a wooden bridge. Before 1946, Kakiat also crossed the brook on this bridge.

In the early 1920s, Frank Place had been reading the fanciful works of Edward Plunkett, Lord Dunsany. One of Dunsany's first books was *The Gods of Pegāna* (London, 1911), a tale about a mysterious kingdom where geography ends and fairyland begins. One of those gods was Slid, "the Lord of gliding waters and of still, Lord of all the waters of the world, and all that long streams garner in the hills; but the soul of Slid is in the sea." About 1920, Frank Place decided to name the cascade for this Dunsany character. Lord Dunsany died in Dublin on October 25, 1957, while Frank Place died on September 8, 1959. In April 1962, his Tramp and Trail Club placed a tablet in Frank Place's memory on a tree near the Cascade. The tablet disappeared about 1970.

The Kakiat Trail continues up the north side of the brook, meeting the Seven Hills Trail (blue on white) at 3.75 miles. The Pine Meadow Trail comes in here, too, and all three trails cross Pine Meadow Brook on a wooden bridge (once called "Hauptman's Bridge," after its first builder, Adolph Hauptman, a member of the Nature Friends Club). Kakiat then turns left and goes up Raccoon Brook, a tributary stream. At 4.1 miles, the Raccoon Brook Hills Trail (RBH) (black on white) starts from the left.

Until 1963, the area to the south of this point was owned by the Ramapo Land Company, controlled by the Pierson family. The Kakiat, HTS, Seven Hills and RBH Trails, as well as the Quartz Brook and Reeves Brook Trails, ran through the Pierson land.

The Boundary Trail also started here, at the junction of Kakiat and RBH. It was marked in 1942 with a black B on white, as well as with the yellow blazes that designated the Park boundary. Little used, the Boundary Trail was abandoned in 1954.

Kakiat now climbs over a ridge and, at 4.6 miles, the RBH Trail joins from the right. The two trails run together for 125 feet, after which RBH turns left, while Kakiat continues straight ahead. At 4.85 miles, Torne Valley Road is crossed, and shortly afterward Kakiat crosses Torne Brook. Soon Kakiat begins to parallel the Columbia Gas Transmission Company pipeline, constructed in 1949 and widened in 2007. The trail then climbs to the Ramapo Rampart (a name invented by Frank Place) at Cobus Mountain. (A rather poetic tale about Claudius Smith, "Cowboy of the Ramapos," said that he had a brother named Jacobus (he didn't)—hence the name Cobus.)

At 6.0 miles, the Suffern-Bear Mountain Trail (S-BM) (yellow) crosses. On the S-BM just south of this junction are two huge boulders (many others are nearby) which were named "Grandma and Grandpa Rocks" by Place and Torrey when they scouted the S-BM in 1926 (*N.Y. Post*, 4/21/36).

Descending Cobus Mountain partly on woods roads, Kakiat reaches the power line service road of Orange and Rockland Utilities at 6.4 miles. Here, the Mountain Trail (orange) leaves to the right, while the Kakiat Trail makes a sharp left turn. After crossing the power line, the trail enters Kakiat County Park and crosses a gas pipeline at 6.65 miles (look carefully here for the blazes). Further down, it goes into Kakiat County Park and once again uses wide woods roads. This county park was created in 1963 when Rockland County acquired 239 acres owned by Anthony Cuccolo (he also owned Kakiat Farm) and the adjoining 105 acres owned by Baillie. At 7.15 miles, the trail approaches the Mahwah River. The old Kakiat Lodge was across the river here. The Kakiat Trail now turns right on a park road, and ends 0.25 mile further, 7.4 miles from the start. A parking area is across the Mahwah River, 0.1 mile to the left.

In the 1920s, the Tramp and Trail Club of New York City rented a lodge at the corner of Route 202 (it was then known as Route 122) and Grandview Avenue. It was called the Kakiat Lodge, probably because it was across the road from the Kakiat Farm. In 1926 that club, led by Frank Place and Raymond Torrey, marked a trail (white K blazes) from the Kakiat Lodge to Stony Brook. They often referred to it as the Tatcony Trail (the initials of Tramp And Trail Club Of New York).

The name Kakiat is derived from a grant of land made in 1696 by Governor Benjamin Fletcher, in the name of King William III, to Daniel Honan and Michael Hawdon. The grant included the land from Sloatsburg to Monsey and Pomona. The Minsi Indians called it Kackyachtaweke. This region, once known as Kakiat, was later named New Hempstead by settlers from Long Island. Eventually it became the Town of Ramapo.

For many years, there was an historical marker at the junction of Route 202 and Grandview Avenue, 0.5 mile northeast of the entrance to Kakiat Park, which read:

KAKIAT LODGE

Aaron (Aurie) Blauvelt (1738-1801), French & Indian War veteran and Orangetown Militia captain in the Revolution, occupied a stone house here and ran a saw and grist mill on the Mahwah River nearby. Son, Cornelius Blauvelt (1766-1843), a colonel in the War of 1812, inherited the farm. His son, Richard, added a foundry to the mill and probably built this homestead c. 1830. It served as an inn in recent decades.

Lichen Trail

Length: 0.45 mile • Blazes: blue "L" on white

The northern end of the Lichen Trail is on the Arden-Surebridge Trail (red triangle on white), about 0.5 mile from the Lemon Squeezer. The trail starts uphill from a rhododendron grove, climbs about 100 feet through a hemlock grove, and then levels out over rocky ledges in a burned-out area, soon passing a beautiful view to the west, over Island Pond. The Lichen Trail ends at the Ramapo-Dunderberg Trail (red dot on white), 0.45 mile north of the Dunning Trail and just east of a large boulder known as "Ship Rock."

"Frank Place of Tramp and Trail Club, with permission of W.A. Welch, is locating a new shortcut trail from A-SB to RD. To be painted white. He strung it last Saturday." (*N.Y. Post*, 4/22/33).

By mid-June, the trail was ready, painted blue. Frank Place called it the Surebridge Shortcut. By mid-September, R.H. Torrey had found the new trail to be rich in common and unusual lichens, especially the one known as "Iceland Moss." The sci-entific name for this species, which grows in brown clumps, is Cetraria Islandica. Torrey also found several varieties of Cladonia. He decided to name the new trail the Lichen Trail (Torreya, *Journal of Torrey Botanical Club*, May 1934; *N.Y. Post*, 9/15/33).

An amusing anecdote relates that Torrey, in his enthusiasm for the new trail, persuaded Major Welch to come with him to hike it. He was greatly embarrassed when he realized that he could not find it.

Long Path

Length: 25.15 miles (Mt. Ivy to Florence Mountain) • *Blazes: aqua*

Miles

0.0	Intersection of Routes 202 & 45 at Mt. Ivy.
0.2	Turn right onto Parkway ramp.
0.4	Leave paved road and enter woods.
1.45	Cross Minisceongo Creek.
2.35	Knob of Cheesecote Mountain.
2.45	Cheesecote Pond.
3.3	Turn left at Letchworth Village Cemetery.
3.5	Turn left onto Call Hollow Road.
4.55	Cross Old Turnpike.
5.45	S-BM Trail joins from right.
5.6	Big Hill Shelter.
5.75	Cross Old Turnpike.
6.25	Cross stream on rocks.
6.35	Site of plane crash.
6.5	Turn right, onto woods road.
6.65	Footbridge over Beaver Pond Brook.
7.05	Bear left (right goes to St. John's).
7.55	Cross Lake Welch Drive.
8.1	Beech Trail goes right.
8.75	Cross Route 106 (Gate Hill Road).
9.2	Cross Seven Lakes Drive (to Lake Skannatati).
10.5	Join Dunning Trail.
10.55	Dunning Trail leaves, left.
11.3	"Times Square"; join A-SB.
11.85	Lichen Trail, left.
12.15	White Bar Trail, left.
12.85	AT crosses.
13.7	View of Upper Cohasset Lake.
13.85	Cross Surebridge Mine Road.
14.0	Old Hurst Trail goes right.

15.0   Cross Arden Valley Road.

16.15   View toward Arden House.

17.0   Hippo Rock.

17.15   Menomine Trail, right.

17.25   Stockbridge Shelter.

17.55   Stockbridge Cave Shelter.

18.75   Join Nawahunta Fire Road.

19.25   Cross Route 6 (parking).

19.7   Junction with Popolopen Gorge Trail.

20.0   Long Mountain summit; Torrey Memorial.

20.2   Go down left.

20.55   Cross Deep Hollow Brook.

21.05   Cross Deep Hollow Trail.

21.6   View from Howell Mountain.

22.0   Cross Brooks Hollow Brook.

23.15   Cross Route 293.

24.5   Join Route 6.

25.15   Go right, off Route 6, down Florence Mountain.

The Long Path (LP) starts at the Fort Lee Historic Park, just south of the George Washington Bridge, and at present ends at John Boyd Thacher State Park in Albany County. The section described in this guide begins at the intersection of Routes 202 and 45 in Mt. Ivy, adjacent to Exit 13 of the Palisades Interstate Parkway. Parking is available at the entrance to South Mountain County Park, on the east side of Route 45, about 0.1 mile south of its intersection with Route 202.

The Long Path goes west on Route 202 and crosses under the Parkway. It then turns right, up the Parkway entrance ramp and past the start of Quaker Road, and enters the woods in a small pine grove. The trail parallels the Parkway for about a mile. For the first 0.7 mile, the trail runs along a narrow strip, with the Parkway to the right and a chain-link fence (beyond which there is residential development) to the left. At 1.3 miles, after passing through a wet area, the trail turns right and continues along a grassy woods road. Shortly after crossing the south branch of the Minisceongo Creek on a culvert adjacent to the Parkway, the trail turns left and continues uphill into Cheesecote Town Park. This mountain—known variously as Cheesecote or Cheesecock Mountain—lies within the royal

Cheesecock's Patent granted by Queen Anne to seven New Yorkers on March 25, 1707.

After reaching the crest of a knob, the trail descends and approaches the east side of Cheesecote Pond. It turns left onto the old Letchworth Village Road, which is "paved" with stones, and goes around the south side of the pond. At the southwest corner of the pond, there is a wide turnaround. (The parking here is for Haverstraw residents only.) The old Letchworth Village Road curves to the right and continues down to Willow Grove Road, while LP turns left, goes up over a rise, and then goes down along a gravel road to the northwest. After passing under a power line, it reaches Letchworth Village Cemetery (where most of the graves are marked only by numbers) and turns left. It soon turns left again and, at 3.5 miles, reaches Call Hollow Road. From this point, Ladentown is 2.6 miles to the left, and the Palisades Interstate Parkway is 0.8 mile to the right (at Willow Grove Road).

In 1921, Major Welch, General Manager of the Palisades Interstate Park, proposed creating a hiking trail from Fort Lee to Bear Mountain via Piermont, Hook Mountain, High Tor and Mt. Ivy (*N.Y. Post*, 3/11/21). Nothing was done, however. In 1928, R.H. Torrey proposed a trail from Englewood landing to Mt. Ivy (*N.Y. Post*, 1/13/28). Again, the proposal was not acted on. In 1932, Vincent J. Schaefer of the Mohawk Valley Hiking Club of Schenectady suggested a new long trail from Bear Mountain to Lake Placid (*N.Y. Post*, 12/23/32). Schaefer laid out his trail in detail on topo maps. He intended that it be followed by map and compass, but did not want it to be blazed. Florence Puller of the New York Hiking Club brought this plan to the attention of W.W. Cady of New York City. In the fall of 1933, Cady began blazing a trail from the George Washington Bridge to Lake Placid (*N.Y. Post*, 11/7/33). Cady's route was described in great detail in R.H. Torrey's Tuesday *New York Post* columns from March 3, 1934 to September 14, 1934. It extended as far as the Adirondack Mountain Club's Johns Brook Lodge in the Adirondacks. It appears that Cady never blazed the trail further north than Route 23, near Windham High Peak, and for years after that, the trail was untended. In 1943, Alexander Jessup again marked the trail as far as Peekamoose Mountain in the Catskills. It included lots of road walking. Again it was left untended. Jessup died on March 11, 1944.

In the spring of 1961, Robert Jessen, Kurt Ramig and Michael Warren of New York City issued a booklet planning a 350-mile route from the George Washington Bridge to

Whiteface Mountain. Jessen was a 21-year-old textile worker (*N.Y. Times*, 10/16/61) and president of the Ramapo Ramblers. By October 1961, the blazing and clearing north from the George Washington Bridge was started. In 1964, the Trail Conference decided on the route through Harriman Park, and in January 1965 it was adopted as a Conference trail. The route chosen was joint with T-MI from Mt. Ivy to Ladentown and across the Park to the Dutch Doctor Shelter. There the new Long Path joined the old Boy Scouts' White Bar Trail over the saddle of Parker Cabin Mountain, over Car Pond Mountain, and north to the AT at Island Pond. Together with the AT, it went up to Fingerboard Mountain (here the R-D also joined) and continued north to a fireplace where it left AT/R-D and

picked up the old route of the Fingerboard-Storm King Trail.

The history of the Long Path was recounted by George Zoebelein in the July 1966 *Trail Walker*.

On September 28, 1971, Secretary of the Interior Rogers C.B. Morton dedicated the Long Path in New Jersey and New York as a National Recreational Trail. Also present for the dedication ceremony were Palisades Interstate Park Commissioners Laurance Rockefeller and Donald Borg, and New York State Commissioner of Parks and Recreation, Alexander Alrich.

In 1981, the Long Path was extensively rerouted to approximately its present line. The purpose of this relocation was to eliminate the two-mile road walk from Mt. Ivy to Ladentown.

The Long Path goes left on Call Hollow Road and after 500 feet turns right, into the woods. Soon it crosses Horse Chock Brook (which drains the three Letchworth Reservoirs) and climbs fairly steeply uphill. About half a mile above the brook, the ruins of the Call family home are visible on the left. At 4.55 miles, the Long Path crosses a wide dirt road known as the Old Turnpike, which is now the route of a buried coaxial telephone cable. Until 1992, this road carried the Long Path for 1.5 miles, but the trail has now been rerouted through more sylvan glades. About 500 feet to the right along the Old Turnpike, a path leaves to the right and goes to the site of ORAK, an old mansion (see pp. 117-18).

Soon the Long Path crosses a small brook and ascends a hill. At the top of the hill, at 5.0 miles, it passes a small swamp to the left. It then goes down and, after a short climb, joins the Suffern-Bear Mountain Trail (S-BM) (yellow) which comes in from the right. A moment later, the joint trails meet a faint woods road, known as the Second Reservoir Trail. To the left, this road goes to the Second Reservoir; to the right, it ends at the

Big Hill Shelter

Old Turnpike nearby.

In another 250 feet, LP/S-BM goes steeply uphill to the Big Hill Shelter, which it reaches at 5.6 miles. Here, the Long Path turns right and goes down to cross the Old Turnpike again. It then goes over another small hill and descends to cross a stream. At 6.35 miles, the trail enters a clearing. This is the site of a 1974 crash of a jet plane which had been enroute to Buffalo to pick up the Baltimore Colts football team. The three crewmen were killed (*N.Y. Times*, 12/2/74).

Beyond the clearing, the trail crosses a boulder field, and at 6.5 miles it turns right, onto a woods road. Until 1981, this road was the route of the Skannatati Trail. Just 100 feet to the left of this junction, the woods road ends at the paved road to Breakneck Pond.

The Long Path now goes down to cross Beaver Pond Brook, which comes from the Breakneck Pond dam. There is a good footbridge across the brook now, but, in years past, hikers crossed on a beaver dam. The bridge was built in 1986 by Park ranger Andy Smith. He named it the Jake Gannon Memorial Bridge in memory of his grandfather, who served for many years as the caretaker of St. John's Church.

At 7.05 miles, a trail to the right leads to St. John's Church. LP bears left and soon crosses Lake Welch Drive at its intersection with St. John's Road. The trail goes northwest along a farm road, passing old cellar holes. This farm—part of the Sandyfield community—was the home of Charles Conklin until September 1938.

LP then goes down a slope and across a low area. At 8.1 miles, the

Beech Trail (blue) starts, to the right. About 0.7 mile further, LP reaches Route 106 (Gate Hill Road). It turns right and follows the road for 250 feet, then turns left and goes up over the shoulder of Rockhouse Mountain (the "Rock House" is a cave to the right of the trail, below the highway). LP passes under a telephone line, rounds the end of Lake Askoti and, at 9.2 miles, crosses the Seven Lakes Drive and reaches Lake Skannatati. At the edge of the lake, LP passes the beginning of the Arden-Surebridge Trail (red triangle on white). LP follows the north shore of the lake, crosses Pine Swamp Brook, and then turns uphill to the right. At 10.5 miles, it joins the Dunning Trail (yellow).

Lake Askoti dam, which carries the Seven Lakes Drive, was built in 1935. Lake Skannatati dam was built three years later. The names of both lakes were chosen by Major Welch. In the Algonquin language, Askoti means "this side," and Skannatati means "the other side." Some time after Lake Skannatati was filled with water, perhaps in 1942, a trail was made by the Boy Scouts from there west to the Hogencamp Mine. On December 1, 1943, the Trail Conference planned a new trail, to be marked with a red cross. It started from the Dunning Trail near Hogencamp Mine, used the Boy Scout route to Lake Askoti, then went up Rockhouse Mountain to Hasenclever Road. After 1947, when the Red Cross Trail was rerouted, this trail route was unblazed. Then in 1961 it was marked as the Skannatati Trail (white) from the Dunning Trail to Lake Skannatati. In 1963, Bill Hoeferlin blazed it to St. John's Church, and in the spring of 1964 he extended it to Big Hill Shelter. In the fall of 1981, most of the Skannatati Trail was taken over by the Long Path.

The Long Path goes west with the Dunning Trail for about 250 feet. It then bears right where the trails diverge, at a fork. A shaft of the Hogencamp Mine is soon visible on the left (the main mine is near the Dunning Trail). LP then goes around a great boulder, called Cape Horn. In the rocks behind the boulder is a cave known as the Cat's Den.

A short distance beyond Cape Horn, LP goes right (here, the original route of the Dunning Trail went left; see p. 38). LP heads north along the side of a little valley and soon joins an old woods road—a continuation of the Surebridge Mine Road—that goes to "Times Square." Here, at 11.3 miles, LP meets the Ramapo-Dunderberg (R-D) (red dot on white) and Arden-Surebridge (A-SB) (red triangle on white) Trails. LP now joins A-SB.

The joint trail briefly follows the Surebridge Mine Road and soon turns left into a hemlock grove. It then descends Surebridge Mountain through rhododendrons, passing the ends of two swamps. This part of the trail was named the "Lost Road" by the blazers of A-SB in 1921.

At 11.85 miles, LP/A-SB passes the end of the Lichen Trail (blue L on white). In another 0.3 mile, it reaches a junction. Here, the White Bar Trail starts to the left and A-SB goes straight ahead to the Lemon Squeezer, while LP bears right (north) and continues along the west side of Dismal Swamp. At 12.85 miles, the Appalachian Trail crosses. Winding now through groves of maple and hemlock, LP climbs the eastern side of Echo Mountain. At 13.7 miles, there is a view of Upper Cohasset Lake, and just below is a shelter that was built in 1937 for the girls' camps on the lake. From here, LP goes down to Surebridge Mine Road and joins a woods road that goes northeast around the end of a swamp. This road is part of the abandoned section of the Hurst Trail (see p. 45). A bushwhack left uphill away from the swamp will take you to Paradise Rock on the summit—a beautiful spot for lunch.

At 14.0 miles, the old Hurst Trail goes right. LP continues northeast along the western foot of Fingerboard Mountain to Arden Valley Road, which it reaches at 15.0 miles. LP crosses the road and follows a woods road to the north.

On the left as one starts up this woods road, a faint trail may be seen going northwest through the saddle between two summits of Bradley Mountain. That path—the Forest Lake Trail—was part of the first road, built in 1760, through the Highlands from Stony Point to Central Valley. It leads into the Harriman estate and should not be used without written permission. The woods road that carries the Long Path here for 0.2 mile was part of that old road, and of the Arden Valley Road before the Park built the present paved road down to Tiorati Circle about 1917.

After 0.4 mile on the woods road, LP diverges left and climbs to the summit of Stockbridge Mountain (named for Elisha Stockbridge, 1826-1916, who owned a hotel near Summit Lake in 1893). From the ridge, Arden House can be seen to the west when there are no leaves on the trees.

Arden House was the home of Edward Harriman. The plans were drawn by architects John Carrere and Thomas Hastings, who are best known for designing the New York Public Library. The house took three years to

Hippo Rock

MICHAEL WARREN

complete, and cost $2,000,000. Edward Harriman moved into his new home in August 1909 and, unfortunately, died of stomach cancer on September 9, 1909. Subsequently, Arden House was used as a conference center for Columbia University.

At about 17.0 miles, a great overhanging boulder named Hippo Rock is to the left of the trail. In another 0.15 mile, the Menomine Trail (yellow) leaves to the right. (The continuation of this trail, going west, is the unmarked Nawahunta Trail.) LP then climbs a ledge to reach Stockbridge Shelter (built in 1928) at 17.25 miles. About 0.3 mile further north, the trail descends a ledge to the Stockbridge Cave Shelter.

The scouting of this trail, the old Fingerboard-Storm King Trail, began in the summer of 1922. In July, the cave was discovered by J. Ashton Allis, who was exploring this section of the trail with his two young sons. The Park improved the cave in 1928 so that it could be used as a second Stockbridge Shelter. Other trails that were first blazed by Allis are the Seven Hills Trail, the Arden-Surebridge Trail, and a long trail from Harrison Mountain in the Wyanokies over Sterling Ridge to Mombasha High Point (1913). A short section of that latter trail is still called the Allis Trail. J. Ashton Allis, a founder of our Trail Conference, died at age 89, on December 29, 1970.

Coming down from the ridge, LP at 18.75 miles joins a fire road that goes north from Lake Nawahunta. In another 0.5 mile, it crosses Route 6

(Long Mountain Parkway). The paved loop, where cars may be parked, is the older (1919) line of Route 6. LP turns left into the woods again and soon reaches a junction with the Popolopen Gorge Trail (red square on white). The path which goes down left from here (known as Deep Hollow Road) was the route of Long Path until September 1988. It is an "ankle breaker" stone road, paved with broken stones in 1934 by the Civilian Conservation Corps.

From its junction with the Popolopen Gorge Trail, LP turns up to the left and climbs to the summit of Long Mountain, which it reaches at 20.0 miles. This was the route of the older and much longer Fingerboard-Storm King Trail, and subsequently was designated the Long Mountain Trail. The 1,155-foot summit affords a fine view to the east, with Turkey Hill Lake below. This was a favorite spot of Raymond Torrey, much loved leader of the Trail Conference who, with J. Ashton Allis, scouted this section of the trail in 1922. Torrey died on July 15, 1938. In his memory, his friends inscribed a memorial on the summit of Long Mountain:

In Memory of
RAYMOND H. TORREY
A Great Disciple of
"THE LONG BROWN PATH"
1880-1938

The memorial was dedicated on Sunday, October 30, 1938, and Torrey's ashes were scattered there to the winds by his friend Frank Place.

0.2 mile north of the memorial, LP turns left and goes down off the ridge (the older markers, which head north into West Point land, can still be seen). The trail descends on switchbacks, following a 1992 relocation. As it approaches Deep Hollow Brook, the trail passes the site of the former Deep Hollow Shelter (1933-1975). The original path down from the ridge was cleared in 1929 by Alexander Jessup, who was at that time the maintainer of the entire Fingerboard-Storm King Trail.

The Long Path crosses Deep Hollow Brook (there may be stepping stones) and then a tributary stream, and goes up a wide firebreak, the boundary of West Point Military Reservation. About 0.4 mile beyond the second stream crossing, an old woods road crosses. This was named the Deep Hollow Trail because it starts at the north end of Deep Hollow, near

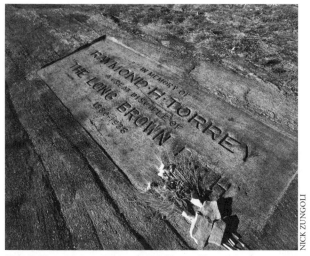

Torrey Memorial on the summit of Long Mountain

Stilwell Lake, and goes southwest along the mountainside to end at Route 6, 0.5 mile west of the LP crossing (see p. 222).

LP continues upward, reaching a fine viewpoint on Howell Mountain (named for William Thompson Howell, 1873-1916, a pioneer hiker in these Highlands). The trail descends steeply into Brooks Hollow, and at 22.0 miles crosses the brook that drains Lake Massawippa. It climbs up Brooks Mountain, turns southwest along the ridge, and then turns right (west) and goes downhill to cross Route 293 (0.15 mile north of Barnes Lake). After going a short way up Blackcap Mountain, the trail turns southwest, down a long ridge, to reach Route 6 just west of its junction with Route 293.

When LP was first blazed in this area in 1962, it went on over Blackcap Mountain to join Lawn Road/Trout Brook Road/Pine Hill Road into Highland Mills. In 1974, it was relocated to approximately its present route to avoid West Point land. Now the trail follows the fence along Route 6 for 0.65 mile, and then, at 25.15 miles, turns right toward Central Valley, using the abandoned line of Route 6 down Florence Mountain.

Major Welch Trail

Length: 2.65 miles · Blazes: red ring on white

Miles

0.0	Start behind Bear Mountain Inn.
0.45	Go left, uphill.
0.95	Turn left and start steep climb.
1.2	Views.
1.4	Cross Perkins Drive.
1.8	Go right, onto Perkins Drive.
1.9	End at Perkins Memorial Tower.

The Major Welch Trail, named in 1944 in memory of Major William A. Welch, the first General Manager of the Park, starts behind the Bear Mountain Inn, and follows the paved path along the west side of Hessian Lake. After 0.45 mile, near the north end of the lake, the trail turns left and goes uphill. It passes the Bear Mountain covered reservoir (see p. 283), on the hillside to the left, and goes above Overlook Lodge, which may be seen below to the right. Soon it levels off on the 400-foot contour on the northeast side of Bear Mountain. At 0.95 mile, the trail turns sharply left (the Appalachian Trail (AT) originally came from below to this point) and climbs steeply 900 feet to the summit. At about 1.2 miles, there are good views of the Hudson River and the hills beyond. The Major Welch Trail crosses Perkins Memorial Drive at 1.4 miles. It continues straight ahead and goes through a picnic area on the summit. At 1.8 miles, it turns right onto Perkins Drive and soon reaches the Perkins Memorial Tower, where it ends, 1.9 miles from the Bear Mountain Inn.

This trail was first marked in 1922 as the route of the new Appalachian Trail up Bear Mountain. The trail builders were expecting a bridge to be erected across the Hudson here. In anticipation, they started the AT up the mountain about a half mile west of the bridge-to-be. There was no Popolopen Drive then, only an old woods road above the gorge. The new Popolopen Drive, started in 1925 (now the route of the Palisades Interstate Parkway), made a 20-foot cut where the AT had started uphill, so the trail was moved 50 yards to the east.

In the fall of 1931, the AT was relocated to pass by the ski jump at the south end of Hessian Lake. The old route was left as an alternative approach trail to the AT, joining the relocated AT on the summit of Bear Mountain (*N.Y. Post*, 1/29/33). In 1934, the old route was repainted white (the AT was blazed yellow, then). In 1940, the Cygian Society added a red ring to the white squares. (In 1991, the blazes were changed to a solid red circle on a white square.) Then, in 1944, Joseph Bartha, Trails Chairman of the Conference, suggested starting the trail from the Inn instead of the Bridge, and naming it for Major William A. Welch, who had died on May 4, 1941. The relocation was done by Charles Luscher in the spring of 1946.

At the top of the mountain, the trail originally ended at Perkins Tower. In June 1960, the Timp-Torne Trail was rerouted away from Bear Mountain, and the former route of that trail, from the summit to the Perkins Memorial Drive, was redesignated the Major Welch Trail, thus extending the trail by 0.75 mile. As part of the Bear Mountain Trails Project (see p. 9), the section of the Major Welch Trail extending from the Perkins Tower down to the Perkins Drive was abandoned in 2010, although a portion of the route was incorporated into the relocated route of the AT.

Also as part of the Bear Mountain Trails Project, most of the half-mile section of the Major Welch Trail that extends from the first crossing of the Perkins Memorial Drive to the Perkins Tower will be relocated onto a newly constructed handicapped-accessible trail (this will also be the route of the AT). It is anticipated that this relocation will be completed in the fall of 2010.

Where the Major Welch Trail comes up from below to cross the Perkins Memorial Drive, there is a point of interest. Uphill, 200 feet above the road and 50 feet east of the trail, a five-foot stone monument, with an iron spike sticking out of the top, may be seen. This is an old boundary marker. When the Park was formed in 1910, the West Point Military Academy retained ownership of a pie-shaped parcel on Bear Mountain. From its apex near the summit, the West Point line went north to Popolopen Creek and west to a point on the old Fort Montgomery Road (a similar monument can be seen there). In 1939, West Point proposed a land exchange with the Park (*N.Y. Times*, 6/4/39). The deal was closed on April 20, 1942 (Commission Minutes, 5/13/42). The Park acquired 50 acres of West Point land on Bear Mountain and a 252-acre parcel north of the brook (which included the Popolopen Torne). In return, West Point acquired 108 acres of Park land northeast of Turkey Hill Lake and 718 acres in the hills northwest of Fort Montgomery (which the Park had bought in 1928 from the Fort Montgomery Iron Corporation). The Park also received a cash settlement of $14,526.19.

DANIEL CHAZIN

Perkins Memorial Tower

West Point was not the only "other" property owner on Bear Mountain. When the Commission acquired the prison site in 1910, their land extended up the mountain to within one-tenth of a mile of the summit. The 237 acres at the very top were the property of Addison Johnson of Port Chester, New York. He also owned the land on the north side of the mountain, down to Popolopen Creek. (The latter tract had, until 1817, been the property of Ithiel June, the first resident of Doodletown.) Johnson sold his land to the Commission on August 19, 1912.

A tenth of a mile west of Perkins Tower was the start of a 23-acre parcel owned by Harriet W. Graham of Queens Village, Long Island. This piece included the land through which the AT and Major Welch Trails were blazed, down to Perkins Drive. Mrs. Graham also had a right-of-way "from the above-described premises to the Dunderberg Turnpike" (now known as Doodletown Road). Except for West Point, she was the last of the "other" landowners on Bear Mountain, selling to the Commission on June 26, 1930.

Menomine Trail

Length: 3.7 miles · Blazes: yellow

Miles

South to William Brien Memorial Shelter (AT/RD) and Red Cross Trail

0.0   Start at south end of Silvermine parking area.

0.45   Join old road which comes out of lake.

0.65   Reach end of Silvermine Lake.

0.95   Turn left on grassy woods road.

1.35   William Brien Memorial Shelter; AT/RD crosses.

1.85   Unmarked trail, right, leads to Bockey Swamp Trail.

2.2   End at junction with Red Cross Trail.

North to Stockbridge Shelter (Long Path)

0.0   Start at south end of Silvermine parking area.

0.25   Cable barrier across road; turn up right.

0.4   Cross Seven Lakes Drive.

0.55   Turn left off Nawahunta Fire Road.

0.65   Cross brook.

0.85   Begin to ascend.

1.1   Cairn; trail, right, leads to Cave Shelter.

1.35   Trail, left, to Stevens Mountain.

1.5   End at Long Path.

The Menomine Trail connects the Silvermine parking area with the Appalachian/Ramapo-Dunderberg Trails (AT/R-D) at the William Brien Memorial Shelter on Letterrock Mountain, and with the Red Cross Trail. It also connects the parking area with the Long Path at the Stockbridge Shelter on Stockbridge Mountain. Since the Menomine Trail primarily serves as a means of accessing these two major trails from the parking area, we will describe the trail in two sections, beginning in each case from the parking area.

South to William Brien Memorial Shelter (AT/RD)

From the southern end of the Silvermine parking area, the Menomine

Trail crosses a bridge and turns left. Just before it reaches the lake, it turns right, and then it turns left and follows along the shore of the lake, passing through a very rocky area. At 0.45 mile, the trail joins a woods road which comes up from the lake. Before the lake was built, this road went along the edge of what was then known as the Bockey Swamp. Since the creation of the lake, the northern section of the road has been submerged, and the remaining portion of the road (now followed in part by the Menomine Trail) became known to hikers as the Bockey Swamp Trail.

After reaching the end of the lake, the Menomine Trail goes up a valley along Bockey Swamp Brook. At 0.95 mile, it comes to an intersection with another woods road. (To the right, this road leads 0.8 mile to the Seven Lakes Drive.) The Menomine Trail turns left on the road, crosses a stream, and begins a steady ascent. At 1.35 miles, it crosses the AT/RD at the William Brien Memorial Shelter.

As it starts down from the shelter, there is a short blue side trail on the right to a spring, which sometimes has water. The Menomine Trail bears left and follows an old woods road downhill. At 1.85 miles, an unmarked trail departs to the right and leads to the Bockey Swamp Trail, just south of the junction of the RD and the AT at the foot of Goshen Mountain. The Menomine Trail now parallels a brook (below to the left), and it ends at 2.2 miles at the Red Cross Trail.

North to Stockbridge Shelter (Long Path)

This part of the Menomine Trail begins just before the bridge at the southern end of the Silvermine parking area. It proceeds west along the guardrail at the edge of the parking area, then follows a dirt road leading through a picnic area. It turns right, uphill, at a cable barrier at the end of the picnic area, crosses a road which leads to an abandoned parking area, and enters an evergreen grove on a knoll above Seven Lakes Drive. To the right of the trail is the grave of "Scobie" Jim Lewis, whose farm was where Lake Nawahunta was created in 1915.

After crossing Seven Lakes Drive at 0.4 mile, the Menomine Trail briefly follows the Nawahunta Fire Road, passing, to the left, the cellar hole of the Lewis family home. At 0.55 mile, near the end of Lake Nawahunta, the Menomine Trail turns down left and crosses the inlet of the lake (Nawahunta Brook) on stepping stones. It passes through a pine grove, crosses a causeway across a swamp, and follows an old wagon road up Stockbridge

Mountain. At 1.1 miles, just beyond a bend in the road, a cairn on the right marks the start of a trail which leads 0.3 mile to the Stockbridge Cave Shelter. This trail, once blazed red, has been painted out with black paint, and the black blazes can still be followed (with care). Now the Menomine Trail begins to level off. At 1.35 miles, a road forks left to Stevens Mountain, and the Menomine Trail again begins to climb. The yellow Menomine blazes end at 1.5 miles, where the Long Path (aqua) crosses. The Stockbridge Shelter is about 0.1 mile up to the right.

The Menomine Trail was created on Labor Day 1994 as a means of linking the AT/RD and the Long Path with the convenient Silvermine parking area. For the most part, it follows the routes of two old woods roads—the Bockey Swamp Trail and the Nawahunta Trail—which had long been used by knowledgeable hikers to access these marked trails from the Silvermine parking area.

The name of the trail, Menomine, was originally given by Major Welch to the lake south of Seven Lakes Drive that was created in 1934 by the Civilian Conservation Corps.

Prior to then, the area was a large swamp, known as the Bockey Swamp. In an attempt to attract birds, the Park planted wild rice in the swamp. But, instead, the rice was eaten by deer. When the lake was built, it was named Lake Menomine, an Indian name for wild rice. It was renamed Silvermine Lake in 1951.

The section of the Menomine Trail that extends from the Brien Memorial Shelter to the Red Cross Trail was originally part of the unmarked Dean Trail. In 2002, the Menomine Trail was extended south from the AT/R-D at the shelter to the Red Cross Trail.

Nurian Trail

Length: 3.6 miles · Blazes: white

Miles

0.0   Former Southfields railroad station.

0.1   Go down, right.

0.25 Cross Ramapo River.

0.35 Cross New York Thruway.

0.65 Turn right and start uphill.

1.1   Top of Green Pond Mountain.

1.4   Turn left onto woods road.

1.6   Cross footbridge over Stahahe Brook.

1.9   Begin steep climb through Valley of Boulders.

2.25 Dunning Trail starts, right.

2.5   Dunning Trail joins briefly.

2.55 Briefly join Island Pond Road.

3.05 White Bar Trail joins from left.

3.15 Turn left and go down.

3.6   End at R-D Trail.

The Nurian Trail is named for its builder, Kerson Nurian. He called it "the Short Trail" to the R-D, making possible a hike from Southfields to Tuxedo.

The trail starts in Southfields, just north of Railroad Avenue, at the site of the former station. The trail continues along the tracks for 0.1 mile, then goes down right, along an old woods road, toward the river, which is crossed on a steel bridge. At 0.35 mile, the trail crosses the New York Thruway on a pedestrian overpass.

In 1824, the old woods road from the railroad tracks to the river was part of the "Monroe and Haverstraw Turnpike," which we now know as Route 106/Gate Hill Road (the railroad did not come through until 1838). The old toll road turned up through the hills past Car Pond (Lake Stahahe), Little Long Pond, and Beaver Pond (Lake Welch).

In 1894, Edward Harriman built a road south from Arden which crossed the Ramapo River 0.25 mile north of the Turnpike bridge. About 1929, Nurian marked his trail to cross the river at a ford where Harriman's bridge had stood. Soon afterward, the Park built a wooden footbridge where the Turnpike had crossed, and Nurian's trail was rerouted to cross that bridge. The bridge was washed away in April 1936 and rebuilt a month later. It was washed out again in December 1938 and replaced in January 1939. That bridge was washed out in 1946, and the present bridge of steel beams was built in 1950. From 1948 to 1950, hikers crossed the river on two steel cables.

During the construction of the Thruway in 1953, the western end of the Nurian Trail was closed. Indeed, it appeared that it would be permanently closed. Agitation for an overpass was started by the Trail Conference in 1954. Initially, Thruway officials rejected a proposed stone-faced bridge on the ground that it would cost $80,000 and serve only a small number of hikers.

William Burton, Conference Trails Chairman, who was a naval architect, then designed a steel-and-concrete bridge, which could be built for half the price. John Coggeshall, a former President of the Conference, who worked for the State, showed the new design to Thruway officials and persuasively argued the need for a bridge

in this location. He was successful in convincing the officials to construct the bridge, which was opened with a ceremony on July 15, 1956. About 1990, the bridge was closed for a year so that it could be raised a few feet to accommodate higher trucks along the Thruway.

Until the early 1970s, passenger trains of the Erie (later Erie Lackawanna) Railroad stopped at Southfields. Although trains no longer stop there, public transportation to Southfields from New York City is still available via Short Line buses. Southfields was also a convenient location to reach by car, as for many years, hikers were permitted to park at the Red Apple Rest—a diner on Route 17 that offered refreshments and a place to warm up after a hike. Beginning about 2004, the owner of the Red Apple Rest refused to allow hikers to park there (the diner closed in 2006). Since, nowadays, most hikers arrive by car, it was determined that the Elk Pen parking area was the most convenient place from which to access the Nurian Trail, and the Stahahe Brook Trail was marked to link the Elk Pen with the Nurian Trail, near the northern end of Lake Stahahe. For the benefit of those hikers who arrive by bus, the western end of the Nurian Trail has been retained as an alternative route.

From the overpass, the trail goes north along Harriman's Level Road (the Old Arden Road), turning right, uphill, at 0.65 mile from the railroad station. It climbs 320 feet to the summit of Green Pond Mountain and then descends. On the way down, at 1.2 miles, a cement box-like structure may be seen on the hillside to the right. That was once a latrine for a camp operated by Grace Church of New York City. The camp's mess hall burned on September 5, 1947, but its fireplace chimney is still standing.

At 1.4 miles, Nurian turns left onto a woods road (the Stahahe Brook Road). In another 0.2 mile, the Stahahe Brook Trail (red horizontal stripe on white) begins and continues ahead along the road. Here, Nurian turns right and goes down to cross Stahahe Brook on a wooden footbridge. It then climbs on switchbacks over a rise and descends to cross Island Pond Brook on rocks, with a pretty waterfall to the left.

In 1929, Torrey described the original route of the Nurian Trail: "Cross the Ramapo River northeast of the station, and follow a trail along the telephone line to Lake Stahahe" (*N.Y. Post*, 6/14/29). That "telephone trail" turned uphill from Old Arden Road a bit south of where the present-day trail starts up, and it reached the paved road along Lake Stahahe about 0.4 mile south of the dam. The trail then followed the road north along the lake. At first, Nurian's trail crossed the Stahahe dam (*Paterson Morning Call*, 8/19/32), but by 1935, it had been rerouted to cross the outlet of the lake on the paved road. In 2001, the trail was again rerouted at the north end of the lake to eliminate the roadwalk.

Across the brook, Nurian turns left and begins to ascend, steeply in places, following the south side of Island Pond Brook (Island Pond has two outlet brooks). The ravine of the brook is known as the Valley of Boulders. After climbing further up, there are great boulders immediately to the left of the trail at 2.1 miles. The Nurian Trail then goes around the end of a long sloping rock, and continues by going up along the rock. Near the top of the rock there is a limited viewpoint to the northeast over Green Pond Mountain.

At 2.25 miles, Nurian reaches the Dunning Trail (yellow), which begins to the right. Bending left, Nurian passes above Green Pond, and it turns left onto the Dunning Trail at 2.5 miles. The two trails run jointly for 50 feet. Dunning then goes off to the left, while Nurian continues ahead. The Boston Mine, an interesting side trip, is 0.15 mile to the north on the Dunning Trail.

Nurian soon turns right onto Island Pond Road. It goes south on the gravel road for about 125 feet, then goes left across a pretty region, with laurels and evergreens, to meet the White Bar Trail at 3.05 miles. Nurian goes south on White Bar for about 0.1 mile, then departs down to the left to cross a small brook. It turns right and briefly follows the brook, then turns left and begins the steep climb up Black Rock Mountain. Nurian ends on the Ramapo-Dunderberg Trail (red dot on white), 3.6 miles from the start. From here, Route 106, where limited parking is available, is 0.4 mile to the right.

Kerson Nurian was born in Bulgaria in 1873. He was a slender man, with gray hair and a gray goatee, and was a member of ADK, AMC, GMC and the Sierra Club. During his trail-building years he was an electrical engineer, working on submarines at the Brooklyn Navy Yard. He was an eager trail marker, but never asked permission of the Park, of the Trail Conference, or of the landowners. In addition to this "Short Trail" (1929), he made the HTS (1928), the Triangle Trail (1939) and the White Cross Trail. Nurian's independence and insistence on having his own way led to several disputes with others over his trails. See p. 39 (dispute with regard to the Dunning Trail's use of a portion of the Nurian Trail), pp. 43-44 (the "Great Ramapo Trail War," involving the HTS Trail, the Seven Hills Trail and the Trail of the Raccoon Hills), and pp. 133-34 (dispute with regard to the Triangle Trail). Kerson Nurian died on November 19, 1948, at the age of 75.

In 2003, the southeastern end of the Nurian Trail at the Ramapo-Dunderberg Trail was slightly relocated to eliminate an eroded trail section.

Parker Cabin Hollow Trail

Length: 1.5 miles • Blazes: orange

Miles

0.0	Route 106, 0.25 mile east of Thruway overpass.
0.1	Join wider woods road that comes in from left.
0.3	Reach crest of rise and begin to descend.
0.8	Cross stream on rocks.
0.95	Marsh to left.
1.2	Another marsh to left.
1.5	End at White Bar Trail.

The Parker Cabin Hollow Trail starts on the south side of Route 106, about 0.25 mile east of the Thruway overpass. It follows a woods road, which soon joins another, wider road. After reaching the top of a rise, it begins to descend. Then, at 0.5 mile, it turns left, leaving the wide woods road, and follows a narrower road parallel to the stream in Parker Cabin Hollow. Portions of the trail have been relocated off wet sections of the road onto parallel footpaths.

At 0.8 mile, the trail crosses the stream on rocks and continues along the south side of the stream. It passes a marsh on the left at 0.95 mile, and it begins to parallel a second marsh at 1.2 miles. Here, the trail narrows to a footpath. After curving around and following the edge of the marsh, the Parker Cabin Hollow Trail ends, 1.5 miles from its start, at a junction with the White Bar Trail.

The Parker Cabin Hollow Trail was adopted by the Trail Conference as an official trail in 2004. For many years prior to that, it was known to hikers as an unmarked woods road.

Pine Meadow Trail

Length: 6.8 miles • Blazes: red square on white

Miles

0.0	Second bridge after Thruway.
0.7	Seven Hills Trail starts, right.
0.9	Reeves Meadow Visitor Center.
0.95	Reeves Brook Trail starts, right.
1.05	Reeves Brook crosses.
1.3	Turn right; Stony Brook Trail continues ahead.
1.4	Quartz Brook Trail goes right.
1.45	Gas line crosses.
2.1	HTS Trail crosses.
2.45	Footbridge across brook.
2.7	Ga-Nus-Quah Rock.
3.1	Diamond Mountain-Tower Trail, left.
3.25	Cross Pine Meadow Road West.
3.3	Road, left, to Lake Wanoksink.
3.7	Conklin Road, left.
3.75	Pumphouse ruin.
3.95	Site of Conklin's Cabin.
4.05	Conklins Crossing Trail, right.
4.45	Cross Pine Meadow Road East.
4.8	Many Swamp Brook crosses.
5.5	Join S-BM Trail.
5.7	Bear left from woods road.
5.95	Leave S-BM and turn right onto woods road along Gyascutus Brook.
6.2	Cross Gyascutus Brook.
6.35	Turn right onto woods road paralleling power line.
6.5	Recross Gyascutus Brook; turn right onto gas pipeline route.
6.7	Turn left, leaving gas pipeline.
6.8	End at Town of Ramapo Equestrian Center.

The Pine Meadow Trail (PM) begins on Seven Lakes Drive in Sloatsburg, at the second bridge after the New York Thruway, 0.7 mile from Route 17. (A more convenient starting place, with parking available, is the Reeves Meadow Visitor Center, 1.4 miles from Route 17.)

From its start at the bridge, PM goes through an abandoned cherry grove and parallels a brook, then climbs slightly and continues along the side of the hill, parallel to the road. At 0.7 mile, the Seven Hills Trail (blue on white) goes uphill, to the right. Then, at 0.9 mile, PM emerges onto a field known as Reeves Meadow, where the Park has erected a visitor center (water and toilet facilities are sometimes available here). Just beyond the building, the Reeves Brook Trail (white) starts up, to the right. PM then follows Stony Brook and, at 1.05 miles, it crosses Reeves Brook on a wooden footbridge.

The Pine Meadow Trail was described by Torrey and Place in the first *New York Walk Book* (1923). They advised hikers to follow Johnsontown Road, "a good dirt road through a picturesque farming country." At 1.5 miles from the Sloatsburg railroad station, the trail crossed Stony Brook on stepping stones and followed a woods road across a meadow (where the visitor center was built many years later). This meadow was part of a 125-acre farm which had been given to the Park in 1921 by wealthy George Grant Mason of Tuxedo Park (see pp. 344-45). (What is nowadays called Reeves' Meadow actually was Mason's Meadow!)

In 1922, Mason's farmhouse was occupied by Chief Park Ranger Bill Gee. During the following years, the Pine Meadow Trail, then unmarked, left Johnsontown Road in Sloatsburg and crossed a bridge (now Greenway) over Stony Brook. It went along the southerly side of Stony Brook and then skirted to the south and east of the Mason farm (which was located between Johnsontown Road and the present-day Seven Lakes Drive). It approached Stony Brook again where the visitor center is now located.

In 1943, the trail was blazed, for the first time, by Frank Place, who used white metal discs (they were changed to red in 1945). He started it then at the cement bridge (demolished 1993) that led into the Mason farm from Johnsontown Road (*Walking News*, Nov. 1943). The trail went between the farm buildings and continued across the meadow to the area of the present-day visitor center.

In those days, Stony Brook flowed through a little pond (Allen's Pond) just south of the junction of Johnsontown Road with Washington Avenue. When the Thruway was built, that road junction was wiped out. A bypass was made around the south side of Allen's Pond, which rejoined Johnsontown Road at the present location of the second left turn from Seven Lakes Drive onto Johnsontown Road.

In 1954, the Pine Meadow Trail was marked to enter the Park from the bypass through a trailer court. The trail crossed Stony Brook on a little bridge. It followed the brook to the demolished Mason farm, then crossed the fields to the woods where the visitor center is now.

The route changed again in 1961, when the new Seven Lakes Drive was built. Allen's Pond was filled in, and Stony Brook was moved over to the south side of the new road where it went under the Thruway. In 1963, the trail was marked from the Sloatsburg railroad station north along the tracks to Seven Lakes Drive, and along that road to the second bridge over Stony Brook. There it turned right and went along the foot of the hill, south of and parallel to Seven Lakes Drive, as it does now.

In 1982, the trail was made to start at that second bridge, but even now some old blazes can still be seen on the poles along the railroad tracks north of the station and along Seven Lakes Drive.

The wooden footbridge over Reeves Brook, as well as the footbridge across Quartz Brook at 1.4 miles, were built in 2005 by Roland Brieault to provide safe crossings of these brooks during periods of high water.

At 1.3 miles, PM turns right, uphill, as the Stony Brook Trail (yellow) goes straight ahead. Quartz Brook is crossed on a footbridge at 1.4 miles. Just before that brook, a vague unmarked trail goes up, to the right. That was the old Quartz Brook Trail, which extended for 0.65 mile to the Seven Hills Trail.

The Columbia Gas Transmission Company pipeline crosses at 1.45 miles. Here, the Pine Meadow Trail is a wide woods road, high above Pine Meadow Brook. At 2.1 miles, the Hillburn-Torne-Sebago Trail (orange) comes up from the Cascade of Slid on the left. It runs jointly with PM for a short distance and then goes up to the right. PM now levels off, following the brook and crossing it (with the Kakiat and Seven Hills Trails) on a log bridge that was first built by Adolph Hauptman, a member of the Nature Friends Club. Bending right, PM follows the brook on an eroded woods road. (If it looks like a road, it is because in the fall of 1965 the Park widened the trail to a 20-foot-wide fire road, up to Pine Meadow Road.) At 2.7 miles, there is a pair of great boulders named Ga-Nus-Quah (Stone Giants). The Tower Trail (yellow) once started here.

A little beyond Ga-Nus-Quah, a fairly clear area can be seen on the left at the foot of the hill. In the spring, two great lilac bushes bloom there.

These bushes are all that remains to mark the place where a tiny cabin stood about 1900.

The 1923 edition of the *New York Walk Book*, describing the Pine Meadow Trail, says on page 102: ". . . it brings you into cleared land with rocky cliffs above you on the left. Here once stood a tiny cabin . . . ." All that can be seen there now are those great lilac bushes, with a piece of an old iron stove among their roots.

That land had been bought by Nicholas Rose in 1865. He also owned land up in Pine Meadow, and a farm near Sloatsburg. He was a woodcutter who carried cordwood down the Pine Meadow Trail with a four-mule team. Sometimes, he lived in that little cabin beside the trail, and he undoubtedly was the one who planted those lilac bushes. Nick Rose sold the place in 1902 to Fred W. Snow. Snow was a well-to-do citizen of Hillburn, son of the founder of that town. He used the little cabin for occasional fishing trips. One day Fred Snow learned that two mountain women had been using his cabin to entertain customers. So he went up the trail and burned the cabin to the ground. In 1921, he sold the parcel to the Park.

When we pass those lilac bushes and see their blooms, we may think of those who lived there over a hundred years ago. Our feelings are expressed in a poem by Jack Chard, of the Union County Hiking Club:

LILACS

Do you remember on that sunny day
We followed through the silence of the woods,
Where birds sang in the leafy green of spring,
That grassy trail where wagons once had passed;
Where grass and bushes crowded on the way;
The woods, advancing, claimed their own at last.
Suddenly lilacs met us in the wood,
Fragrant with mauve flowers of a rich delight.
Here must some long-forgotten home have stood
Where patient hands tended their simple herbs,
Some apple trees, still standing gnarled and lost,
And these sweet lilacs to adorn their life.
Some grass-grown stones recall the vanished house.

But those who lived and loved and died within,
Calling it home, their names we do not know;
Can only guess their heartbreak, joys and fears.
If men recall us at some distant day,
Long after death has closed our busy scene,
We did not live in vain if they can say:
"They left us lilacs where their life had been."

At 3.0 miles, the marked trail goes up to the left, past the foundation of a Civilian Conservation Corps building (the headquarters of the three CCC camps in the Pine Meadow area). A wide path goes straight ahead, across a level area bounded by a low stone wall (many hikers assume that the wide path is the official trail). Soon the Diamond Mountain-Tower Trail (yellow) goes off to the left.

PM now turns right, goes down to cross Christie Brook and continues along a rocky road to Pine Meadow Road West. On the right, this road crosses a dam and continues halfway around the lake. The Pine Meadow Trail now crosses the road and follows the north shore of the lake. For much of the way it follows old water and sewer pipes, usually buried but sometimes placed above ground on a rock causeway, which serves today as the trail route. This pipeline, and others around Lakes Wanoksink and

DANIEL CHAZIN

Pine Meadow Lake

Minsi, were built in 1934 to service the camps which were to be built on the lakes. The pipelines all terminate in a large (but never used) concrete septic tank on Christie Brook.

At 3.3 miles, a road leaves, left, to Lake Wanoksink. Shortly afterward, a trail goes right, out to a point in the lake often used as a lunch stop. Conklin Road begins to the left at 3.7 miles. Until 1934, when Pine Meadow Lake was created, this was the Woodtown Road, which crossed the swampy meadow on a corduroy roadbed and went down Torne Valley to Ramapo. Just beyond is the ruin of a stone-faced building. This is often thought to have been Conklin's Cabin, but it was actually constructed to house the pumps which were to supply water to the (never built) camps around the lakes. A path uphill behind the ruin leads to a very large water tank.

The actual site of Conklin's Cabin, 0.2 mile further on the trail, is a flat area, bounded by a steep rock on the left and the lake on the right. The cabin was next to a single large walnut tree, which stands near the middle of the area. Against the steep rock are the remains of a wall which was part of Conklin's cow barn.

The Conklin family lived there from 1779 to 1935, when the new lake was flooded. In 1933, the CCC built a camp for 200 young men across the meadow to the south. Ramsey Conklin's three sons, Steve, Nick and Theodore—then in their 30's—also worked on the new lake. When the water covered their spring and garden, the Conklins departed to Ladentown. There the town supervisor, Pin-

Hikers at Conklin's Cabin

PALISADES INTERSTATE PARK COMMISSION

cus Margulies, allowed them to live in an old schoolhouse at the corner of Camp Hill and Quaker Roads. By 1942, the cabin at Pine Meadow was in ruins (*Walking News*, Nov. 1942) despite the wire fence the Park had built around it.

The Pine Meadow Trail continues eastward along the lake. In sight of the end of the lake, the Conklins Crossing Trail (white) departs, down to the right, while the Pine Meadow Trail goes up to the left, leaving the pipeline. At 4.45 miles, Pine Meadow Road East is crossed. Then, 0.35 mile further, Many Swamp Brook is crossed. There was once a little bridge here, called Turtle Bridge.

At 5.5 miles, the Pine Meadow Trail joins the Suffern-Bear Mountain Trail (S-BM) (yellow). The joint trails cross Pittsboro Hollow Brook and continue along an old woods road. In another 0.2 mile, the trails turn left from the road and descend to the gully of Gyascutus Brook. Here, at 5.95 miles, S-BM turns left and crosses the brook, while PM continues down the gully of the brook on a woods road. After bearing left and crossing the brook, PM curves right and follows another woods road parallel to the power lines at the base of the mountain.

The Pine Meadow Trail recrosses the brook at 6.5 miles and joins a service road that runs along a buried gas pipeline. In 0.2 mile, it turns sharply left and descends on a footpath to the Town of Ramapo Equestrian Center on Route 202, where it ends, 6.8 miles from the trailhead on Seven Lakes Drive.

Until 1943, PM ran jointly with S-BM for 0.2 mile, then continued down the woods road to cross Gyascutus Brook and come out at another woods road (now the power line service road). The eastern end of PM, beyond S-BM, was abandoned in 1943. The Trail Conference reinstated this end of the trail in 2006, thus providing another access point to the trails in Harriman from Route 202 on the east. Instead of departing from S-BM after 0.2 mile, PM now continues along S-BM for another 0.2 mile, then heads down along Gyascutus Brook on a woods road. PM joins the original trail route just before crossing the brook (the original trail route is a wide woods road that can be easily followed).

Popolopen Gorge Trail

Length: 4.5 miles • Blazes: red square on white

Miles

0.0	Popolopen viaduct, south end.
0.2	Old bridge site.
0.7	Go right on aqueduct.
1.4	Timp-Torne, 1777W and 1779 Trails join, right.
1.45	Leave aqueduct.
2.1	Cross Queensboro Brook.
2.45	Left on Fort Montgomery Road.
2.55	Leave road, right.
2.75	Queensboro Lake on left.
3.2	1779 Trail leaves, left.
3.4	Go left on Summer Hill Road.
3.95	Anthony Wayne Trail, left.
4.5	End at Long Path.

Hikes on the Popolopen Gorge Trail (PG) often start from the Bear Mountain Inn. To reach the trailhead, take the paved path along the east side of Hessian Lake to the traffic circle near the bridge, then cross the Palisades Interstate Parkway. The blazes start on the left, in a clearing, just before reaching the Popolopen Viaduct. The trail goes down an old road to a point where there once was a bridge across the gorge.

Before the Popolopen Viaduct was opened on July 15, 1916, the road that "straggled past Highland Lake [i.e., Hessian Lake] was little more than a stony track which went down to a little iron bridge over Hell Hole" (*N.Y. Post*, 1/4/29). A dam had been built near there in 1901 to generate water power for a mill downstream. The little lake behind the dam is known as Roe Pond.

The Popolopen Gorge Trail climbs to Roe Pond and runs along it. It soon turns left and begins a steep ascent to the Bear Mountain Aqueduct, which was built in 1929-30 to bring water from Queensboro Lake to the Bear Mountain area. PG follows the aqueduct, and at 1.4 miles it joins the Timp-Torne Trail (T-T) (blue) and the two Revolutionary trails, which come up from the brook on the right.

At 1.45 miles, PG goes up left, away from the aqueduct. PG soon begins to follow Queensboro Brook, which it crosses on a concrete pipe aqueduct at 2.1 miles. It then goes along a woods road and, after 0.35 mile, turns left on a gravel road. This is the Fort Montgomery Road, which runs from Queensboro Lake to Fort Montgomery, mostly on West Point property.

After 0.1 mile on the gravel road, PG/1779 turns right, while T-T/1777W turns left. PG/1779 soon passes Queensboro Lake (built in 1915), where a good spot can be found for a lunch stop. At 3.2 miles, the 1779 Trail leaves to the left, and 0.2 mile further PG turns left on a gravel road below the dam at Turkey Hill Lake. This road, known as Summer Hill Road, was built in 1933 by the Civilian Conservation Corps. It runs 1.4 miles from Route 6 to the north end of the lake.

Leaving the road, PG now climbs around the west end of the dam and follows the lake shore. At 3.95 miles, near the end of the lake, the Anthony Wayne Trail (white) starts to the left. PG then goes uphill, turns right on a woods road and, at 4.5 miles, ends at a junction with the Long Path (aqua).

In 1940, Alexander Jessup marked a route with metal discs from the Bear Mountain Circle to the hikers' bridge that carried the Timp-Torne Trail across Popolopen Creek. He used the aqueduct path. The trail soon was neglected (it was wartime, and Jessup died in 1944). After the Popolopen Drive had been widened to four lanes, it was expected that the crossing of the Drive by the Timp-Torne Trail would be eliminated. As an approach to that trail, the aqueduct path was again marked by Meyer Kukle and Bob Bloom of the College Alumni Hiking Club. They used square white marks, and named it the Popolopen Gorge Trail (Trail Conference Minutes, 6/8/55). In 1960, the blazes were given a vertical red bar, and the trail was extended by Sam Wilkinson and Bill Burton to Long Mountain, passing the Queensboro and Turkey Hill Reservoirs. The bridge over Queensboro Brook was built by the Park in 1954. It carries a pipe which delivers the treated sewage from the Anthony Wayne Recreation Area into Queensboro Brook. In 2004, the blazes were changed from red dot on white to red square on white.

Raccoon Brook Hills Trail

Length: 2.95 miles · Blazes: black dot on white

Miles

0.0   Leave Seven Hills Trail.

0.3   Reeves Brook Trail, left.

0.35 Start climb.

0.7   HTS Trail crosses.

1.1   Gas line crosses.

1.4   Right, on woods road.

1.55 Kakiat Trail crosses.

1.9   Viewpoint from Raccoon Brook Hill.

2.4   Viewpoint over Pine Meadow Lake from second summit.

2.5   Poached Egg Trail, right.

2.9   Caves, right.

2.95 End at Kakiat Trail.

The Raccoon Brook Hills Trail (RBH) starts east from the Seven Hills Trail (blue on white), 0.35 mile south of the junction of the Seven Hills Trail with the Reeves Brook Trail. This point is 0.1 mile north of the cliff known as Torne View. (On Bill Hoeferlin's maps after 1960, this height is labeled Reeves Mountain.)

Heading downhill, RBH at 0.3 mile passes the end of the Reeves Brook Trail. It then crosses a little brook and climbs up a steep fault scarp. Looking up from below, one can see a jutting rock which was called "The Pulpit" by old-time hikers. From the top of the scarp, RBH goes down a bit, then climbs again to a ridge where the Hillburn-Torne-Sebago Trail (orange) crosses on a bare rock. At 1.1 miles, a gas line crosses (Columbia Gas Transmission Company, laid in 1949 and widened in 2007). After another 0.2 mile, RBH goes fairly steeply downhill and turns right on a woods road. The woods road soon disappears into laurels, and RBH goes down to the left.

At 1.55 miles, the Kakiat Trail (white) joins from the left. The two trails run together for 125 feet, after which RBH turns left, while Kakiat contin-

Ladder on the RBH Trail

ues straight ahead. RBH now climbs Raccoon Brook Hill, which has two 1,150-foot summits. The climb is rather steep in places, with a wooden ladder placed at a particularly steep spot just below the first summit.

Just before the trail climbs to the first summit, it crosses an old Park boundary. Until 1963, the land from this point south to Suffern was owned by the Ramapo Land Company of the Pierson family.

The first summit, at 1.9 miles, offers a view to the south, while the northernmost summit, at 2.4 miles, affords a view of Pine Meadow Lake when there are no leaves on the trees. RBH then descends. At 2.5 miles, a short rocky trail (yellow on white) leaves to the right to Pine Meadow Road West. The trail was marked by Conrad Schaefer about 1985 and is known as the Poached Egg Trail. It was officially adopted by the Trail Conference in 1989. RBH now goes up a bit, over the top of a hill, and then down again to cross Raccoon Brook. Look for caves at the foot of the hill, where Indian artifacts (now in the Bear Mountain Museum) were found. At 2.95 miles, RBH ends at the Kakiat Trail, 0.5 mile north of its first crossing of this trail.

The Raccoon Brook Hills Trail was first blazed in 1931 by Paul H. Schubert of Ridgewood (Queens), who also made the Red Disc (now Blue Disc) Trail (see p. 24). He named the trail the "Trail of the Raccoon Hills" (TRH). The original markers were half discs, red with white centers. They were later changed to red discs with vertical white bars. Schubert started his trail on Ramapo Torne, going north from there to the top of the third hill (Reeves Mountain or Torne View), where it starts today. The route from the Torne coincided with Nurian's HTS Trail and with the Seven Hills Trail which was maintained then by Jack Spivack of the New York Ramblers. When Nurian began painting out the others' blazes, a dispute arose, which was known as the "Great Ramapo Trail War" (see pp. 43-44). Schubert gave in and started his trail from the third hill (Torne View). The extension of the Seven Hills Trail to Suffern, although reblazed, was not maintained because of opposition from the Ramapo Land Company (of the Pierson family), on whose property the trail was located.

In 1939, the TRH blazes were changed to discs which were half white/half red. In 1940, the southern 1.75 miles of the trail were closed by the landowner. Hikers then created a "northern loop" which followed the park boundary southward from the Kakiat Trail to just west of Raccoon Brook Hill, and then continued along the northern portion of the route of the original TRH for the remainder of the loop. This loop, which became known as the Raccoon Brook Hills Trail (RBH), was marked in 1942 by Frank Place with black R's on white. This situation continued until March 14, 1963, when the Park acquired 1,796 acres of Pierson land, thus permitting the reopening of the southern end of this trail (as well as other trails on the newly-acquired land).

The Woodland Trail Walkers maintained this trail from 1949 to 1991.

Ramapo-Dunderberg Trail

Length: 23.05 miles · Blazes: red dot on white

Miles

0.0 Tuxedo railroad station.

0.6 Go uphill from Grove Drive.

0.8 Triangle Trail starts, left.

1.15 Viewpoint over Tuxedo.

1.4 Cross gas line; T-MI starts, up right.

2.15 Tri-Trail Corner.

2.7 Black Ash Mountain summit.

3.1 White Bar Trail crosses.

3.4 White Cross Trail starts, right.

3.65 Triangle Trail crosses.

4.2 Victory Trail crosses.

4.35 Tom Jones Shelter, right.

4.5 Summit of Tom Jones Mountain.

4.9 Route 106 crosses.

5.3 Nurian Trail leaves, left.

6.25 Bald Rocks Shelter, right.

6.4 Dunning Trail crosses.

6.65 Goldthwaite Memorial.

6.85 Lichen Trail starts, left.

6.9 Ship Rock.

7.55 Times Square: A-SB/LP crosses.

7.65 Pothole in cliff, left.

8.3 Bottle Cap Trail crosses.

9.05 AT joins, left.

9.15 Hurst Trail to Fingerboard Shelter, right.

9.7 Fireplace (old FB-SK).

10.15 Lake Tiorati Trail starts, right.

10.2 Cross Arden Valley Road.

10.9 Turn right, leaving AT.

11.25 Cross Seven Lakes Drive.

12.3   Turn right and begin steeper climb.

12.6   Summit of Goshen Mountain.

12.9   AT joins, left; Bockey Swamp Trail crosses.

13.7   William Brien Memorial Shelter; Menomine Trail crosses.

14.1   Intended ski trail crosses.

14.65 Silvermine Road crosses.

15.05 Summit of Black Mountain.

15.65 1779 Trail crosses.

15.85 Palisades Interstate Parkway crosses.

16.05 AT leaves, left.

16.35 Beechy Bottom East Road crosses.

16.85 Cats Elbow; S-BM Trail joins, right.

16.9   S-BM Trail leaves, left.

17.9   Timp Pass; Red Cross Trail leaves, right.

18.8   T-T Trail crosses.

19.1   1777 Trail crosses.

19.5   Fireplace; Bockberg Trail, left.

19.55 Bockberg Trail leaves, right.

19.9   Summit of Bald Mountain.

20.05 Cornell Mine Trail, left.

21.0   Bockberg Trail joins briefly.

21.2   Viewpoint over Bear Mountain Bridge.

21.45 Eastern summit of Dunderberg Mountain.

22.1   White-blazed side trail leads ahead to viewpoint.

22.2   Begin to follow railway grade.

22.55 Turn left at stone abutment and descend on route of cable incline.

22.8   Timp-Torne Trail joins from right.

22.9   Pass lower railway tunnel, right.

23.05 Route 9W; left to parking.

The Ramapo-Dunderberg Trail (R-D) was the first trail in Harriman State Park to be built by the New York hiking clubs, organized in October 1920 as the Palisades Interstate Park Trail Conference. The route of the trail was suggested by Major William Welch, the General Manager of the Park.

The trail starts at the Tuxedo railroad station. It heads north on a paved path to East Village Road, where it turns right and crosses the railroad tracks. After passing the entrance to a parking area on the left (free parking on weekends; fee charged on weekdays), R-D crosses the Ramapo River. Continuing along East Village Road, it bears right to parallel the Thruway, then curves left, goes under the Thruway, and turns left onto Grove Drive. At 0.6 mile, at a concrete catch-basin where the paved road bears left, R-D turns right and starts uphill on a switchback. The Kakiat Trail (white) also starts here. At 0.8 mile, the Triangle Trail begins to the left, and R-D soon starts a steep climb up Pine Hill. At 1.15 miles, there is a viewpoint to the left of the trail over the village of Tuxedo. From here, the trail descends briefly.

At 1.35 miles, R-D turns right on a woods road which comes up from below and crosses the route of the Columbia Gas Transmission Co. pipeline (built in 1949 and widened in 2007). Just beyond, the Tuxedo-Mt. Ivy Trail (red dash on white) starts to the right, up a rock face. R-D goes straight ahead, soon passing a mine down to the left and another, uphill on the right. Those mines were probably the reason for the old road, which ends near the mines. The ore must have gone to Solomon Townsend's Augusta Works at Tuxedo, about 1800.

Continuing straight ahead and downhill, R-D turns right onto a woods road that follows the south side of Black Ash Brook (the Black Ash Swamp Road). At 2.1 miles, it crosses the brook below a natural dam that backs up the water in Black Ash Swamp. In another 250 feet, R-D reaches Tri-Trail Corner, where the Victory Trail (blue V on white) and the Blue Disc Trail (blue dot on white) begin. R-D goes uphill, under a telephone line. The 1,130-foot summit of Black Ash Mountain is reached at 2.7 miles. At 3.1 miles, in the saddle between Black Ash Mountain and Parker Cabin Mountain, the White Bar Trail crosses, and 0.3 mile further the White Cross Trail leaves to the right.

R-D now climbs Parker Cabin Mountain, meeting the Triangle Trail (yellow) again at 3.65 miles. After 150 feet, Triangle leaves to the right (there is a view here of Lake Sebago), while R-D goes down the north end of the mountain to a fireplace in a notch where the Victory Trail crosses. Now the trail climbs Tom Jones Mountain (named for one of the Claudius Smith gang, who shot Parker, another horse thief, at his cabin in Parker Cabin Hollow). At 4.35 miles, the Tom Jones Shelter (built in 1927) is on the right. The 1,280-foot summit is then crossed, after which the trail goes steeply down to a brook and Route 106, which it reaches at 4.9 miles.

In 1920, when the trail was first blazed, the land south of Black Ash summit was owned by the Tuxedo Park Association. The trail was marked with their permission and was called the Tuxedo-Tom Jones Trail (from Tuxedo to Route 416— later Route 210 and now Route 106). In those days, that road was called Seven Lakes Drive.

The trail we have described so far was blazed in November 1920 by an AMC group led by J. Ashton Allis. At that time, Allis was a bank examiner, but he later became vice-president of Grace National Bank and chairman of Fairchild Aviation Company. The trail was marked with galvanized iron squares, inscribed "T-TJ." In the beginning, T-TJ crossed the Ramapo River on East Village Road, then turned north past a group of houses. Leaving the road, it crossed Black Ash Brook and went up its north side, then crossed to its south side (where the Triangle Trail crosses now) and so to the rock dam.

On August 10, 1930, Raymond Torrey suggested to Joseph Bartha that he relocate the T-TJ Trail. At that time, the Tuxedo-Mt. Ivy Trail (T-MI) was joint with T-TJ from Tuxedo until it turned right, uphill, on an old woods road that went high above Black Ash Brook. It then left the road and turned right, up over a rock face, towards Claudius Smith Rock. Torrey's suggestion was for T-TJ to follow T-MI up the woods road and then continue down to rejoin the earlier T-TJ route near the upper crossing of Black Ash Brook. The job was soon done (*N.Y. Post*, 9/16/30). In 1932, the trail was remarked as the R-D Trail, from Tuxedo to Jones Point.

In January 1955, after the Thruway was built, the Adirondack Mountain Club marked a new route for R-D in Tuxedo. From the railroad station, R-D followed the tracks south for 500 feet, then turned left to cross the Ramapo River on a steel footbridge. After passing a town playground, it turned right onto East Village Road, crossed under the Thruway, then turned left onto Grove Drive. When a new parking area north of the station was opened, parking at the station became off-limits to hikers (even on weekends), so R-D was relocated in 2006 to cross the tracks on East Village Road and go by the new parking area. In 1997, the section of the trail just east of Grove Drive was relocated from an eroded gully to a newly constructed switchback.

Until 1935, there was a "pole" fire tower on Parker Cabin Mountain, about where the Triangle Trail crosses R-D (*N.Y. Post*, 2/20/35). During 1930, a 115-foot well was drilled near the shelter on Tom Jones Mountain and equipped with a hand pump. This pump was repaired many times after vandals broke it, and in 1967 it finally was abandoned.

DANIEL CHAZIN

Bald Rocks Shelter

After crossing Route 106, R-D gradually climbs Black Rock Mountain. At the top, at 5.3 miles, the Nurian Trail (white) departs on the left, while R-D continues north along the ridge. After descending to a valley, it climbs to the Bald Rocks—at 1,382 feet in elevation, the highest point in the park. The trail passes just east of the summit and goes by the Bald Rocks Shelter (built in 1933) at 6.25 miles. 0.15 mile further, the Dunning Trail (yellow) crosses. R-D soon goes over an open rock surface (known as the Whaleback), passing through an area burned by a forest fire but now starting to regenerate with evergreen trees.

At 6.65 miles, a bronze plaque may be seen on a boulder to the right of the trail. This was placed on July 13, 1964 by the Fresh Air Club in memory of George Goldthwaite (1889-1960). On December 22, 1929, he hiked the entire R-D Trail in 4 hours and 51 minutes—the record time for hiking this trail. He is also remembered for his great knowledge of Park trails and as a hike leader.

After descending to cross a stream on a log bridge, R-D comes to another open rock where the Lichen Trail (blue L on white) leaves to the left at 6.85 miles. Just beyond is "Ship Rock," a boulder beside the trail that looks like a ship's prow, bottom up.

R-D now turns east and goes down about 40 feet, then up over Hogencamp Mountain. (When the trail was first marked in 1920, there was also a ruined fire tower here on the 1,353-foot summit; *N.Y. Post*, 4/1/21.) "Times Square," marked by a fireplace next to a great boulder, is reached at 7.55 miles. Here, R-D crosses the Arden-Surebridge Trail (red triangle on white) and the Long Path (aqua).

Continuing north, 0.1 mile from Times Square R-D climbs a rocky ledge. On this ledge, to the left of the trail, a large pothole was discovered by Frank Place on March 9, 1924 (*N.Y. Post*, 4/22/30). At 8.3 miles, as R-D goes down through a hemlock grove, the Bottle Cap Trail crosses. After climbing several more ledges, R-D swings east and joins the Appalachian Trail (AT) (white) on Fingerboard Mountain. The joint trails go north, reaching a junction with the Hurst Trail (blue), which leaves to the right at 9.15 miles. The Fingerboard Shelter (built 1928; *N.Y. Herald Tribune*, 10/7/28) is 0.1 mile down the Hurst Trail.

At 9.7 miles, R-D/AT passes a stone fireplace. The old Fingerboard-Storm King Trail (FB-SK) (built in 1922) used to start here. In 1964, its route was taken over by the new Long Path. Descending gradually now, R-D/AT reaches a junction with the Lake Tiorati Trail (blue) at 10.15 miles. This short trail, built in 2004, leads in 0.3 mile down to the Tiorati Circle, where water, restrooms and swimming are available in season. In another 200 feet, R-D/AT crosses Arden Valley Road. Across the road, an old road to the right leads to the site of the Fingerboard Fire Tower (erected 1922; removed in 1987).

The trail from Route 106 up Black Rock Mountain and over Hogencamp Mountain was first blazed on December 11, 1920 by J. Ashton Allis and William W. Bell, both of the AMC. Then on December 18th they marked the trail from Surebridge Mine Road (Times Square) to Arden Valley Road. Also, in December 1920 a team from the Tramp and Trail Club (Frank Place) blazed the trail from Tiorati Circle to Beechy Bottom.

In 1920, Arden Valley Road going west from Tiorati Circle was a dirt road 12 feet wide (*N.Y. Post*, 5/18/23). Going east from the circle, Tiorati Brook Road was "being improved."

Until 2004, R-D turned right at Arden Valley Road, followed the road down to Tiorati Circle, continued east on Tiorati Brook Road for 0.35 mile, then turned left into the woods, soon rejoining the present trail route. To avoid the roadwalk, the R-D was relocated in 2004 to follow the AT across Arden Valley Road, continue north along the AT for 0.7 mile, then turn right on a woods road and follow it to rejoin the original trail route. Although the roadwalk has been eliminated, the trail has been lengthened by about one mile.

R-D/AT continues north until it reaches a woods road at 10.9 miles.

Here, R-D turns right, leaving the AT, and descends to the east along the woods road. (To the left (west), the woods road leads in 0.3 mile to the Long Path (aqua).) After passing the Youmans Flats park maintenance area on the left and joining the dirt road leading to this facility, R-D crosses Seven Lakes Drive at 11.25 miles. R-D now begins a steady climb on a woods road, then levels off.

After rejoining the original trail route (which came in from Tiorati Brook Road), the R-D leaves the woods road at 12.3 miles and starts its final climb of Goshen Mountain. It goes northeast along the 1,320-foot ridge, then descends to the valley between Goshen and Letterrock Mountains. Here, at 12.9 miles, the AT joins from the left and the unmarked Bockey Swamp Trail comes up from below, crosses R-D/AT, and continues south. After some ups and downs, R-D/AT reaches the William Brien Memorial Shelter at 13.7 miles. In front of the shelter, a blue-blazed side trail goes to a spring-fed well nearby, and the Menomine Trail (yellow) crosses. To the left, the Menomine Trail goes down to the Silvermine parking area on Seven Lakes Drive in 1.35 miles; to the right, it leads in 0.85 mile to the Red Cross Trail.

On old trail maps, the unmarked Dean Trail started at this shelter, going downhill 0.85 mile to the Red Cross Trail. This section of the Dean Trail (which is now blazed yellow as part of the Menomine Trail) was once (1922) part of the Boy Scouts' White Bar Trail system. The Dean Trail is an old trail that went down to Stillwater Brook and then southeast to Bulsontown. The broad road that comes up to the shelter from Seven Lakes Drive was built in 1935 by the Civilian Conservation Corps.

The shelter here, built in 1933, was known as the Letterrock Shelter. William Brien, a naturalist, was the first president of the New York Ramblers (1923). He died on October 12, 1954. In his will, he left funds to build a new shelter in the Park. Such a shelter was built at Island Pond in 1957, but because of later vandalism it was demolished in 1973, and the Letterrock Shelter was renamed in his memory.

Originally, this mountain was called "Lettered Rock Mountain." In the early Park days, a Weyant family lived in Beechy Bottom near Queensboro (their graves are still there, in the road maze at Long Mountain Circle). They told a tale (*N.Y. Post*, 6/12/24) about a Frenchman who made periodic trips from Caldwell's Landing (Jones Point) into the mountains with his slave, returning with sacks of silver coins. He boasted of the "lettered rock" and of a silver hoard that lay due east of that rock. No one could find that lettered rock—until 1934.

In that year, a group of four treasure hunters was arrested after they had spent months blasting various places on Letterrock Mountain (*N.Y. Times*, 11/10/34). They had obtained a 1690 map from the Morgan Library, old, yellowed and cracked, that gave directions to the mine where Spaniards had hidden a silver treasure. They pointed to marks on a great boulder, but William Carr of the Trailside Museum said the marks had been caused by weathering.

R-D/AT climbs over rocks behind the shelter and continues northeast. About ten minutes from the shelter, a faint trail crosses. Followed to the right, this eventually becomes the wide ski trail that goes down to Silvermine Lake. To the left (indistinct) it becomes a woods road that slabs down off the mountain to join the CCC trail out to the Seven Lakes Drive. R-D/AT then descends to a valley where, at 14.65 miles, it crosses a wide gravel road—the Silvermine Road. Before it was "paved" in 1934 by the Temporary Emergency Relief Administration, it was known as the Black Mountain Trail (red blazes). R-D/AT now climbs steeply up Black Mountain, passing over ledges which afford beautiful views of Silvermine Lake. The trail levels off along the top at 15.05 miles, with grand views toward the south and east. To the left as the trail starts down, one can find a prospector's hole and, a little further along, a much deeper, water-filled hole. This hole came to be called the "Spanish Silver Mine," although there is not a trace of silver there. It was sufficiently romantic, however, to give its

View looking east from Black Mountain

name to a nearby ski slope that was opened in 1936, and later to the lake beside the ski slope.

Now the trail starts steeply down the east end of Black Mountain. After going up and over a low ridge, the 1779 Trail crosses. Soon afterwards, R-D/AT crosses the old Beechy Bottom West Road (rather vague just here) and then, at 15.85 miles, the Palisades Interstate Parkway. About 0.2 mile after going up steps on the east side of the Parkway, the AT leaves sharply to the left, while R-D goes down to Beechy Bottom Brook. Against the high bank, just west of the brook, Major Welch built the first trail shelter in the Park—a half-hexagon of corrugated iron (*N.Y. Post*, 11/25/21). It was removed in 1936, after extensive damage by the CCC boys.

Beyond the brook, R-D turns left and briefly follows the Horn Hill Bike Trail, with blue-on-white plastic markers. Then, at 16.25 miles, R-D turns off to the right. After climbing stone steps, it crosses Beechy Bottom East Road (made into a fire road by CCC), also blazed with bike trail markers. It continues up West Mountain, steeply in places. On the way up, R-D passes an old iron mine, and it meets the Suffern-Bear Mountain Trail (S-BM) (yellow) at the top of the Cats Elbow. There are good views here. The two trails are joint for about 300 feet. On a ledge, at 16.9 miles, S-BM leaves to the left. R-D climbs around another spur, then drops down to Timp Pass where it meets the Red Cross Trail at 17.9 miles. Here the un-marked Timp Pass Road goes left, down to Doodletown. R-D now bends to the right and descends, first gradually, then more steeply. At 18.4 miles, it turns sharply left and climbs very steeply up a rocky slope. It continues to climb for 0.3 mile, then descends to cross the Timp-Torne Trail (T-T) (blue) at 18.8 miles. To the left, T-T leads in 0.3 mile to the summit of The Timp, with panoramic views.

The R-D on the south crown of West Mountain was marked in 1920 by A.B. Malcolmson. As origi-nally laid out, R-D followed a route up the Timp face known as the Six Chins Trail, which had been located and named by Frank Place in 1917. Both men were from the Tramp and Trail Club. From The Timp to Jones Point, the trail was blazed in January and February 1921 by E. Cecil Earle and A.B. Malcolmson of the Tramp and Trail Club and J. Ashton Allis of AMC.

By the 1990s, the very steep route that R-D (and T-T) followed up the face of The Timp had become badly eroded, so it was decided to construct new routes for both R-D and T-T that would bypass this steep climb. A new route for the T-T was located north of Timp Pass, and the relocated trail was opened in the summer of 1998. R-D was relocated to a route south of Timp Pass, with the new trail route being completed in the fall of 1999. As a result of the relocation, R-D no longer reaches the top of The Timp.

About 0.3 mile beyond the T-T intersection, R-D crosses the 1777 Trail. In the past, this old road was called the Lumberjack Trail and Steep Street. It is the route taken by the British troops in 1777 from Stony Point to attack Forts Clinton and Montgomery. Going now northeast, R-D climbs through laurels, then descends to a brook where there is a fireplace. The road which comes from the hill ahead, and departs down left, is the Bockberg Trail. R-D follows it briefly uphill, leaves it, then briefly rejoins it. At 19.55 miles, the Bockberg Trail departs to the right for the second time, while R-D continues its steep climb to the 1,115-foot summit of Bald Mountain (the Bockberg), with great views. The Cornell Mine is passed 250 feet beyond the summit, and the end of the Cornell Mine Trail (blue) is reached at 20.05 miles.

Continuing now toward Dunderberg proper, R-D at 21.0 miles meets the Bockberg Trail again, and then crosses a grade of the old Dunderberg Spiral Railway (see pp. 285-90). After a short descent, R-D climbs to a panoramic viewpoint, with the Bear Mountain Bridge to the north, and the Hudson River to the south. R-D continues over the 900-foot summit and steeply descends its eastern face.

After passing another viewpoint (just to the right of the trail) over the Hudson River (with Peekskill directly ahead), R-D turns sharply right at 22.1 miles. Here, a short white-blazed side trail leads ahead to another viewpoint over the river. Soon, R-D begins to follow a section of the graded railbed. In 0.35 mile, it turns left at a stone abutment and descends steeply along the route of the proposed cable incline, on which the railway cars would have been pulled up the mountain. At 22.8 miles, at the bottom of the incline, R-D joins the Timp-Torne Trail (blue) just above a 100-foot-long masonry tunnel (through which the final descending leg of the railway would have passed), and it runs jointly with Timp-Torne for 0.25 mile to its terminus on Route 9W. Parking is available on the west side of the road, a short distance to the north, opposite the intersection with Old Route 9W (which leads to Jones Point).

DANIEL CHAZIN

Stone abutment of the Dunderberg Spiral Railway

Until 2000, R-D headed east from the viewpoint at 22.1 miles, descended to Route 9W, and continued to Jones Point, located along the river. In 1999, a forest fire obliterated part of this section of the trail, and it was decided to relocate it along a graded section of the Dunderberg Spiral Railway and then down the route of the cable incline to a junction with the R-D Trail. This relocation eliminates a dangerous crossing of Route 9W and facilitates loop hikes using the T-T and R-D Trails, both of which now use the same trailhead on Route 9W in a location where ample parking is available.

The old road at Jones Point that goes around Dunderberg at the river level was built in 1907, 12 feet wide. The new road was built 30 feet wide, higher up, in 1930 (*N.Y. Times*, 6/29/30). Until 1930, the road was designated N.Y. Route 3. An even old-er road, the Dunderberg and Clove Turnpike, had been built in 1809.

Jones Point and part of the mountain, including much of the spiral railway, were purchased by the Park in 1928 from Mary E. Jones and Charles and Anna Jones. They were a wealthy Westchester/Long Island family. Their ancestor, Joshua T. Jones, bought 100 acres in 1836 at what was then known as Caldwell's Landing.

On Thursday night, May 11, 1967, a single-engine plane crashed on Dunderberg Mountain. The pilot, Arnold Shaefer of New York City, was killed. Three hikers found the wreck on the following Saturday morning (*Journal News* (Nyack, N.Y.), May 15, 1967). Part of the wreckage may still be seen a little way north of the R-D, about 0.5 mile from Route 9W, just west of where the R-D crosses a loop of the spiral railway.

Red Arrow Trail

Length: 0.35 mile · Blazes: red arrow

Miles

0.0   Start up from T-MI.

0.15 Old Limekiln Mountain Trail, right.

0.35 End at S-BM.

This short trail presently connects the Tuxedo-Mt. Ivy Trail (T-MI) (red dash on white), which comes up from Ladentown, with the Suffern-Bear Mountain Trail (S-BM) (yellow), which descends Circle Mountain.

Going up T-MI from Ladentown, Red Arrow starts steeply up to the right at 0.95 mile. At 0.15 mile from the T-MI, Red Arrow goes uphill, to the northwest, beside a stone wall. Off to the right is another stone wall, which goes uphill to the north. The old Limekiln Mountain Trail begins on the east side of that stone wall. At 0.35 mile, the S-BM comes in from the left. The Red Arrow Trail now officially ends here.

The Red Arrow Trail once continued ahead, running jointly with S-BM over Ladentown Mountain, down past the Third Reservoir, and up to Breakneck Mountain. Here the S-BM departs to the right, up over a big rock, and the Breakneck Mountain Trail (white) starts to the left. Red Arrow continued straight ahead, and soon began to go steeply down to the camp road, where it ended, 1.45 miles from the T-MI.

In older editions of the *New York Walk Book*, the Red Arrow Trail was described as a "fisherman's short-cut from Ladentown to Breakneck Pond." It is not known how the trail was first marked. About 1931, the Interstate Hiking Club cleared and remarked it (*Paterson Morning Call*, 9/20/35). It was restored again by Frank Place in 1943, then maintained by Joseph Bartha until the NYU Club took it over in 1948.

Red Cross Trail

Length: 7.9 miles • Blazes: red cross on white

Miles

0.0	Start from A-SB on Pine Swamp Mountain.
0.45	Cross Seven Lakes Drive.
1.15	Telephone line crosses.
1.35	Hasenclever Mountain Trail, left.
1.65	Turn left on woods road from Lake Askoti.
1.9	Hasenclever Road joins, right.
2.45	Cross Tiorati Brook Road.
2.55	Cross Tiorati Brook.
3.1	Bockey Swamp Trail, left.
3.2	Beech Trail starts, right.
4.45	Menomine Trail, left.
4.75	Stillwater Trail, right.
5.65	Cross Palisades Interstate Parkway.
5.85	1779 Trail joins, left.
5.95	S-BM joins, left.
6.02	S-BM leaves, right.
6.05	Red Cross turns left.
6.55	Cross Beechy Bottom Road.
7.0	Turn left onto woods road.
7.15	Turn left onto Horn's Route.
7.4	Turn left onto North "Ski Trail."
7.45	Turn right onto stone road.
7.9	End at Timp Pass.

The Red Cross Trail was first blazed in April 1944, but it has been re-located several times since then. It now starts from the Arden-Surebridge Trail (A-SB) (red triangle on white) on Pine Swamp Mountain, 0.25 mile from the parking area at Lake Skannatati. After ascending briefly, parallel to the A-SB, it descends the mountain and crosses Seven Lakes Drive. Red Cross then passes the north end of Lake Askoti and climbs up the ridge on the far side of the lake. About 0.2 mile after Red Cross crosses a telephone line, the Hasenclever Mountain Trail leaves to the left. Red Cross crosses a swampy area on a wooden bridge and, at 1.65 miles, turns left onto a woods road which comes from Lake Askoti. It follows this woods road for 0.25 mile and then turns left onto the Hasenclever Road. Just beyond the junction, the old water-filled Hasenclever Mine is visible on the right.

In 1765, Peter Hasenclever, a German mining engineer working for a London company, discovered this mine on the old woods road. In the years before the Interstate Park was created, this road, then known as Cedar Ponds Road, was maintained by the Town of Stony Point. An occasional cement town marker may be seen in the grass by the roadside. The history of "Baron" Hasenclever and his mine is related in J.M. Ransom's *Vanishing Ironworks of the Ramapos* (pp. 130-35).

After crossing Tiorati Brook Road at 2.45 miles, the trail goes across an unused ballfield, enters the woods and goes down to Tiorati Brook. A little way up the brook, hidden in weeds, is an earth mound. This is all that remains of the Orange Furnace, planned by Hasenclever but built by James Brewster about 1800. The trail crosses the brook and proceeds with Goshen Mountain on the left. Going gently downhill, it crosses another brook. Just past the brook, an unmarked woods road starts to the left. That old road crosses the brook again and goes north for about 0.9 mile, with Goshen Mountain on the left and swamps on the right.

Red Cross now rounds the south end of Letterrock Mountain. At 3.1 miles, the southern end of the Bockey Swamp Trail (unmarked) is on the left. The junction is marked by a cairn. The Beech Trail (blue) starts to the right in another 0.1 mile. Red Cross then goes down a long valley, with Letterrock Mountain on the left and Flaggy Meadow Mountain on the right, and crosses several streams. At 4.45 miles, the Menomine Trail (yellow) comes in on the left. Red Cross now crosses a brook on a wooden footbridge. Just beyond, the cellar hole of the Burnt House is visible to the left of the trail. A local story relates that this was the home of a boss woodcutter named Jonas Lewis.

Before it was marked with red crosses, the trail down from Tiorati Brook had been called the Burnt House Trail. Here it briefly coincided with the Dean Trail, then crossed to the right side of Stillwater Brook and followed that brook around the end of Flaggy Meadow Mountain, ending on Tiorati Brook Road. (The lower end of the trail, from the crossing of the brook to Tiorati Brook Road, is now known as the Stillwater Trail.) About 1920, the Boy Scouts made it part of their White Bar Trail system (*N.Y. Post*, 6/23/33).

During the 1930s, George Goldthwaite of the Fresh Air Club researched the trails in this area. His hand-drawn map dated February 22, 1940 shows the Dean Trail passing the Burnt House and continuing east to end at Bulsontown (Cedar Flats Road). This is the present route of the Red Cross/1779 Trail. In 1944, the newly-marked Red Cross Trail incorporated the Burnt House Trail from Tiorati Brook Road and then followed the Dean Trail, until it turned off that trail just beyond the S-BM crossing. In 1965, the Park widened the Red Cross Trail to 20 feet, from the Hasenclever Mine to the Burnt House.

There was a local story told by Harvey Bulson, a blacksmith, that a woodcutter named Jonas Lewis lived in the Burnt House beside the trail. One day in 1910, Bulson stopped to visit Jonas. Opening the door, he found Jonas and his four sons sitting on one side of the room. A spittoon was on the other side. The five tobacco chewers were competing to see who could hit the mark, and line of tobacco juice crossed the floor from each of them. (Isn't it odd what things go down in history?)

Footbridge over a brook

DANIEL CHAZIN

At 4.75 miles, the Stillwater Trail (unmarked) leaves to the right. Red Cross continues east and passes a swamp to the right. At 4.95 miles, it crosses a wet region where Owl Swamp Brook comes down from the left. On the west side of that brook are traces of an (intended) old road, started in 1934 but abandoned. At 5.6 miles, the trail reaches the Palisades Interstate Parkway. It turns left along the southbound lanes for 150 feet, then crosses the road opposite the end of the guardrail and enters the woods on the median strip. Red Cross then crosses the northbound lanes and turns left. Again, it runs along the guardrail for 150 feet, then turns right and enters the woods. East of the Parkway, it passes through a level region, with the 1779 Trail joining from the left at 5.85 miles. (This point is the end of the old Black Mountain Trail.) Soon the Suffern-Bear Mountain Trail (yellow) comes in from the left and departs again after 400 feet. About 150 feet further along, Red Cross suddenly turns left, while the 1779 Trail goes on down the wide old Dean Trail.

For the next mile, Red Cross follows a route that was first marked about 1940 by J. Ashton Allis, who was then treasurer of the Trail Conference. On the way, Red Cross crosses Beechy Bottom Road (built in 1740 from Stony Point to Central Valley). Red Cross then descends steadily and, at 7.0 miles, turns left onto an old woods road, once known as the Bulsontown-Timp Road. In another 50 feet, a trail marked with "A-B" blazes (by the Addisone Boyce Girl Scout camp) joins from the right. To the right, the A-B blazes go across a stone wall and continue down to Mott Farm Road. Red Cross once followed that route, but it now goes north on the old road for 0.15 mile, crosses a stream on a short suspension bridge erected by the Girl Scouts, and then turns left at a T-junction onto another old road (Horn's Route). A little way up that road, a faint trail goes off to the left near the ruin of an old cabin. After another 0.2 mile, Red Cross departs to the right from Horn's Route, crosses a little brook and then an old woods road, and turns left onto the North "Ski Trail" at 7.4 miles. In another 275 feet, it turns sharply right onto another "stone road" which, for much of its distance, is a real "ankle-breaker"! This "stone road" climbs (often steeply) to Timp Pass, which it reaches at 7.9 miles. Here the Red Cross Trail ends at a junction with the Ramapo-Dunderberg Trail (red dot on white) and the unmarked Timp Pass Road.

When it was first blazed in 1944, Red Cross started from the Dunning Trail (now Long Path) near a shaft of the Hogencamp Mine, and followed an older Boy Scout trail to Lake Skannatati (the first dam of which was built in 1938). The trail went around the south end of Lake Askoti and climbed the hill to the east on an old woods road. That road, which more or less followed the county line, joined the present route near Hasenclever Mine. From there the route was the same as now, except at the eastern end. There, instead of turning up toward Timp Pass, it went on down to Bulsontown Road (now known as Mott Farm Road). In 1951, when the Rockland County Girl Scouts began to build Camp Addisone Boyce, they asked that the Red Cross Trail be relocated. This was done in 1952, sending the trail to the road across the dam of the new lake. Finally, in 1964, Red Cross was sent uphill to end at Timp Pass.

In 1947, the western end of the trail was relocated. It was made to start from Seven Lakes Drive, at the entrance to Camp Thendara. That made the trail one mile shorter. The original western end, from near the Hogencamp Mine shaft to Lake Skannatati, was demarked but still maintained (Trail Conference Minutes, 2/6/57), and it became the Skannatati Trail in 1961. (In 1981, the Skannatati Trail became part of the Long Path.)

In 1978, the beginning of Red Cross was again relocated, this time to the route it follows at present. That was done to avoid parking congestion and vandalism at Camp Thendara.

Red Timp Trail

Length: 1.0 mile (about 0.6 mile on Park property) • Blazes: two red T's in red-outlined quadrants on a white background in a red circle

Miles

0.0 Start at R-D/T-T junction; go east, turn right in 150 feet.

0.4 Junction with old Timp-Torne Trail.

0.55 Old Timp-Torne Trail leaves, right.

1.0 End at Girl Scout camp (private property).

This Trail, which is not an official Trail Conference trail, was blazed by the Girl Scouts of Camp Addisone Boyce on Mott Farm Road. Although the route of this trail is currently marked with blazes and is easy to follow, it is not officially maintained, and portions of the treadway are in relatively poor condition. The first 0.4 mile of the trail down from The Timp is fairly steep and severely eroded in places.

The Red Timp Trail starts from the junction of the Timp-Torne (T-T) (blue on white) and Ramapo-Dunderberg (R-D) (red dot on white) Trails, 0.2 mile east of the summit of The Timp. Red Timp heads east on the T-T for about 150 feet, and then leaves to the right and goes steeply down the hillside, following an old road that is severely eroded in places. At 0.4 mile, it reaches the former route of the T-T Trail at the beginning of a region that was lumbered in 1986. The trail here crosses outside of the Park boundary.

Red Timp turns right (southwest and then west) and reenters the Park, following the former route of the T-T Trail (the old T-T is still marked by a few blue-on-white blazes, as well as a few newer blazes apparently added by the Girl Scouts). At 0.45 mile, a side trail with yellow-on-red wooden blazes goes left onto private property. The Red Timp Trail continues straight, passing a swampy area on the left which occasionally invades the road.

At 0.55 mile, a junction is reached. Here, Red Timp bears left, leaving the old T-T, and goes around a great cliff called the Boulderberg. The trail soon enters Girl Scout property and follows an old road, along a stream, down into their camp on Mott Farm Road. From the junction, the old T-T, still marked by old and new blue-on-white blazes, bears right (northwest) and heads uphill on a woods road. It can easily be followed to its intersection with the R-D Trail just east of Timp Pass.

To the east of its junction with the Red Timp Trail at 0.4 mile, the route of the old T-T (which is on private property) has been obliterated for a few hundred feet by logging operations. Past the logged area, the old T-T route can, with some difficulty, be found heading diagonally left on a faint old road, uphill, and it soon reenters the Park. However, there are no remaining blazes in this area and the trail is quite difficult to follow.

The Red Timp Trail is a very old trail, which was shown on the Park's 1927 topo map as the Timp Trail. For many years it was known to hikers as the Timp Bypass, since, when used together with the old Timp-Torne Trail, it enabled hikers to bypass the very steep descent of the Timp on the Ramapo-Dunderberg (R-D) Trail. Now that the Timp-Torne Trail has been rerouted over the summit of The Timp and avoids the steep descent by using a more gentle route to the north, it is no longer necessary to use Red Timp as a bypass, and the trail has fallen into relative disuse.

Reeves Brook Trail

Length: 1.65 miles · *Blazes: white*

Miles

0.0   Reeves Meadow.

0.2   Reeves Brook, left.

0.5   Woods road leaves, right.

1.35   Seven Hills Trail crosses.

1.65   End at Raccoon Brook Hills Trail.

The Reeves Brook Trail starts near Seven Lakes Drive, at the far edge of Reeves Meadow. (To reach the beginning of the trail from the visitor center parking lot, turn left on the Pine Meadow Trail and follow it for 300 feet to the start of the Reeves Brook Trail, which goes off to the right.) Going uphill on a woods road, the trail approaches Reeves Brook at 0.2 mile. Then at 0.5 mile the woods road (once known as the Fishline Trail) departs to the right. The Reeves Brook Trail goes straight ahead, fairly steeply up, following the brook which flows down along a geologic fault. At 1.35 miles, the Seven Hills Trail (blue on white) crosses, and at 1.65 miles the Reeves Brook Trail ends at the Raccoon Brook Hills Trail (black dot on white). 0.2 mile to the east, on top of a cliff, is the rock known as "The Pulpit."

The Reeves Brook Trail was first mentioned in the Trail Conference minutes of April 4, 1956, which stated that this "unofficial trail" had "not been accepted by the Park." When the Park purchased 1,796 acres of Pierson land in 1963, the Reeves Brook Trail was made a Conference trail, and Bob Bloom of the College Alumni Hiking Club, who probably first blazed it, became its maintainer. Bloom, who served for many years on the Board of the Trail Conference, maintained the trail until his death on April 4, 1986.

Seven Hills Trail

Length: 6.65 miles · Blazes: blue on white

Miles

0.0 Entrance to Sebago parking area.
0.35 Buck Trail goes left.
0.6 Turn left, up Woodtown Road (West).
0.7 Turn right, off road.
0.9 T-MI crosses.
1.1 Fire road joins, left.
1.4 Diamond Mountain-Tower Trail, left.
1.5 HTS joins, right.
1.75 Diamond Mountain-Tower Trail, left.
1.77 Diamond Mountain summit.
1.8 HTS leaves, right.
2.5 Cross Pine Meadow Brook.
3.0 HTS crosses.
3.3 Gas line crosses; Quartz Brook Trail, right.
3.7 Reeves Brook Trail crosses.
4.05 RBH Trail starts, left.
4.15 Torne View.
4.5 HTS joins, left.
4.7 HTS leaves, left; 7H turns down, right.
5.25 HTS begins, left, at foot of hill.
6.3 Fishline Trail crosses.
6.65 End at Pine Meadow Trail.

The Seven Hills Trail (7H) starts opposite the entrance to the Lake Sebago hikers' parking area on Seven Lakes Drive, four miles from Route 17. For 0.3 mile, the trail goes fairly steeply up Conklin Mountain on an old woods road, once known as the Monitor Trail. (In November 1988, the lower end was slightly relocated.) Near the top of the climb, the Buck Trail (yellow) begins to the left.

The Seven Hills Trail goes down the slope of Conklin Mountain and, at 0.6 mile, turns left, up Woodtown Road (West). Here the trail crosses Diamond Creek, and after going up 0.1 mile, it leaves the road and turns sharp right. On the left at this point, a white-blazed trail goes about 300 feet to a ledge on which there is a large quartz boulder known as Monitor Rock.

When the Seven Hills Trail was first blazed, it started from Monitor Rock. The rock was so named by the Fresh Air Club when they found tucked under it a copy of the *Christian Science Monitor* newspaper. The road up to the rock from the parking area at Old Sebago Beach was named the Monitor Trail. That trail was forgotten until hiker parking at Sebago Dam was ended in 1977. At that time, 7H was rerouted down to the present parking area.

Woodtown Road (West) is a very old road that started at the Burnt Sawmill Bridge (where Sebago Dam is now). It crossed the saddle between Conklin and Diamond Mountains, then went across the south end of a swamp on Christie Brook (now Lake Wanoksink) to join the main Woodtown Road which ran from Willow Grove to Ramapo.

Diamond Mountain, too, has changed its name. The 1923 edition of the *New York Walk Book* showed it as Halfway Mountain. Then in 1927 the Park's large topographic map named the higher eastern end Diamond Mountain, while the western end remained Halfway Mountain.

Seven Hills Trail now goes along the ridge of Diamond Mountain. At 0.8 mile, it passes a great boulder, called the "Cracked Diamond," and at 0.9 mile, the Tuxedo-Mt. Ivy Trail (red dash on white) crosses. At 1.1 miles, 7H briefly joins a fire road (which goes from Pine Meadow Road up to the site of the fire tower). A little further, at 1.4 miles, the Diamond Mountain-Tower Trail (yellow) leaves to the left. There was once an 80-foot steel fire tower, 75 yards east of this junction, erected in 1935 from the steel of the tower that stood on Bear Mountain. It was removed in 1955, erected again in 1966, and removed again in 1986.

At 1.5 miles, the Hillburn-Torne-Sebago Trail (HTS) (orange) joins from the right. The Diamond Mountain-Tower Trail (yellow) ends on the left at 1.75 miles, just before 7H reaches the 1,242-foot summit of the mountain. At 1.8 miles, HTS departs to the right, while 7H goes steeply down to Pine Meadow Brook, where it turns left briefly on the Kakiat Trail (white). Both trails (along with the red-blazed Pine Meadow Trail) cross the brook on an often-washed-away log bridge. Kakiat then departs to the left, following Raccoon Brook, while the Pine Meadow Trail goes right, down along Pine Meadow Brook. 7H follows the Pine Meadow Trail for about 450 feet beyond the bridge, and then turns left at a fireplace and begins to climb Chipmunk Mountain.

At 3.0 miles, HTS again joins from the right, and leaves left 100 feet further on. 7H turns right onto the route of a buried gas pipeline at 3.3 miles, and in another 100 feet 7H turns left and soon crosses Quartz Brook. The Quartz Brook Trail, abandoned in 1969, went down the left side of the brook to the Pine Meadow Trail. Until 1963, this trail was on private property, as was the Seven Hills Trail south of the summit of Chipmunk Mountain.

At 3.65 miles, 7H drops very steeply down from a fault scarp (good view) to cross the Reeves Brook Trail (white). Climbing again, 7H passes the start of the Raccoon Brook Hills Trail (black dot on white) to the left at 4.05 miles. Shortly afterwards, 7H reaches a viewpoint from the south end of this hill, known as Torne View (1,170 feet). 7H then drops steeply down into a gully, and climbs back up to meet HTS once again at 4.5 miles. In another 0.2 mile, at a dip in the ridge, 7H bears right, while HTS turns left and continues ahead to Ramapo Torne.

This is a good place to relate the early history of the Seven Hills Trail. It was first blazed by J. Ashton Allis about 1922. At that time, he was President of the Fresh Air Club, which had been organized in 1876 by "Father Bill" Curtis (there is a monument on the way up Slide Mountain to Curtis and his companion Allen Ormsbee, both of whom died in June 1900 in a snowstorm on Mt. Washington). Allis was a compulsive trail blazer. His marks were tiny nicks, called "bird's eye blazes," and his cairns were soon hidden by weeds. His trail started in the village of Ramapo, went up the Torne, and continued over Torne View and Chipmunk, Halfway, Diamond and Conklin Mountains, end-ing at Monitor Rock.

After he marked the trail, Allis broached the idea to Major Welch who, in 1923, suggested the need for such a trail, landowners permitting. (*N.Y. Post*, 11/29/23). In 1926, Allis' faint trail was discovered by Jack Spivack of the New York Ramblers. On December 18, 1927, with two friends, Spivack blazed Allis' trail white from the Torne to Pine Meadow Brook. He later continued the blazes to Monitor Rock (Mountain Magazine, Jan. 1928). Spivack intended to start the trail up Nordkop Mountain at Suffern, then over the hill above Hillburn to the Torne. It was Spivack who named it "Trail of the Seven Hills." The seven hills he had in mind were: (1)

Nordkop Mountain (above Suffern); (2) Hillburn Mountain (above Hillburn); (3) Ramapo Torne; (4) Torne View; (5) Chipmunk Mountain; (6) Diamond Mountain; and (7) Conklin Mountain.

During 1928, Kerson Nurian blazed the HTS Trail from Hillburn partly on Allis' older route, and used Spivack's trail for 0.2 mile north of the Torne. Eight years later, in the fall of 1936, Spivack at last extended his Seven Hills Trail (now blazed blue) to Suffern, using part of Nurian's HTS

and part of the S-BM. In that year, there began the "Great Ramapo Trail War," as a result of which parts of the Seven Hills Trail were painted out by Nurian (see pp. 43-44). When the "war" was over, Spivack repainted his blue blazes to Suffern. But the Seven Hills Trail, as well as other trails in the area south of the Park boundary (just south of Pine Meadow Brook) were closed in 1940 by order of the Ramapo Land Company (Pierson Estate).

From the saddle in the Torne ridge, 7H turns down right on a woods road. At the bottom (5.25 miles), the trail turns right, as the HTS Trail begins to the left (the road to the left, now the route of HTS, was once the route of 7H into Sloatsburg). The trail passes a beaver swamp, crosses Beaver Brook, and goes down around the north side of Middle Hill, now following the old Mason Trail. At 6.3 miles, the Fishline Trail crosses, and at 6.65 miles the Seven Hills Trail ends at the Pine Meadow Trail (red square on white).

James R. Pierson, president of the Ramapo Land Company, died on May 3, 1959, at the age of 85. In 1963, after several years of negotiation, the Park acquired 1,796 acres of Pierson land by condemnation. This included the land south to the Ramapo Torne, and the acquisition enabled all trails in this area to be reopened. The Seven Hills Trail was extended to Suffern, using Spivack's old route. But the extended trail still passed over some private land, so by 1965 it had been rerouted onto the woods road at the

foot of the Torne. That road went to the Thruway fence (the "Going East" Trail), and then continued north along the fence to Greenway, the first street in Sloatsburg east of the Thruway. Local residents protested (since there was no room to park near the trailhead), and in November 1976 the Seven Hills Trail was given its present route from Ramapo Torne to the Pine Meadow Trail, where it ends, 0.2 mile south of the visitor center on Seven Lakes Drive.

Stahahe Brook Trail

Length: 0.75 mile · Blazes: horizontal red stripe on white

Miles

0.0 Start on Arden Road; A-SB leaves to left.

0.3 Cross bridge over Stahahe Brook and turn left, leaving road.

0.35 Turn right onto Stahahe Brook Road.

0.5 Cross stream.

0.75 End at Nurian Trail.

The Stahahe Brook Trail begins on Arden Road, 0.4 mile south of Arden Valley Road. Here, the Arden-Surebridge Trail (red triangle on white) leaves to the left to begin its climb of Green Pond Mountain, and the Stahahe Brook Trail heads south along the road. At 0.3 mile, the trail crosses a wood-and-stone bridge over Stahahe Brook. Just beyond, the trail turns left, leaving the road, and climbs on a footpath.

In another 250 feet, the Stahahe Brook Trail turns left onto a woods road, the Stahahe Brook Road, and continues to climb more gradually. It crosses a stream at 0.5 mile and ends, 0.75 mile from the start, at a junction with the Nurian Trail (white). To the left, the Nurian Trail goes down to cross Stahahe Brook, then climbs through the Valley of Boulders. Straight ahead, it continues along the road for 0.15 mile, then turns right to climb the southern ridge of Green Pond Mountain.

The Stahahe Brook Trail, which follows old woods roads for almost its entire length, was marked by the Trail Conference in 2004 to provide alternate access to the Nurian Trail when the owner of the Red Apple Rest in Southfields (a traditional parking spot for hikers on the Nurian Trail) closed his parking lot to hikers. The Stahahe Brook Trail enables one to park at the Elk Pen and follow marked trails to the Nurian Trail, near the north end of Lake Stahahe.

Stony Brook Trail

Length: 1.85 miles · Blazes: yellow

Miles

0.0   Begin at Pine Meadow Trail.

0.1   Cross Quartz Brook on footbridge; cross gas pipeline.

0.4   Kakiat Trail joins, left.

0.55 Cross Pine Meadow Brook on footbridge; Kakiat Trail leaves, right.

1.7   Cross Diamond Creek.

1.85 End at Hillburn-Torne-Sebago Trail.

The Stony Brook Trail begins at the Pine Meadow Trail (red square on white), 0.4 mile from the Reeves Meadow Visitor Center. At first, it follows a woods road along the aptly-named Stony Brook. In 500 feet, it crosses Quartz Brook on a footbridge and traverses a wide clearing for a gas pipeline. The trail soon narrows to a footpath.

At 0.4 mile, the Kakiat Trail (white) joins from the left, having crossed Stony Brook on a footbridge. Then, at 0.55 mile, both trails cross Pine Meadow Brook on a footbridge. Just beyond, the Kakiat Trail leaves to the right, while the Stony Brook Trail continues ahead, now following a footpath along Stony Brook. It continues along the brook for over a mile, following an old woods road for part of the way.

At 1.7 miles, the trail crosses Diamond Creek and passes through a dense stand of mountain laurel. It ends, 1.85 miles from the start, at a junction with the Hillburn-Torne-Sebago Trail (HTS) (orange). To reach Seven Lakes Drive, continue ahead for 400 feet on HTS to its terminus at the Tuxedo-Mt. Ivy Trail (T-MI) (red dash on white), then turn left and follow T-MI for 0.15 mile to its intersection with Seven Lakes Drive, just north of the dam at the south end of Lake Sebago.

Until 2003, the Stony Brook Trail was unmarked, although it was well known among hikers. At the suggestion of the Park, the trail was adopted by the Trail Conference in 2003 and blazed yellow.

About 1.1 miles from the start of the Stony Brook Trail, an old unmarked trail may be seen coming downhill on the west side of the

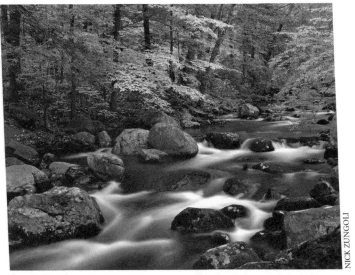

Stony Brook

brook. In 1921, this was part of the Boy Scouts' White Bar Trail. It came from their Camp Leatherstocking (where the Dutch Doctor Shelter is now), went up Diamond Creek, crossed Woodtown Road and went over Conklin Mountain on the Buck Trail. The land east of the brook to the top of Halfway Mountain was sold to the Park in 1916 by Miss Julia Siedler of Montclair, N.J. She had inherited it from her father, Charles Siedler, who built a mill at Dater's Crossing in 1882. The land on the west side of the brook, to the top of the ridge, was sold to the Park in 1921 by Fred Snow, a notable citizen of Hillburn.

Suffern-Bear Mountain Trail

Length: 23.35 miles · Blazes: yellow

Miles

0.0 Suffern; Route 59.

0.2 Viewpoint.

0.35 Viewpoint to right; woods road joins.

0.6 Gas line crosses.

0.8 Summit of Nordkop Mountain.

1.0 Seven Hills Trail went left (1944-63).

1.3 Seven Hills Trail went left (1936-44).

1.45 Climb Kitchen Stairs.

1.9 Gas line crosses.

2.15 Cross outlet of cattail swamp.

2.75 Power line crosses.

3.15 Cross Os-Sec Brook in Valley of Dry Bones.

3.7 Sky Sail Farm.

4.2 Gas line crosses.

4.4 MacIlvain's Rocks; Grandma and Grandpa Rocks.

4.5 Kakiat Trail crosses.

4.65 Summit of Cobus Mountain.

5.6 Conklins Crossing Trail, left.

5.75 The Egg.

5.95 Stone Memorial Shelter; cross Sherwood Path.

6.5 Hawk Cliff.

6.8 Pittsboro Trail joins from right.

7.0 Pine Meadow Trail joins from left.

7.2 Old Pine Meadow Trail went right.

7.45 Pine Meadow Trail leaves, right; Gyascutus Brook crosses.

7.7 Summit of Panther Mountain.

8.3 Many Swamp Trail crosses.

8.65 T-MI Trail (Two Bridges Road) crosses.

9.4 Red Arrow Trail, right.

9.5 File Factory Brook crosses.

9.55 Woodtown Road crosses.

10.15 Third Reservoir, right.

10.3 Breakneck Mountain Trail, left.

11.15 Big Hill Shelter; Long Path joins.

11.35 Long Path leaves, right.

11.5 Old Turnpike crosses.

12.1 Jackie Jones Mountain; fire tower.

12.8 Ruins of ORAK.

13.2 Cross Gate Hill Road (Route 106).

13.75 Irish Potato.

15.55 Turn right on Lake Welch Drive.

15.75 Palisades Interstate Parkway crosses.

15.95 Scutt Memorial tablet.

16.45 Pingyp summit.

17.0 Brook crosses; fireplace.

17.25 Pines summit.

17.6 Turn left onto Red Cross/1779 Trail.

17.65 Leave Red Cross/1779 Trail.

18.2 Beechy Bottom Road crosses.

18.3 Horn Hill summit.

18.6 Horn Hill Bike Trail crosses.

18.75 North "Ski Trail" crosses.

19.1 Cats Elbow; R-D Trail joins.

19.15 R-D Trail leaves, right.

19.8 Timp-Torne Trail joins, left.

20.1 Timp-Torne leaves, right.

20.7 Knob of West Mountain.

21.1 Doodlekill crosses.

21.5 Turn left onto Bridle Path.

21.65 Turn right, leaving Bridle Path.

21.85 Rejoin Bridle Path at Doodletown Road.

22.35 Turn left, leaving Bridle Path.

22.5 Seven Lakes Drive crosses.

23.35 End at trail junction near Bear Mountain Inn.

The Suffern trailhead of the Suffern-Bear Mountain Trail (S-BM) is on

Route 59, about 500 feet north of the Thruway crossing. The trail leaves the sidewalk and goes steeply up a ravine, over rocks, to a good viewpoint. It continues to climb steeply until it reaches another viewpoint to the right. S-BM then joins a woods road and, at 0.6 mile, crosses a gas pipeline. After reaching the summit of Nordkop Mountain, the trail passes under a power line and descends into a hollow. Near this location, from 1944 to 1963, the Seven Hills Trail joined S-BM. (The route of this old trail is no longer obvious.) From this hollow, S-BM climbs a broken fault face which Frank Place in 1925 named the Kitchen Stairs. Beyond the Stairs, S-BM goes up and continues across a fairly level area. At 1.9 miles, it crosses another gas line, with an especially wide right of way. To the west, this gas line comes down in Hillburn, near where Route 59 crosses the Ramapo River. The trail then dips down across the outlet of a cattail swamp, goes up again over irregular ridges, and passes beneath a power line. At 3.15 miles, a deep notch, full of boulders, is crossed. Frank Place called this area the "Valley of Dry Bones" (a reference to the Bible—Ezekiel, chapter 37) because he felt that some rocks resembled animals. The little stream through this notch was named Os-Sec Brook.

After climbing the next hill, S-BM runs along the eastern edge of the Ramapo Rampart, passing the stone walls of the long abandoned Sky Sail Farm. In another 0.5 mile, the Columbia Gas Company pipeline crosses, and the trail passes through boulders known as MacIlvain's Rocks. At 4.5 miles, just beyond two great boulders that have been named "Grandma and Grandpa Rocks," S-BM crosses the Kakiat Trail (white). To the right on this trail, it is 1.5 miles to Route 202. S-BM now climbs over Cobus Mountain (1,150 feet), named after Jacobus Smith, said to have been the brother of Claudius Smith, the bandit (see p. 49). After descending through mountain laurel on a rocky footpath, S-BM climbs the next hill. A short distance beyond the summit, a viewpoint looks down into the glacial cirque behind Horse Stable Mountain, with New York City visible in the distance on a clear day. The trail now descends to the Conklins Crossing Trail (white), which ends here.

The S-BM Trail was proposed in 1924 by Major Welch, General Manager of the Palisades Interstate Park, as a project for the Trail Conference. Under the general direction of Frank Place, the trail builders divided the task into sections. Place himself, with Torrey's help, took the southern portion from Suffern to Conklin's Crossing. He reported: "I have already started scouting over the ridges at the lower end of the Ramapo Rampart" (*N.Y. Post*, 10/28/24). It was Frank Place who, in 1925, named the Kitchen Stairs, the Valley of Dry Bones, and the Grandma and Grandpa Rocks.

The pipeline over Nordkop Mountain was built in 1952 by the Algonquin Company. Before crossing the mountain, this pipeline goes south from Ladentown along the foot of the hills, parallel to Route 202. The Columbia Gas Transmission Company pipeline, crossed by S-BM near the Kakiat Trail, was built in 1949 and widened in 2007.

The trail makers named MacIlvain's Rocks after William J. MacIl-vain of the Fresh Air Club. They said he had chosen the most difficult route possible through those rocks (*N.Y. Post*, 5/1/27).

Until 1963, the Park boundary was 0.5 mile north of the Kakiat Trail. The first 5.0 miles were on land belonging to the Ramapo Land Company (of the Pierson family). At times they closed their land to hikers who, when allowed to hike on the property, were required to pay a fee for a permit to hike the S-BM, Kakiat, HTS and Seven Hills Trails.

The original route of the S-BM Trail is described in detail in the second (1934) edition of the *New York Walk Book*, pp. 158-62.

Continuing north from the Conklins Crossing Trail, S-BM passes a great boulder named "The Egg," with views to the east and southeast. It then descends to cross Many Swamp Brook and climbs up a ledge to the E.D. Stone Memorial Shelter (built 1935), which it reaches at 5.95 miles. Just beyond the shelter, the unmarked Sherwood Path, a wide woods road, crosses. S-BM now climbs gently for 0.3 mile. It then crosses back to the edge of the ridge and passes along a height called Hawk Cliff, with panoramic views. The land on the hillside below this cliff was once terraced for the gardens of Albert and Grace Pitt, a mountain couple who lived in a shack nearby.

Going down now, S-BM at 6.8 miles joins the Pittsboro Trail (unmarked) which comes up from the right. At the junction is the Witness Oak, a huge fallen white oak tree. In generations past, this tree marked the boundary of long-forgotten mountain farms. In another 0.1 mile, S-BM bends to the right, while the Pittsboro Trail (now invisible) continued straight ahead. At 7.0 miles, the Pine Meadow Trail (red square on white) comes in from the left. The joint S-BM and Pine Meadow Trails now cross Pittsboro Hollow Brook and continue along an old woods road.

In another 0.2 mile, S-BM/Pine Meadow turns left from the old road and descends into the gully of Gyascutus Brook. (The woods road, which

wɛ
fu
U:
re
rc

tɛ
f
ʌ
l
]

Mountain to T-MI, joint with T-MI to Woodtown Road, then over Squirrel Swamp Mountain to Hawk Cliff, etc. (*N.Y. Post*, 11/19/25), but by January 1926 the route the trail presently follows had been worked out. The shelter on Big Hill was scouted by R.H. Torrey and Park officials Raymond Adolph and John Tamsen in March 1927 (*N.Y. Post*, 3/18/27). A steel fire tower was erected in 1928 on Jackie Jones Mountain to replace an older one made of wood. The AT&T microwave tower was built early in 1947.

The original route of S-BM came down from the Jackie Jones Mountain fire tower almost due north, reaching Gate Hill Road about where the dam was later built. In 1954, it was rerouted to go down the road from the new relay tower. In 1993, it was rerouted

through ORAK.

ORAK was a mansion on the east side of Jackie Jones Mountain that belonged to George Briggs Buchanan, a vice-president of the Corn Products Refining Co., which made KARO syrup. Buchanan bought the land and built his house in 1923. He named his estate for KARO, which he spelled backwards. The dining room of the house resembled a ship's cabin, with portholes for windows, and a floor that rocked gently to simulate a ship's motion. Buchanan died on April 13, 1939, and his heirs sold the property to the Park in 1947. The home, gardens and outbuildings were rented to Park employees until 1973, when the main house and hothouse were demolished. The foundations are still impressive.

S-BM turns right on Gate Hill Road to cross Minisceongo Creek. It immediately turns left and follows a woods road for about 0.15 mile, then turns right and goes up Irish Mountain. (The woods road continues to the tent camp area northeast of Lake Welch.) At the summit of Irish Mountain (1,174 feet), the trail passes a huge boulder, named the Irish Potato by Bill Hoeferlin. Here, S-BM turns right and descends gently from the summit. On the way down, Upper Pound Swamp, which usually looks like a lake rather than a swamp, can be seen below, to the right of the trail. After briefly climbing Pound Swamp Mountain, S-BM turns left before reaching the summit and goes down towards Lake Welch Drive.

At 15.55 miles, S-BM reaches Lake Welch Drive. It follows this road east for about 0.15 mile and then bears left and crosses the southbound lane of the Palisades Interstate Parkway and a brook on an overpass. It br left, crosses the northbound lanes of the Parkway, turns left again the a short distance, goes north along the Parkway. Watch carefully turns yellow blazes—about 50 yards from the overpass, the trail sud right and goes up over rocks.

Here, the climb of the Pingyp begins. The way up is over steep ledges. After about 0.15 mile (and a climb of 300 feet!), you will reach a rock ledge, with pitch pines, with a broad view to the southeast. Just beyond, if you can manage to look up (rather than at your feet), you may notice on a rock face, just above the trail, a memorial plaque to Harold B. Scutt, who first scouted this trail in May 1925. The grade moderates soon after the plaque is passed. After continuing upward for another 0.5 mile, you will come to another ledge with a grand view down the Hudson River, and then reach the 1,023-foot summit of Pingyp.

Now the trail drops down the north side of the mountain to a woods road in the valley between Pingyp and The Pines. It turns right briefly on this road (the Pines Trail), parallel to a little brook. To the east, this road goes to Bulsontown; to the west, it goes to Stillwater Brook at the Palisades Interstate Parkway. After about 300 feet, S-BM turns left, crosses the brook, passes a fireplace, and climbs 250 feet to the summit of The Pines. As it begins to go down the north side, S-BM passes a ledge which affords a nice view of West Mountain and The Timp.

At 17.6 miles, S-BM turns left on the Red Cross/1779 Trail. After 400 feet, it turns right again, and soon crosses two streams and goes steeply up a rocky ledge. About 0.5 mile from the Red Cross Trail, it crosses a small brook and then crosses old Beechy Bottom Road, now marked with blue-on-white plastic blazes as a bike path. From here, a 120-foot climb leads to the summit of Horn Hill (930 feet). S-BM then descends gradually. It crosses the Horn Hill Bike Trail, then crosses a "stone road," known as the North "Ski Trail." S-BM now goes up the southern spur of West Mountain. After a climb over steep ledges, at 19.1 miles S-BM joins the Ramapo-Dunderberg Trail (R-D) (red dot on white) at the top of a curve called the Cats Elbow. Here, there are excellent views to the south and southeast from a rock ledge.

This section of S-BM, from Gate Hill Road to Cats Elbow, was scouted in the spring of 1925 by Harold B. Scutt of Douglaston, L.I., who also had a summer home in Tomkins Cove (*N.Y. Post*, 5/25/25). He died on April 2, 1930 in an airplane accident at Attica, N.Y. Scutt was a member of AMC and GMC. He and Torrey had been the first to go over the route proposed for the Northville-Lake Placid Trail which ADK was building. In Harriman Park he also worked on the Timp-Torne Trail (*N.Y. Post*, 8/11/22). At 11:00 a.m. on Sunday, October 19, 1930, the tablet on Pingyp was dedi-

Tree Planting on The Pines, 1948

cated in his memory by his friends. Thirty people were present.

Gate Hill Road was built in 1824 as the "new turnpike" from Monroe to Haverstraw. It replaced the Old Turnpike, which was the route of the Long Path from 1981 to 1992. The new turnpike was a toll road, with a toll gate just east of the bridge over Minisceongo Creek—hence the name "Gate Hill Road."

When first built in 1925, S-BM crossed Gate Hill Road near the location of the present-day dam. The Hasenclever Road also crossed at this point. That road has been cut off by the Lake Welch Drive and drowned by Lake Welch.

Scutt followed a suggestion by Herb Hauptman of ADK (*N.Y. Post*, 12/24/24) to cross the brook on stepping stones. (In 1949, the brook crossing was moved 0.2 mile east of the dam.) S-BM then proceeded across the fields east of Hasenclever Road (where the tent camping area was built in 1953), entered the woods at the foot of Grape Swamp Mountain and followed a woods road around the north side of Grape Swamp to a fireplace at a junction with an unmarked trail above the south side of Tiorati Brook. S-BM turned right on this trail and, in another 0.3 mile from the fireplace, it crossed Tiorati Brook on a wooden footbridge and reached Tiorati Brook Road a short distance west from where the trail presently arrives at the road. The abutments of that bridge are still there. The trail then went to the right on Tiorati Brook Road. In 0.2 mile, the road crossed Tiorati Brook, and 0.25 mile further, S-BM turned left off the road, crossed Stillwater Brook on stepping stones, and started up Pingyp. In 1953, when the Lake Welch tent campsites were built, the trail was rerouted over Irish Mountain. After reaching the Irish Potato near the summit, it went down to the northwest. It passed the campsites and went around the east side of Grape Swamp to a junction with the older route of the trail. Most of this portion of the trail has been obliterated by Lake Welch Drive.

In 1969, when Lake Welch Drive was being built, S-BM was rerouted to the northeast. It went over Pound Swamp Mountain and down along Grape Swamp Brook until it reached the paved road. About 1972, it was relocated to the hillside above the brook.

At present there is a level area just south of the brook, near the junction of Lake Welch Drive with Tiorati Brook Road. On old maps this was labeled the "Jimmy Stalter Place," a reference to the Stalters, a family of wood-cutters. The Boy Scouts adopted this area in 1922 for their Camp Pathfinder, part of their White Bar Trail system.

Pingyp is a name which was put on the first park map in 1920 by Major Welch. It is a very old name, which he had heard from local residents. There had been a wooden fire observatory on the summit, but by 1925 it had fallen down. After descending from Pingyp, S-BM climbs The Pines where, according to the

fifth edition of the *New York Walk Book* (p. 90), "there is not a single pine tree to be found." When the trail was made, this was private land, but even then there were only a couple of pines on it (*Paterson Morning Call*, 6/3/32). In 1945, the owner cut down all the trees and sold the land to the Park. Then, on April 25, 1948 (Arbor Day), led by Trails Chairman Joseph Bartha, sixty Trail Conference members planted eight-inch trees on The Pines. This was repeated in 1949 and 1950.

After The Pines, S-BM briefly joins the Red Cross/1779 Trail. This woods road, once known as the Dean Trail, is now thought to have been the route followed in 1779 by General Anthony Wayne and his men on their way to attack the British at Stony Point. A half mile further, S-BM crosses Beechy Bottom Road. This was the first road built across the Highlands in 1740 from Stony Point to the Queensboro Road. After going over Horn Hill, S-BM crosses a "stone road" known as the North "Ski Trail." This once was a trail marked with aluminum H's by Jim Horn, Vice President of the Fresh Air Club (*N.Y. Post*, 9/9/21). In 1934 it was "paved" by the CCC as a fire road, and it was subsequently marked as a ski trail. The Cats Elbow, where S-BM meets the R-D Trail, was named by Frank Place (*N.Y. Post*, 6/8/28).

The section of S-BM from Cats Elbow to Bear Mountain Inn was first scouted by Raymond Torrey in 1926. From the Cats Elbow ledge, S-BM

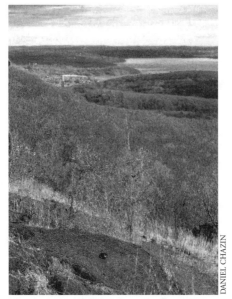

View over the Hudson from the Cats Elbow

and R-D run together for a short distance. R-D then goes off to the east, while S-BM turns north to cross the hollow between two summits of West Mountain. It formerly went up a steep route, named the Fire Escape by Torrey, but has been rerouted to climb on a more moderate grade. On the crest of West Mountain, the Timp-Torne Trail (T-T) (blue) joins for 0.3 mile. T-T then departs right to the West Mountain Shelter, while S-BM goes northwest to a knob, with views of the Perkins Memorial Tower on Bear Mountain. A rocky descent, soon followed by a steep ascent, leads to another knob, a high point of West Mountain. From here, S-BM goes steeply down and continues to descend along an old woods road, following the gully of the Doodlekill. After crossing the brook, S-BM turns left onto the Doodletown Bridle Path at 21.5 miles, and both run together for 0.15 mile. S-BM then turns right, goes over a low ridge, crosses two branches of a brook and goes up a bank to rejoin the Bridle Path at the old Doodletown Road. The 1777W Trail crosses here. After 150 feet, S-BM and the Bridle Path turn left and leave Doodletown Road. S-BM follows the Bridle Path northeast for 0.5 mile until, at a bend in the path, the yellow blazes turn left uphill to Seven Lakes Drive.

From the Drive, S-BM ascends the shoulder of Bear Mountain, following a telephone line. Soon, it begins to descend toward the Bear Mountain playground. Just south of the old ski jump, S-BM turns right onto a park service road and goes down to a large playing field behind the skating rink. It follows the western edge of this field to a trail junction behind the Bear Mountain Inn, where S-BM ends at 23.35 miles.

S-BM originally climbed West Mountain on a very steep route up a cliff, known as the Fire Escape. In 1985, Chief Ranger Tim Sullivan requested that the trail be rerouted because the Fire Escape's precipitous descent made it dangerous in winter conditions. The new route, which is much less steep, adds about 0.5 mile to the trail.

Coming down northeast from West Mountain, or southwest from Seven Lakes Drive, S-BM encounters the Doodletown Bridle Path. In 1926, when Torrey described his section of S-BM from Bear Mountain to the Fire Escape (*N.Y. Post*, 12/17/26), the Bridle Path had not yet been built. His trail crossed Doodletown valley just about where it does now. From Doodletown Road, near the last house, Torrey cut a new trail which roughly paralleled the Seven Lakes Drive for half a mile, then went uphill to cross the Drive.

In 1934-35, a path was built around Doodletown by men of the Temporary Emergency Relief Administration. Known as the Doodletown Bridle Path, it was used as a bridle path for some years, but also became popular as a cross-country ski trail. This new path used part of the route of Torrey's S-BM Trail from where it came down from the Drive to the junction with Doodletown Road. For years, S-BM followed its original line, but in 1949, at the suggestion of Park Police Chief Hlavaty, the northern loop of the Bridle Path was included in the S-BM. This made the trail 1.1 miles longer. About 1965, the northern loop was again left out.

Concurrently with the opening of the relocated Appalachian Trail on the east face of Bear Mountain on National Trails Day in 2010, the final half mile of the S-BM (from the ski jump to the trail junction behind the Inn) was relocated to a more attractive route.

In 1925, only four years after T-T had been blazed, the Park started construction of Popolopen Drive. It opened in 1927, and was widened to three lanes in 1934. In 1947, the construction of the Palisades Interstate Parkway was begun. Popolopen Drive, widened to four lanes, was opened again on November 30, 1953.

Gradually, it became clear that crossing that high-speed road was dangerous for hikers, especially after August 28, 1958, when the Parkway was opened all the way to the George Washington Bridge. So the Trail Conference rerouted T-T to avoid that crossing. From West Mountain, where T-T/AT had gone down to Doodletown Road, there was an old white-blazed Queensboro-West Mountain Trail (Q-W) that went down the ridge line. This had been scouted and cairned in 1934 by Frank Place and the Tramp and Trail Club as a short cut to the T-T/AT (*N.Y. Post*, 3/18/35). In June 1960, T-T was routed down the old Q-W Trail to the Fort Montgomery Road at the water treatment plant. It followed that road, past the Queensboro Furnace, to the old route coming up from the footbridge across the creek. This arrangement lasted until 1971, when West Point closed the Fort Montgomery Road. T-T was rerouted to join the Popolopen Gorge Trail (then marked with a vertical red bar on white), which had been blazed in 1960 to Long Mountain by Sam Wilkinson and Bill Burton. Once again, T-T crossed the creek on the often washed-out footbridge.

The footbridge over Popolopen Creek was washed out once again during Tropical Storm Floyd in September 1999. This time, both the Park and the Trail Conference decided that the time had come to construct a more durable bridge that was less susceptible to being washed out. A site for the new bridge was located a short distance east of the original bridge location, a grant was obtained to cover the cost of the bridge, and the new bridge opened in June 2004.

In 2006, the eastern end of T-T was relocated so that it continued under Route 9W and ended at the newly-opened Fort Montgomery State Historic Site.

Shortly after the junction with the AT, the trail arrives at a viewpoint over Bear Mountain and the Hudson River. T-T/AT then crosses to the west side of West Mountain, where there is an excellent view of Beechy Bottom and the Anthony Wayne Recreation Area. For the next 0.65 mile, the joint trails run along the ridge, with a number of additional viewpoints. T-T then turns left as the AT continues straight ahead and begins its descent (that was the original "western leg" of T-T). At 6.3 miles, the Suffern-Bear Mountain Trail (S-BM) (yellow) comes in from the right and runs jointly with T-T for 0.3 mile. S-BM then departs to the left. At 6.7 miles, the trail

Burros carrying materials for West Mountain Shelter, 1928

passes the West Mountain Shelter. This shelter was built in 1928, with burros being used to carry up the lumber and cement. A gradual descent (there are some steep sections), with good views to the south, brings the trail to a fireplace at a brook. T-T then continues down an eroded road.

At 7.3 miles, T-T turns left and goes down to Timp Pass Road. It turns left again and follows the road for 300 feet. (To the right, Timp Pass Road leads in 350 feet to Timp Pass, and a junction with the Ramapo-Dunderberg and Red Cross Trails.) T-T then turns right and begins its climb to the summit of The Timp. At 7.8 miles, it reaches a beautiful viewpoint over the Bear Mountain Bridge, and then, in another 500 feet, it comes out at the 1,080-foot summit of The Timp, with a view over Haverstraw Bay to the south.

T-T now heads east, descending gently. At 8.1 miles, the Ramapo-Dunderberg Trail (red dot on white) crosses. Here, the Red Timp Trail begins, and in 150 feet it leaves to the right. This trail was blazed by Girl Scouts from Camp Addisone Boyce, who utilized the route of an old trail once called the Timp Bypass. A short distance further along, T-T passes a good viewpoint from the top of a large rock. The 1777 Trail crosses at 8.55 miles. At 8.95 miles, the Escalator—a steeply slanting crack in the face of the cliff—is to the right. Now zig-zagging downward, with a number of good views along the way, T-T crosses the Jones Trail and a little brook at 10.05 miles. Ahead and a bit to the left is one end of the unfinished upper Dunderberg Spiral Railway tunnel. The trail follows the descending grade of the railway through a cut and fill—with a beautiful view over Haverstraw Bay—and then follows a work road up to the other end of the tunnel. The trail crew which blazed the trail here also cleared the debris from this quite impressive tunnel. Unfortunately, it is likely to be water-filled in wet weather.

A few yards further along, the trail goes down to the next lower descending railway grade, which it follows for 0.25 mile. At 10.5 miles, the grade ends, and T-T goes down to the right. It zig-zags downward, at times steeply, passing a beautiful viewpoint over the Hudson River. Then, at 10.95 miles, it turns sharply right, again joining the Ramapo-Dunderberg Trail (red dot on white). After passing the lower railway tunnel, it descends on steps built into the hillside, and, at 11.2 miles from the start, T-T ends at Route 9W, just south of Jones Point. Parking is available on the west side of the road, a short distance to the north, opposite the intersection with Old Route 9W (which leads to Jones Point).

When it first was blazed, the Timp-Torne Trail, a highline branch of the R-D Trail, started from the R-D at Timp Pass. In 1947, it was extended from Timp Pass to Tomkins Cove (Trail Conference Minutes, 4/2/47). It went down from Timp Pass on the 2.6-mile-long, white-blazed Timp Trail which went around the east side of a 680-foot knob known as the Little Timp, or Boulderberg. At Mott Farm Road the trail turned east and was blazed all the way to the railroad station at Tomkins Cove.

The land where the T-T and Red Cross Trails met Mott Farm Road was acquired in 1951 by the Rockland County Girl Scout Council, who built a camp and a lake there. They asked that the trails be rerouted. In 1952, T-T was rerouted from the foot of the Boulderberg, paralleling the Park boundary until it intercepted

the Jones Trail. It followed that trail out to Route 9W, 0.5 mile south of the Anchor Monument. In 1967, slight relocations were made to move the trail away from homes in the Tomkins Lake Colony. Then, in 1986, disaster struck! Lumberjacks were clear-cutting the south side of Dunderberg Mountain. Even the trees with the T-T blazes were cut, from the Red Timp Trail to the 1777 Trail. It turned out that the trail had been blazed outside the Park boundary and was actually on private property!

With the help of the Park authorities, a new route for the Timp-Torne was devised: the one described above. The new section, from Jones Point to a junction with the R-D Trail just east of The Timp, was built in the fall of 1987 by an AMC crew led by Bob Marshall and Tom McCarthy. The new section of the Timp-Torne Trail was designed to include many viewpoints, a section of the old railway bed, and both tunnels of the spiral railway.

Then, in 1998, the route of the Timp-Torne in the area of The Timp was changed again. The 1987 relocation had rerouted the T-T onto the R-D Trail for the descent of The Timp. But this very steep trail had become badly eroded, so it was decided to construct new routes down The Timp for both the T-T and R-D Trails. A new route for the T-T was located north of Timp Pass, and the trail was constructed by the West Hudson Trail Crew, under the direction of Bob Marshall, and opened in the summer of 1998. A relocation of the R-D descent of The Timp was built by the same trail crew in 1999.

Triangle Trail

Length: 5.25 miles · Blazes: yellow triangles

Miles

0.0	Start at R-D Trail.
0.5	Telephone line.
0.95	Cross Black Ash Brook.
1.25	Cross Deep Hollow Brook.
1.7	Old Park boundary.
2.5	Cross brook, bear right and ascend.
2.6	White Bar Trail joins.
2.75	Turn left and leave White Bar Trail.
3.3	Parker Cabin Mountain; R-D Trail crosses.
4.0	Telephone line.
4.1	Victory Trail crosses.
4.2	Cross brook; swamp to right.
4.5	Cross into Rockland County.
4.8	Trail, left to ADK camp.
5.05	Trail, left, to ADK camp.
5.2	Old Rectangle Trail, right.
5.25	End at White Bar Trail.

The Triangle Trail starts at the Ramapo-Dunderberg Trail (R-D), 0.2 mile from Grove Drive in Tuxedo. After 0.5 mile, it briefly runs along a telephone line and then turns right onto a woods road. After again passing under the telephone line, it turns left onto the woods road that runs along Black Ash Brook. This road was once the route of the R-D Trail. It then crosses the brook and soon turns right onto another woods road. Triangle continues gently uphill and, at 1.25 miles, crosses Deep Hollow Brook. As the trail goes north, Black Ash Mountain is on the right. At 1.7 miles, the trail crosses the old boundary line on Fox Mountain between Harriman Park and the Tuxedo Park Association. After crossing a fairly level region, the trail crosses a brook at 2.5 miles and goes up to join the White Bar Trail, which comes in from the left. Soon Triangle leaves White

Bar and climbs up Parker Cabin Mountain. It joins the R-D Trail briefly on the summit. Until 1935, there was a wooden fire tower here.

Triangle then leaves the R-D Trail and goes to the eastern edge of the summit for a view of Lake Sebago—a favorite lunch stop. The trail now goes steeply down for a short distance, and then continues to descend more gradually. At 4.1 miles, Triangle crosses the Victory Trail (blue V on white) near Lake Skenonto. Soon afterwards, it crosses a brook that drains a swamp on the right. At this point, a woods road goes right; in 0.6 mile it reaches the White Bar Trail. After skirting the south end of Lake Skenonto, Triangle goes over several small ridges and comes down near an arm of Lake Sebago. It joins the Sloatsburg Trail that goes along the western edge of the lake. Near this point, an unmarked trail goes left along the lake edge to ADK Camp Nawakwa. A little further along, by a huge boulder, another unmarked trail goes to Camp Nawakwa. At 5.2 miles, the old Rectangle Trail goes northwest to the Victory Trail. In another 250 feet, the Triangle Trail ends at the White Bar Trail. The Dutch Doctor Shelter is 0.15 mile farther down the White Bar Trail, about 100 feet up to the left.

The Triangle Trail was first marked in 1939 as the Yellow Bar Trail. It was blazed by Kerson Nurian, with yellow bands around the trees, starting from the the woods road along Black Ash Brook, the former route of the R-D Trail. Nurian used already existing roads and trails, ending on Parker Cabin Mountain. In October 1939, he offered his trail to the Trail Conference. They accepted, and assigned Harry Zilverman as its maintainer.

Early in 1942, the Conference marked a Yellow Triangle Trail from Parker Cabin Mountain to the arm of Lake Sebago, and continuing to ADK Camp Nawakwa. At the lake edge, it crossed an older trail that ran past the Old Dutch Doctor's place to Johnsontown at the northwest end of Lake Sebago (the Sloatsburg Trail).

Nurian was a Bulgarian electrical engineer who worked on submarines at the Brooklyn Navy Yard (see p. 71). In 1943, he returned to Bulgaria, and the Conference then decided to mark the whole trail, from Black Ash Brook to Lake Sebago, with yellow metal triangles (Trail Conference Minutes, 4/4/44). By 1946, it was marked to the Dutch Doctor Shelter. The Conference (probably Joe Bartha) also eliminated an 0.75-mile loop which followed the old Park boundary on Fox Mountain.

Then, in 1947, Nurian returned! Joseph Bartha's Trail Committee minutes for September 24, 1947 reported that all 80 metal markers had been removed from the Triangle Trail from Black Ash Brook to Parker Cabin Mountain (that had been the route of Nurian's Yellow Bar Trail). By the spring of 1948, it was clear who had done it, because the yellow bars had been repainted around the trees. After heated discussions with Bartha and the Conference, Nurian agreed to leave the trail alone, provided that painted triangles were used instead of metal ones. And so it was. Nurian died on November 19, 1948, at the age of 75.

In 1951, 1,200 acres of land were sold by the Tuxedo Park Association to the Palisades Interstate Park. Half of the required funds were supplied by New York State, and half by Commissioners W. Averell Harriman and George W. Perkins. Now the R-D, Kakiat, Blue Disc and Triangle Trails were no longer on private property. In 1954, the new Thruway cut off the original R-D route from Tuxedo up Black Ash Brook. Although R-D had not used that route since 1930, the Triangle Trail did start there until 1955. In the spring of 1955, Triangle was relocated onto its present route.

Tuxedo-Mt. Ivy Trail

Length: 8.2 miles · Blazes: red dash on white

Miles

0.0	R-D Trail, 1.4 miles from Tuxedo station.
0.35	Claudius Smith Rock.
0.7	Horseshoe curve at swamp.
1.55	Join White Bar Trail.
1.65	Turn left, uphill.
2.05	Camp road crosses.
2.4	Sebago Dam.
2.65	HTS Trail begins, right.
2.8	Diamond Creek crosses.
3.35	Seven Hills Trail crosses.
3.55	Woodtown Road (West) crosses.
4.3	Pine Meadow Road West crosses.
5.1	Pine Meadow Road East crosses.
5.15	Breakneck Mountain Trail, left.
6.0	Woodtown Road; go right.
6.05	Turn left, leaving road.
6.65	Fireplace; S-BM Trail crosses.
7.25	Red Arrow Trail starts, left.
7.8	Power line; go left, then right.
8.1	Turn left onto dirt road.
8.2	End at road to power substation.

The Tuxedo-Mt. Ivy Trail (T-MI) starts from the Ramapo-Dunderberg Trail (R-D), 0.8 mile from Grove Drive, and 1.4 miles from the Tuxedo station. Both T-MI and R-D have red blazes on white backgrounds (although T-MI is blazed with a red dash, while R-D has a red dot). After 0.35 mile, the trail reaches the base of Claudius Smith Rock. It then curves left and climbs the rock. On the way up, the Blue Disc Trail (blue dot on white) crosses. At the top, a path to the left leads to a viewpoint. In another 125 feet, the White Cross Trail starts to the left.

Claudius Smith was of English stock, born in Brookhaven, Long Island. He was descended from Richard Smith, the founder of Smithtown. His father bought 200 acres in Orange County at Smith's Clove, later named Monroe. Claudius, a man of large stature, married and had three sons: William, Richard and James. The sons, and perhaps a dozen others, formed a gang of thieves who operated in the southern part of Orange County around Suffern and Haverstraw. They robbed local farms, and during the Revolution they hijacked the arsenal trains of the Continental Army. They hid out in places like the cave on Horse Pond Mountain near Tuxedo, and Horse Stable Mountain near Ladentown.

Claudius was captured and jailed at Kingston on July 17, 1777, but he escaped. With a reward posted for the arrest of him and his three sons, Claudius fled to the British in New York City. Later he settled near Smithtown. He was recognized there by Major John Brush of the Continental Army. On a December night in 1778, Brush and five comrades crossed Long Island Sound and found Claudius asleep in bed. They took him prisoner and transported him to the jail in Goshen. There he was hanged on Friday, January 22, 1779.

Sons Richard and James were later captured and hanged. Son William died in the Goshen jail of wounds inflicted by Continental soldiers who chased the gang on Schunemunk Mountain. The rest of the gang fled to Canada. (This story is from the *New York Sun* of October 26, 1927.)

Going gently downhill now, T-MI at 0.7 mile makes a horseshoe turn around the right end of a swamp. From the south end of that swamp, a faint old road goes up a slope. In 0.4 mile, this road forks. To the right, it goes to the Blue Disc Trail at the point where the gas pipeline crosses. To the left, it goes more steeply down, with many turns, to the old Johnsontown Road.

T-MI now goes over a low ridge and down to a woods road, the route of the White Bar Trail. (0.1 mile to the left is the Dutch Doctor Shelter, built in 1935.) At 1.55 miles, T-MI turns right on this road, which was once known as the Sloatsburg Trail.

In another 0.1 mile, T-MI leaves the White Bar Trail to the left and goes uphill over another ridge. T-MI then goes down to Lake Sebago. It crosses the paved camp road that serves the American Canoe Association and the Adirondack Mountain Club (Nawakwa) camps, and then runs along the southwest shore of the lake. At 2.4 miles, it reaches the Sebago Dam on Seven Lakes Drive and turns left. After crossing to the north end of the

PALISADES INTERSTATE PARK COMMISSION

Sebago Dam, 1951

dam, it descends the embankment and drops down to the brook level. T-MI goes right on a wide trail which runs along Stony Brook and crosses a tributary stream. At this point, the Hillburn-Torne-Sebago Trail (HTS) (orange) starts to the right. T-MI now starts to climb Diamond Mountain. At 2.8 miles, it crosses Diamond Creek. The ridge top, where the Seven Hills Trail (blue on white) crosses, is reached at 3.35 miles.

Here, on Diamond Mountain, we can stop to reflect on the history of the T-MI. It was a favorite project of Major William A. Welch, the Park's first General Manager. It was he who persuaded the Tuxedo Park Association to let the Trail Conference blaze the trail in the spring of 1923 (*N.Y. Post*, 5/11/23). He provided copper markers for the trail crew: Place, Holt, Lewis and Torrey. The route from Tuxedo was joint with T-TJ until T-MI turned right, up a woods road, towards Claudius Smith Rock (see p. 88). There were no Blue Disc or White Cross Trails then, and it was not until 1951 that Claudius Smith Rock became "ours." Going past the Dutch Doctor's clearing, and over the ridge to Burnt Sawmill Bridge (there was no dam or lake there then), the trail went up Halfway Mountain (named Diamond Mountain in 1927) on the old Woodtown Road (West). That road, a narrow overgrown trail, was used in 1933 by the Civilian Conservation Corps to get their trucks and machines over the mountain to build Pine Meadow, Wanoksink and Minsi Lakes. The road became so muddy and eroded that T-MI was relocated in the spring of 1935 to its present route up Diamond Mountain by Ernest Dench and W.P. Bottomley of the Interstate Hiking Club (*N.Y. Post*, 3/16/35).

After crossing the Seven Hills Trail, T-MI crosses old Woodtown Road (West) and, at 4.3 miles, reaches Pine Meadow Road West. It then goes over a rocky knob and passes by a swamp. Pine Meadow Road East crosses at 5.1 miles. In another 400 feet, the Breakneck Mountain Trail (white) starts to the left. Shortly afterward, T-MI turns left onto an old woods road that crosses the north end of Big Green Swamp. At 6.0 miles, T-MI reaches Woodtown Road, which it follows to the right, crossing a little brook that connects Big Green Swamp (on the right) with Squirrel Swamp (on the left).

In 1923, there was a little bridge across the brook, called Tim's Bridge. In 1927, Frank Place nailed a sign on a tree there: "Tim's Bridge," in memory of a faded sign that hikers remembered. Frank's sign, and the bridge too, were gone by 1930. The present bridge was built in 1986.

About 250 feet beyond the bridge, T-MI turns left on what was once known as the Two Bridges Road. It passes through an area with dense mountain laurel thickets and reaches a fireplace at 6.65 miles, where the Suffern-Bear Mountain Trail (yellow) crosses. Going down gradually, T-MI passes the start of the Red Arrow Trail at 7.25 miles. Soon afterwards, T-MI turns off to the right onto another woods road, and continues to descend more steeply. As the trail descends, Limekiln Mountain is on the left and Eagle Rock is on the right. At 7.8 miles, T-MI reaches a power line and, turns left briefly, then right again, along a gas pipeline. After another 0.25 mile, the trail goes down left on a dirt road to end at a parking area on paved Diltz Road, which leads to a power company substation. This road starts at Mountain Road in Ladentown.

In December 1974, Art Beach, for the Trail Conference, and Tim Sullivan, for the Park, arranged with officials of Orange and Rockland Utilities to allow parking on their land for access to the T-MI Trail (*Trail Walker*, Jan./Feb. 1975). Do not block the road and do not park on the land near the private home on the hill.

The route down the Two Bridges Road is the same as the one blazed in 1923. From Ladentown the trail was marked along Route 62 (now Route 202) northeast for 1.5 miles to the Erie Railroad station at Mt. Ivy. In 1936, the Interstate Hiking Club, which maintained the trail, rerouted it to avoid the long walk on the highway; instead of taking the Two Bridges Road from Tim's Bridge, the blazes went north 0.7 mile on Woodtown Road and turned right on the File Factory Hollow Trail. This led downhill 1.0 mile to Call Hollow Road at Krucker's Farm. The trail then turned right on Camp Hill Road, which it followed to Quaker Road, which led to Mt. Ivy. After some years, Mr. Krucker asked the hikers not to go through his farm. So, in 1944, T-MI was sent from Woodtown Road down the S-BM/Red Arrow Trail to rejoin the Two Bridges route. In 1946, some inexperienced trail worker blazed T-MI down the Two Bridges Road again and blacked out the "real" route (Trail Conference Minutes, 10/2/46). The Trail Conference decided to let the new route remain (Trail Conference Minutes, 4/2/47). In the fall of 1965, the Park widened T-MI to a 20-foot fire road for 2.5 miles, from Ladentown to Pine Meadow Road East. This accounts somewhat for the appearance of the trail today. In 1951, when the Erie Railroad stopped service to Mt. Ivy, T-MI was made to end at Lad-entown. Then, in 1961, it was again marked to Mt. Ivy to join the Hook Mountain/Tors Trail, in expectation that the latter trail would become part of the new Long Path. In October 1961, the Long Path was started from the George Washington Bridge, and in 1964 the Conference determined its route through Harriman Park. It joined the T-MI at Mt. Ivy and both trails coincided to the Dutch Doctor Shelter where the Long Path took over the White Bar Trail. This route remained until 1981, when the Long Path was routed from Mt. Ivy over Cheesecote Mountain.

Across the road from the parking place in Ladentown is a grove of small trees. This grove shades an old cemetery of several graves, dating to 1858: Eliza Secor, James and Fannie Haring, one stone with the initials "E.S.," and one stone with a weathered, illegible inscription. Eliza Secor was the daughter of Isaac and Mary Secor who in 1836 had bought the land of Michael Laden. In 1865 they donated land for the Methodist Church. The road from the little cemetery to Mountain Road was called Dilts' Lane; it led to farmer Dilts' place, where the Orange and Rockland substation is now.

Twin Forts Trail

Length: 0.4 mile · Blazes: vertical blue stripe on white

Miles

0.0   Start at gate in back of Historical Museum.

0.05 Side trail from Bear Mountain Bridge joins, left.

0.15 Cross short footbridge over stream.

0.25 Cross 340-foot suspension bridge over Popolopen Creek.

0.5   End at Fort Montgomery Visitor Center.

To reach the start of the Twin Forts Trail from the parking area at the Bear Mountain Inn, follow the Appalachian Trail under Route 9W and through the Trailside Museum and Zoo. In front of the Historical Museum, where the Appalachian Trail turns left, continue straight on a paved path towards the museum, then turn right at a sign for "scenic views." Follow this path around the right side of the museum and past a viewpoint overlooking the Hudson River to a gate in a fence, where a triple blaze marks the start of the Twin Forts Trail. (The gate is closed daily at 4:00 p.m.; if you arrive later than that, proceed to the west end of the north sidewalk on the Bear Mountain Bridge, where a side trail marked with a red vertical stripe on white descends to join the Twin Forts Trail.)

The Twin Forts Trail descends stone steps and crosses under the Bear Mountain Bridge, where there is a panoramic viewpoint over the Hudson River. In another 100 feet, a side trail, marked with a red vertical stripe on white, leaves to the left and climbs to the western end of the bridge. The Twin Forts Trail descends gradually to a short footbridge over a stream, built in 2004 by volunteers from the New York-New Jersey Trail Conference. It then climbs a little and descends to reach, at 0.25 mile, the southern end of a 340-foot suspension bridge over the Popolopen Creek.

The trail continues across the bridge, with views to the right of the railway bridge over the creek, the Bear Mountain Bridge and the Hudson River. Above to the left is the truss bridge that carries Route 9W over the creek. From the northern end of the bridge, the trail follows an old road uphill. At the top of the ascent, the trail bears left, and it ends, 0.5 mile

Suspension bridge over Popolopen Creek

from the start, at the Fort Montgomery Visitor Center. The trailhead of the Timp-Torne/1777W/1779 Trails is ahead, on the left.

The Twin Forts Trail was built by the Park in 2002 to provide a direct connection between the historic Forts Clinton and Montgomery. The 340-foot suspension bridge over Popolopen Creek, constructed by the New York State Bridge Authority at a cost of $1.9 million and dedicated by Governor Pataki on October 6, 2002, is situated at the site of a pontoon bridge that was built during the Revolutionary War. The Trail Conference was asked to assist in improving the trail, and it was adopted by the Conference in 2004.

Victory Trail

Length: 3.4 miles • *Blazes: blue V on white*

Miles

0.0	Tri-Trail Corner.
0.2	Telephone line crosses.
0.3	Detour left if wet.
0.4	Old Park boundary.
0.7	White Cross and White Bar Trails cross.
0.8	Old Rectangle Trail, right.
1.25	Triangle Trail crosses.
1.95	Left on camp service road.
2.15	Hemlock Hill Road, left.
2.25	Turn left off road.
2.65	Join Hemlock Hill Road.
2.85	Trail, right, to Tom Jones Mountain.
3.15	Fireplace; R-D Trail crosses.
3.4	End at Route 106.

The Victory Trail starts at a natural rock dam on Black Ash Brook, at Tri-Trail Corner, where the Victory, Blue Disc and Ramapo-Dunderberg Trails meet. The trail is rather level for its first 2.25 miles. It follows an old road along the western side of Black Ash Swamp, and generally parallels a telephone line. At 0.3 mile, the trail is on the very edge of the swamp; in wet weather, it might be better to stay on the road higher up. The original boundary between Harriman Park and lands of the Tuxedo Park Association is crossed about ten minutes from the start.

At 0.7 mile, the White Cross Trail crosses. In another 300 feet, the White Bar Trail joins Victory for 100 feet, then departs up right. At 0.8 mile, the old Rectangle Trail starts to the right. (It ends near the Dutch Doctor Shelter.) Then, at 1.25 miles, the Victory Trail reaches Lake Skenonto, where the Triangle Trail (yellow triangle) crosses. Along the lake shore there are several good lunch spots. At 1.95 miles, Victory joins a paved camp road.

At 2.15 miles, the old Hemlock Hill Road (Continental Road) goes left. Victory continues on the paved road a little farther, then turns left and starts a climb to the foot of Tom Jones Mountain. In another 0.4 mile, it joins the old Hemlock Hill Road. At 2.85 miles, an unmarked trail enters right from Tom Jones Mountain. Soon afterwards, the Ramapo-Dunderberg Trail (R-D) crosses at a fireplace. Victory continues along Hemlock Hill Road another 0.25 mile to end at Route 106, 0.5 mile west of the point where the R-D Trail crosses.

Before 1930, hikes from Tuxedo often went north on an old woods road, known as the Black Ash Swamp Road, that ran along the east side of the Ramapo River. After 0.3 mile, the road turned right and went up the south side of Black Ash Brook. It crossed to the north side just below the rock dam that backs up Black Ash Swamp. The road followed the same route it does now, ending at Sebago Beach on Johnsontown Road, except that it crossed over Big Swamp, the predecessor of Lake Skenonto (which was not built until 1935). For one of their hikes, the ADK planned "to take the Black Ash Swamp Trail from Tuxedo to Sebago, thence to Allis' Trail of Seven Hills, etc." (*N.Y. Post*, 1/16/31).

In 1942, J.A. Allis, then Chairman of the Conference Trails Committee, proposed to make Black Ash Swamp Road a Conference trail (Trail Conference Minutes, 6/3/42). In October 1942, Bernard Landau, President of the C.C.N.Y. Hiking Club, volunteered to blaze the trail, but he was recruited into the Army. On April 4, 1943, the trail was cleared and marked with blue V's by a group led by Abe Shechter.

At first, the trail went up Hemlock Hill Road from the camp road and ended at the junction with the R-D Trail. Hemlock Hill Road once was used by the American Continental troops to go from the Ramapo Valley to Johnsontown and points east. It was replaced in 1824 by the Monroe-Haverstraw Turnpike (now Route 106).

In 1949, the trail was extended from the fireplace at the foot of Tom Jones Mountain out to Route 210 (now Route 106). In 1960, the Park created a dump on the old Hemlock Hill Road and, to avoid the dump, the Victory Trail was routed around it in 1964. As of 2010, the dump is still used to dispose of tree limbs. Ignore the dump and enjoy a walk up that old road for 0.15 mile to rejoin the Victory Trail.

White Bar Trail

Length: 7.4 miles · Blazes: horizontal white bar

Miles

0.0	Start from A-SB/LP.
0.3	Join Crooked Road.
0.9	Dunning Trail joins, left.
1.15	Dunning Trail leaves, right.
1.7	Nurian Trail joins, right.
1.75	Site of Camp Deerslayer.
1.8	Nurian Trail leaves, left.
2.0	Island Pond Road joins.
2.05	Turn left and parallel Route 106.
2.15	Cross Route 106 to parking area.
2.3	Hilltop Shelter, right.
2.7	Car Pond Mountain (second summit).
3.1	Parker Cabin Hollow Trail, right.
3.55	Triangle Trail joins, right.
3.7	Triangle Trail leaves, left.
3.9	R-D Trail crosses.
4.4	White Cross and Victory Trails cross.
5.5	Woods road from Lake Skenonto, left.
5.65	Triangle Trail ends, left; join old Sloatsburg Road.
5.8	Dutch Doctor Shelter, left.
5.85	T-MI Trail joins from right.
5.95	T-MI Trail leaves, left.
6.0	Homestead site of "Old Dutch Doctor," right.
6.3	Unmarked Springbrook Trail begins, right.
6.75	Reach gate; White Bar goes down, right.
6.9	Old Johnsontown Road joins, left.
7.05	Kakiat Trail joins, left.
7.1	Kakiat Trail leaves, right.
7.4	End at Johnsontown Circle.

The White Bar Trail starts from the Arden-Surebridge Trail (A-SB) (red triangle on white), about 0.2 mile from the Lemon Squeezer, at the point where the Long Path (aqua) comes from the north to join the A-SB. After a fairly level 0.3 mile, White Bar joins a woods road that comes from the east side of Island Pond (the "Crooked Road") for 0.6 mile. At 0.9 mile, the Dunning Trail (yellow) comes in from the left, and both trails run together for a quarter of a mile. Dunning then departs to the right, while White Bar continues southwest, going gently upward through a wide valley that is dotted with straight, tall trees.

At 1.7 miles, the Nurian Trail (white) comes in from the right. In 1922, this area was the site of the Boy Scouts' Camp Deerslayer, a part of their White Bar Trail system. In 1926, Camp Deerslayer was moved to Parker Cabin Hollow. After 0.1 mile, the Nurian Trail leaves to the left. In another 0.2 mile, White Bar joins Island Pond Road and, at 2.05 miles, approaches Route 106. It turns left and parallels the road for about 500 feet, then crosses the road to a parking area. The trail now begins a rather steep climb of Car Pond Mountain. On the first 1,080-foot summit, there is a shelter made of corrugated iron, off the trail on the right (but not visible from the trail). White Bar then goes steeply down into a notch and up again to the second 1,100-foot summit, which it reaches at 2.7 miles.

On the current USGS topographic map (Sloatsburg Quadrangle), these two summits, as well as the two summits to the west, are unnamed. On the Park's 1927 topo map, the peak just to the west (which is south of Lake Stahahe, i.e., Car Pond), is named Hemlock Hill. Bill Hoeferlin in his 1944 handbook called our second summit "Car Pond Mountain," although his maps named it "Hemlock Hill." All editions of the Trail Conference map call the second summit "Car Pond Mountain."

White Bar now goes steeply down into Parker Cabin Hollow, where it crosses a brook and reaches the eastern end of the Parker Cabin Hollow Trail (orange) at 3.1 miles. A long steady climb up a shoulder of Parker Cabin Mountain follows. At 3.55 miles, the Triangle Trail (yellow triangle) joins from the right, then soon leaves to the left. After another 0.2 mile, the Ramapo-Dunderberg Trail (red dot on white) crosses in the saddle between Parker Cabin and Black Ash Mountains. Dropping gently down, White Bar crosses the White Cross Trail and briefly joins the Victory Trail (blue V on white). It then climbs over Blauvelt Mountain. At 5.5 miles, a woods road from Lake Skenonto comes in from the left. White Bar passes the end of the Triangle Trail, then passes the Dutch Doctor Shelter (on a rise to the left of the trail) and, at 5.85 miles, joins the Tuxedo-Mt. Ivy Trail (T-MI) (red dash on white). T-MI leaves at 5.95 miles, and immediately afterwards one sees on the right an old cellar hole, with a hundred-year-old tree growing from the center.

The cellar hole is all that remains from the homestead of John Frederick Helms, the "Old Dutch Doctor," who lived here from 1874 to about 1892. He bought six marshy acres from David Demarest and built a cabin. He made a living by raising medicinal herbs, such as ginseng. His son, John Wilbur, born in 1866, was brain-damaged at birth. Both father and son were illiterate. The son became the owner of the property in 1884. When the "Old Dutch Doctor" died, the son was taken in and cared for by John Waldron, whose farmhouse was on the hillside where Johnsontown Circle is now. A grove of tall pines marks the site where the farmhouse once stood. Waldron's blacksmith shop was across the road, above Spring Brook. In 1927, John Wilbur, then 61 years old, was committed to the County Home by Dr. Gillette, and he died there in 1950. He is buried near the entrance to the Sloatsburg cemetery, beside a mortuary which once belonged to Warren Waldron (John Waldron's son).

Continuing southward, the beginning of the unblazed Springbrook Trail, an old woods road, is visible to the right at 6.3 miles. That trail goes northwest and, at 0.3 mile, meets the Fox Trail, which goes toward Almost Perpendicular. The Springbrook Trail then bends southward and soon rejoins the White Bar Trail.

Soon White Bar comes to a gate, where it turns down, right. At 6.8 miles, it reaches the end of the Springbrook Trail and then joins old Johnsontown Road, which comes in from the left. (To the left, Johnsontown Road is cut off by the Seven Lakes Drive.) In this vicinity was the 64-acre farm of William Lewis Becraft.

At 7.05 miles, the Kakiat Trail (white) goes up left to cross the Seven Lakes Drive. Shortly thereafter, Kakiat leaves to the right. Our White Bar Trail ends at 7.4 miles, at the Johnsontown Road circle. From the circle, the paved Johnsontown Road continues another 2.2 miles to Route 17 in Sloatsburg.

The White Bar Trail was first marked in 1921-22 by the Boy Scouts from the 17 camps on Kanawauke Lakes, led by Archibald T. Shorey of Brooklyn. Their marker was a red metal disc which had a white bar across it. They used mostly old roads, making a 35-mile circle around the Kanawauke Lakes with five spokes radiating from the center. On those spokes were six camps where Scouts could stay overnight: Camp Forest Ranger, where Lake Skannatati was later built, Camp Leatherstocking at the Old Dutch Doctor's place (until 1926), Camp Hawkeye at the western foot of Jackie Jones Mountain, Camp Pathfinder at the junction of Tiorati and Stillwater Brooks (moved to Hasenclever Mine in 1926), Camp Prairie at Youman Flats near Tiorati Circle, and Camp Deerslayer in the wooded valley north of Car Pond Mountain (moved to Parker Cabin Hollow in 1926). Meals at the camps were thirty-five cents (fifty cents for guests). The camps were connected with headquarters by wireless (Shorey, *N.Y. Post*, 8/12/22).

The piece of the White Bar system that is still known today by that name started on the Crooked Road at the north end of Island Pond. From there, a branch went uphill to the east to join the A-SB Trail. The Appalachian Trail, marked through there in 1922, used the White Bar route up to the Lemon Squeezer. (From the Lemon Squeezer, this branch of White Bar followed A-SB to "Times Square," and then continued on the R-D Trail.)

Going south on Crooked Road past Island Pond, White Bar departed when the road turned left uphill (now the route of the Dunning Trail). It continued south, as it does today, to the Old Dutch Doctor's place and beyond.

Sometimes during the next twenty years, the markers were changed to a white blaze with two green stripes. The trail apparently was neglected because in 1943, the Conference minutes state that "an effort is being made by Mr. George Goldthwaite to locate the old White Bar Trail north of Island Pond" (Trail Conference Minutes, 12/1/43). He apparently succeeded because, in 1944, the trail was restored and maintained by H.F. Hamm of the ADK.

This continued until 1964, when the Trail Conference routed the new Long Path along the White Bar route from the Dutch Doctor Shelter to Island Pond. For the next 17 years, only hints of the older blazes could be seen under the new aqua color. Then in 1981 the white bars were seen again! The Long Path was rerouted and the White Bar Trail was restored (*Trail Walker*, Oct./Nov. 1981, p. 9).

In January 1995, the White Bar Trail was extended south for 1.55 miles from the Dutch Doctor Shelter to the Johnsontown Circle. This extension facilitated access to the park trails from the end of Johnsontown Road, where parking is available.

White Cross Trail

Length: 2.15 miles · Blazes: white cross

Miles

0.0   Claudius Smith Rock.

0.85   Black Ash Swamp, left.

1.0   Old Park boundary.

1.45   White Bar and Victory Trails cross.

1.6   Parker Swamp, down right.

2.15   End at R-D Trail.

The White Cross Trail connects the Tuxedo-Mt. Ivy Trail (T-MI) (red dash on white) at Claudius Smith Rock with the Ramapo-Dunderberg Trail (R-D) (red dot on white) on Parker Cabin Mountain. It starts by going north, downhill from T-MI (in icy weather, it is safer than the parallel Blue Disc Trail), and soon passes to the left of a swampy area. At 0.85 mile, the trail goes along the east side of Black Ash Swamp and soon crosses the old Park boundary. At 1.45 miles, the White Bar and Victory Trails cross. White Cross then ascends gently, with Parker Swamp visible down to the right. At 2.15 miles, White Cross ends at the R-D Trail, just below the steep ascent to Parker Cabin Mountain.

The first mention of this trail appears in the *New York Post* of January 31, 1936, which announced that the Interstate Hiking Club planned to hike on February 2nd on the White Cross Trail, "new to most Interstaters." It had been blazed earlier by Kerson Nurian, the builder of several other trails (HTS in 1928, Nurian in 1929, and Triangle in 1939). In 1939, he asked the Trail Conference to take over the maintenance of this trail. The New York Chapter of the Adirondack Mountain Club (to which Nurian belonged) was assigned the task, and they have continued to maintain it since then.

THE
REVOLUTIONARY
TRAILS

1777 Trail

Length: 2.95 miles (joint section) • *Blazes: red 1777 on white diamond*

Miles

0.0	Route 9W; Jones Trail.
0.05	Cross grade of spiral railway.
0.4	Cross footbridge.
0.65	Turn left, leaving Jones Trail.
0.7	Second Jones leg goes right.
1.1	Turn up, right.
1.35	Timp-Torne Trail crosses.
1.4	R-D Trail crosses.
1.7	Bockberg Trail joins, right.
2.0	Timp Pass Road, left.
2.05	Cross brook; begin Pleasant Valley Road.
2.35	Cross Timp Brook.
2.65	Bridle Path crosses.
2.9	Road, right, to Herbert Cemetery.
2.95	Trails divide.

The 1777 Trail marks the route taken by British troops under Sir Henry Clinton on October 6, 1777 from Stony Point to attack the American forces at Fort Clinton and Fort Montgomery. To avoid private property, the present-day trail starts from Route 9W, 0.75 mile south of the intersection of the road leading to Jones Point. There is a small parking area about 200 feet south of the trailhead.

At first, the trail follows an old road known as the Jones Trail, which was built about 1890 to take workmen up to the various levels of the Dunderberg Spiral Railway. In 300 feet, it crosses the lowest grade of the railway. Then, at 0.4 mile, the trail crosses a stream on a wooden footbridge, built in 1987 as an Eagle Scout project by Enoch Namenson, and rebuilt in 2004, also as an Eagle Scout project, by Clint Aylward (note the wide stone abutments from the original bridge).

At 0.65 mile, the trail has been rerouted to the left to avoid an eroded section of the original road. Then, in 150 feet, the 1777 Trail turns left, while the Jones Trail continues straight ahead (on the old road to the right). In another 150 feet, a branch of the Jones Trail comes in from the right. Now the 1777 Trail runs close to the Park boundary, with homes visible to the left. At 1.1 miles, after passing a small wet area to the left, the 1777 Trail turns right and goes steeply up an old road to a saddle on the ridge between The Timp (on the left) and Dunderberg Mountain (on the right). At 1.35 miles, the Timp-Torne Trail (blue) crosses.

This is a good place to look back down the trail towards the valley below. About 0.4 mile to the south is Tomkins Lake (you can glimpse it on the way up), and beyond is Buckberg Mountain. The route taken from Stony Point by the British troops in 1777 went over Buckberg, past the lake and up this road over the ridge. In those days, it was called the King's Road. In later years, it has been known as Steep Street or the Lumberjack Trail.

In 1900, the lake and the surrounding land belonged to Laura E. Woods, a relative of the local Tomkins family. Her daughter married James Fowler, who was president of Scott and Bowne Co., makers of "Scott's Emulsion." In 1912, Fowler built a house on Bird Hill Road (the old King's Road). The house burned in 1928. Then in 1952 the ruin was bought by Vladimir Sunguroff, who began to restore it. He died before he had finished the restoration, but his wife still lives there in the part of the house that was rebuilt.

In 1947, Mrs. Fowler sold the land around the lake (including Bird Hill Road) to a private developer (Tomkins Lake Colony), and in 1951 she sold the land west of the lake to the Rockland County Girl Scouts. Until then, many hikes started from Tomkins Cove, going up either "Steep Street" or the old Timp Trail from Bulsontown Road.

Now the 1777 Trail continues north, soon crossing the Ramapo-Dunderberg Trail (red dot on white), and then heading down into Doodletown Valley. At 1.7 miles, the Bockberg Trail joins from the right. (Bockberg is another name for Bald Mountain.) Near the bottom of the slope, the faint Timp Pass Road joins from the left. The trail crosses a little brook on a wooden bridge, and the blazes continue along Pleasant Valley Road through the abandoned settlement of Doodletown. Just past the brook crossing, an old dam and a shelter are visible to the right. This is all that remains of a camp that was maintained there until the 1950s by Riverside

Church of New York City. (For more information on this history of this area, see the section on Doodletown, pp. 265-80.)

At 2.35 miles, Timp Brook crosses, and at 2.65 miles the Bridle Path crosses. At 2.9 miles, a road goes right to the Herbert Cemetery. Then at 2.95 miles the trail reaches the point where the British forces divided into two columns. The east column turned to the right to attack Fort Clinton (where the Trailside Museum is located now). The west column went northwest, up an old road which brought them to Queensboro and the road there to Fort Montgomery.

1777E Trail to Fort Clinton

Length: 2.35 miles · Blazes: red 1777E on white diamond

Miles

0.0	Trails divide; continue straight ahead.
0.1	Turn right on Doodletown Road.
0.3	Reservoir on right.
0.35	Lemmon Road, left.
0.5	Go left, off road.
0.6	Join Bridle Path.
0.95	Cornell Mine Trail begins, right.
1.35	Tunnel under South Entrance Road.
1.4	Tunnel under Seven Lakes Drive.
1.65	Pass Bear Mountain Inn.
1.8	AT joins, left.
1.95	Tunnel under Route 9W.
2.35	Trailside Historical Museum.

From the point where the 1777 Trail divides, the 1777E Trail continues along Pleasant Valley Road. After 0.1 mile, it turns right on Doodletown Road and passes the Doodletown Reservoir (built in 1975) and Lemmon Road (which goes up left to Seven Lakes Drive). At 0.5 mile, the trail leaves Doodletown Road (which goes downhill to Route 9W) and goes up to join the Bridle Path. Soon the Cornell Mine Trail (blue) begins on the right, and then the 1777E Trail goes through two tunnels (under the South Entrance Road and the Seven Lakes Drive). After passing the south parking lot and restrooms, 1777E continues ahead on a paved path. It passes to the left of the Bear Mountain Inn, and follows a path above Hessian Lake. At 1.8 miles, the AT (white) joins from the left, and both trails go through a tunnel beneath Route 9W into the museum grounds. 1777E ends at the Trailside Historical Museum, near the site of Fort Clinton. Behind the musuem, the Twin Forts Trail (vertical blue stripe on white) leads down to a footbridge over Popolopen Creek and up to the Fort Montgomery Visitor Center.

1777W Trail to Fort Montgomery

Length: 5.3 miles • Blazes: red 1777W on white diamond

Miles

0.0	Trails divide.
0.05	Cross Doodlekill.
0.5	S-BM Trail crosses.
1.0	AT joins briefly.
1.05	Go left, leaving AT.
1.3	Cross parking area.
1.95	T-T Trail joins.
2.05	Cross Parkway on overpass.
2.25	Go right, leaving road.
2.45	Rejoin road; PG/1779 comes in.
2.55	Turn right, off road.
2.9	Cross Queensboro Brook.
3.6	Go down left with T-T/1779.
3.65	Cross Popolopen Creek; go right on West Point Aqueduct.
3.75	T-T Trail leaves, left.
3.95	T-T Trail rejoins from left.
4.6	Turn right on Mine Road.
4.7	Turn left, leaving road.
4.9	Brooks Lake Trail joins briefly.
5.0	Turn left on Mine Road.
5.15	Climb embankment and continue on paved road.
5.4	Cross under Route 9W and end at Fort Montgomery Historic Site.

After the 1777 Trail divides, the 1777W Trail goes through a small clearing, crosses a little brook (the Doodlekill) and goes gently uphill on an old road, past the ruins of some Doodletown homes. At 0.5 mile, an intersection with the Suffern-Bear Mountain Trail (yellow) and Doodletown Road is reached. Here, 1777W turns left onto Doodletown Road, which it follows gently uphill towards the Seven Lakes Drive. At 1.0 mile, the Appalachian Trail joins from the left, and the two trails briefly follow the same route. Just before reaching the Seven Lakes Drive, 1777W leaves the old road and goes left into the woods. Soon a parking area is reached. The trail continues to run roughly parallel to the Seven Lakes Drive until, at 1.95 miles, it joins the Timp-Torne Trail (blue), and both cross the Palisades Interstate Parkway on an overpass. The trails then pass the Queensboro Dam (1915) and a water treatment plant (1929). They then turn right, off the gravel road, to avoid a pistol range. At 2.45 miles, PG/1779 joins, and all four trails continue north along the road for 0.1 mile. The trails then turn right, leaving the Fort Montgomery Road. The road beyond this point is on land of West Point Military Academy, where hiking is allowed only with written permission. In another 0.35 mile, Queensboro Brook is crossed on a footbridge, and the trails turn left and continue along the brook. At 3.6 miles, the Popolopen Gorge Trail continues straight ahead while 1777W/1779/T-T turns left and goes down across Popolopen Creek. Up the bank on the north side, the trails turn right onto the West Point "Patrick" Aqueduct. This 20-inch pipeline was opened on August 31, 1906. It is 33,000 feet long and carries water from Queensboro Brook and Popolopen Creek to the Lusk Reservoir on the Academy grounds.

In another 500 feet, the Timp-Torne Trail turns left and goes up to the Popolopen Torne, while the 1777W/1779 Trails continue along the aqueduct path. The Timp-Torne Trail rejoins from the left in 0.2 mile. All three trails continue on the aqueduct path until it crosses Mine Road at 4.6 miles. The trails turn right and follow the paved road for 500 feet. They then turn left, leaving the road, and continue downhill on a footpath, briefly joining the Brooks Lake Trail (red square on white) at 4.9 miles.

At 5.0 miles, the three trails turn left onto Mine Road. In 150 feet, they turn right, leaving the paved road, and continue along an old woods road. Then, at 5.15 miles, they climb an embankment and continue on a paved road. In 275 feet, they turn right and follow a footpath under Route 9W to end, 5.4 miles from the start, at the access road to the Fort Montgomery State Historic Site.

In 1975, when these trails were first marked, they all went to the Trailside Museum, where there was a Dan Beard exhibit. Medals and patches were awarded for hiking either trail.

The Revolutionary trails were first scouted and blazed in 1974-75 as a joint project of the Rockland County Boy Scout and Girl Scout Councils, the Palisades Interstate Park, the Cooperative Extension Association of Rockland County, and the NY/NJ

DANIEL CHAZIN

Footbridge over Popolopen Creek

Trail Conference. The routes were determined by Jack Mead, Director of the Trailside Museum. He used information from military records in London and maps drawn by Robert Erskine, Surveyor General of the American army in 1778-79.

For the first hike on the 1777 Trail, a ceremony was held on March 27, 1975. Leading the hike were Brad Bobb, Captain of Shore Guard, Orange County Militia, and John Walker of the 42nd British Regiment Foot "Black Watch." Also present were Jack Focht, who had put up the blazes (he used a stepladder), Tim Sullivan, representing the Park, and representatives of the Scouts and the Trail Conference. This first hike started at the junction of the Buckberg and Mott Farm Roads. It went over Bird Hill, to the right of Tomkins Lake, and up over Dunderberg—the actual route the British troops had taken in 1777. Musket fire was heard again, on Dunderberg and in Doodletown.

A second ceremony, with the same participants, was held on April 12, 1975 for the 1779 Trail. This one started at the Cliff House near the Bear Mountain Viaduct. It proceeded along the Forest of Dean Mine Road and Fort Montgomery Road, past the ruins of the Queensboro Furnace, to Queensboro, and ended at the Bullowa Scout Camp (the old Springsteel farm).

In the years since 1975, the trails have been maintained by the Boy Scouts' Order of the Arrow, and most recently by the Trail Conference. The trails have been rerouted in places to avoid private or West Point property. In some places, they depart from the original route to avoid dangerous highway crossings.

1779 Trail

Length: 8.6 miles · Blazes: blue 1779 on white diamond

Miles

0.0 Start on access road to Fort Montgomery Historic Site.

0.2 Left on paved road.

0.45 Left on Mine Road.

0.55 Brooks Lake Trail joins briefly.

0.7 Right on Mine Road.

0.8 Go left on West Point Aqueduct.

1.45 Continue straight ahead; T-T turns right.

1.65 T-T rejoins.

1.75 Turn down left and cross Popolopen Creek.

1.8 Go right with Popolopen Gorge Trail.

2.5 Cross Queensboro Brook.

2.85 Go left on Fort Montgomery Road.

2.95 Turn right, with PG Trail.

3.2 Pass Queensboro Lake.

3.65 Go left (leave PG).

3.8 Left again, onto Summer Hill Road.

4.3 Cross Route 6.

4.4 Cross Seven Lakes Drive.

4.65 Cross Anthony Wayne Trail.

5.8 Orange/Rockland county line.

6.1 Cross AT/R-D.

6.6 Cross Owl Lake Road.

7.05 Cross Palisades Interstate Parkway.

7.15 Join Beechy Bottom Road.

7.25 Go right, off Beechy Bottom Road.

7.6 Join old Black Mountain Trail.

7.7 Go left on Red Cross Trail.

7.8 S-BM joins, briefly.

7.9 Red Cross leaves, left.

8.4 Pines Trail joins from right.

8.55 Beechy Bottom Road joins from left.

8.6 Bulsontown.

The 1779 Trail starts on the access road that leads from Route 9W to the Fort Montgomery State Historic Site, 0.2 mile north of the north end of the Popolopen Viaduct. For the first 1.45 miles, it runs jointly with the 1777W and Timp-Torne (T-T) Trails.

After climbing stone steps, the joint trails cross under Route 9W, and they turn left onto a paved road at 0.2 mile. At the end of the road, the trails go down and continue along an old woods road. Then, at 0.45 mile, the joint trails reach Mine Road (old Forest of Dean Road). They turn left and follow the road for 150 feet, then turn right onto a grassy woods road. In another 300 feet, the trails turn left, leaving the road, and briefly join the Brooks Lake Trail (red square on white). After crossing a wet area on puncheons, the Brooks Lake Trail leaves to the right, and 1779/1777W/T-T continues up a steep, rocky path. At 0.7 mile, the trails turn right onto Mine Road, and in another 500 feet (immediately after Wildwood Ridge goes off to the left), they turn down left on a path which is the route of the West Point Aqueduct.

Of course, the aqueduct was built 127 years after General Wayne passed this way. The Boy Scouts who originally blazed this trail followed Wayne's route—along the Mine Road to its junction with the Fort Montgomery Road. Those early blazes can still be seen on the telephone poles along Mine Road, beyond the aqueduct crossing, but the newer blazes turn left with the blue Timp-Torne Trail and follow the aqueduct path.

At 1.45 miles, the Timp-Torne Trail turns up, to the right, to cross Fort Montgomery Road and Mine Road and ascend Popolopen Torne. Our 1779 Trail (along with the 1777W Trail) goes straight ahead along the aqueduct path. After 0.2 mile, our trails meet Timp-Torne again and, in a few hundred feet, all turn left, going down to cross Popolopen Creek. After passing a fireplace, they go up and join the Popolopen Gorge Trail (PG) (red square on white), and all four trails go west on the Bear Mountain Aqueduct (built in 1929-30). In another 300 feet, the trails leave the Aqueduct (it is walkable and can be followed to rejoin the trail 0.4 mile further up the brook). At 2.5 miles, the trails cross Queensboro Brook on a concrete pipe aqueduct bridge, and in another 0.35 mile, they turn left on Fort Montgomery Road.

Two years after Forts Clinton and Montgomery had been destroyed by British troops, General George Washington instructed General Anthony Wayne to drive the British from the fort at Stony Point. Starting from several camps north of Fort Montgomery, Wayne led about 1,150 men in four regiments around Bear Mountain by way of the Fort Montgomery Road.

They stopped for lunch on July 15, 1779 near where our present trail joins the old Fort Montgomery Road. They continued south through the valley now called Beechy Bottom and took an old road down to Springsteel's farm (now the Boy Scouts' Camp Bullowa). At midnight, Wayne's troops attacked the fort from three directions and quickly subdued its defenders.

At 2.95 miles, 1779/PG turns right, off the road, while 1777W/T-T goes straight ahead towards West Mountain. Now following an old woods road, the trail approaches Queensboro Lake, a pretty spot to stop for lunch. At 3.65 miles, our 1779 Trail turns left from the PG route, and soon joins a wide fire road that goes through a Park work area to Route 6. This fire road, known as the Summer Hill Road, was built by the Civilian Conservation Corps in the spring of 1933. It goes around the foot of Summer Hill to the site of a dam in Curtis Hollow.

After crossing Route 6 (Long Mountain Parkway) near Long Mountain Circle, at 4.3 miles, the trail crosses the Seven Lakes Drive. Easily seen on the opposite side of the traffic circle is a cemetery of perhaps 100 graves, where the residents of Queensboro hamlet—the Weyants, Brooks and Coons—lie buried. The most recent burial there was in 1993.

Going uphill now toward Black Mountain, the 1779 Trail crosses the Anthony Wayne Trail (white) and joins an old woods road (the Leisure Trail) which goes along the west side of a low ridge.

This ridge was designated DeGaffles' Ridge on a map of the area drawn by Robert Erskine for General Washington in 1778. On his map, a road appears to run along the crest of the ridge. In fact, in those days there was no road on the ridge. There was a well-used road, known as Beechy Bottom Road, on the east side of the ridge. Most of that road was destroyed when the Palisades Interstate Parkway was built in 1953. Since, from the Seven Lakes Drive south, it was no longer possible for the trail to follow the historical route used in 1779, the blazers of our historical trail chose the Leisure Trail on the west side of DeGaffles' Ridge.

At 5.8 miles on the 1779 Trail (1.4 miles south of Seven Lakes Drive), the old Leisure Trail departs down to the left. This point (marked by cairns on both sides of the trail) is on the Orange/Rockland county line. The Leisure Trail continues for another 0.25 mile until it ends at the Appalachian/Ramapo-Dunderberg Trail (AT/R-D), 75 yards above Beechy Bottom West Road.

From the junction, our 1779 Trail proceeds straight ahead. At 6.1 miles, it crosses the AT/R-D, which comes down from Black Mountain. Soon afterward the ridge ends abruptly, and our trail descends to the Owl Lake Road. It crosses this road and picks up another woods road (once named the Black Mountain Trail) which passes through a swampy region. At 7.05 miles, it reaches the Palisades Interstate Parkway.

After crossing the Parkway, the 1779 Trail briefly joins the Beechy Bottom Road, then turns right, off that road, and crosses a little stone viaduct. Continuing through a rocky region (where General Wayne certainly never went), it soon joins a woods road (the Black Mountain Trail), and 0.1 mile further joins the Red Cross Trail. Red Cross and 1779 here follow a well-worn old road which was known as the Dean Trail when the Park was formed in 1910.

At 7.8 miles, the Suffern-Bear Mountain Trail (yellow) joins for about 400 feet and leaves again. Red Cross then departs to the left, while 1779 continues downhill. At 8.4 miles, the unmarked Pines Trail (the trail along the brook between Pingyp and The Pines) joins from the right. Then, at 8.55 miles, 1779 meets Beechy Bottom Road on the left, and all reach a paved road at 8.6 miles. This is Bulsontown. The houses in this area are mostly owned by Bulson families who have lived here for generations. Just ahead is Cedar Flats Road, where a street sign says that the road we have just left (Beechy Bottom Road) is called Queensboro Road.

Wayne's route went briefly left on Cedar Flats Road, and then continued on Bulsontown Road. After 0.7 mile, it turned left onto Franck Road past the Boy Scouts' Camp Bullowa (where the American troops rested at Springsteel's farm to prepare for their midnight assault on the fort at Stony Point). To reach the Stony Point Battlefield Park, go left on Wayne Avenue 0.7 mile to Route 9W. Turn right on Route 9W for 0.3 mile, then turn left onto Park Road, which goes downhill to the battlefield park. Old 1779 blazes may be occasionally found along these roads.

THE WOODS ROADS

Besides the marked hiking trails, Harriman-Bear Mountain State Parks feature an extensive network of woods roads. Described in this section are about 50 miles of woods roads. Some are maintained by the Park as fire roads, while others are not formally maintained. Except for the Horn Hill Bike Trail (and several other roads which are used for part of their length by marked hiking trails), these woods roads are not blazed. They can, however, be readily followed by hikers equipped with a map, and they may be combined with the marked trails to form interesting and varied loop hikes.

Arden Road

Length: 2.8 miles

Miles

0.0 Begin at Arden Valley Road.

0.05 Wide path to Elk Pen leaves, right.

0.1 AT leaves, left; A-SB begins.

0.4 A-SB leaves, left; Stahahe Brook Trail begins.

0.7 Cross Stahahe Brook; Stahahe Brook Trail leaves, left.

1.5 Road monument.

1.55 Nurian Trail joins, left.

1.75 Nurian Trail leaves, right, at Thruway pedestrian overpass.

2.8 End at Route 106.

The Arden Road (also known as the Old Arden Road) presently begins on Arden Valley Road, a short distance east of the road leading into the Elk Pen parking area. The Appalachian Trail (AT) (white) briefly follows the road, but soon turns left and starts up the hill. Just before the AT turns off the road, a wide path, right, leads to the Elk Pen parking area, and the Arden-Surebridge Trail (A-SB) (red triangle on white) begins and runs south along the road. At 0.4 mile, the A-SB leaves to the left and the Stahahe Brook Trail (horizontal red stripe on white) begins and heads south along the road. Then, at 0.7 mile, the road crosses Stahahe Brook on a wooden bridge. On the south side of the brook, the Stahahe Brook Trail goes off to the left, and Arden Road continues south as an unmarked route. A road monument is passed at 1.5 miles, soon after which the Nurian Trail (white) joins from the left. The trail runs south along the road for 0.2 mile, then turns right and crosses the pedestrian overpass across the Thruway.

About 1894, Edward Harriman requested permission from Orange County to close a road through his estate. That road went south from Florence Mountain (east of Central Valley) past Forest Lake to join the road from Twin Lakes (Baileytown Road). Despite some protests from local residents, permission was granted. In order to show his gratitude to his neighbors, Harriman built a new road from Arden to Southfields. A monument erected later by the County explained that the road had been made "to show the value of level roads in hilly countries." The road started from the Greenwood Furnace at Arden and went south above Arden Brook and the Erie Railroad. After 0.65 mile, it reached the site of Arden Valley Road (completed in 1934). This section of the road has been partly obliterated by the Thruway, which was built in 1954.

At the Elk Pen (built 1919), Harriman's road turned up to the foot of the mountain (where a branch went up the valley and across some meadows to Echo Lake) and then continued south. This section of the road remains and is still used by hikers. When it was first built, Harriman's

"level road" crossed the Ramapo River on a bridge located 0.25 mile north of the bridge that presently carries the Nurian Trail over the river. No trace of Harriman's bridge remains. It probably was washed away in the great flood of October 8, 1903. Hoeferlin's older maps indicate a ford at the site of Harriman's bridge.

The road south of the Nurian Bridge was part of the old Monroe-Haverstraw Turnpike (see p. 196). Sometime before 1920 (perhaps after the 1903 flood), a connection was made on the east side of the Ramapo River between the Turnpike and Harriman's "level road." The connecting road was obliterated during the construction of the Thruway, but in 1954 the two roads were again connected, higher on the hillside.

Baileytown Road (Twin Lakes Road)

Length: 2.1 miles

Miles

0.0   Route 6 (Long Mountain Road).

0.3   Lake Te Ata, right; Lower Twin Lake, left.

0.8   Cross brook from Upper Twin Lake.

1.4   Trail, left, to Cave Shelter.

1.75 Cemetery, left.

1.85 Old boundary, right.

1.95 Nawahunta Trail, left.

2.1   Harriman Estate gate.

Baileytown Road begins as a paved camp service road, starting from Long Mountain Parkway and passing between Lake Te Ata and Lower Twin Lake. (Hikers should note that the nearest parking area is 0.35 mile west on Route 6, requiring one to walk back along this high-speed road. This parking area should be approached heading east on Route 6.) At 0.6 mile, a branch goes off to the right and leads to the camps on Upper Twin Lake. A brook from Upper Twin Lake is crossed at 0.8 mile. At 1.4 miles, directly opposite a "one way" sign (for vehicular traffic), a faint trail on the left goes 0.5 mile up to the Stockbridge Cave Shelter. A short distance beyond, the pavement ends at the last camp building, and Baileytown Road continues straight ahead (the paved road to the right leads into a camp). A cemetery may be seen on the left at 1.75 miles—the names on the stones are Bailey and Lewis. At 1.85 miles, a stone wall is visible on the right. Until 1942, this was the boundary of the Park. A faint path beyond that wall leads down to a brook. More stone walls are above the brook, and on the other side of the brook is the overgrown farm of William and Mary Bailey. William died in 1924 at the age of 87, and Mary sold the farm to the Park in 1925.

The unmarked Nawahunta Trail (an easily followed woods road) comes in on the left at 1.95 miles. The Lewis family lived at the other end of that trail, where Lake Nawahunta is now. There were many marriages between the Baileys and the Lewises, so naturally a road was built to connect their lands.

At 2.1 miles, our road ends at a gate, the entrance to the Harriman estate. Baileytown Road actually continues for 4.5 more miles through the Harriman estate to Arden. In the early 1920s, Roland Harriman bought the last Parrott family home on that road, and when the last Bailey farm was sold to the Park in 1930, the County gave permission to close the road to the public. In 1942, Averell Harriman gave the Park a quarter-mile-wide strip, from the top of Stockbridge Mountain, northwest across Summit Lake, and down nearly to the line of the Thruway.

Standing by the Harriman gate, an old woods road may be seen going to the right. That road leads to the William and Mary Bailey farm in about 0.25 mile. The determined hiker will have to fight his way through the barberries and proceed to the northwest corner of the farm, where the road will be found again. It goes up over the ridge and down to Summit Lake.

About 0.1 mile up that old woods road from the Harriman gate, an even fainter road goes left. That one, very faint in places, leads to the south end of Summit Lake in about 0.65 mile from the Harriman gate and continues along the west side of the lake to some camp buildings.

Late in the day on Friday, October 23, 1942, Lester Bailey, 72 years old, the son of Samuel Bailey, left a note: "I have gone to the fields." Lester still farmed 60 acres of the family farm south of Upper Twin Lake and tended the family cemetery. When he had not returned a day later, a search was organized. He was found, the following Sunday, November 1st, two miles from home. He had a 16-pound raccoon on his shoulder, a kerosene lantern and a shotgun (*N.Y. Times*, 11/2/42).

Only Lester's cousin Irving remained. He lived as a recluse in a stone veneer cottage near the road. Irving died on Christmas Day 1947—the last of the Baileys (Commission Minutes, 1/13/48).

Beechy Bottom East Road

Length: 3.95 miles

Miles

0.0	Seven Lakes Drive (0.3 mile west of overpass).
0.05	Anthony Wayne Trail joins briefly.
0.15	AW Trail rejoins, right, on original Beechy Bottom Road.
0.2	Original Beechy Bottom Road leaves, left.
0.45	Fawn Trail starts, left; Anthony Wayne Trail leaves, right.
0.8	County line.
0.85	Gravel Park road crosses.
0.9	Mica Mine, below on right.
1.6	Appalachian Trail crosses.
1.85	Ramapo-Dunderberg Trail crosses.
2.1	North "Ski Trail" (stone road), left.
2.25	Branch of Horn Hill Bike Trail joins, right.
2.45	Beechy Bottom West Road joined, right.
2.65	1779 Trail joins, right.
2.75	1779 Trail leaves, right.
2.85	Suffern-Bear Mountain Trail crosses.
3.0	Horn Hill Bike Trail leaves, left.
3.5	Red Cross Trail crosses.
3.7	Bulsontown-Timp Trail, left.
3.9	1779 Trail joins, right.
3.95	Park boundary; Bulsontown.

When the park was created in 1910, there were two roads going south through Beechy Bottom Valley, on the hillsides above the brook—Beechy Bottom East Road and Beechy Bottom West Road. Beechy Bottom West Road was largely destroyed by the construction of the Palisades Interstate Parkway in 1953.

Beechy Bottom East Road started just east of Beechy Bottom Brook, 0.25 mile east of the junction of Seven Lakes Drive with Long Mountain Parkway. That road can still be found going south from the Drive. Another route of the eastern road, built in 1933, starts 0.1 mile to the east of the earlier route. We will describe the 1933 road.

The 1933 road starts above a bank on the Drive (now also the route of the Palisades Interstate Parkway). The first part of this road is largely overgrown with barberry and other vegetation. After about 200 feet, the Anthony Wayne Trail (AW) (white) comes in from the left and joins Beechy Bottom East Road. In another 200 feet, AW leaves to the right. The road ahead is now covered with dense barberry, but it is possible to follow a cleared path along the iron pipe. At 0.15 mile, the older route of Beechy Bottom East Road (now followed by AW) comes in from the right, and AW rejoins the newer road (which is now covered with grass and much easier to follow). Immediately afterwards, the road passes two concrete blockhouses. Just before the second blockhouse, the older road leaves the 1933 road and goes up to the left (it joins the Fawn Trail a bit farther south). At 0.45 mile, the Fawn Trail (red F on white) starts up to the left, and just beyond, the Anthony Wayne Trail leaves sharply to the right and goes down to the parking area on a gravel Park service road. Beechy Bottom East Road continues straight ahead along the gravel road (now blazed with blue-on-white plastic markers as the Horn Hill Bike Trail).

At 0.85 mile, a gravel Park road goes off to the left, up to a concrete reservoir (the large pipe along the road also goes to the reservoir). In another 100 feet, this road goes down to the right and leads to the south parking area of the Anthony Wayne Recreation Area. About 300 feet south of that road junction, the Mica Mine may be found, about 50 feet below the level of Beechy Bottom Road.

At 1.6 miles, the Appalachian Trail (AT) (white) crosses. Then, at 1.85 miles, the Ramapo-Dunderberg Trail (R-D) (red dot on white) crosses. One of the "stone roads," known as the North "Ski Trail," comes down on the left at 2.1 miles. This "stone road" is an old trail, once part of Horn's Route, which had been blazed with aluminum H's by Jim Horn, who was vice president of the Fresh Air Club in 1921. It is now the route of the Horn Hill Bike Trail. At 2.25 miles, another branch of the bike trail comes up on the right, from the R-D and the AT near the brook.

At 2.45 miles, Beechy Bottom West Road once joined, and at 2.65 miles, as the trail rounds the southern end of West Mountain, our modern 1779 Trail comes in on the right (on a path that once was a branch of the Black Mountain Trail). In another 400 feet, the 1779 Trail departs again, to cross a little stone bridge.

Soon the Suffern-Bear Mountain Trail (yellow) crosses, with Horn Hill to the north. Then, 0.15 mile further, the bike trail, with the blue-and-white markers, departs to the left (100 feet down this trail, the South "Ski Trail" goes right and leads 0.85 mile—on a rather rough route—down to the Red Cross Trail.) At 3.5 miles, the Red Cross Trail crosses. Now we are getting pretty far down the hill, and the road becomes rockier and more difficult to follow. At 3.7 miles, sharp eyes will see the old Bulsontown-Timp Trail depart on the left. That trail, now marked A-B (Addisone-Boyce), goes past the Girl Scout camp and up to The Timp (following the route of the Red Timp Trail).

The 1779 Trail (the old Dean Trail) comes in on the right at 3.9 miles, and Beechy Bottom Road ends at the Park boundary at 3.95 miles. Cedar Flats Road is another 0.1 mile ahead.

Starting just before the point where the Horn Hill Bike Trail departs to the left, highway markers can be seen on both sides of the road, roughly every 150 feet, all the way down to Queensboro Road in the hamlet of Bulsontown. These are low concrete benchmarks, about eight inches high, with a metal highway department plate on the top. They are mostly obscured in the brush but can be spotted by a keen eye.

Beechy Bottom valley is full of history. At the north end, where the Beechy Bottom East Road starts, there was the hamlet of Queensboro—a road center. From here, roads led to the Forest of Dean Mine to the north, and to Kings Ferry (Stony Point) to the south. In 1774, a farm there was owned by Moses Clement. In later years, the Weyant and Brooks families lived there. A cemetery 250 feet north of the road junction (now on the side of the Long Mountain Circle) contains the graves of those families. The earliest stone is dated 1868, but many graves are unmarked.

The valley for half a mile south, and the hills to the west, belonged to the Weyant family. Their home was on Beechy Bottom East Road, about 0.3 mile south of Long Mountain Parkway. The home of John Wesley Van Wart, who owned most of the valley south to the junction of the East and West Roads, was a half mile further south.

In 1859, there was a little schoolhouse at the start of the West Road. (The schoolhouse was demolished in 1927.) The next building to the south belonged to T.H. Ferris, and the home of Abraham J. Rose was at 1.55 miles (just north of the AT and just east of the Parkway). His cellar hole and well are still there. Still further south, at 1.85 miles, was the home of William

Rose. George Bulson lived at 1.95 miles, and his neighbor George Nickerson was just beyond.

Except for George Bulson's 42 acres, the land in the valley from Nickerson's place north to the Weyant farm (0.1 mile above the county line) was acquired by John Wesley Van Wart between 1869 and 1882. Van Wart died in 1892, and his heirs sold the 680-acre estate (1.1 square miles) to the Park in 1916. It seems possible that the Van Warts were related to Isaac Van Wart who, together with John Paulding and David Williams, had captured the British spy Major André at Tarrytown on September 23, 1780.

The 260 acres of the Nickerson and Rose places were shown as the "Brush Place" on General Robert Erskine's military map of 1778. The 1790 census of Orange County lists the three families of John, Peter and Caleb Brush as living in Haverstraw Town. The 1880 census lists William Brush as a boarder on the Van Wart farm.

There were two farms on the Beechy Bottom East Road—those of Weyant and Van Wart. From the Van Wart home at the county line, a footpath went south along the hillside to join Beechy Bottom West Road (then a county road known as the Queensboro Road). Also, from the Van Wart home a farm road went down across the farm (which is now the south parking area of the Anthony Wayne Recreation Area) and angled uphill to join the West Road about where the

AT/R-D crosses now. Two more Van Wart homes were on that farm road, which can still be followed from the southwest side of the south parking area. After passing two cellar holes, the faint old road vanishes beneath the Parkway, about 0.1 mile south of the visitor center.

In 1933, the first CCC camp was set up on the Van Wart farm (near the location of the present-day south parking area). Their task was to build a road into Curtis Hollow, and to build a reservoir (Turkey Hill Lake) there. A second camp was set up on the West Road just north of the AT/R-D crossing. Their task was to build a road to Owl Swamp, and to construct a lake there. A third camp was set up on the east side of Beechy Bottom Brook where the West Road joined the East Road (this location has been obliterated by the Parkway). Their task was to build fire roads in the region to the south (we call them "stone roads").

One project of the CCC camps was to extend the old Beechy Bottom Roads and transform them into northbound and southbound motor roads which would connect Tiorati Brook Road in the south with Seven Lakes Drive and Long Mountain Parkway at Queensboro. The East Road was to be for northbound traffic, and the West Road for southbound traffic.

The CCC boys widened Beechy Bottom East Road, leveled it, and extended it south of the Van Wart house. The plan was for it to cross the valley and continue to the east side of Owl Lake. From there it was to follow the north side of Stillwater Brook and join the West Road in the notch between the Pingyp and Flaggy Meadow Mountain. The route of this road was cut in 1953 by the construction of the Parkway, but west of the Parkway, evidence of road construction—rock piles gathered for the roadbed, and an "avenue" where trees were cut down—is still visible. Parts of the proposed route along Stillwater Brook were also cleared and can still be followed.

Beechy Bottom West Road, known since Revolutionary days as the Queensboro Road, was shown on General Robert Erskine's 1778 map, drawn for General George Washington. When the Park was created in 1910, this was the most-used road in the Beechy Bottom valley. The several farms along it had been bought out by the Park by 1917. The West Road started from Long Mountain Parkway, 0.1 mile southeast of the cemetery, and ran along the hillside.

In 1933, the CCC started to improve the old Beechy Bottom West Road. Some of their work near the north end can be seen where the Anthony Wayne Trail crosses it, on the way uphill, west of the Palisades Interstate Parkway overpass. For the next mile, however, their new road, as well as the older road, has been destroyed by the Parkway. The part which remains begins, on the hillside above the Parkway cut, about 0.25 mile north of the Park visitor center (former gas station). In the next 0.6 mile, three county road markers can be seen. They were placed there by the WPA in 1934.

About half a mile down the road (beginning at the Parkway cut), a Civilian Conservation Corps camp was set up in 1933. The AT/R-D Trail crosses in another 0.1 mile. For a short distance south of the AT/R-D, the old road is indistinct, lost in barberry bushes. But then it can be seen again, and at 0.95 mile, it turns down left to the Parkway (the newer Owl Lake Road goes straight ahead). Near here, traces of walls are visible in the bushes; this is where George Bulson lived until 1917. A story has it that he moved his house down the road to Bulsontown, but the Bulson families living down there now have not heard that story. Just beyond here, Beechy Bottom West Road crossed the brook and was joined by Beechy Bottom East Road.

Neither of the Beechy Bottom Roads was ever opened to general traffic after 1934. Parts of the East Road are still used by Park vehicles, though.

Bockberg Trail

Length: 1.85 miles

Miles

0.0   End of Pleasant Valley Road.

0.05   Timp Pass Road leaves, right.

0.3   1777 Trail leaves, right.

0.65   R-D Trail joins briefly; fireplace to right.

0.75   Go right; R-D continues straight ahead.

1.05   Go right at fork.

1.4   Hairpin turn; R-D is straight ahead.

1.85   R-D Trail; Spiral Railway.

Bockberg (Bald Mountain) is the Dutch name for Goat Mountain. The Bockberg Trail starts in Doodletown valley and goes over Dunderberg Mountain. It originally continued down to Route 9W via two separate routes, but significant sections of both routes are now eroded and no longer visible.

The trail starts at the south end of Pleasant Valley Road, where it crosses a brook. Just north of the brook are the remains of a summer camp that once was run by the Riverside Church of New York City. The woods road which continues south from the bridge and goes uphill is the Bockberg Trail. (It is also marked here as the 1777 Trail.) About 250 feet beyond the bridge, the faint Timp Pass Road begins to the right. The 1777 Trail departs to the right at 0.3 mile, while the Bockberg Trail continues up, parallel to a brook.

At 0.65 mile, just before the Bockberg Trail crosses a brook, the Ramapo-Dunderberg Trail (R-D) (red dot on white) joins. The trails run jointly for only a short distance, and the R-D leaves to the left at a fireplace. Soon the trails again join briefly. A bit further up the hill, the Bockberg Trail turns sharp right, while R-D continues straight ahead. At 1.05 miles, a broad path goes up to the left. That is not our trail, but a side trail that goes nearly to the R-D on Dunderberg Mountain. The Bockberg Trail turns down to the right, around a swampy area. At 1.4 miles, it makes a hairpin turn (here, the R-D Trail is only 75 feet ahead) and goes steeply down. It then levels off, turns left about 100 feet from the bottom of the hill, and meets the R-D once again at 1.85 miles. Just beyond this point, the trail ends at a level section of the Dunderberg Spiral Railway. To the right, 0.2 mile down the railway bed, is the Jones Trail.

The Bockberg Trail formerly divided at the Spiral Railway and continued down a gorge between two summits of Dunderberg Mountain. Although portions of each of the two routes are still visible, other sections are eroded to the point that they cannot be followed.

From the Spiral Railway, one route starts on a woods road to the left. It soon becomes indistinct, but stays to the left of a little brook and several swamps lower down. If the brook and swamps are kept to the right, the hiker will eventually enter a gorge (the gorge is shown on the 2010 edition of Harriman-Bear Mountain Trails Map #119, but the brook is not). For the last 0.2 mile in the gorge (which is quite steep at this point), it is possible to follow a faint woods road that parallels the stream at a distance of 20 to 50 feet. Upon reaching Route 9W, 0.75 mile from the Spiral Railway, the hiker may choose to cross the highway and bushwhack down to the older road, 100 feet lower. The older road (which is now part of the Hudson River Greenway Trail and is much more pleasant to walk along) can be followed to the left for 0.4 mile until it joins the modern highway.

The other branch of Bockberg Trail goes left along the Spiral Railway for 0.2 mile, then turns left, through a gap in a stone wall (about 100 feet from the end of this section of the railway). This route formerly followed a distinct path with switchbacks, but the path has eroded, and hikers must bushwhack down the very steep hillside. Eventually, a distinct but quite eroded woods road will be seen. That road goes down the gorge, fairly high above the brook, and reaches Route 9W 0.75 mile from the Spiral Railway. This point is 0.25 mile up the road from the end of the first route, described above. Again, it is best to bushwhack down to the lower old road, taking care to avoid a gravel pit there.

The Bockberg Trail is passable for most of its length by Park trucks or jeeps. From 1985 to 1991, it was used to maintain the stations that were erected in several places on Dunderberg Mountain to monitor the air quality around the power plant at Tomkins Cove.

The left-hand trail down the gorge was once the route of an iron pipe that carried water from the spring at the head of the brook down to the old

ELIZABETH "PERK" STALTER

John Stalter

road near the river level. This route was described by William T. Howell, in his diary for May 17, 1908 (*The Hudson Highlands*, vol. II, pp. 77-78). The pipe had been laid by John Stalter, a woodcutter who lived in Doodletown, to supply water to the men who were building the new state road there in the summer of 1907. The Stalter Spring, usually leaf-covered, can still be found on the mountain, a short distance below the junction of the Bockberg Trail and the R-D.

Conklin Road

Length: 1.5 miles

Miles

0.0   Begin at Pine Meadow Road East.

0.55 Trail to former Lake Minsi dam leaves, right.

1.15 Lake Wanoksink.

1.5   End at Pine Meadow Trail.

This road, originally part of Woodtown Road, was given its present name by Bill Hoeferlin in 1945. It leaves Pine Meadow Road East about 0.1 mile south of the junction of Woodtown Road and Pine Meadow Road East. It is the road on the right (west). Cisterns along the right (west) side of the road, beginning at 0.15 mile, were part of the water system for the unfinished Lake Minsi. At 0.55 mile, a pleasant woods road goes off to the right. It leads in 0.15 mile to the site of the former Lake Minsi dam. The dam was destroyed and the lake drained in 1984. All that remains is a wet but scenic meadow (remnants of the high wall of the dam may been seen on the left at the end of the road).

Continuing southwest, Conklin Road reaches the shore of Lake Wanoksink at 1.15 miles. Although the old road is now under water here, a path continues south, near the edge of the lake, for about 425 feet, then turns right and continues along the top of the dam. From the end of the dam, follow a short, steep path down the embankment to rejoin Conklin Road as it emerges from under the dam. The old Conklin Road heads south for another 0.25 mile, through a notch in the hills, to end at the Pine Meadow Trail (red square on white).

Cranberry Mountain Trail

Length: 0.85 mile

Miles

0.0 Begin at Pine Meadow Road.

0.85 End at camp service road.

The Cranberry Mountain Trail, a woods road, begins on Pine Meadow Road, 0.8 mile from Seven Lakes Drive. Here, Pine Meadow Road turns right and begins to head southeast, while the Cranberry Mountain Trail continues straight ahead (northeast), following the route of a buried telephone cable that was installed in 1969. In 50 feet, the unmarked High Hill Trail begins to the left. Then, at 0.85 mile, a woods road begins to the right, leading 0.15 mile to the top of the hill, from where Breakneck Pond is visible and camp trails continue down to the northern shore of Breakneck Pond. In another 150 feet, the Cranberry Mountain Trail ends at a paved camp service road.

Crooked Road

Length: 3.3 miles

Miles

0.0	Begin at Arden Valley Road.
0.35	AT joins, right.
0.4	AT leaves, left.
0.55	A-SB joins, left.
0.7	Cross brook draining Dismal Swamp.
0.75	A-SB leaves, right.
0.85	White Bar Trail joins, left.
1.45	Dunning Trail joins; White Bar Trail leaves.
1.8	R-D Trail crosses.
2.25	Bowling Rocks.
2.4	Abandoned Dunning Trail route goes off, left.
2.8	Turn right, leaving Dunning Trail.
3.3	End at Route 106.

Hikers in 1920 were familiar with the "Crooked Road." On the first Park trail map, it was shown as starting from the Arden Valley Road on the Harriman estate. It skirted Echo Lake and then went southwest to the south side of Island Pond.

The road today starts from the south side of Arden Valley Road, 0.2 mile east of the gravel road leading to Island Pond. At 0.35 mile, near the edge of Island Pond, the Appalachian Trail (AT) (white) joins briefly, on its way down from the Lemon Squeezer.

The old road continues south, high above the pond. The Arden-Surebridge Trail (A-SB) (red triangle on white) joins from the left at 0.55 mile, and then, at 0.7 mile, the Crooked Road crosses a brook which drains the Dismal Swamp. Soon afterwards, the A-SB departs to the right. At 0.85 mile, the White Bar Trail joins from the left. The clear, wide trail continues south.

At 1.45 miles, the Dunning Trail (yellow) joins, and the White Bar Trail leaves. Here the Crooked Road, now following the route of the Dunning

Trail, turns left and soon goes steeply up the slope of Black Rock Mountain. On the way up, it crosses a fairly level region, and then another short, steep climb through laurels brings it to the Ramapo-Dunderberg Trail (red dot on white) at 1.8 miles. Now heading gradually down, the road crosses a stream and then goes over a level area of bare rock dotted by boulders (named "Bowling Rocks") at 2.25 miles. The abandoned Dunning route goes off to the left at 2.4 miles, and a junction is reached at 2.8 miles. Straight ahead, the Dunning blazes continue to the Hogencamp Mine. But our Crooked Road turns right and goes south down to Little Long Pond. On the way, it passes through an abandoned Girl Scout camp, and it reaches Route 106 at 3.3 miles.

When the Park was formed in 1910, Island Pond remained in the Harriman estate. The Park boundary followed the Crooked Road from Echo Lake to the point where the Dunning Trail joins it now, at the foot of Black Rock Mountain. In 1921-22, the Boy Scouts marked their White Bar Trail along this road. Their trail came down from the Lemon Squeezer on the route later adopted by the AT trail blazers in 1922. While one leg of the White Bar Trail continued south to the highway, as it does today, another leg followed the Crooked Road to Little Long Pond.

On the hillside above Little Long Pond, the Park, in 1919, built Camp Matinecock for the Boy Scouts. In

the winter of 1920-21, when the new Trail Conference was building the R-D Trail, the volunteers were accommodated with bed and board at Camp Matinecock. In 1930, the Queens Council Girl Scouts took over the camp, calling it Camp Quid Nunc (Latin = What Now?). In order to enable the girls safely to cross the road to the lake, a rustic footbridge was built over the road.

The Girl Scouts vacated the camp in 1969, and the camp was demolished in 1976. Its dining hall was moved to "Merritt Bank" (a Park storage area for scrap materials), off Seven Lakes Drive between Silvermine and Tiorati Lakes. The footbridge over the road was demolished in June 1987.

File Factory Hollow Trail

Length: 0.95 mile

Miles

0.0 Begin at Woodtown Road.

0.1 Limekiln Mountain Trail crosses.

0.35 Trail, left, to Horse Chock Mountain.

0.95 End at power line service road.

The File Factory Hollow Trail starts on Woodtown Road, 0.7 mile north of the Tuxedo-Mt. Ivy Trail (red dash on white), and 0.15 mile north of the Suffern-Bear Mountain Trail (yellow). It goes down to the power line above Call Hollow Road. At 0.1 mile, the Limekiln Mountain Trail crosses, from the nearby File Factory Brook (which drains Squirrel Swamp). At 0.35 mile, a trail (formerly used by horses) goes off to the left, up to Horse Chock Mountain. Other trails will be passed—one on the right goes to the top of Limekiln Mountain. Then, at 0.95 mile, the power line service road is reached. Below is Krucker's picnic grove. The Diltz Road hikers' parking area is 1.05 miles southwest.

Where the trail ends at the power line service road, the remains of an old dam can be seen in the brook. Here, in 1832, a file factory was built by a 21-year-old Englishman named James Slinn and his brother. In 1850, the Slinns sold the factory to John F. Anderson, who had married a local girl named Catherine Secor. Anderson operated the factory until his death in 1883, when it passed to Catherine's brother John H. Secor. Green's *History of Rockland County*, published in 1886, said that Anderson's file factory still employed four or five men.

Hasenclever Road

Length: 1.85 miles

Miles

0.0   Tiorati Brook Road, 0.25 mile below dam.

0.05 Woods road, right.

0.45 County line.

0.55 Hasenclever Mine, left; Red Cross Trail departs ahead.

0.6   Overgrown woods road, left, goes to Beech Trail.

0.7   Old trail, right, to Red Cross Trail.

1.2   Beech Trail crosses.

1.6   Trail, right, to Charleston farm.

1.65 Grape Swamp Mountain Trail, left.

1.85 End at Lake Welch Drive.

Hasenclever Road begins at Tiorati Brook Road, about 0.25 mile east of the dam at the southeast corner of Lake Tiorati. It proceeds south along the route of the Red Cross Trail. After 275 feet, a woods road goes up to the right. This road (which probably was the route of Hasenclever Road before Tiorati Brook Road was built) goes around the end of the mountain, above and parallel to Tiorati Brook Road, and ends near the camp road just south of the dam. The Hasenclever Mountain Trail branches west from this road and goes up along the ridge of Hasenclever Mountain.

At 0.45 mile, there is a county line marker on the right. The letters on the top are "O" (Orange) and "R" (Rockland). Then, at 0.55 mile, the Hasenclever Mine is on the left. The mine is 100 feet deep, filled with water and mud. Here, the Red Cross Trail bears right, while our road goes left around a low knob. On the far side of the knob, at 0.6 mile, a Rockland County highway monument may be seen on a rock on the left, about 15 feet from the road. Then, in another 50 feet, a woods road begins to the left. For the first 25 feet, it is obscured by low bushes, but it soon becomes visible. In many places, it is overgrown with laurel, but an experienced hiker may be able to follow it for 0.75 mile to the Beech Trail, 0.1 mile south of Tiorati Brook Road (at this point, when approaching from Tiorati Brook Road, the Beech Trail turns left, while the old woods road, obscured by vegetation, continues straight). At 0.7 mile, two vague woods roads begin to the right. They soon join and, although becoming progressively more overgrown, can be followed for 0.2 mile to the Red Cross Trail (for 10 years, 1948-58, that was the route of the Red Cross Trail).

At 0.8 mile, the road crosses a little concrete bridge—a reminder that until 1910 this was a county road. Then, at 1.2 miles, the Beech Trail (blue) crosses. At 1.6 miles, a woods road goes down to the right (it leads 0.25 mile to the old Charleston farm on the Beech Trail). Just beyond, another woods road goes off to the left. If one takes this woods road and then almost immediately bears left onto a faint trail, it will lead to the summit of Grape Swamp Mountain. At 1.85 miles, Hasenclever Road ends at Lake Welch Drive.

Hasenclever Road, built in 1760 from Stony Point to Central Valley, is one of the oldest roads in the Park. Its significance is apparent from the many woods roads (most of which are overgrown) that branch off of it. Hasenclever Road was mapped by General Robert Erskine in 1778 for General Washington. It was also described in a press release by Major Welch (Press Release #205, 1/9/30). From Cedar Pond (now Lake Tiorati), it went past Hasenclever Mine to Beaver Pond (now Lake Welch). It followed the brook down old Gate Hill Road to Call Hollow Road, and then continued out to Stony Point.

Going north from Cedar Pond dam (Hasenclever had built the dam about 1765), the road coincided with our Tiorati Brook Road for 0.5 mile, and then went right, away from the lake, around a knob to the north of the lake. It continued to the northwest down a hill, and crossed the Seven Lakes Drive 0.5 mile north of Tiorati Circle. It followed what is now a Park road up past an abandoned girls' camp, and then curved to the south. Just about where it reaches our present Arden Valley Road, the old road turned up sharp right, passing between two peaks of Bradley Mountain. It went gently down past Slaughters Pond (Forest Lake) and north to June's Tavern (Central Valley). The road from Bradley Mountain past Forest Lake is on Harriman land, which is not open to the public. This part of the road is not shown on an 1859 map of Orange County, and probably was abandoned about 1838, when a new road was built to the Greenwood and Bradley Mines.

Horn Hill Bike Trail

Length: 4.8 miles • *Blazes: blue on white*

Miles

0.0   South end of parking area.

0.2   Fenced enclosure, right; cross first bridge.

0.4   Sharp left over second bridge.

0.45 Cross third bridge.

0.5   Cross fourth bridge.

0.6   AT crosses.

0.7   R-D comes in, left.

0.75 R-D leaves, right.

1.05 Turn left onto Beechy Bottom East Road.

1.15 Turn right onto North "Ski Trail."

1.3   Turn right onto woods road.

1.5   S-BM crosses.

2.05 Turn right onto Beechy Bottom Road.

2.2   S-BM crosses.

2.3   1779 comes in, left.

2.4   1779 leaves, left.

2.8   First section of trail comes in, left.

2.95 Branch of trail leaves, right.

3.2   R-D crosses.

3.45 AT crosses.

4.2   Turn right at T-intersection.

4.6   Turn left onto Anthony Wayne Trail.

4.8   End at entrance road to Anthony Wayne Recreation Area.

The Horn Hill Bike Trail, blazed with blue-on-white markers, forms a figure-eight loop, starting at the southern parking area of the Anthony Wayne Recreation Area. (The first mile of this trail was designated as the Anthony Wayne South Ski Trail in previous editions of this book.) It is the only trail in Harriman-Bear Mountain State Parks on which bicycles are permitted. Bicyclists are asked to follow the trail in a designated di-

Bike rider on the Horn Hill Bike Trail

rection, which is how it is described here (hikers may choose to walk in either direction).

The bike trail begins at the southeast corner of the parking area and soon enters a pine forest where, at 0.2 mile, a fenced-in enclosure can be seen on the right (the fence has been broken by a fallen tree). That was a demonstration area, built to show how the vegetation looks where browsing deer are excluded.

At 0.4 mile, the trail turns sharply left, across Beechy Bottom Brook. Here, there is a little dam across a stream that comes down from the right. Two more bridges are crossed, and the trail passes to the right of a small knoll. Just beyond, where the bike trail joins another old road, the Appalachian Trail (white) crosses. Then, at 0.7 mile, the Ramapo-Dunderberg Trail (R-D) (red dot on white) comes down from the left.

After crossing two culverts, the R-D leaves to the right. Soon, the bike trail turns up to the left, with Beechy Bottom Brook to the right of the trail. At 1.0 mile, the trail bears right, and at 1.05 miles it reaches Beechy Bottom East Road.

Across Beechy Bottom Road is another unfinished road. Judging from the piles of stone along the way, it, too, was a CCC project. After 0.1 mile, it goes down and crosses Beechy Bottom Road, to end 100 feet beyond at a "T." Here another unfinished road begins to run parallel to Beechy Bottom Road. It ends 0.1 mile to the south, where it has been cut by the Parkway. The continuation of that intended road can still be seen, on a knoll west of the Parkway (see p. 173).

Before the Park was created in 1910, the south parking area was part of a farm that had belonged to John Wesley Van Wart. He died in 1892, and his wife Elizabeth died in 1911.

In 1916, the heirs sold their 630 acres in Beechy Bottom to the Park. This section of the bike trail was one of John Wesley's farm roads. The little dam we see at 0.35 mile probably provided a pool where his cattle could drink.

The Horn Hill Bike Trail turns left and follows Beechy Bottom Road for 0.1 mile, then turns right onto the North "Ski Trail." At 1.3 miles, it turns right onto another woods road (designated as the "North-South Connector" in previous editions of this book). It goes steeply up Horn Hill, then levels off near the top at 1.45 miles. Going gently down, it crosses the Suffern-Bear Mountain Trail (yellow) at 1.5 miles. It then levels off, and for a while goes gently up. After going down more steeply at 1.9 miles, it levels off, and it reaches Beechy Bottom Road at 2.05 miles. At the junction, there is a Rockland County highway monument—a reminder that Beechy Bottom Road was once a county road from Bulsontown to Queensboro. The bike trail turns right and follows Beechy Bottom Road for the next 2.55 miles.

The Suffern-Bear Mountain Trail crosses at 2.2 miles, and in another 500 feet, the 1779 Trail (blue 1779 on white diamond) joins from the left. The bike trail runs concurrently with the 1779 Trail for 400 feet, and then the 1779 Trail departs to the left. At 2.8 miles, the first section of the bike trail joins from the left. You retrace your route for 0.15 mile (this is the center of the "figure-eight") but continue ahead on Beechy Bottom Road when a branch of the bike trail leaves to the right at 2.95 miles.

The Ramapo-Dunderberg Trail crosses at 3.2 miles, and the Appalachian Trail crosses at 3.45 miles. At a T-intersection, reached at 4.2 miles, turn right to continue on the bike trail, then bear left in 100 feet as another Park road goes off to the right.

At 4.6 miles, the bike trail turns left, leaving Beechy Bottom Road, and descends on a gravel Park road, the route of the white-blazed Anthony Wayne Trail. The Horn Hill Bike Trail ends, 4.8 miles from its start, at a gate along the entrance road to the Anthony Wayne Recreation Area. To return to the start, bicyclists (and hikers) can turn left and follow the paved entrance road to the southern parking area.

Island Pond Road

Length: 2.35 miles

Miles

0.0 Arden Valley Road; proceed south on wide gravel road.

0.05 CCC road leaves, right.

0.2 Turn right onto original route of Island Pond Road.

0.3 AT joins, left.

0.35 AT leaves, right.

0.95 A-SB joins, right.

1.15 Road, left, to old cabin.

1.2 A-SB leaves, left.

1.5 Dunning Trail joins; Boston Mine, left.

1.55 Dunning Trail leaves, right.

1.6 Nurian Trail crosses.

1.8 Trail, right, to Stahahe High Peak.

2.3 White Bar Trail joins, left.

2.35 Route 106.

Island Pond Road starts at a gate on Arden Valley Road, 1.1 miles east of the Elk Pen parking area. The wide gravel road straight ahead, built in 1963, is the start of our route, but it is not the original Island Pond Road. To find the original Island Pond Road, take the Civilian Conservation Corps (CCC) road that begins on the right a short distance beyond the gate. Like many other CCC roads, it is easily distinguished by its remarkable stone work. The CCC built this road in 1934 as a level approach to Island Pond from the new (1930) Arden Valley Road. About 0.15 mile down the CCC road, the original Island Pond Road, built about 1905, comes up from the right and crosses the CCC road. The route to the left was widened by the CCC in preparation for enlarging Island Pond, but that plan was abandoned.

Since it is not possible to follow the start of the original Island Pond Road as a through route, we will begin by following the wide gravel road south from Arden Valley Road. At 0.2 mile, turn right, leaving the gravel road, and continue on a woods road that is the original Island Pond Road. Then, at 0.3 mile, near the northern end of Island Pond, the Appalachian Trail (AT) (white) joins from the left. The AT leaves to the right at 0.35 mile. Island Pond Road then parallels the edge of the pond. At 0.95 mile, the Arden-Surebridge Trail (A-SB) (red triangle on white) joins from the right. Island Pond Road soon crosses the southern outlet of the pond, and at 1.15 miles, a road goes left to a point on the south end of the lake. The stone ruins there are all that remain of a cabin built by the Park for the use of Park rangers.

The road now heads south and begins to climb. The A-SB soon leaves to the left and, at 1.5 miles, the Dunning Trail (yellow) joins from the left. The Boston Mine is 200 feet to the left along this trail. The Dunning Trail soon goes off to the right, and shortly afterward the Nurian Trail (white) joins briefly and then leaves to the left. At 1.8 miles, as the vegetation changes from evergreen to deciduous, an unmarked trail leads right to Stahahe High Peak. Going gently down now, the White Bar Trail joins from the left at 2.3 miles, and at 2.35 miles, Island Pond Road ends where it meets Route 106 at a gate (here, the White Bar Trail bears left, parallels Route 106 for 0.15 mile, then crosses the road and reaches a parking area).

Island Pond was acquired by Edward Harriman in 1885. It seems likely that he built the original road to Island Pond about 1905. The *Rockland County Times* for February 13, 1908 mentions the road around Island Pond "which Mr. Harriman built two or three years ago." The road came up by switchbacks from the meadows on Harriman's farm. The old road then turned south toward the lake.

After the Park acquired Island Pond in 1927, they widened the road to 20 feet. Then, in 1934, the CCC built a level approach from the new (1930) Arden Valley Road. They widened the road by cutting out the laurels in preparation for enlarging Island Pond. That plan, fortunately, was abandoned. In 1966, the road from Island Pond to Route 210 (now Route 106) was covered with gravel.

Jones Trail

Length: 1.55 miles

Miles

0.0 Begin at Route 9W.

0.05 Cross grade of spiral railway.

0.4 Cross wooden bridge.

0.7 1777 Trail departs, left.

1.25 Timp-Torne Trail crosses.

1.55 End at railway bed.

The Jones Trail, which is a woods road, starts at Route 9W, 0.5 mile south of the Anchor Monument. There is a parking area about 300 feet south of the trailhead. For the first 0.7 mile, the Jones Trail is marked with the blazes of the 1777 Trail (red 1777 on white diamond). About 300 feet from the start, it crosses the lowest grade of the old Dunderberg Spiral Railway. After 0.4 mile, it goes over a wooden bridge. Then, at 0.7 mile, after a brief detour to the left to avoid an eroded section of the old road, the 1777 Trail departs to the left, while the Jones Trail continues straight ahead.

The Jones Trail goes north, up along the face of the eastern Dunderberg cliffs, and, in 0.2 mile, begins to parallel a little brook. At 1.25 miles from Route 9W (0.55 mile from the 1777 Trail junction), the Timp-Torne Trail (blue) crosses the Jones Trail. Across a brook, the Timp-Torne Trail leads to the unfinished tunnel of the Spiral Railway.

Uphill, beyond the Timp-Torne crossing, the Jones Trail is somewhat eroded. It crosses the brook and ascends through laurels. The Jones Trail ends at 1.55 miles, where it reaches the next-higher level of the railway. Here, there is a panoramic view over the Hudson River. It is possible to follow the railbed to the left for 0.2 mile to a junction with the Ramapo-Dunderberg Trail (red dot on white).

The Jones Trail was built about 1890 as a work road to get work- men with their tools and animals up to the several levels of the Spiral

View over the Hudson

Railway. It was named for the family that owned most of the mountain. In 1836, Joshua T. Jones of Westchester County bought 100 acres of the Bradley/Jameson Patent at Caldwell's Landing (later renamed Jones Point). Through the years, the family bought more of the mountain. Then in 1951, with a gift of $25,000 from Laurance S. Rockefeller, the Park purchased all 640 acres of the Charles H. Jones estate. That tract included all of the Jones Trail, as well as most of the Spiral Railway.

If one continues on the 1777 Trail for about 125 feet beyond the Jones Trail turn-off, one will notice a woods road (with some old, faded orange blazes) that departs to the right. This road soon rejoins the Jones Trail, but about 200 feet up this road, another faint woods road goes up to the left. This road winds uphill and then becomes an obscure path that continues up toward the cliff. At the cliff face, the path leads left to the Escalator, a steep, slanted crack in the cliff. One can climb this steep crack, but it is necessary to use your hands as well as your feet, and the climb is particularly difficult (and even dangerous) when covered with ice in the winter (or by wet leaves in other seasons). At the top, the crack reaches a ledge where there is a beautiful view to the east and south. From the Escalator, a vague route marked with occasional cairns leads to the Timp-Torne Trail.

Nawahunta Fire Road

Length: 1.8 miles

Miles

0.0   Begin at Seven Lakes Drive.

0.1   Cellar hole, left.

0.15 Menomine Trail leaves, left.

0.3   Lewis (Dunn) Mine, right.

0.45 Trail to Silvermine parking area leaves, right.

1.4   Long Path joins, left.

1.8   End at Route 6.

This wide road starts at a gate on the Seven Lakes Drive near Lake Nawahunta. It goes north 1.8 miles and ends at Route 6, near the Long Path crossing.

For the first 0.15 mile, the yellow-blazed Menomine Trail runs along the fire road. On the left side, 0.1 mile from the gate, is the cellar-hole of the Lewis family home. A short distance beyond, the Menomine Trail goes down to the left, while the Nawahunta Fire Road continues straight ahead. At 0.3 mile, the Lewis Mine (also known as the Dunn Mine) is on the right, at the foot of the hill. An old woods road goes up to the right at 0.45 mile, over the ridge and down to the entrance of the Silvermine parking area.

After another 0.95 mile, on the way downhill, the Long Path (aqua) joins from the left. The fire road ends at 1.8 miles, at the top of a cut on Route 6.

There is an older trail through this valley which parallels the fire road, although portions of this route are now invisible. To find this old trail, follow the yellow blazes of the Menomine Trail across the brook at the north end of the lake. At 0.35 mile from the brook, just before the Menomine Trail makes a sharp left turn, look to the right for a faint old woods road that turns north. This road can be followed for about 0.15 mile, after which it disappears. It is possible to find the road by bushwhacking downhill to the northeast, where the old road can be seen again at about 0.5

Entrance to the Lewis Mine

mile. At 0.7 mile, the old road disappears again at the edge of a swamp, but from that point it is only 0.2 mile north to the Long Path. At 0.9 mile, the Long Path comes down from the left, and both trails go together along the swampy valley for 0.3 mile. They then join the fire road.

Before it was built in 1915, Lake Nawahunta had been the site of "Scobie" Jim Lewis' farm. The family graveyard is across Seven Lakes Drive from the entrance to the fire road. The Lewis family was related by marriage to the Bailey family on the west side of Stockbridge Mountain. That probably accounts for the old road (Nawahunta Trail) that connects the two places.

Bill Hoeferlin's 1941 trail map shows a road going south 0.75 mile from Long Mountain Parkway (Route 6). The Fingerboard-Storm King Trail (later the Long Path) left that road after 0.5 mile. Things remained that way until 1954 when the present fire road was built from Seven Lakes Drive to Long Mountain Parkway. (Before 1954, the "Lewis Road" ended at the mine.)

Nawahunta Trail

Length: 1.45 miles

Miles

0.0   Seven Lakes Drive.

0.15 Turn left off fire road.

0.25 Cross brook.

0.7   Trail, right, to Cave Shelter.

1.1   Long Path crosses.

1.2   Trail, right, to Stockbridge Shelter.

1.7   Baileytown Road.

The Nawahunta Trail starts at a gate on the north side of the Seven Lakes Drive, about 1.8 miles north of Tiorati Circle, and 0.4 mile west of the entrance to the Silvermine parking area. For the first 1.1 miles, it runs concurrently with the yellow-blazed Menomine Trail (see pp. 65-67).

The Nawahunta Trail begins by running along the Nawahunta Fire Road. After 0.15 mile, the trail turns left, crosses a brook (the inlet of Lake Nawahunta) on stepping stones and continues through a pine grove. The Nawahunta Trail then crosses a causeway across a swamp and climbs Stockbridge Mountain on an old road. At 0.7 mile, just beyond a bend in the road, a side trail with blacked-out blazes goes off to the right and leads to the Cave Shelter and to the YMCA camp on Baileytown Road. This junction is marked with a cairn.

The Long Path (aqua) crosses at 1.1 miles. The Stockbridge Shelter is to the right, while Hippo Rock is to the left. The yellow blazes of the Menomine Trail end at the Long Path crossing, but the continuation of the Nawahunta Trail along the old road is obvious. At 1.2 miles, the trail reaches a junction with a branch road leading right to the shelter, and at 1.7 miles it ends at Baileytown Road.

It seems likely that this old road over the mountain was made many years before the Park was created in 1910. The Baileys to the west were related to the Lewises to the east, and it would seem that this road might have been used by them to visit each other. The route has always been known to hikers, but it appears to have been first blazed in 1946. "An outlaw trail has been discovered: from Lake Nawahunta to FB-SK, painted white" (Bartha's Trail Committee Minutes, 1/29/47). And to this day, the blazes (now the yellow blazes of the Menomine Trail) go only to the FB-SK (now the Long Path).

Old Turnpike

Length: 3.0 miles

Miles

0.0	Dam of First Reservoir.
0.15	Trail, right, to Long Path.
0.6	Long Path crosses.
0.7	Trail, right, to ORAK.
1.25	S-BM crosses.
1.35	Second Reservoir Trail, left.
1.5	Long Path crosses.
2.0	Plane crash site, right.
2.1	Join paved camp service road.
2.4	Cranberry Mountain Trail, left.
3.0	Lake Welch Drive.

To reach the Old Turnpike from Call Hollow Road, take the gated paved road leading west to the water treatment plant (the route of Woodtown Road) and head towards the First Reservoir. (Parking for a few cars is available along Call Hollow Road at the trailhead.) As one walks up the paved road, remnants of the original Old Turnpike can be seen on the right. The section of the old road that cuts across Horse Chock Brook is somewhat overgrown, but it can still be followed.

The present-day Old Turnpike starts at the northwest end of the First Reservoir, 0.4 mile from Call Hollow Road. The rather wide road is the route of a buried telephone cable. At 0.6 mile, the Long Path (LP) (aqua) crosses, and then an unmarked trail departs to the right—it goes to the paved road which leads from Gate Hill Road to the AT&T microwave relay towers. Just before it reaches the road, the Suffern-Bear Mountain Trail (S-BM) (yellow) crosses that trail; to the right, S-BM leads to the site of the Buchanan mansion, known as ORAK.

S-BM crosses the Old Turnpike at 1.25 miles, and at 1.35 miles the obscure Second Reservoir Trail goes off to the left (it crosses the LP/S-BM and is more easily followed after that). Soon afterwards, the Long Path comes down from the Big Hill Shelter and crosses the Old Turnpike.

At 2.1 miles, the Old Turnpike joins a paved camp road that comes from Breakneck Pond. The Old Turnpike follows this road to Lake Welch Drive. From this point, St. John's Church is 0.7 mile east, while the Seven Lakes Drive is 0.9 mile west.

The Old Turnpike was a road from Monroe (now known as Southfields) to Haverstraw. It is not known when it was first built, but it became the "old" turnpike in 1824, when a new turnpike (now Gate Hill Road/Route 106) was built. The Old Turnpike was rather overgrown until 1969, when AT&T widened it to 20 feet and buried a coaxial cable along one side.

Originally, the Old Turnpike continued both east and west of the present route. From the vicinity of the present First Reservoir (built in 1912), it continued east (downhill), crossed Horse Chock Brook, and followed Call Hollow Road to Willow Grove Road (which was then known as Gate Hill Road).

Going west, the Old Turnpike followed the old Johnsontown Road. Beyond Johnsontown (now the site of Sebago Beach), it may have used the road known as Continental Road or Hemlock Hill Road (part of the route of the Victory Trail) out past Car Pond to the Orange Turnpike.

In 1921, the Boy Scouts used the Old Turnpike as part of their White Bar trail system. This trail followed the Cranberry Mountain Trail to the Old Turnpike, then left it above the First Reservoir to go down to Gate Hill Road where they had their Camp Hawkeye.

Pine Meadow Road

Length: 4.35 miles (Pine Meadow Road West) or 3.65 miles (Pine Meadow Road East)

Miles

0.0   Seven Lakes Drive.

0.05 Little Doe Trail, right.

0.4   Ski trail joins, right.

0.8   Cranberry Mountain Trail, straight ahead.

1.0   Buck Trail branch, right.

1.1   Woods road, left, to Breakneck Pond.

1.5   Trail, left, to lake.

1.7   Road divides:

Pine Meadow Road West

1.7   Buck Trail starts, right.

2.35 T-MI Trail crosses.

3.0   Woodtown Road (West), right.

3.25 Road, left, to Lake Wanoksink.

3.7   Pine Meadow Trail crosses.

3.75 Dam.

4.05 Poached Egg Trail, right.

4.35 Road ends at Torne Valley Road.

Pine Meadow Road East

1.8   T-MI Trail crosses.

1.9   Old woods road, left.

2.45 Woodtown Road joins, left.

2.55 Tri-Trail Junction; take center road.

3.35 Many Swamp Trail, left.

3.4   Faint trail, right, to Pine Meadow Lake.

3.55 Pine Meadow Trail crosses.

3.6   Sherwood Path, left.

3.65 Road ends.

Because it is closed to motor traffic, Pine Meadow Road is an attractive route for hikers and cross-country skiers. It starts on the east side of Seven Lakes Drive, 0.4 mile north of the hikers' parking area at Lake Sebago. In about 325 feet, at a cairn, the unmarked Little Doe Trail leaves to the right. After 0.4 mile, a ski trail, with red markers, comes in from the right and joins Pine Meadow Road. To the right, this ski trail crosses Seven Lakes Drive 0.15 mile south of the end of Pine Meadow Road.

At 0.8 mile, the Cranberry Mountain Trail continues straight ahead, while Pine Meadow Road turns right and goes up a notch between Cranberry Mountain on the left and Conklin Mountain on the right. On the way up this notch, at 1.0 mile, a branch of the Buck Trail (marked with black-stripe-on-yellow blazes) starts to the right. A little farther, at 1.1 miles, an unmarked woods road goes north, leading to the west side of Breakneck Pond (there is a cairn at the junction and some faded white blazes along the road). At 1.5 miles, an unmarked trail goes left to the east side of Breakneck Pond (the junction with this trail is marked with a cairn). Then, at 1.7 miles, the road divides into the east and west branches. On the right side, about 50 feet beyond this junction, the Buck Trail (yellow) begins.

Pine Meadow Road West now bears right and heads southwest, crossing the Tuxedo-Mt. Ivy Trail (T-MI) (red dash on white) at 2.35 miles. At 3.0 miles, Woodtown Road (West) from Sebago Dam comes in from the right. Here, also, a gravel road goes off to the right, then bears left up Diamond Mountain to the site of the old fire tower.

At 3.25 miles, the road crosses a stone bridge over the outlet of a swamp. In another 150 feet, a road begins to the left. It goes up to the top of the Lake Wanoksink dam and continues to the Pine Meadow Trail on the shore of Pine Meadow Lake. Then, at 3.7 miles, the Pine Meadow Trail (red square on white) crosses, after which the road goes over a dam (built in 1933-34) and continues along the west shore of the lake. At 4.05 miles, a trail on the right is marked white with a yellow center. Known as the Poached Egg Trail, it was made about 1985 by Conrad Schaefer as a shortcut to the Raccoon Brook Hills Trail. It was officially adopted by the Trail Conference in 1989. At 4.35 miles, Pine Meadow Road West reaches the unmarked Torne Valley Road, which comes in from the right. This point is actually the end of Pine Meadow Road West. The road ahead, which continues to the edge of the lake, is the continuation of Torne Valley Road.

Pine Meadow Lake from Pine Meadow Road

It is a part of the old road from Ramapo to Willow Grove, which crossed Pine Meadow before the lake was built.

Pine Meadow Road East bears left and heads south from the junction. At 1.8 miles, the Tuxedo-Mt. Ivy Trail crosses, and 0.1 mile farther, a very faint woods road (the original route of the T-MI) goes left. Woodtown Road joins from the left at 2.45 miles, and at about 2.55 miles, the hiker is confronted with a three-trail junction. The trail to the right is Conklin Road, a continuation of Woodtown Road. The middle trail is Pine Meadow Road East. The left trail is a road that goes steeply up, and returns to Pine Meadow Road East at about 2.95 miles. It seems to have also been built in 1933, but there is no apparent need for it (it is good for a ski run, however).

Pine Meadow Road East bears left at 3.0 miles, where the road appears to go straight ahead (that road leads only to an old CCC campsite). At 3.35 miles, on the way down a gentle slope, if one watches carefully on the left, the unmarked Many Swamp Trail can be seen. A pretty but somewhat overgrown woods road, it leads to the Starr Clearing and beyond. In another 350 feet, a faint trail leaves to the right and soon turns left. The first 0.15 mile of this trail is nearly invisible (marked by only one or two cairns), but the remainder of this 0.8-mile trail, which leads to the north shore of Pine Meadow Lake, is well marked by cairns and unofficial yellow plastic blazes. The Pine Meadow Trail crosses Pine Meadow Road East

199

at 3.55 miles. Soon the Sherwood Path to the Suffern-Bear Mountain Trail at Stone Memorial Shelter goes left, and then Pine Meadow Road East ends at 3.65 miles.

When it was built in 1933-35, Pine Meadow Road was intended to circle the lake, but the project was suspended before the road was completed. Long planned by Major Welch, construction of Pine Meadow Road was begun in 1933 by workers of the Temporary Emergency Relief Administration. The first trucks and equipment for building the dam were brought over Diamond Mountain from Sebago Dam on old Woodtown Road (West). Because that road was too steep and muddy, a better but longer route was built. They chose a country road called the Cranberry Mountain Trail. That trail started east from Johnsontown Road, at a point opposite the NYU Camp (now Sebago Cabin Camps). Until 1917, this had been the site of a large white farmhouse, the home of Mary Waldron. On a ski trail through a hemlock grove nearby, one can still read the inscription on a Waldron tombstone:

IN MEMORY OF
FATHER & MOTHER,
SISTERS & BROTHERS
WHO WE MISS.
ABRAM WALDRON
BORN 1819
DIED MAY 5, 1897

The Waldron farms extended for 0.5 mile on both sides of the Cranberry Mountain Trail. Beyond, at the foot of the hill, was the farm of Charles Schoonover.

Pine Meadow Road used existing trails until it joined Woodtown Road. At this junction, where Christie Brook starts from Big Green Swamp, there was once a sawmill operated by the Christie family. In 1865, the beams for the Methodist Church in Ladentown were sawn there. Raymond H. Torrey wrote (*N.Y. Post*, 7/21/33): "There was a sawmill, Christie's, on the Woodtown trail, about two miles north of Pine Meadow, the dam of which still remains. The new road to the CCC camp passes along it."

The TERA workers improved old Woodtown Road. The portion south of our "triplet junction" is now known as Conklin Road, a name which first appeared on Bill Hoeferlin's maps in 1945. It went to the south end of a swamp on Christie Brook (now Lake Wanoksink), where it met the other arm of Woodtown Road which came over the mountain from the Burnt Sawmill Bridge (now Sebago Dam).

Woodtown (Conklin) Road went on south through a notch in Pine Meadow Mountain, crossed swampy Pine Meadow, and continued down the Torne Brook Valley to the hamlet of Ramapo. At the edge of Pine Meadow, a short side road turned east to Ramsey Conklin's cabin.

Second Reservoir Trail

Length: 0.75 mile

Miles

0.0   Begin at west end of Second Reservoir dam.

0.25   Right on woods road.

0.75   Reach S-BM Trail/Long Path.

This woods road connects the Second Reservoir with the Suffern-Bear Mountain Trail (S-BM) (yellow)/Long Path (LP) (aqua) and the Old Turnpike near Big Hill Shelter. From Woodtown Road at the Second Reservoir, go west to the end of the dam, and then follow around the edge of the reservoir for about 0.25 mile. The Second Reservoir Trail starts up to the right. There used to be a sign there on the roadside, but there are just two metal posts there now. The trail is a distinct woods road that goes up to the S-BM/LP at 0.75 mile (0.5 mile from the reservoir). Here, the Second Reservoir Trail turns left and runs jointly with the S-BM/LP for a short distance. In about 75 feet, the S-BM/LP turns left, but the Second Reservoir Trail continues straight ahead. This section of the trail is completely overgrown, although it can still be followed with care. Never fear—the Old Turnpike is only 0.1 mile farther ahead. To avoid bushwhacking, you can take the S-BM to the right. It reaches the Old Turnpike in 0.15 mile. Or you can go up left 0.15 mile to the shelter, and then follow the aqua blazes of the Long Path back to the Old Turnpike.

It probably was the Wood family who made this old road. They had a sawmill at the old millpond (the site of the present-day Second Reservoir), and the road was a shortcut to the Old Turnpike.

Sherwood Path

Length: 1.6 miles

Miles

0.0	Pine Meadow Road East.
0.15	Many Swamp Brook crosses.
0.5	S-BM Trail crosses; shelter to right.
1.0	Pittsboro Trail, left.
1.05	Turn right onto power line road.
1.1	Turn left and descend.
1.2	Cross under power line.
1.25	Pittsboro Hollow Brook crosses.
1.3	Gas line crosses.
1.6	End at Mahwah River.

The Sherwood Path, although no longer an official Conference trail, runs along a woods road for its entire length, and can be easily followed. Most of the hiking trail markers have been obliterated, but a few red markers may still be visible on the lower portion of the trail.

The Sherwood Path begins near where the Pine Meadow Trail (red square on white) crosses Pine Meadow Road East. About 300 feet south of that junction, the Sherwood Path leaves the road, and goes off to the left. It, too, is a wide woods road, and begins on fairly level terrain. At 0.15 mile, Many Swamp Brook crosses, and at 0.5 mile, the Suffern-Bear Mountain Trail (yellow) crosses. Just to the right is the Edgar D. Stone Memorial Shelter (built 1935). Soon the trail begins to go down the mountain on a very rocky and eroded road. The Pittsboro Trail goes off to the left at 1.0 mile. At 1.05 miles, after passing a wrecked car in the middle of the trail, the Sherwood Path turns right onto a service road built to maintain the power lines further down the mountain. In another 200 feet you will reach a T-junction. The road going straight ahead (and then curving uphill to the right) is the continuation of the power line service road. Here the Sherwood Path turns left and continues downhill. It goes under the power lines and, at 1.25 miles, crosses Pittsboro Hollow Brook.

Just beyond the brook, the Sherwood Path crosses another open strip of land, the route of a buried gas pipeline. It then descends and turns left along the Mahwah River. At 1.6 miles, the trail ends at the site of a former bridge (large pieces of the bridge can be seen here and downstream). Until the bridge was removed in the 1990s, the Sherwood Path crossed the river on the bridge, turned right, and continued uphill to end at Route 202.

The Sherwood Path once was a narrow mountain trail. It was first blazed in 1943 by Frank Place of the Tramp and Trail Club. He named it after Judson Sherwood, who owned the land through which the trail ran. The Sherwoods are descended from Rev. James Elias Sherwood, who owned much land in the vicinity, and who, in 1829, founded the Methodist Church known as Wesley Chapel. Many "mountain folk" lived on James Sherwood's land. One of the best known was Silas Pitt, who lived on the Pittsboro Trail. In 1963, the Park acquired the land above the Algonquin pipeline from Harold T. Sherwood, son of Judson Sherwood. Harold died in 1977, but his son Jonathan, of Pomona, remembers hiking the trail with his father many years ago. In 1965, the Park widened the footpath to a 20-foot fire road, which later became very much eroded.

Summer Hill Road

Length: 1.45 miles

Miles

0.0   Begin at Route 6.

0.25 Leave park work area.

0.5   1779 Trail leaves, right.

0.7   Popolopen Gorge Trail crosses.

1.45 Road terminates near north end of lake.

Built by the Civilian Conservation Corps in 1933, Summer Hill Road starts from the north side of Route 6, about 0.15 mile west of the Long Mountain Circle (a park sign here reads "Brooks Place"). For the first 0.5 mile, it follows the route of the 1779 Trail (blue 1779 on white diamond). At first, it goes along a park road which turns right about 100 feet from Route 6 and continues into a work area (the road to the left is the old line of Route 6). The work area is the site of a large house which once belonged to the Brooks family and later became Camp Quannacut (see p. 308).

At 0.25 mile, Summer Hill Road—now a wide woods road—leaves the work area (at its northwest corner) and continues along the east side of Summer Hill. At 0.5 mile, the 1779 Trail leaves to the right. Then, at 0.55 mile, an old woods road comes up from the right (it goes down along a brook that runs into Queensboro Lake). At 0.7 mile, the Popolopen Gorge Trail (red square on white) comes in from the left and leaves to the right in 100 feet. Summer Hill Road then rises to the north end of the dam at Turkey Hill Lake. It continues along the lake, with Turkey Hill on the right, and, at 1.45 miles, terminates near the end of the lake.

Before the lake was built, an old road continued up the valley another 1.6 miles, to the Mine Road near the Forest of Dean. A remnant of that old road can be found at the northeast corner of the lake, past a swampy area. The road vanishes in a swamp at the northern tip of the lake, but if you continue north a short distance, cross the brook and go back towards the lake, you can easily find the road near the lake, on the west side of the brook. The road soon heads north and, with care, it can be followed to the Park boundary.

Surebridge Mine Road

Length: 2.2 miles

Miles

0.0 "Times Square"; head northwest on A-SB/LP.

0.1 A-SB/LP leaves, left.

0.15 Surebridge Swamp, left.

0.5 Surebridge Mine, right.

0.6 Bottle Cap Trail crosses.

1.15 AT joins, left.

1.17 Greenwood Mine, right.

1.2 AT leaves, right.

1.45 Long Path crosses.

1.7 Turn right onto paved road.

2.2 End at Arden Valley Road.

"Times Square," the junction of the Ramapo-Dunderberg Trail (R-D) (red dot on white), Arden-Surebridge Trail (A-SB) (red triangle on white) and Long Path (LP) (aqua), is a good place to start on Surebridge Mine Road. The road, which heads northwest along the route of A-SB/LP, is about 20 feet wide. A-SB/LP soon departs to the left in an evergreen grove and, a little further on, the Mine Road turns north. Soon, the Surebridge Swamp is seen on the left. In fact, since the firefighters' bulldozers went that way in 1988 (their scars can still be seen on the rocks), the swamp has invaded the road. In wet seasons, the road may be flooded for about 500 feet, but it is usually passable (if necessary, this wet region can be avoided by going up the hillside to the east, where there is a faint trail that leads down to the Bottle Cap Trail near the Surebridge Mine). Many of the high-bush blueberries along the Mine Road in the swampy area were uprooted by the bulldozers; some have recovered.

At 0.5 mile, there is a water-filled mine hole on the right—the Sure-bridge Mine. On the hillside beyond (about 225 feet from the road), more impressive mine openings can be found. At 0.6 mile, the Bottle Cap Trail crosses. Then, at 1.15 miles, the Appalachian Trail (AT) (white) joins from the left. Just beyond, the large water-filled opening of the Greenwood Mine may be seen on the right, with a large pile of tailings on the left. There are other openings higher up and a little further to the north.

The AT leaves to the right at 1.2 miles. A short distance beyond, it is necessary to cross Surebridge Brook (on a pile of mine tailings) and to continue the pleasant walk along the other side of the brook. A swamp is soon passed, and there are more mine openings on both sides of the road at 1.4 miles, just before the Long Path crosses. In another 0.25 mile, Upper Lake Cohasset is approached. Before the lake was made in 1922, the Surebridge Mine Road crossed along the edge of a swamp to end at Arden Valley Road. After the lake was completed, a camp road was constructed around the east side of the lake. Turn right on this paved road, and follow it past an abandoned group camp and Camp Ma-Kee-Ya to Arden Valley Road, where the road ends at 2.2 miles (no parking is available here).

The Surebridge Mine Road also went 0.25 mile south of Times Square; the Long Path follows that part of the old road. There, where the land begins to dip into a valley, the mineworkers came with their carts from the Greenwood Furnace (now known as Arden). In the valley beyond was the Hogencamp Mine. The ore from the mine was loaded into buckets on an overhead cable and carried up from the mine, through the valley, to the carts waiting at the hilltop. The stone piers of that cable system may still be seen along the valley, beginning at the cliff above the mine. The overhead cable system was about 0.35 mile long.

Some hikers have referred to the Surebridge Mine Road as the "Lost Road." This happened because of an error on Bill Hoeferlin's 20th edition of his Hikers Region Map No. 17 (May 1970). That was when he first applied the name "Lost Road" to this well-known road that had never been lost. In fact, Lost Road was the name that had been given by J.A. Allis in 1921 to a section of the Arden-Surebridge Trail, from a brook at the foot of Surebridge Mountain up to the R-D Trail

at Times Square (*N.Y. Post*, 11/11/21).

Another branch of the Surebridge Mine Road (now the route of the Arden-Surebridge Trail) went downhill from Times Square 0.5 mile to the Pine Swamp Mine. From that point, in 1936, the Park cut a fire road to Seven Lakes Drive, using the route of the A-SB Trail. In the fall of 1965, the fire road was extended up to Times Square and along the Surebridge Mine Road to Upper Lake Cohasset.

Torne Valley Road

Length: 1.8 miles

Miles

0.0   Start at Pine Meadow Lake.

0.15 Unmarked trail, left.

0.35 Pine Meadow Road West junction; turn left.

1.05 Kakiat Trail crosses.

1.15 Pipeline crosses.

1.55 Metal gate.

1.8   Metal gate (Park boundary).

Torne Valley Road is a very old and important road that ran from the factory center at Ramapo to the Monroe-Haverstraw Turnpike at Willow Grove. North of Pine Meadow, it was called Woodtown Road, because it passed the sawmills of the Wood family. The road was straighter and drier than the alternate route (now known as Route 202). It was in constant use until about 1854, and it is shown on the 1859 Cory/Bachman map of Rockland County. Since the southern sections of this road have been obliterated or are on private property, we will describe the route in a southerly direction, from what is now Pine Meadow Lake to the Park boundary.

Torne Valley Road begins on the south shore of Pine Meadow Lake (appropriately, in a pine grove). At first, it is a pleasant, wide road which passes through the site of a Civilian Conservation Corps camp (established in May 1933). At 0.15 mile, an unmarked trail begins to the left. This trail follows the unfinished sewer system around the south side of the lake to the Conklins Crossing Trail (white). At 0.35 mile, a junction is reached. The road straight ahead is Pine Meadow Road West, but Torne Valley Road turns left and heads south. At this point, the character of the road changes. For the next 0.8 mile, the road has been bulldozed and now has a sticky clay surface which retains moisture, resulting in the formation of many puddles in shallow depressions in the roadway. These puddles often exist even during relatively dry periods.

At 1.05 miles, the Kakiat Trail (white) crosses, and at 1.15 miles the road crosses the pipeline cut of the Columbia Gas Transmission Company (built in 1949 and widened in 2007). The road now starts gently downhill, and it reaches a metal gate at 1.55 miles. At 1.8 miles, the road reaches another metal gate at the Park boundary. The road can be followed straight ahead to the power substation (at 2.05 miles, just before a brook, there is an unmarked trail right to the site of a Starr family home).

At 1.55 miles, there is a hidden side trail which is well worth following by experienced hikers. Just south of the metal gate, enter the woods to your left (east). In about 100 feet, a clear woods road can be seen heading east-northeast. Follow this road which, at 0.2 mile, turns east-southeast and crosses Torne Brook. For the next 0.7 mile the road is generally easy to follow (there are cairns at the few spots where the road becomes rather vague), and it reaches the gas pipeline about 0.4 mile west of the S-BM crossing. From this point, one can follow the grassy pipeline route east, cross the S-BM and continue downhill along the pipeline (with excellent views of the Hudson Valley), which leads to the orange-blazed Mountain Trail in Kakiat County Park. Turn right onto the Mountain Trail, which affords more views, and follow it down to the parking area at the entrance to Kakiat Park on Route 202.

Woodtown Road

Length: 3.8 miles

Miles

0.0	Start at Call Hollow Road.
0.3	Letchworth Water Works; paving ends.
0.35	First Reservoir dam.
1.25	ron Mountain Trail, left.
1.35	Second Reservoir dam; turn left.
1.95	Limekiln Mountain Trail, left.
2.15	File Factory Hollow Trail, left.
2.3	S-BM Trail crosses.
2.85	T-MI Trail joins, right; Tim's Bridge.
2.9	T-MI Trail leaves, left.
3.2	Fire road, left, to Starr Place.
3.6	Pittsboro Trail, left.
3.7	Pine Meadow Road East joins.
3.8	Tri-Trail Junction: Woodtown Road ends.
	right: Conklin Road; center: Pine Meadow Road East; left: Crescent Trail.

This old road across the Ramapo Plateau starts from Call Hollow Road in the hamlet of Willow Grove. There is parking for three or four cars on the side of Call Hollow Road.

The beginning of Woodtown Road is paved. At 0.25 mile, the route of the Old Turnpike goes diagonally right. At 0.3 mile, the road passes a water treatment plant. Here the paving ends and the road bears left, past a gate. It soon comes to the east end of the dam of the First Reservoir.

Woodtown Road goes gently uphill, with Horse Chock Brook to the right. At 0.65 mile, a concrete culvert crosses under the road. In another 100 feet, an overgrown woods road departs to the left. It can be followed south, northeast and then east to the saddle between the two summits of Horse Chock Mountain. To the right, about 200 feet beyond the culvert, there is a beech tree with several horizontal indentations in the bark. The carving "J. Christie is coming, Lord" was once visible on this tree. The

Cloud reflections in the Second Reservoir

Christie family owned much land in this region since 1829. Joseph E. Christie, who lived in nearby Thiells, is probably the one who carved the tree. He died on November 28, 1943.

At 0.9 mile, a largely overgrown and little used trail begins on the left. It goes up to a pretty notch between Horse Chock and Iron Mountains. Then, at 1.25 miles, the unmarked Iron Mountain Trail starts to the left. It ends at the power line on the east side of the mountain.

Woodtown Road soon crosses Horse Chock Brook. At this point, there is a stone wall along the bank on the right. Above the bank is the site of the Wood family home. Also on the right is another, older road which follows the wall. This road—the original Woodtown Road—goes down along the hillside on the left side of the brook, ending at the First Reservoir. Although this road was abandoned about 1854, it remains in remarkably good condition and can easily be followed.

At 1.35 miles, just below the dam of the Second Reservoir, Woodtown Road turns left. (The more obvious route that continues straight ahead and then bears right is a service road which leads to the Third Reservoir.) Beside the brook that runs down from the dam are the foundations of the Wood family sawmill. A little further on, a trench crosses the road. This is part of a sluice that diverts water into the reservoir from a swamp higher up.

Continuing southwest, the reservoir is visible on the right. Shortly afterward, the cellar hole of another Wood home may be seen on a briar-covered bank on the right. The road continues gently up, with stone walls on either side. A brook on the left feeds a swamp which, in turn, drains into the reservoir. Then, at 1.95 miles, the Limekiln Mountain Trail comes in from the left at a cairn. The File Factory Hollow Trail departs to the left at 2.15 miles. At 2.3 miles, the Suffern-Bear Mountain Trail (yellow) crosses, and at 2.85 miles, the Tuxedo-Mt. Ivy Trail (T-MI) (red dash on white) comes in from the right.

The T-MI Trail runs along this road for only about 300 feet and soon departs to the left. In that short distance, the road crosses a tiny brook, which connects Big Green Swamp on the west with Squirrel Swamp on the east. A wooden footbridge crosses the brook.

Many years ago, before the first New York Walk Book was published in 1923, there was a bridge there, big enough to carry wagons. On a nearby tree there was a faded sign: "Tim's Bridge." In 1927, Frank Place, president of the Tramp and Trail Club, put up a new sign (*Mountain Magazine*, Jan. 1928), but by 1930 that sign, too, was gone (*N.Y. Post*, 9/19/30). Nevertheless, for many years the spot was shown on hikers' maps as "Tim's Bridge."

At 3.2 miles, a fire road leaves to the left. It goes to the Starr Clearing, where it meets the Many Swamp Trail. Then, at 3.6 miles, the faint Pittsboro Trail (barely visible here) also goes left to the Starr Clearing (if one does not lose it in the laurels).

Going gently downhill now, Woodtown Road at 3.7 miles joins Pine Meadow Road East. Just beyond the junction, there is a little swampy pond on the left. That was the millpond for Christie's sawmill, which stood there in 1865. In 1933, when the Temporary Emergency Relief workers built Pine Meadow Road, they ran it over Christie's mill dam. No trace of the dam or of the mill remains.

At 3.8 miles, the hiker is faced with a choice of three trails. The center one is Pine Meadow Road; the left one is a crescent-shaped trail that rejoins Pine Meadow Road in about 0.4 mile; the right one, called Conklin Road, is the continuation of Woodtown Road. It was much improved by the TERA as an approach to the three lakes the CCC was building (Pine Meadow, Wanoksink and Minsi).

Woodtown Road is named after a family of woodcutters who had several homes, a sawmill and a barkmill at the site of the Second Reservoir. In the 1800s, much of the land in that area belonged to Ralph Bush. In 1829, he sold several parcels to Henry Christie, who built millponds and sawmills on Horse Chock Brook and also at the source of what was named

Christie Brook. He also owned Horse Chock Mountain (sometimes known as Iron Mountain), where he opened several mines. In 1848, Christie sold his sawmill and millpond on Horse Chock Brook to Jonas Wood.

Jonas, who was born in 1801, had two children: Angeline, who married John Secor, and Daniel (born 1845). Daniel left the mountain homestead in 1864 to go to Oneida County, N.Y. In 1870, he returned to Stony Point, where he started a lumber business, and later sold carriages and farm implements. In 1873, he married Mary E. Waldron.

It seems that Jonas was still alive in 1899, when he sold the mills and millpond to Isaac and Mary Bedford. In 1908, they in turn sold a portion of their land south of the millpond to New York State for Letchworth Village.

The Christies continued to own property in the hills east of the millpond. Their last parcel was sold to the Park in 1951 by Lucy Christie of Thiells.

In 1910, the 50-acre Parcel #30, known as the Bedford Pond property (the old Wood millpond), was acquired by Letchworth Village for $538.84 (the pond was 14 acres). During 1912, the dam for the First Reservoir was completed. This served until 1924, when two dry years showed the need for another reservoir. Accordingly, plans were made in 1926 for a new dam at the old Wood millpond. Joe Rose, who was living on Call Hollow Road in 1985, said that he worked on that job in 1927—the old mill dam was broken down then, and only a muddy little pond was there. In 1928, the new dam and Second Reservoir were complete. Then, in 1951-52, a third reservoir was built on Horse Chock Brook (not on Woodtown Road). This necessitated the relocation of the S-BM Trail by about 400 feet.

Ramsey Conklin, one of the better known Ramapo mountain people, died in 1952 on the bank above Woodtown Road, near the site of the Wood home (see p. 307).

Woodtown Road was used for hauling iron, charcoal and wood to Haverstraw. A hiker, Ruth Gillette Hardy, described the road as she knew it in 1912: "This was a town road until 1854, if not later, straighter and drier than the valley road we now call Route 202, from the iron furnaces in Ramapo Village to Haverstraw" (*Trail Walker*, Sept. 1971).

Raymond Torrey described the road as "rather obscure, the brush being so thick. At one place it crosses an old mill dam (Christie's dam) where the path in summer is quite overgrown with young trees" (*N.Y. Post*, 7/15/21). That overgrown condition was changed when the TERA built Pine Meadow Road, and again in 1957 when Park bulldozers cleared Woodtown Road from the First Reservoir to Pine Meadow Road East (*Trail Conference News*, Feb. 1957). In the fall of 1965, the road was again widened, this time to 20 feet (*Trail Walker*, Mar. 1966).

Woodtown Road (West)

Length: 2.0 miles

Miles

0.0   Leave Seven Lakes Drive at Sebago Dam.

0.2   Cross brook.

0.5   Turn briefly south.

0.9   Seven Hills Trail joins; cross Diamond Brook.

1.0   Seven Hills Trail leaves, right; Monitor Rock, left.

1.05 Land levels; path, left, to incinerator.

1.1   T-MI Trail crosses.

1.35 Pine Meadow Road West ahead; Woodtown Road turns right, parallel to Pine Meadow Road.

1.55 Cross Christie Brook.

1.6   Cross Pine Meadow Road West.

1.65 Top of Wanoksink Dam.

1.75 Road, right, to Pine Meadow Lake.

1.9   Cross second dam.

2.0   End at Conklin Road.

This old woods road starts at the foot of Sebago Dam. In 500 feet, it is briefly joined by the Tuxedo-Mt. Ivy Trail (T-MI) (red dash on white). After crossing a brook at 0.2 mile, the old road rises gently, turns briefly south at 0.5 mile, and continues up through a pretty glade, with Diamond Creek to the right.

At 0.9 mile, the trail passes a cascade. Here, the Seven Hills Trail (blue on white) joins from the left, and the road immediately crosses the brook. Seven Hills leaves to the right at 1.0 mile. Here, an unmarked trail on the left goes up a short distance to a large quartz boulder on a ledge, known as Monitor Rock. After a bit, the land levels, and a path goes left to an incinerator (built in 1933 by the Civilian Conservation Corps). Just beyond that path, the T-MI Trail crosses. Woodtown Road now goes gently downhill and at 1.35 miles approaches Pine Meadow Road West.

Across Pine Meadow Road here, a path leads through laurels toward

Lake Wanoksink. Just beyond the laurels is the foundation of a 1933 Civilian Conservation Corps building. To the right, just before the junction with Pine Meadow Road, another woods road heads back up Diamond Mountain. It goes to the site of the former fire tower (dismantled in 1986).

Woodtown Road was here long before Pine Meadow Road was built. Most hikers will want to continue ahead on Pine Meadow Road West, which again meets Woodtown Road at 1.6 miles. If you are determined to try to follow the original route of Woodtown Road, you should turn right just before reaching Pine Meadow Road and head south through the bushes. You may notice an overgrown path leading through the laurels. This nearly invisible path, which runs parallel to Pine Meadow Road, follows the route of the old Woodtown Road. After 0.2 mile, the path reaches Christie Brook. The little bridge here has long been gone, but the stone abutments are still visible. Raymond Torrey described the road here in 1921: "a fairly open wood road—a wagon width in winter but very narrow in summer . . . . This crosses Christie Brook, a considerable stream in winter, a belt of moss-covered rocks in summer" (*N.Y. Post*, 7/15/21).

After crossing Christie Brook (which drains Lake Wanoksink), Woodtown Road again reaches Pine Meadow Road West at 1.6 miles. Our old road is now under the dam and in the lake, but a wide path straight ahead (on the left, if you followed Pine Meadow Road) leads to a large rock on the shore near the top of the dam. A bit further, a stone-paved road departs to the south—it goes to the Pine Meadow Trail on the north shore of Pine Meadow Lake. Our path, cut through laurels in the 1960s by Jim Stankard of the Westchester Trails Association, continues around the lake edge. In another 0.15 mile, it crosses a second, smaller dam, where a trail goes down the southern face of the dam to Conklin Road. Our path continues straight and reaches a T-junction in about 100 feet, where it turns left and proceeds north. To the right, another trail goes south to Conklin Road. Our path continues around the southeast corner of the lake and, at 2.0 miles, ends at the old Conklin Road, where it comes up from the lake.

This old road started from the Burnt Sawmill Bridge, which crossed Stony Brook where Sebago Dam was built in 1926. The road went east, up over what was then known as Halfway Mountain. This mountain was designated as Diamond Mountain on the large topographic map published by the Park in 1927.

The road itself had no name until 1943 when, on the seventh edition of his Hikers Region Map No. 5, Bill Hoeferlin labeled it "Deer Trail." On the same map, he named for the first time the "Buck Trail" and the "Little Doe Trail." Then, in 1945, Hoeferlin changed the name to Woodtown Road. Maps issued by the Park used this name only after 1966. It can be regarded as having been a leg of the main Woodtown Road which ran south from Willow Grove to Pine Meadow.

In the spring of 1923, when Raymond Torrey and Frank Place first blazed the T-MI Trail, they used this road from Burnt Sawmill Bridge to the top of Halfway Mountain. In the years that followed, the road was used for dragging dead chestnut logs from the Pine Meadow area (*N.Y. Post*, 4/24/28). Then in 1933 the Civilian Conservation Corps used the road to get their machines over the mountain to build Pine Meadow, Wanoksink and Minsi Lakes. The road became so muddy and eroded that the T-MI was rerouted to avoid it.

When they began their work at Pine Meadow, the CCC established an electric generator near Sebago Dam. The power line and telephone line were put on poles erected along Woodtown Road. Some of those poles can still be seen along the road on the west side of the mountain, and several sawed-off pole stumps are still visible on the east side.

When Sebago Dam was built, the road that had crossed Burnt Sawmill Bridge was rerouted across the dam and the nearby wingdam. That work was completed in 1926. Then in 1932 the Park built an area below the dam for overnight motor camping. The ruin of the comfort station there can still be seen on the left at the beginning of Woodtown Road (West). The camp was abandoned when the new Seven Lakes Drive was built in 1961.

Before Lake Wanoksink was built, our Woodtown Road crossed the little bridge on Christie Brook and proceeded east along the foot of Pine Meadow Mountain. It crossed a swampy region (now the south end of Lake Wanoksink), then rose to higher land where it joined the north-south Woodtown Road (now known as Conklin Road).

THE UNMARKED TRAILS

This section describes 12 unmarked trails in Harriman-Bear Mountain State Parks. These trails generally do not have a clear and obvious treadway for the entire route. Sometimes, hikers can find their way with the help of cairns, but cairns are unofficial and unmaintained markers which may be absent, infrequent or difficult to locate. Although we believe that these unmarked trails can be followed with care by experienced hikers, even they will occasionally lose the trail, as the treadway may be faint or invisible in places, and there often are other plausible routes that lead the wrong way. Those who choose to follow these unmarked trails should take along a map and compass and possess good navigation skills.

Bockey Swamp Trail

Length: 2.95 miles

Miles

0.0   Begin at Silvermine parking area.

0.45   Old road comes out of lake.

0.65   Reach end of lake.

0.95   Cross woods road; Menomine Trail leaves, left.

1.0   Pass swamp to left.

1.3   Begin to climb.

1.4   Flat-sided rock to right.

1.55   Cross brook.

1.7   AT/R-D crosses.

1.8   Turn right near top of rise.

2.1   Summit of Letterrock Mountain to left.

2.45   Start down.

2.7   Join old woods road.

2.95   End at Red Cross Trail.

The Bockey Swamp Trail starts from the bridge at the east end of the Silvermine parking area. Until Silvermine Lake was built in 1934, the big swamp there was called the Bockey Swamp. The name "bockey" refers to the baskets that were woven by the mountain people for carrying charcoal to the local furnaces. For the first 0.95 mile, the Bockey Swamp Trail follows the route of the yellow-blazed Menomine Trail. At 0.45 mile, the trail joins an old wagon road coming up out of the lake.

After reaching the end of the lake at 0.65 mile, the old road climbs briefly and comes to a woods road at 0.95 mile (this junction is marked by a cairn). That road starts at Seven Lakes Drive (with the AT) and goes up to the shelter on Letterrock Mountain. Here, the yellow blazes of the Menomine Trail follow the woods road to the left. Our Bockey Swamp Trail crosses the road and heads south along the foot of a hill. The trail in this section is faint, but is marked by frequent cairns and occasional faded white blazes. It passes a swamp on the left and continues along Bockey

Swamp Brook (this portion of the trail is often wet). At 1.3 miles, the trail begins to climb, passing through an area with many blowdowns. Then, at 1.4 miles, the Bockey Swamp Trail passes a large rock, to the right of the trail, with a smooth, flat side. It continues to climb along a woods road on the west side of the brook until, at 1.55 miles, it bears left, crossing the brook (which runs under rocks at this point), and climbs through a boulder field. The footpath is nearly invisible here, but the cairns can be followed to the top of the hill (be sure to keep the brook to your right).

At 1.7 miles, the Bockey Swamp Trail crosses the joint Appalachian (AT) (white)/Ramapo-Dunderberg (R-D) (red dot on white) Trails. Here, the character of the trail changes. Cairns become much less frequent, but the trail follows a discernable footpath (marked by some faded white blazes) for the next mile. At the AT/R-D crossing, the Bockey Swamp Trail bears slightly left and follows a well-worn path (this path might be blocked off by branches). At a cairn in an open area near the top of a rise, at 1.8 miles, our trail turns right (straight ahead, the footpath continues east to the Menomine Trail). The Bockey Swamp Trail continues through an area of dense blueberry bushes, gently climbing towards the summit of Letterrock Mountain. Although the bushes may grow over the trail, the footpath is clearly evident to an experienced hiker. It is particularly delightful to hike this trail section in late July, when the blueberries are ripe!

The trail passes just to the right of the summit, which affords limited views through the trees, at 2.1 miles. After a level section through dense blueberry bushes, it begins to descend at 2.45 miles. With the southern peak of Letterrock Mountain in view ahead, the trail bears left, skirting the peak. At 2.7 miles, it continues its descent, rather steeply in places, on an old woods road, with sections of the road overgrown with blueberries. After another relatively level section, it ends at the Red Cross Trail at 2.95 miles. Here, the Beech Trail is 0.1 mile to the left.

The Bockey Swamp Trail formerly continued across the Red Cross Trail. The trail here is now obscured by bushes, but if you continue straight ahead, an old woods road will soon be seen. This road can be followed for 0.3 mile to Tiorati Brook, the outlet of Lake Tiorati. There used to be a wooden bridge here, but it was removed in 1990, and it is often impossible to cross the brook after heavy rains. Tiorati Brook Road is reached 500 feet beyond the brook. The parking area on the Beech Trail is 0.35 mile to the left, while Tiorati Dam is 0.9 mile to the right.

Brooks Hollow Trail

Length: 1.6 miles

Miles

0.0   Begin at Route 6.

0.45 Start down to Brooks Hollow.

0.7   Cross stream.

0.75 Long Path crosses.

1.6   Park boundary.

The Brooks Hollow Trail starts from Route 6, just east of Lake Massawippa. It proceeds north, following a road along the east side of the lake and passing an abandoned camp, and then heads down into Brooks Hollow at 0.45 mile. The trail becomes obscure as it nears a stream at 0.7 mile, but you should continue straight ahead, crossing the stream and reaching the Long Path (aqua) at 0.75 mile. The continuation of the Brooks Hollow Trail, an old woods road, is clearly visible on the north side of the Long Path. The Brooks Hollow Trail may be followed until the park boundary is reached at 1.6 miles. Although the trail continues for another 0.4 mile to Mine Lake, on the property of the West Point Military Academy, this section of the trail is closed to the public.

Deep Hollow Trail

Length: 0.7 mile

Miles

0.0   Begin at Long Path.

0.7   End at Route 6.

This is not Deep Hollow Road, a "stone road" that the Long Path followed until 1988, down along Deep Hollow Brook (see p. 259). To reach the Deep Hollow Trail, take the Long Path (aqua) north from the parking area on Route 6 and head west on the Long Path from Deep Hollow Brook. At 0.25 mile from the second brook crossing, a trail to the right heads into the West Point Military Reservation (closed to the public). In another 500 feet, an old woods road crosses the Long Path (the junction is marked by a cairn). This is the Deep Hollow Trail. To the north, 0.6 mile on West Point land (closed to the public), it comes down to Deep Hollow Brook, and at 1.5 miles it reaches Mine Lake at the same place as the Brooks Hollow Trail.

Going south from the Long Path, the Deep Hollow Trail (occasionally marked with blacked-out blazes) goes over a hill and reaches Route 6 at 0.7 mile.

Flaggy Meadow Mountain Trail

Length: 1.35 miles

Miles

0.0 Begin at gate on Tiorati Brook Road.

0.25 Cross boggy area.

0.35 Faint connector trail begins, right.

0.85 Blue-blazed trail begins, right; bear left, following green metal blazes.

1.35 End at Red Cross Trail.

The Flaggy Meadow Mountain Trail begins at a gate on Tiorati Brook Road, 0.4 mile east of the parking area for the Beech Trail. For the first 0.85 mile, it follows a woods road which, although somewhat overgrown in places, can be followed without undue difficulty by an experienced hiker. Near the start, the trail curves to the right and, at 0.25 mile, it crosses a boggy area and a small stream. The trail then ascends and bears right. At 0.35 mile, a faint trail marked with cairns leaves to the right. (In about 750 feet, this faint trail connects with a trail (described below) marked in places with blue metal disks.)

At 0.5 mile, the Flaggy Meadow Mountain Trail heads more steeply uphill, and it reaches a height of land at 0.65 mile. Then, at 0.85 mile, it reaches a fork (here, the summit of Flaggy Meadow Mountain is about 0.15 mile to the left). To the right, a blue-blazed trail leads to the Stillwater Trail (despite the presence of occasional blue discs, this side trail can be difficult to follow in places). To stay on the Flaggy Meadow Mountain Trail, bear left, now following dark green metal blazes along a footpath.

After passing some interesting rock outcroppings, the trail begins a gradual descent at 1.05 miles, and it curves right just before it ends at the Red Cross Trail at 1.35 miles.

Grape Swamp Mountain Trail

Length: 0.65 mile

Miles

0.0   Begin at Tiorati Brook Road.

0.35 Turn right onto woods road.

0.65 Nickel Mine.

Grape Swamp Mountain is on the south side of Tiorati Brook Road, as it heads toward a junction with Lake Welch Drive. There are a number of old woods roads and unmarked trails in the area but, except for the main Grape Swamp Mountain Trail, which leads to the Nickel Mine (see p. 369), these routes are difficult to follow.

The Grape Swamp Mountain Trail starts on the south side of Tiorati Brook Road at the point where the road crosses Tiorati Brook, 0.15 mile below the parking area at the Beech Trail crossing. The main trail, an old woods road, begins by running along the right side of the brook. In about 150 feet, a branch trail goes off to the right. Continue straight ahead on the main trail, which soon leaves the brook and continues east. The trail is often wet and overgrown with mountain laurel, but it is marked by occasional cairns and can be followed with care. At 0.25 mile, the laurel ends, and the old road becomes clearly visible.

At 0.35 mile from the start, a distinct woods road, marked by cairns, goes up to the right. Turn right and follow this road for 0.3 mile, until mine tailings are visible to the left at about the 940-foot contour. Here, you will notice a long mine trench. Behind the tailings, you will find another mine trench. Follow the second trench to reach the larger opening of the Nickel Mine. To reach the smaller opening of the mine, bushwhack uphill to the west for about 500 feet. The Nickel Mine marks the end of this branch of the trail.

If, instead of turning right on the woods road at 0.35 mile, you continue straight ahead, you will reach, in another 0.3 mile, a cut, high above Lake Welch Drive. An old road uphill near there was the route of the Suffern-Bear Mountain Trail until 1969.

One can also reach the Nickel Mine by following the branch trail that goes off to the right at the junction about 150 feet from the trailhead. However, this trail is overgrown in many places and is quite difficult to follow. If you wish to attempt this route, continue for 0.4 mile from the brook and then, at the 1,020-foot contour, bushwhack 0.1 mile east. Watch for a hill of mine tailings. Next to it is the smaller opening of the Nickel Mine. (The other, larger opening is 0.1 mile to the east and downhill.) This branch of the trail once continued on over the mountain, reaching Lake Welch Drive at 1.0 mile, but it is now overgrown and nearly invisible.

Hasenclever Mountain Trail

Length: 0.85 mile

Miles
0.0   Begin at Tiorati Brook Road.
0.1   Make sharp right turn.
0.2   Make sharp left turn.
0.85 End at Red Cross Trail.

The Hasenclever Mountain Trail starts from Tiorati Brook Road, about 350 feet west of the Red Cross Trail crossing. Follow a dirt road south for about 50 feet, briefly turn left on another dirt road, then immediately turn right (at a cairn) onto a fainter woods road, which begins to ascend gradually. In about 400 feet, as the old road curves sharply to the right, a short section of the road is overgrown with barberry. In another 400 feet, the road narrows to a footpath and curves sharply to the left. The trail soon reaches the ridge of Hasenclever Mountain, where it levels off. It continues along the ridge (occasionally obscured by blueberry bushes) until it ends at the Red Cross Trail at 0.85 mile. From this point, on the Red Cross Trail it is 0.9 mile west to Seven Lakes Drive near Lake Askoti, or 0.55 mile east to Hasenclever Mine, and 0.55 mile further to Tiorati Brook Road.

Pines Trail

Length: 1.35 miles

Miles

0.0   Start at 1779 Trail.

0.1   Unmarked trail, left, towards Park boundary.

0.4   Unmarked trail, left, to Pingyp Mountain.

0.6   S-BM Trail joins from right.

0.65 S-BM Trail leaves, left.

1.2   Trail starts to fade out as it nears Parkway.

1.35 End at Palisades Interstate Parkway.

The Pines Trail was once a major route through the valley between the Pingyp and The Pines, and it connected near its west end with the Stillwater Trail to the northwest and the Flaggy Meadow Mountain Trails to the west. However, a portion of the Pines Trail, as well as both of those connections, was obliterated when the Palisades Interstate Parkway was constructed in the 1950s, and today the Pines Trail is mainly used as a connector between the 1779 and Suffern-Bear Mountain Trails.

The Pines Trail begins at the 1779 Trail, about 0.2 mile west of the end of the paved Queensboro Road at the Park boundary (unfortunately, there is no convenient parking at the end of the road). At 0.1 mile, a woods road goes left towards the Park boundary. At 0.4 mile, a trail goes left up the eastern side of Pingyp. At 0.6 mile, the Suffern-Bear Mountain Trail (yellow) joins from the right and soon leaves to the left. Up until this point, the trail is an easily followed old woods road, but it gradually fades out as it approaches the Parkway.

At 1.2 miles, the Pines Trail—now quite faint—turns sharply right at a cairn at the bottom of a gentle descent. In another 100 feet, it turns left at another cairn (the turns are designed to avoid as much as possible of the swampy area just ahead). After the left turn, follow an old woods road along the high ground towards the Parkway. In the last 50 feet before reaching the Parkway cut, it is necessary to cross first a swampy area and then Stillwater Brook. The best route is probably diagonally left, but there is no clear path, and the crossing can be very wet in times of high water.

From this point, it is possible to cross the Parkway, find the clearly visible woods road which was once a continuation of the Pines Trail, and follow that road south until it connects with a heavily overgrown woods road, which leaves to the right and heads up Flaggy Meadow Mountain.

Pittsboro Trail (First Pittsboro Trail)

Length: 0.8 mile

Miles

0.0   Just before Sherwood Path, turn right from gas pipeline service road and enter woods.

0.1   Cross power line.

0.2   Cross power line service road.

0.3   Clearing; continue straight.

0.6   Cross to left side of stream.

0.65 Sharp left uphill (cairn and blue paint blaze).

0.8   Meet S-BM Trail at "Witness Oak."

This trail, as well as the Second Pittsboro Trail, are named after the Pitt family, mountain people who lived in the valley until 1947.

To reach the First Pittsboro Trail from the Town of Ramapo Equestrian Center off Route 202, follow the red-on-white-blazed Pine Meadow Trail uphill for 0.1 mile to the gas pipeline service road. Here, the Pine Meadow Trail turns right, but you should turn left onto the level gas pipeline service road.

After following the pipeline service road for 0.7 mile, you will notice concrete barriers across the road. These barriers delineate a road that goes up to the power line (this is the route of the Sherwood Path). About 50 feet before reaching the barriers, turn right and enter the woods. Almost immediately, an old woods road, bordered by large rocks, will be seen. This is the First Pittsboro Trail. Follow this road uphill for 0.1 mile, with a stream visible below to the left, and continue straight across the power lines (you may have to detour to the right if the power line clearing is overgrown). On the far side of the power line clearing, the old woods road we are following is badly eroded and obstructed by blowdowns, so it is convenient to walk uphill to the right of the road. At 0.2 mile, you will reach the power line service road (this is a continuation of the road that began at the concrete barriers mentioned above).

The continuation of the First Pittsboro Trail (still a clearly visible woods road) can be seen across the power line service road, about 20 feet to the left. Follow this road uphill, crossing a small clearing at 0.3 mile. Beyond the clearing, the road goes through mountain laurel thickets and descends slightly to come out close to the stream. Here, a path to the left leads down to the stream, but you should continue ahead on the woods road on the right side of the stream (the woods road on the other side of the stream is the Second Pittsboro Trail; see p. 231).

Our (First) Pittsboro Trail continues uphill, through a pretty valley, until it reaches a three-way fork at 0.6 mile. The right fork, barely visible, continues uphill to the right and eventually joins other woods roads near Catamount Mountain. The middle fork, much clearer, continues along the right side of the stream for some distance and then ends (there are two old cellar holes about 200 feet ahead). The left fork, heavily eroded by the stream, is the First Pittsboro Trail, which crosses the stream diagonally to the left.

The First Pittsboro Trail continues for a short distance along the left side of the stream and then turns sharply left, uphill (the turn is marked by a cairn and by an extra-large blue paint blaze, the only blaze on this trail). Follow the woods road (and occasional cairns) uphill to meet the Suffern-Bear Mountain Trail (yellow) at the "Witness Oak," where the First Pittsboro Trail ends, 0.8 mile from the gas pipeline service road (and 1.6 miles from the Town of Ramapo Equestrian Center).

The "Witness Oak" was a huge white oak that marked the boundaries between long-forgotten farms (a few stone walls that also delineated the boundaries of these farms can still be seen). Although the "Witness Oak" died many years ago, its massive seven-foot-high stump and an equally massive trunk remain. The trunk makes a pleasant place to sit and rest after the climb up from the parking lot.

Second Pittsboro Trail

Length: 0.4 mile

Miles

0.0   Start from power line service road at wrecked car.

0.4   At three-sided stone structure, cross stream to First Pittsboro Trail.

To reach the Second Pittsboro Trail from the Town of Ramapo Equestrian Center off Route 202, follow the red-on-white-blazed Pine Meadow Trail uphill for 0.1 mile to the gas pipeline service road. Here, the Pine Meadow Trail turns right, but you should turn left onto the level gas pipeline service road.

After following the gas pipeline service road for 0.7 mile, you will notice concrete barriers across the road. These barriers delineate a service road that goes up to the power line (this is the route of the Sherwood Path). Turn right onto this service road and follow it uphill, crossing Pittsboro Hollow Brook. At a junction with another service road, turn right, then turn left (uphill) on a woods road marked by a wrecked car. This marks the start of the Second Pittsboro Trail. The power line service road continues to the right (0.1 mile down that road, the First Pittsboro Trail crosses).

Bear right along the trail, passing more wrecked cars. When the woods road turns right in a few hundred feet, the route of the trail becomes somewhat vague. However, follow the gentle slope north and then northeast, keeping the steep hillside to the left and the stream valley to the right. Soon, more wrecked cars and a clear woods road will be found.

The cars were left there by several Conklin families who formerly lived along the trail. (There were once eight Conklin cabins along the trail, and they housed 16 adults and 21 children.) One car belonged to Jim Conklin; another pick-up truck was used by Jess Conklin to supply electricity to a washing machine and television set. Jonathan Sherwood, whose father owned the land on which these squatters lived, said that he saw some of them living in the old cars. All of these Conklin families probably arrived and built their shacks after 1947. These Conklin families were described in an article in the *Rockland County Leader* of November 15, 1956.

Beyond the wrecked cars, to the

left of the trail, the remains of old cabins and garden terraces can be seen. These structures were built by the Pitt family, which preceded the Conklins into the valley. In 1935, former Scout leader A.T. Shorey sent a picture of Maggie Gannon pulling a plow guided by Gil Pitt. The plow was a piece of stove iron, bolted to a piece of oak root (*N.Y. Post*, 1/7/35).

About 0.4 mile from the start of the Second Pittsboro Trail, the remains of a three-sided stone structure can be seen to the right of the trail, near the stream. At this point, it is preferable to cross the stream and follow the woods road on the other side (the First Pittsboro Trail), as the continuation of the Second Pittsboro Trail is nearly impossible to follow.

From the stone structure, the Second Pittsboro Trail headed left (uphill) for about 200 feet, turned right, and eventually reached the "Witness Oak" on the Suffern-Bear Mountain Trail (S-BM). (The end of the First Pittsboro Trail is about 20 feet to the right along the S-BM Trail.) Here, the Second Pittsboro Trail turned right and followed the S-BM. In another 0.1 mile, where the S-BM bends to the right, the Second Pittsboro Trail turned left, leaving the S-BM (there is a cairn to the right of the S-BM at this location). The Second Pittsboro Trail continued for another mile to Woodtown Road, reaching it about 250 feet northeast of its junction with Pine Meadow Road East. However, this section of the Second Pittsboro Trail is heavily overgrown and largely invisible (although a determined hiker can find some sections of the trail, particularly near Woodtown Road, where a cairn marks the end of the trail).

The last of the Pitts to live in the valley was Gilbert (Gil) Pitt, 1865-1947. He was a 6-foot 3-inch tall mountaineer who spoke good English with an antique accent. Gil claimed to be descended from Richard Pitt, the son of William Pitt (Lord Pitt of England, first Earl of Chatham, 1708-78). Richard, who remained here after the Revolution, is listed in the 1790 census of Orange County as living in Haverstraw Town. His grandson was Silas Pitt, who settled in Hogencamp Hollow (now known as Sky Meadow Road), where Gil Pitt was born.

When he was 22 years old, Gil Pitt married Mildred Conklin. She left him. At the age of 41, he married again to Amy Pose. She died of pneumonia. After many lonely years, Gil found Maggie Gannon in the county almshouse, and took her to keep house for him. He was about 60 years old then, and she was about 70.

Margaret (Maggie) was born in Southfields and raised in Sandyfield (now Lake Welch). Her mother died in childbirth, and Maggie was raised by her father's aunt, Marg Odell, and by her husband Jacob. On March 22, 1886, she married Bill Gannon,

ROCKLAND COUNTY HISTORICAL SOCIETY

Baskets made by mountain people

a Civil War veteran. They had a son, Jake, but eventually separated. She married Levi Bulson, a barge captain from Tomkins Cove, after nursing his wife for eleven years. When Levi died, Maggie went back to live with her stepmother. After a brief marriage to Charlie Youmans in 1906 and other mishaps, Maggie went to live in the county almshouse, where Gil Pitt found her.

Gil and Maggie built two cabins in the hollow, on the left side of the stream, along the Second Pittsboro Trail—a summer house lower down, and a winter house further uphill. About 1938, Gil's older brother Albert moved into the summer house with his wife Gracie. They said they would stay only until they could build a shack of their own. But the years went by, and Albert and Gracie continued to live there until they died.

To get what money they needed, the Pitt brothers worked for farmers in nearby towns. They were also excellent basket makers. Gil made his baskets, which resembled Adirondack pack baskets, from white oak splints which he cut with a spokeshave. He also carved spoons and scoops of basswood. Those things were exchanged at Pincus Margulies' store in Ladentown for various items that the mountain family needed. "Pinky" Margulies extended credit during the winter, but the mountaineers always paid their bills.

During the 1940s, Bill Hoeferlin would lead his group, the Wanderbirds, on hikes to visit Gil and Maggie, bringing canned goods. Usually these hikes were held on Palm Sunday or Easter Sunday, and the notice of the hike in *Walking News* would include a reminder to all participants to bring along a can of food for Gil and Maggie.

Maggie and Gil became seriously ill in March 1946. They were rescued by the Ramapo Police. They stayed for three months in the County Home, then went back to their cabin (*N.Y. Times*, 7/4/46).

Brother Albert died in December 1946, at the age of 82. Gil Pitt died on May 12, 1947, also aged 82. Gracie Pitt died alone in her cabin January 5, 1948, at the age of 80. She was discovered by a neighbor, Norman Conklin, and a party was dispatched to carry her down the mountain on an improvised sled. As they passed Maggie Gannon's place, they stopped to ask Maggie to step out and say goodbye to Gracie. Maggie declined, and turned to put more wood on her fire (*N.Y. Times*, 1/6/48). Sometime later,

rather than live alone on the mountain, Maggie went to live with friends down in the valley. She died in a Garnerville nursing home on February 5, 1955 at the age of 99.

The Pitts had neighbors on the mountain. Up above the Pitt cabins, where the Pittsboro Trail reaches the S-BM, there is a level region to the left of the trail, below Hawk Cliff. This is probably where Norman Conklin lived with his wife and niece. A half mile north of the S-BM junction was the Starr Clearing—occupied until 1925.

All the Conklins were evicted by the Park about 1965, after the Park had taken Harold Sherwood's land. Bill Hoeferlin noted the event in his *Walking News* of March 1965.

Pound Swamp Mountain Trail

Length: 1.05 miles

Miles

0.0   Begin at Irish Potato.

0.35 Faint side trail leaves, right.

0.55 S-BM leaves, left.

0.7   Reach Upper Pound Swamp.

0.8   Turn left, uphill, on wide woods road.

1.05 End at ruins of Redard estate.

The main trail on Pound Swamp Mountain is the Suffern-Bear Mountain Trail (S-BM) (yellow), which goes north from Irish Mountain. It is convenient to describe our trail as starting from the Irish Potato, on the summit of Irish Mountain. From the Irish Potato, proceed north on the S-BM Trail. At 0.35 mile, a faint side trail (marked by cairns at the start) begins to the right, but it soon becomes a steep and rocky bushwhack to the southwest corner of Upper Pound Swamp, which is really a little pond. To follow the Pound Swamp Mountain Trail, continue ahead on S-BM for another 0.2 mile. At 0.55 mile, S-BM turns left, while the Pound Swamp Mountain Trail proceeds ahead as a faint woods road, reaching Upper Pound Swamp at 0.7 mile. Follow the woods road around to the southeast corner of the swamp, at 0.8 mile, where a wide woods road on the left heads gently uphill. Continue on this wide road for another 0.25 mile to a paved road that comes up from Gate Hill Road, near its junction with Blanchard Road. Here, 1.05 miles from the Irish Potato, the Pound Swamp Mountain Trail ends.

To the left are the ruins of an old mansion. This was the estate of Rose O. Redard, heiress and namesake of the Red Rose Tea fortune. The estate was acquired by the Park in April 1961, and the mansion was demolished in December 1961.

Rockhouse Mountain Trail

Length: 1.1 miles

Miles

0.0 Begin at Route 106; head north on Beech Trail.

0.6 Turn left, leaving Beech Trail.

0.85 Cross brook.

1.1 End at woods road.

The Rockhouse Mountain Trail starts from the north side of Route 106, about 1.1 miles east of the Kanawauke Circle. For the first 0.6 mile, it follows the blue blazes of the Beech Trail. At 0.45 mile, it climbs up along the mountain for a short distance, then begins to descend. Soon, at 0.6 mile, the Rockhouse Mountain Trail leaves to the left on a footpath, while the Beech Trail continues straight ahead. (The junction is marked by a cairn.) For the rest of the way, the Rockhouse Mountain Trail is marked with small, faded white paint blazes and cairns. After going up gently for about 600 feet, the trail begins to descend until it reaches a shallow brook, which it crosses at 0.85 mile (from Route 106). The trail now climbs, reaching the top of a rise at 0.95 mile, Here, it bears right (north) and descends on an old, but clearly evident, woods road. It ends, 1.1 miles from the start, at a junction with a well-worn woods road (this junction is also marked by a cairn). That woods road, followed to the left, goes down in 0.8 mile to Seven Lakes Drive at the southern end of Lake Askoti. To the right, it leads in 0.35 mile to the Red Cross Trail (0.25 mile from the Hasenclever Mine).

The "rock house," a cave which gives its name to the mountain, is below (south of) the highway, about 0.2 mile east of the Long Path crossing.

Sloatsburg Trail

Length: 2.6 miles

Miles

0.0 Begin at Seven Lakes Drive.

0.75 T-MI Trail joins from right.

0.85 T-MI Trail leaves, left.

0.95 Dutch Doctor Shelter, right.

1.05 White Bar Trail leaves, left; Triangle Trail starts.

1.25 Trail to Camp Nawakwa, right.

1.5 Second trail to Camp Nawakwa, right.

1.6 Triangle Trail leaves, left.

2.4 Rejoin old road.

2.6 End at Sebago Beach parking area.

The Sloatsburg Trail begins as a woods road, starting from a gate on Seven Lakes Drive, 1.15 miles northeast of the Reeves Meadow Visitor Center. About 150 feet from the gate, the Sloatsburg Trail turns left, and the White Bar Trail soon joins from the left. After 0.75 mile, a cellar hole with a large tree in the middle may be seen to the left of the trail. This is where the "Old Dutch Doctor," John Frederick Helms, lived from 1874 to about 1892 (see p. 146). In another 150 feet, the Tuxedo-Mt. Ivy Trail (T-MI) (red triangle on white) comes down from the right and joins the Sloatsburg/White Bar Trail.

At 0.85 mile, T-MI leaves to the left, and the Sloatsburg Trail continues along the route of the White Bar Trail. Soon afterwards, a path to the right leads to the Dutch Doctor Shelter, up on the hillside. At 1.05 miles, the White Bar Trail goes left, and the Triangle Trail starts. The Sloatsburg Trail now follows the route of the Triangle Trail.

At 1.25 miles, a trail goes off to the right, over the hill, to the ADK Camp Nawakwa on the lake. Another trail to the camp starts at 1.5 miles, and then the Sloatsburg Trail (and Triangle Trail) reach the lake edge. They go along together to 1.6 miles, where Triangle departs to the left. Our trail now follows the edge of Lake Sebago. Before the lake was made in 1925, our trail was a road along the edge of Emmetsfield Swamp. The old road here has now been covered by the lake, so the present-day trail is a relatively level footpath which parallels the old road.

The footpath rejoins the old road at about 2.4 miles, and it ends at the Sebago Beach parking area, 2.6 miles from Seven Lakes Drive. Parking at Sebago Beach is available only when the beach is open to the public.

THE HISTORICAL TRAILS

The ten trails described in this section can be extremely difficult to follow, even for an experienced hiker. In many instances, sections of the trail simply no longer exist (which is why we call them "historical" trails). Nevertheless, experienced hikers may enjoy attempting to follow these routes. Such hikers should be prepared for the possibility that they will be unable to follow the trail and will have to backtrack or bushwhack to reach their destination.

Not all unmarked trails in Bear Mountain/Harriman Park are described in this book. It is a delightful feature of the Park that the number of trails seems endless. It often happens that as one walks again on a well-known trail, a faint side trail will be noticed for the first time. Take the time to follow it—an unexpected pleasure lies ahead.

High Hill Trail

This trail, marked by cairns in places, goes around the south side of High Hill, which is south of Lake Welch Drive and just east of Seven Lakes Drive. An interesting way to approach this trail is to take the old Johnsontown Road north from Baker Camp Road (which goes off Seven Lakes Drive just north of Lake Sebago). About 0.2 mile north, just before old Johnsontown Road ends at a high cut, scramble down and cross Seven Lakes Drive. On the opposite bank, the beginning of the High Hill Trail is marked by a great boulder with a cairn (obscured by low branches) on its top.

Although the start of the trail is obscured by bushes, if you go 100 feet to the east, you will notice a faint woods road going uphill. About 300 feet from the boulder, at a cairn, the trail bends to the right and soon becomes more obvious. At 0.35 mile, the trail enters an evergreen grove. On the left is the cellar hole of Henrietta Conklin's home. She sold her farm to the Park in 1915. Past the cellar hole, the trail proceeds straight ahead, but is obscured by barberry.

At 0.4 mile, the High Hill Trail begins to descend slightly to the right. In another 250 feet, it joins a woods road and curves to the left. Beginning at 0.55 mile, the trail route has been cleared and is easier to follow. Then, at 0.75 mile, the trail turns sharply right and crosses a stream. It ends in another 500 feet at the Cranberry Mountain Trail, about 50 feet north of Pine Meadow Road (the last 100 feet of the trail are somewhat obscured by the brush).

It is possible to leave the trail at 0.4 mile and bushwhack up to the hilltop, then head northeast along the ridge through a pleasant landscape of open forest and low grass, passing several old cellar holes and remnants of woods roads, and eventually come down to a camp service road near its junction with Lake Welch Drive.

Horn's Route

On the North "Ski Trail," about 0.1 mile east of where the Suffern-Bear Mountain Trail crosses, a cairn will be seen on the right. Here, at a very gentle angle, a faint woods road departs toward the slope on the right. The faint old road is marked with an occasional cairn as it crosses a fairly level area to the southeast. A big boulder, with a cairn on its top, will be seen on the left at 0.1 mile. The trail goes down a valley and at 0.2 mile reaches the lip of a swampy hollow. Follow cairns along the left edge of the swamp, and cross the brook at 0.25 mile. Just beyond, turn left (do not follow the faint path that continues ahead, slightly uphill). The trail now is a perfectly visible old road going down the right side of the brook.

At 0.65 mile, a side trail goes right, down to a branch of the South "Ski Trail." Further downhill, Horn's Route approaches the brook, where it meets the Red Cross Trail. Here, Red Cross crosses the brook to the left, on its way up to Timp Pass. Horn's Route turns right onto the route of the Red Cross Trail. In another 0.2 mile, it passes the sites of two old cabins. Here, the branch of the South "Ski Trail" joins from between two stone walls on the right. Then, at 1.15 miles, Horn's Route ends at the Bulsontown-Timp Road (A-B Trail), while Red Cross turns right (southwest). Horn's Route once went left here, and continued another 0.15 mile to a road that went south (through the Scout camp) to a farm road leading to Tomkins Cove (named Mott Farm Road after it was paved about 1935).

This trail was first marked about 1920 by James T. Horn, the vice president of the Fresh Air Club and a founding member of the New York-New Jersey Trail Conference. Horn lived at 15 East 53rd Street, New York City.

Jim Horn's personal trail—marked with a metallic letter H, stamped from sheet aluminum—started at the Tomkins Cove railroad station and followed the route we have described. Continuing on the North "Ski Trail" to Beechy Bottom Road, Horn's Route followed Beechy Bottom Road around Horn Hill to the point where the 1779 Trail now comes up from the Parkway. (That bit of road, up from the Parkway, was part of the Beechy Bottom West Road, where it crossed over to join Beechy Bottom East.) Horn then followed the woods road, once known as the Black Mountain Trail, that went over toward Owl Swamp. Of course, there was no Owl Lake Road then (it was built in 1933), but Horn's trail can still be seen (and followed) in several places in the bushes below Owl Lake Road.

If one climbs the hill from the west end of the dam, the continuation of Horn's Route will be found on an old woods road that goes over the hillside and comes down at the Burnt House. Horn then went up the Dean Trail (now Menomine Trail) for 0.35 mile to a left fork. That led to the foot of Goshen Mountain, where the Appalachian Trail and the R-D sepa-

rate. Then it continued over Goshen Mountain to Seven Lakes Drive at Tiorati Circle on a path later adopted by the R-D and (for a time) the AT. To follow Horn's Route, continue west over Goshen Mountain on the R-D until the R-D turns right onto a woods road. Horn's Route continued straight ahead to reach Tiorati Brook Road in 0.15 mile, then followed Tiorati Brook Road to Tiorati Circle.

Jim Horn's Route was taken by hikers who were in a hurry to catch the train at Tomkins Cove (*N.Y. Post*, 11/16/28). Horn died in the mid-1930s on a hike in the Hudson Highlands. He was over 80 years old.

Iron Mountain Trail

Iron Mountain is the southwest end of a ridge labeled Horse Chock Mountain on Trail Conference Map #118. Bill Hoeferlin first called it Iron Mountain on his May 1945 map. On O'Connor's 1845 map, it is called Hasha Hill. It is shown as the property of the Christie Mining Company on an 1876 map. A deep ravine divides the ridge, the portion to the north (to the east of the First Reservoir) being Horse Chock Mountain.

Several trails start up the hill from Woodtown Road. The best of them was described by Bob Marshall in the *Trail Walker* of June/July 1987. It starts from Woodtown Road 500 feet northeast of the point where that road crosses Horse Chock Brook at the Second Reservoir, or 0.85 mile southwest of the dam at the First Reservoir.

The trail—which, at this point, is a clearly visible woods road—goes up at a moderate pitch. At 0.5 mile, a trail goes right to File Factory Hollow. Then, at 0.6 mile, the woods road reaches a ridgetop. Here, the Iron Mountain Trail, now marked by cairns, goes off to the left. There is no view at this point, but about 200 feet straight ahead (slightly downhill), there is an excellent view of the New York City skyline.

Follow the cairns, which mark a faint trail that heads east for about 0.2 mile, then northeast for another 0.2 mile. Portions of this section of the trail (as it heads northeast) are invisible, but the route can be followed by heading compass northeast, looking for cairns (as well as tin can lids nailed to the trees), and keeping the downslope as close to your right as possible. At 1.0 mile, there is a spectacular view from near a large vertical boulder. The Hudson River and High Tor above Haverstraw are clearly visible, with the New York City skyline in the far distance. The huge white building on the hilltop directly to the east is a private residence (known to many hikers as "the Shapiro residence").

From the boulder, one is tempted to continue northeast, soon starting down a gentle slope. However, this route is not recommended, as it soon becomes steep and eroded. A much better route is to follow a faint road to the north, heading slightly away from the ridge. In 300 feet, the road becomes more obvious, and it soon loops around to the southeast. The next 0.15 mile of the road is faint in spots but is marked with cairns (and, at one point, with tin can blazes). Eventually, the road becomes much clearer, and it ends, 1.4 miles from the start, at the Orange and Rockland Utilities power line. Both the power line service road and the wide gas line below are easily walkable, but the service road is the better route, as the gas line is blocked in places by fences that indicate private property. To the right (southwest), File Factory Brook is reached in another 0.2 mile, the Tuxedo-Mt. Ivy Trail (red dash on white) joins 0.75 mile beyond the brook (bear left here onto the gas line), and the Diltz Road parking area is 0.3 mile further.

Limekiln Mountain Trail

This trail, as shown on maps made by Bill Hoeferlin, starts from the Red Arrow Trail and ends at Woodtown Road. At present, the southern end of the trail is obscured by thick brush, and other portions of the trail are nearly invisible. However, some parts of the trail can more easily be followed.

One possible approach is from the Red Arrow Trail. About 500 feet from its start on the Tuxedo-Mt. Ivy (T-MI) Trail, at the top of a small rise, two faint paths go east (right). The two paths soon join, and this heavily overgrown route (an old woods road, now barely visible) can be followed east, through thick laurel. It soon turns north, crosses a small brook, and reaches an open area near the Red Arrow Trail at 0.1 mile. (This point can also be reached by following the Red Arrow Trail for 0.15 mile from its start at the T-MI. At this point, the Red Arrow Trail is at the base of a fairly steep pitch, with a stone wall immediately to the right. About 200 feet to the right, another stone wall can be seen. The Limekiln Mountain Trail is an old woods road on the hillside, about 100 feet east of that stone wall.)

For the next 0.15 mile, the Limekiln Mountain Trail is nearly invisible. However, the trail can be found by continuing about 500 feet to the northeast and then about 250 feet north. At that point, a faint woods road can be seen going left, uphill.

The trail, faint but visible, soon crosses Squirrel Swamp Brook and, 150 feet further, it crosses the File Factory Hollow Trail. Woodtown Road is 0.1 mile to the left (west). The Limekiln Mountain Trail continues northward, up through a rocky notch. Beyond that, the trail becomes even more faint, but it can be followed to its end at Woodtown Road, about 0.2 mile north of its junction with the File Factory Hollow Trail (this end of the trail is marked by cairns).

Little Doe Trail

The Little Doe Trail, an old woods road, starts from Pine Meadow Road, about 325 feet from the gate on Seven Lakes Drive. A cairn is there, behind a row of barberry bushes on the right side of the road. The trail is faint at first, but it is marked by cairns, and it soon becomes more obvious. At 0.2 mile, the Little Doe Trail crosses a ski trail (the junction is marked by a cairn). Seven Lakes Drive is 0.2 mile to the right on the ski trail. The Little Doe Trail then crosses a small brook and bears up left, following cairns. After crossing a fairly level region, it approaches a laurel grove. Here, it bears right, and it soon turns right and slabs up the mountain on a clearly defined woods road. Where the land levels off at 0.5 mile, the road becomes fainter. From here on, the trail is marked with cairns, with some interesting boulders to the left of the trail.

At 0.6 mile, the treadway seems to end at a boulder field. The Buck Trail is only about 300 feet straight ahead, but the most direct route to the Buck Trail is not practical, as it crosses the boulder field, a swamp and a laurel thicket. The most obvious line of cairns bears right to skirt the boulder field and swamp, and it reaches the Buck Trail in about 500 feet. The fork in the Buck Trail is 0.2 mile to the left. (It is very difficult to find the intersection of the Little Doe and Buck Trails when starting from the Buck Trail.)

Fractured boulder along the Little Doe Trail

Many Swamp Trail

This old trail starts from the hikers' parking area at Ladentown. Follow the Tuxedo-Mt. Ivy Trail (red dash on white) blazes up to the buried gas pipeline and, almost immediately, turn left onto a short connecting road that leads to the power line service road. Directly across the power line service road, hidden in the bushes, you will see a stone-lined road going uphill. That is the Many Swamp Trail. Follow this road uphill (at this point, the road resembles a streambed). At 0.45 mile, the road crosses Squirrel Swamp Brook. Here, the road (easy to follow up to this point) bends right and continues uphill, with the brook on the right, until the land begins to level off. At 0.7 mile, the trail bends left (southwest), with a swamp on the right.

At 0.85 mile, the trail bears right at a fork. Just beyond, the Suffern-Bear Mountain Trail (S-BM) (yellow) crosses. To the left, it has come down from Panther Mountain; to the right, in 0.35 mile, it will cross Squirrel Swamp Brook and meet the Tuxedo-Mt. Ivy Trail. Watch for cairns at the S-BM crossing, since the Many Swamp Trail here is obscured by the low shrubbery. The trail goes straight ahead towards a low hill, and then bends to the left (southwest).

At 0.95 mile, the trail approaches the laurel-covered edge of a swamp and then continues through the swamp. It is not feasible to follow the trail through the swamp, so it is necessary to skirt the swamp to the left. Soon, you will come to a woods road, with a stream visible just down the road to the left (both the road and the stream are shown on the 2010 edition of Trail Conference Map #118, with the woods road shown as a dashed red line). Continue straight ahead for another 100 feet (do not turn onto the road), and you will reach the continuation of the Many Swamp Trail—a clear woods road that comes out of the swamp.

Follow this road for about 500 feet until it turns sharply right and goes uphill. Here, at 1.05 miles, the Many Swamp Trail leaves the woods road and continues straight ahead. The route (which is shown on Map #118 as a dashed red line) is marked by a line of closely-spaced cairns. Although they are partially obscured by bushes, the cairns can be easily followed for the next 0.1 mile. Beyond this point, though, the cairns are spaced further apart, and the trail becomes very difficult to follow.

At 1.15 miles, an old road comes out of the swamp. Follow the road for the next 0.1 mile (it heads southwest and uphill, away from the swamp) until it fades out. At this point, a line of cairns, partially hidden by bushes, goes uphill diagonally to the right. There is also a large circular cairn on the top of a large flat boulder (left there by Franz Alt) about 40 feet to the left of the trail, but the main cairn line—which represents the route of the trail—bends to the right (west).

Follow this line of cairns to the top of a small rise. From this point, the cairns that mark the trail route are very difficult to follow, but the general direction is west. At 1.3 miles, the cairns begin to follow a faint old road, and at 1.45 miles, the remains of old stone walls appear to the left. Bear left, following these old stone walls and some cairns. There are several lines of cairns and herd paths in this area, but they all lead to the Starr Clearing at 1.5 miles. The clearing is marked by many piles of stones, with only a few trees.

From the south end of the Starr Clearing, head northwest, following a fairly obvious trail marked by a few cairns. At 1.6 miles, at a cairn, the trail turns left onto a woods road (to the right, this road leads for 0.5 mile to Woodtown Road). Then, at 1.7 miles, the Second Pittsboro Trail crosses. While this trail can no longer be detected, its route is approximated by a trail shown on Map #118 as a dashed red line (and presently marked by unofficial orange blazes) that goes off to the left. The Many Swamp Trail continues southwest. At 2.05 miles, the trail crosses Many Swamp Brook. At 2.4 miles, our trail arrives at Pine Meadow Road East. The junction is marked with a cairn. The Pine Meadow Trail (red square on white) is 0.2 mile to the left.

The ruin of an old shack can be seen just north of where the trail starts, on the power line service road. It was built there about 1936 by Ramsey Conklin and his sons. After they left their cabin at Pine Meadow in 1934, they moved into an abandoned schoolhouse at the corner of Camp Hill and Quaker Roads in Ladentown. Ramsey did not like that new set-up. He complained that seven or eight cars passed his place each day. "Not good for the livestock," he said. So he built two shacks at the foot of Limekiln Mountain, on land that belonged to Ira Hedges of Ladentown. Ramsey paid $1 per month rent. He lived there until 1952, when his body was found near the Second Reservoir. Son Theodore (Dory), who was on the Park payroll, continued to live in the shacks until he was evicted in 1963.

Along the trail, up in the hills at the foot of Squirrel Swamp Mountain, is the Starr Clearing. This was one of many Starr family farms—another was near Torne Valley Road, below the Russian Bear. A third was said to be the site named "Sky Sail Farm" by the men who blazed the S-BM Trail.

Aaron Starr (1862-1956) owned the farm at the junction of the Pittsboro and Many Swamp Trails. He was also a partner in the sawmill that had been built by the grandfather of Joseph E. Christie (of Thiells) at the junction of Woodtown and Pine Meadow Roads.

Aaron also owned the Big Green Swamp, where blueberries and cranberries grew in profusion. Each year, mountain folk came from afar to pick the berries there. Then Aaron got the idea to charge a fee to pick berries in his swamp. The neighbors resented this and made veiled threats. Finally, one summer, Aaron's house and barn were set afire. That was in 1919. Aaron's son Daniel sold their 39 acres to the Park, and the family moved to Orangeburg. When he died in 1956, old Aaron Starr was buried in the cemetery at Ladentown. His sister Eliza had married Nicholas Conklin. They are buried in St. John's Cemetery. Her grandson, Ben Jones of Lindbergh Road, Stony Point, a member of St. John's Church, died in 1989. Old Aaron's brother Charlie Starr was for a time the owner of Anderson's file factory at File Factory Hollow. Aaron's grandson James Aaron Starr, Jr., who was born in 1916, remembered as a boy going back up to the Starr Place to pick ginseng.

In the *New York Evening Post* of November 9, 1923, Brooklyn Boy Scout leader Archibald T. Shorey described a hike to the clearing known as the Starr Place, at the foot of Squirrel Swamp Mountain. There was a fine spring and a campsite there. Shorey and his scouts built a cabin near the summit of Squirrel Swamp Mountain. A side trip up from the Starr Clearing will lead to that site. Far over on the north end of the mountain, against a great boulder, are the remains of Shorey's cabin.

The Many Swamp Trail now ends at Pine Meadow Road East. That road, built in 1934, actually followed two branches of the Many Swamp Trail—it followed the left branch of the trail to a junction with another trail that in 1934 was blazed as the Pine Meadow Trail; and it followed the right branch of the Many Swamp Trail to the site of Christie's sawmill, where Woodtown Road comes in.

Owl Lake Road

Owl Lake Road is on the hillside along Beechy Bottom valley, parallel to the Palisades Interstate Parkway. Built in 1933-34 by the Civilian Conservation Corps, it was intended to be the southbound lane of a motor road from Queensboro Circle to Tiorati Brook Road.

We usually encounter this trail as we go up the Appalachian/Ramapo-Dunderberg Trail (AT/R-D) toward Black Mountain. About 275 feet up from the Parkway, just past a stand of evergreens on the right, the AT/R-D crosses two old roads. The lower one is the even older Beechy Bottom West Road that went to Bulsontown. The upper road is the 1933 highway. Both roads are overgrown by barberry and difficult to see from the AT/R-D. To follow the roads north from the AT/R-D, it is best to avoid the worst of the barberry by walking in the woods parallel to and east of the roads.

A quarter mile north of the AT/R-D, the two roads join and become relatively free of vegetation, but they end at 0.65 mile above a cut for the Parkway. (This location is north of the Visitor Center/Book Store and south of the north parking area for the Anthony Wayne Recreation Area.)

South of the AT/R-D, the roads are hard to find in a mass of barberry. 0.3 mile from the AT/R-D, Beechy Bottom West Road turns left (southeast), while Owl Lake Road goes straight ahead. It continues south and then southwest through the barberry, crossing the 1779 Trail in another 0.4 mile. At 0.5 mile (from the Owl Lake Road/Beechy Bottom West Road junction), the unmarked Black Mountain Trail goes right (uphill) at a cairn. Then, at 0.8 mile, another trail comes steeply down from the mountain. This trail, known as Black Mountain II, goes up to the end of Silvermine Road, and was to be a "stone road" (see p. 261).

The Owl Lake dam (destroyed in 1988) is reached at 0.9 mile. Here the road ends. Owl Lake Road was originally intended to go down to Stillwater Brook, crossing the brook near the Burnt House. There it was to take over the route of the old Burnt House Trail (now known as the Stillwater Trail) and continue east and then south, around the end of Flaggy Meadow Mountain, down to Tiorati Brook Road. Although this section, too, was cut by the construction of the Parkway, its continuation further south, along Flaggy Meadow Mountain, can still be followed.

Quartz Brook Trail

Quartz Brook, which the trail follows, starts from a swamp on Chipmunk Mountain and runs down one mile to Stony Brook, 0.4 mile below its junction with Pine Meadow Brook. Quartz Brook crosses the Pine Meadow Trail (red square on white) a few yards below the gas pipeline crossing.

The Quartz Brook Trail goes up from the Pine Meadow Trail, about 325 feet east of the junction of the Pine Meadow and Stony Brook Trails. At the start, the Quartz Brook Trail follows a faint woods road diagonally uphill, to the right. Just beyond the woods road are what appear to be two streambeds. When the road crosses the second "streambed," turn right and follow it—it is actually another old woods road. This old road, which roughly parallels Quartz Brook, is heavily eroded, but it can be easily followed for 0.35 mile (several side roads branch off to the right, so you should bear left at each fork).

At 0.35 mile, the trail joins a wider woods road, which leads left, towards the pipeline cut. You can follow this wider road for 0.15 mile, almost to the brook and the pipeline. Old maps and trail descriptions indicate that the trail once turned right here and continued uphill along the west side of the brook, reaching the Seven Hills Trail in about 0.15 mile, at a point roughly 250 feet southwest of the pipeline crossing, but this segment of the trail can no longer be followed.

This little-used trail became "legal" in 1963, when the Park purchased a large part of the Pierson Estate. It had never been blazed (except by wine bottles stuck on branches by a "Frenchman"). In 1962, it was blazed white by Bob Bloom of the Trail Conference, but it was abandoned again in 1969.

South "Ski Trail"

Beechy Bottom Road, after it leaves the vicinity of the Palisades Interstate Parkway, continues around Horn Hill. The 1779 Trail soon departs to the right, and shortly thereafter the Suffern-Bear Mountain Trail (S-BM) (yellow) crosses. 0.15 mile east of the S-BM crossing, the Horn Hill Bike Trail (blazed with blue-on-white markers) joins from the left (at a highway monument). Go just over 100 feet along the bike trail, and you will see a cairn on the right. This marks the start of the South "Ski Trail." The trail is almost invisible here, being covered with low blueberry bushes. But it soon becomes more distinct, and it crosses a little brook at 0.1 mile. It then curves to the left and goes uphill on an old woods road. It soon turns right onto another old, eroded road (this turn may be hard to find when proceeding in the reverse direction) and heads east, down a valley with a steep hillside on the left. Several faded pink ski markers may be seen—remnants of its former status as a ski trail.

At 0.35 mile, the old road temporarily disappears as it enters a level area overgrown with barberry. If you bear slightly left, avoiding the thickest part of the barberry, you will see the old road reappear in about 250 feet. Then, at 0.55 mile, just after the trail comes out onto another level area, you will notice a large rock with a flat top, about 50 feet to the right (south) of the trail. The South "Ski Trail" (which is virtually invisible at this point) turns right here, leaving the old road (which continues straight ahead). It passes just to the right (west) of the rock and soon crosses a brook. On the other side of the brook, the faint route of the trail can again be located.

The trail now begins to descend gently (avoid the steeper and more obvious routes which go down to the left), and it ends, 0.85 mile from the start, at the old Bulsontown-Timp Road (the route of the Red Cross Trail). It should be noted that the final 100 feet of the South "Ski Trail" are invisible. To the left on the Red Cross Trail, there is a T-junction in 0.15 mile. Here, the Red Cross Trail goes left on Horn's Route. To reach the North "Ski Trail," turn right at the T-junction and continue for another 0.1 mile until you see the trail start up on the left.

Stillwater Trail

The unmarked Stillwater Trail starts from the Red Cross Trail, 0.3 mile east of its junction with the Menomine Trail (yellow) and 0.85 mile west of the Palisades Interstate Parkway. This point is 0.2 mile east of the Burnt House site.

The trail crosses Stillwater Brook (the wide wooden bridge that formerly crossed the bridge here no longer exists, and it is often impossible to cross the brook without getting wet) and heads southeast along the hillside, just above the brook. After 0.25 mile, it joins a wider dirt road which comes in from the right. The wide trail is now fairly high above the brook, and at 0.7 mile it reaches the Palisades Interstate Parkway.

The route of the trail was cut when the Parkway was built in 1952. It is possible to bushwhack up along the Parkway cut, or simply follow the Parkway south for 0.3 mile. Then, where the steep hillside comes down to the level of the road, climb over the guard cables and follow a dirt road to the west.

The trail soon proceeds south, with Flaggy Meadow Mountain on the right. At 1.2 miles, the overgrown Flaggy Meadow Mountain Trail goes up to the right. That trail goes northwest, up to the 970-foot level, then branches, with one branch continuing northwest, and another branch turning south, ending at a gate on Tiorati Brook Road. At times, it is hard to find the trail in the tall grass.

The Stillwater Trail gradually becomes more difficult to follow. It ends, 0.6 mile beyond the junction with the Flaggy Meadow Mountain Trail, at Tiorati Brook Road, just east of its junction with Lake Welch Drive.

Before the Red Cross Trail was first blazed in April 1944, what is now known as the Stillwater Trail was the southern end of the Burnt House Trail. In 1922, this part of the Burnt House Trail was made a part of the Boy Scouts' White Bar Trail system. Their Camp Pathfinder was located at the junction of the Burnt House Trail and Tiorati Brook Road.

The Burnt House Trail appeared on a New York State Conservation Department map of 1882 and on O'Connor's 1854 map of Rockland County. It was undoubtedly a wood-cutters' road.

In 1933-34, Major Welch set the Civilian Conservation Corps workers to building a pair of roads from Tiorati Brook Road north, past the Owl Lake Dam and through the Beechy Bottom valley. An unfinished portion of one of those roads coincided with the Burnt House Trail where it went around Flaggy Meadow Mountain. To reach the beginning of that CCC road, bushwhack south for 0.15 mile from the site of the Burnt House, cross Stillwater Brook and another little brook, and climb a little way up the hillside. The unfinished road starts there and goes east to the Parkway.

THE STONE ROADS

*In 1933-36, the Temporary Emergency Relief Administration and the
Civilian Conservation Corps built a number of fire roads for the Park.
Mostly, they followed already-existing woods roads. The TERA and CCC
workers laid a base of broken stone (Telford base) on the old roads, in
preparation for a final coat of gravel. With certain exceptions, the final
gravel surface was never finished, so the roads became known as the
"stone roads." These roads are described below in two groups:*

Stone Roads West of the Palisades Interstate Parkway:
1. Deep Hollow Road
2. Silvermine Road
3. Black Mountain Trail
4. Black Mountain II

Stone Roads East of the Palisades Interstate Parkway:
5. North "Ski Trail" (and its branch to Timp Pass)
6. Timp Pass Road

*The North "Ski Trail," the South "Ski Trail" (see p. 253) and Timp
Pass Road were marked with red plaques as ski trails by the Youth Conservation Corps in 1980. It turned out that they were too long and, in
places, too dangerous. In 1987, these ski trails were officially de-marked,
but some of the red plaques can still be seen. So, although these trails are
no longer maintained for skiing, it is still convenient to call them
"ski trails."*

Deep Hollow Road

This "stone road" is approached from the hikers' parking area off Route 6. Follow the Long Path (aqua) heading north. At 0.3 mile (from the parking area), the Popolopen Gorge Trail (red square on white) begins to the right, and the Long Path goes up Long Mountain. Here, Deep Hollow Road begins on the left. It goes down to the site of an old shelter at 0.75 mile (from the parking area), where the Long Path comes down from the ridge and crosses the brook. This may be the first "stone road" new hikers encounter; they will wonder why it was made that way. Deep Hollow Road was the route of the Long Path until 1988 (some faded or blacked-out blazes are still visible).

Silvermine Road

We usually meet this road at the east side of the dam at Silvermine Lake. The road and dam were both built in 1934. (In previous editions of this book, the road was called the Silvermine Ski Road. However, it is not designated as a ski trail and, according to Park Ranger Tim Sullivan, it never has been. So we now call it simply Silvermine Road.).

Silvermine Road actually starts from Seven Lakes Drive, at a stone comfort station (now closed) where a motor camp had been built in 1926 (about 0.8 mile from the Long Mountain Circle). From the comfort station, the road goes up along the brook for 0.25 mile, crosses it, and reaches Silvermine Lake in another 0.2 mile. It heads south along the east shore of the lake for 0.25 mile, crosses a brook, and goes up through the notch between Black and Letterrock Mountains, crossing the Appalachian/Ramapo-Dunderberg Trail (AT/R-D) at 0.65 mile (from the east side of the dam). The faint Black Mountain Trail, another "stone road," leaves to the left 0.2 mile above the AT/R-D crossing, while the Silvermine Road bends right, around a knob.

At 0.75 mile from the AT/R-D, the "paved" road goes down a short slope, where the "paving" ends. The remains of a TERA work shed may still be seen here. To the left, a faint "stone road" (which we designate as "Black Mountain II") starts down to Owl Lake Road. The continuation of the road, now an old footpath, is occasionally marked by cairns, but is

Silvermine Road at the AT/R-D crossing

quite difficult to follow, even for an experienced hiker. At 1.25 miles, the old trail reaches the AT/R-D on the Letterrock ridge, 0.3 mile east of the Brien Memorial Shelter.

Black Mountain Trail

Before the TERA improved it, this old trail started from the Seven Lakes Drive, 0.3 mile east of the present Silvermine parking entrance. It went down to the edge of Bockey Swamp, and crossed Queensboro Brook there. From there it followed the route of the present-day Silvermine Road up the notch. At a cairn 0.2 mile beyond the AT/R-D crossing, the faint Black Mountain Trail departs down left. Here and there along the way the beginnings of the TERA "paving" can be seen. They give the hiker confidence that he is on the trail but, in many places, the trail is overgrown and difficult to follow, despite the presence of occasional cairns. For much of the way, the trail is at the foot of a high cliff to the left; the AT/R-D is on the top of that cliff. At 0.25 mile down from Silvermine Road, the trail becomes easier to follow. It turns right and crosses a brook at 0.4 mile, and it ends at a cairn on Owl Lake Road at 0.5 mile.

This old trail continued east along Owl Lake Road and turned right in 0.1 mile onto the route of the present-day 1779 Trail. Part of its original route has been obliterated by the Palisades Interstate Parkway. But east of the Parkway, the original route is used again by the 1779 Trail for about 0.15 mile, until it ends at the Red Cross Trail (the old Dean Trail).

Black Mountain II

This stone road never had a name. The 1989 Conference map shows it as a dashed red line (it is not shown on the 2010 edition of Conference Map #119). It leaves Silvermine Road 0.55 mile from the Black Mountain Trail junction (0.75 mile beyond the AT/R-D crossing) at the end of the "paved" section, near the remains of a TERA work shed. Here and there along the way the TERA workers began to lay their stone base. For 0.3 mile, the trail practically tumbles down the mountainside. It ends at Owl Lake Road, about 0.4 mile west of the 1779 Trail crossing.

North "Ski Trail"

This "stone road" starts up (east) from the Beechy Bottom Road, 0.25 mile south of the Ramapo-Dunderberg Trail (red dot on white) crossing. It was formerly designated as a ski trail, but it is no longer maintained, and nearly all of the red ski markers have been removed (especially at both ends of the trail). The "pavement" of broken stone, laid on the trail by the CCC in 1934, was largely bulldozed to the edges of the trail by the firefighters in 1988.

The first part of trail is now the route of the Horn Hill Bike Trail, with blue-on-white plastic blazes. At 0.15 mile, the bike trail leaves to the right (the section of the bike trail to the right was designated in previous editions of the book as the North-South Connector). At 0.2 mile, the Suffern-Bear Mountain Trail (yellow) crosses. At 0.3 mile, a cairn on the right shows the faint beginning of Horn's Route. Soon the North "Ski Trail" begins to go down, and it curves to the southeast.

At 0.85 mile, just beyond a fairly level wet region, a faint trail departs to the right. This pretty "no-name" trail leads in 0.25 mile to the Red Cross Trail, coming up from the valley below, at a stream crossing.

Continuing down the North "Ski Trail," now more steeply, there is a fork at 1.0 mile. Straight ahead, the Red Cross Trail comes up from below and turns to join the left fork—another stone road which goes up 0.4 mile

Torger Tokle, ski jump champion, 1941

to Timp Pass. The North "Ski Trail" continues straight ahead, following the right fork. At 1.05 miles, the Red Cross Trail leaves abruptly to the right, and the North "Ski Trail" continues steeply downward. The trail levels off and, soon after a steep S-curve, it ends, 1.25 miles from the start, at the old Bulsontown-Timp Road, marked with A-B blazes. Directly ahead, beyond a stone wall, are buildings of Girl Scout Camp Addisone Boyce. 0.25 mile to the right, the old road leads to the start of the South "Ski Trail."

Timp Pass Road

Timp Pass Road really is an ankle breaker! It starts just beyond the little brook at the end of Pleasant Valley Road in Doodletown. A jeep trail (the 1777 Trail) crosses the brook and continues straight ahead. In another 250 feet, Timp Pass Road begins to the right. It goes up the valley for 0.7 mile to the pass. In 0.2 mile, a cairn may be seen on a rock to the right. This marks the start of an old road which leads to the Herbert Mine (see p. 366). Timp Pass Road now begins to ascend more steeply. Near the top of the climb, at 0.55 mile, the Timp-Torne Trail (T-T) (blue) joins from the left and runs along Timp Pass Road for 250 feet, then leaves to the right. Timp Pass Road officially ends at the pass, 0.7 mile from its start, at a junction with the Red Cross and Ramapo-Dunderberg Trails.

Of course, the old road continues south from Timp Pass. To continue along this road, follow the red-dot-on-white blazes of the Ramapo-Dunderberg Trail to the left for 150 feet, then continue ahead on the road where the red-dot-on-white blazes turn left. This was formerly the route of the T-T Trail. Although T-T was relocated in 1987, the old blue-on-white blazes of the trail are still visible. At 0.55 mile below the pass, the old road reaches a junction with the Red Timp Trail. Timp Pass Road follows the Red Timp blazes to the right, soon passing an elevation known as the Boulderberg, or Little Timp. The road goes down the west side of the Boulderberg to the Girl Scouts' Camp Addisone Boyce (private property). Mott Farm Road is just beyond.

In a letter dated October 2, 1935 to C.H. Halevy, Secretary of the New York Mountain Club, Raymond H. Torrey said: "The road through Timp Pass is intended, I am told by the Park officials, as a fireroad only." It used to be a farmers' road. When the cows on the farms in Doodletown stopped giving milk, they were driven up over Timp Pass and down to the farm in Tomkins Cove (the Springsteel farm, now the Boy Scouts' Camp Bullowa). There the bulls "freshened" them, and they went back over the pass with a new outlook on life.

It is interesting to note that, at one time (in January 1950), the Evergreen Outdoor Club blazed the Torger Tokle Memorial Ski Trail, which extended 7.5 miles from the Silvermine Ski Tow to the Bear Mountain Inn. The trail was marked with 2" x 6" red blazes. It went up the Silvermine Road, down

the Black Mountain Trail, and across Beechy Bottom Brook, where the new Parkway was being built. It then followed the North "Ski Trail" and the leg to Timp Pass, which was described as very dangerous. It continued down Timp Pass Road, through Doodletown, to the Bridle Path and up to the Inn.

Torger Tokle was a young skier from Trondheim, Norway. In 1941, he won the National Ski Jumping championship with a 181-foot leap at Bear Mountain. He served during World War II in the 10th Mountain Division, and was killed in Italy. In 1947, the Torger Tokle Memorial Ski Jump was won by Torger's younger brother, Arthur.

The Tokle Memorial Trail was abandoned in 1960 (*Walking News*, June 1960).

DOODLETOWN AND IONA ISLAND

Doodletown is the site of a former hamlet just south of Bear Mountain and north of Dunderberg Mountain. The picturesque valley was inhabited at least since 1762, when Ithiel June arrived from Connecticut. The Junes (or Jouvins) were descended from the French Huguenots, a group who arrived here about 1700.

Iona Island, originally named Salisbury Island, lies in the Hudson River, connected to the mainland by a road across a marsh. On July 13, 1683, in the reign of Charles II, Salisbury Island, the valley later named Doodletown, and all of Bear Hill (as Bear Mountain was then known) were sold to Stephanus van Cortlandt, Mayor of New York City, by Sakaghkemerk, sachem of the Haverstraw Indian tribe. The same land was sold in 1685 to Thomas Dongan, Governor of New York, by the Haverstraw chief Werekepes.

Not to be outdone by the Native Americans, King George II granted Bear Hill on July 30, 1743 to Richard Bradley, then Attorney General of the colony. Salisbury Island and the lower part of what was to be Doodletown, a total of 500 acres, was granted to Bradley's children, Sarah, Catherine, George, Elizabeth and Mary. The 500 acres in the upper end of the valley were granted to Thomas Ellison and Lawrence Roome on November 12, 1750.

The Junes and other settlers in the valley were aware that a fort had been built in the summer of 1776 at the foot of Bear Hill. They were taken by surprise on October 6, 1777, when 900 British soldiers marched over Dunderberg and down Pleasant Valley Road through Doodletown. The soldiers turned up Doodletown Road toward Queensboro. Twelve hundred more troops arrived and waited in Doodletown until the first division approached Fort Montgomery. Then the second division marched to attack Fort Clinton. (Today, the 1777 Trail follows the route of the British march of October 6, 1777.)

A romantic story, repeated many times, tells us that the British derided the settlers by playing the tune "Yankee Doodle" as they marched through, giving rise to the name Doodletown. Actually, records show that the hamlet was already called Doodletown when the British arrived. Another possible derivation of the name has been suggested by C.C. Vermeule of East Orange, N.J. He thought that "Dood" may refer to the Dutch word for

Iona Island from Anthony's Nose

dead timber, etc., and that "Del" means valley (*N.Y. Post*, 11/4/27).

Until World War I, only about 75 people lived in Doodletown. One of these was John Stalter, a woodcutter. William Thompson Howell, in his diary, *The Hudson Highlands*, tells how John Stalter worked on the new road being built in 1908 around Dunderberg to Jones Point. John Stalter (1852-1920) is buried in the Herbert Cemetery in Doodletown. His grave is marked by a monument in a fenced-off portion of the cemetery.

Of course, the June family also lived there. In 1860, Caleb A. June (a bachelor) was the preacher in the first church, built in 1851, near the old (1809) road to Jones Point. Others who lived in Doodletown probably worked on Iona Island, or perhaps were employed by the Knickerbocker Ice Company at Hessian Lake.

Iona Island, originally called Salisbury Island, then Weygant's Island, was bought in 1847 by John Beveridge for his son-in-law Dr. E.W. Grant. Dr. Grant planted 20 acres to Iona grapes, imported from the Hebrides, and several thousand fruit trees. He went bankrupt in 1868, and the island was taken over by his creditor, the Bowery Savings Bank. The bank built an amusement park, a hotel and picnic grounds to entertain thousands of visitors who arrived on the West Shore Railroad (built in 1882) and by boat from New York City. It was probably at that time that a dam was built on lower Doodletown Brook, and a pipeline was installed to carry fresh water out to the island.

In 1900, the U.S. Navy bought the island for $160,000 for use as a naval ammunition depot. This provided employment for the Doodletown wage earners. In the 1930s, the dam on the brook was supplemented by a deep cistern further upstream (where the reservoir is now). A pipeline took the water to the island; our Cornell Mine Trail follows that aqueduct for a short distance. Between 1917 and 1945, the population of Doodletown increased. During those years, the Park gradually bought many of the homes. Some were demolished, others rented. The Navy abandoned Iona Island in 1947. On September 16, 1965, the Park acquired it for $290,000. The plans were to develop the island as a recreation area, and Doodletown was intended to become a ski center.

In 1962, the remaining private holdings in Doodletown were condemned, and by 1965 the hamlet was completely vacated. The last to leave, on January 16, 1965, was Clarence June, Jr. Gray's Hill, the old road down to Route 9W, was blocked off in 1966.

For a comprehensive history of Doodletown, including a detailed hiking guide to Doodletown today, see *Doodletown: Hiking Through History in a Vanished Hamlet on the Hudson*, by Elizabeth "Perk" Stalter (a former resident of Doodletown), published by the Palisades Interstate Park Commission.

A Guided Tour of Doodletown

The various sites in Doodletown are indicated by numbers on the accompanying map.

1. Somewhat off the beaten track, on the north side of the Old Caldwell Turnpike (facing Iona Island), is the site of the first Doodletown church. It was built in 1851 by John Beveridge of Newburgh, who had bought Salisbury (Iona) Island in 1847. He also supplied a Presbyterian pastor, but the local people were mostly Methodists. As a result, attendance at services was poor. For a time, the church was used during the week as Schoolhouse #11 of the Haverstraw School District (it later became Schoolhouse #7 of the Stony Point School District, when that town was incorporated in 1865). About 1860, Beveridge gave the church to the parish, who installed Caleb A. June as their "exhorter." After a new church was built on Doodletown Road (see #13), the old church became a private dwelling and was eventually destroyed. The site of the church, which is about 0.1 mile northwest of the point where the Old Caldwell Turnpike crosses a stream, is now surrounded by barberry bushes, but the impressive stone foundation is still visible.

2. To the north of the church, a building was erected in the 1850s as a parsonage. By 1859, it had become a private residence. In the early part of the twentieth century, it was the home of Joseph and Julia Jerminario (Julia was a daughter of John Stalter). The building was acquired by the Park about 1930 and soon demolished. All that can be seen now are the cellar walls and a cement walk.

3. Gray's Hill, closed as a road since 1966, starts uphill from Route 9W just north of the bridge that crosses Doodletown Brook leading into the marsh. (At present, it begins as a grass-covered road, blocked off by boulders, and marked with a Park sign giving the background of Doodletown.) On the right side, just up where the road bends sharply to the left, there was once a small hotel, operated until 1921 by Antonio Manglass. A branch of the road passed in front of the hotel and ended on the South Entrance Road that goes up to the Bear Mountain Inn. On the right side

Doodletown N

0   0.1   0.2   0.3 mile

Historical marker for the Steinman home (#7)

of the road, at the sharp bend and for some distance beyond, there is a low stone retaining wall. The home above the wall belonged to Knut and Alma Magnell. A bit further up the road, where a boulder barrier has been made, was the home (right) and garage (left, on a flat area) of the Horace Herbert family.

4. The Cornell Mine Trail comes down here along an old road. A little way up that road was the five-room home of John Magnell, Knut's son, built in 1935. It was sold in 1950 to Angelo and Ruth Donato, who worked for the Park. The Park acquired it in 1962. A driveway which goes off the Cornell Mine Trail parallels Gray's Hill, then soon joins it. The home of Mr. Wamble was up to the right of the driveway.

5. To the left of the road (Gray's Hill) as it goes uphill, the land falls steeply down to the brook. Down there is an old dam, known as Gray's Dam, now filled with gravel and mud. The hillside down to the brook was once the terraced garden of Dr. and Mrs. Thomas Gray. The Grays, who were from New York City, had adopted a girl named Millicent Eady. Sometime in 1899, Millicent came up the Hudson in a motorboat, and discovered Doodletown. She decided to buy the house and land of Amelia Thomas so that her adoptive parents could live there. During the next ten years, Millicent (who later married a musician named Phillip James) acquired much of the land on both sides of Doodletown Brook, including the first church, which was still standing in 1903.

After the Grays died, Millicent James rented the Gray home to Harold and Hilda Herbert. Harold was a plumber who worked for the Navy at Iona Island. In 1930, the Park acquired part of Millicent's property for $55,000, and it obtained the remainder of the property for $20,000 in 1941.

6. Next on the left was the home of William and Olivia Herbert. Their home, on an 0.7-acre parcel, was a wedding gift to them in 1910 from Mrs. Gray. Olivia, a Swedish girl, was Mrs. Gray's cook and housekeeper. William worked as a blacksmith on Iona Island and had a shop on the hillside below his home.

7. The Bridle Path crosses, and then on the right, above a low rock wall (partially obscured by barberry), was the home of Edward Steinman, who worked for the Park. On the roadside are the stone walls of a garage built for the Park by the WPA in 1934.

8. A little further along, on the right side, was a home that Harold Herbert (brother of William Herbert) built in 1923. It was sold to the Park in 1958.

9. A work road leads to the left, down to the water plant below the reservoir. A home to the left of that road was the birthplace of retired Park employee Denzel Livingston (of the June family). It was called "The Beehive" because of a swarm of bees in the attic.

"The Beehive"

PALISADES INTERSTATE PARK COMMISSION

Montville Community Church, 1910

10. A wide road enters from the right—Lemmon Road, which goes for 0.3 mile up to the Seven Lakes Drive. It was named for Newton and Rebecca June Lemmon, who owned 107 acres in the area. Their home was on the east side of Lemmon Road, just south of Seven Lakes Drive. Rebecca sold the house to the Park in 1917, and it became the home of Chief Park Ranger Bill Gee. Later, it was occupied by Raymond Adolph, Park Forester and subsequently Park Superintendent. Adolph retired in 1947, and the house was demolished in 1952. The land below the house was devoted to the Park nursery, the lower edge of which was marked by a stone wall. Near that wall, east of Lemmon Road, was the first cemetery of the June family. The graves were marked with simple fieldstones. The first to be buried there was Charity Baxter June, wife of Ithiel June. The flat gravestones were taken by the TERA workers in 1933 to line the ditches of the new Bridle Path. A possible location for this long-lost cemetery has recently been established, and a commemorative monument has been placed there by members of the June family.

11. The name of the road that we have been following now changes to Doodletown Road. Just west of Lemmon Road, a large tree with broken macadam paving and a few large rocks around its base may be seen on the right. Behind that tree was the second Doodletown school, built in the late 1800s as Schoolhouse #7 of the Stony Point School District. After 1926, the old school was used for square dances and community events. It was demolished by the Park in 1960.

12. Paved Doodletown Road sweeps around the reservoir and crosses Doodletown Brook on a culvert. Before the reservoir was built, the road went straight down to the water and crossed the brook on a low cement bridge. The old road can still be seen, and the surface of the bridge (known as "The Riding Bridge") is just below the surface of the reservoir. The old Dunderberg Turnpike (formerly known as the Caldwell Turnpike) crossed this low region just north of the June cemetery on the knoll. The old road is now under the reservoir.

13. At the end of the reservoir, there is a T-intersection. The road to the left goes to the Second June Cemetery. Doodletown Road turns right and goes uphill for about 500 feet to a junction with Pleasant Valley Road, which departs to the left and goes uphill, while Doodletown Road continues straight ahead. At the junction, on the right side, was the Montville Community Church (Montville was another name for Doodletown). Although it was a Methodist Church, it was not a member of the Methodist Conference. This was Doodletown's second church, built in 1889. There were five rows of pews in the church, but no stained glass. When the church was demolished in 1965, the pews and the bell were given to the Episcopal Church of Jones Point.

14. Across from the church was the home of Mildred Stember, who married Mr. Seigel. She sold it to Schoenfeld, who in turn sold it to the Park in 1962. The driveway and the clearing for the house are covered with vines and other undergrowth.

15. Up the road from the church there is a clearing on the right—the site of the new (1926) school, near a great hickory tree. It was a impressive fieldstone building. From the front lobby, a set of steps led up to a hallway, off of which were two classrooms. In the basement, there was a coal furnace for hot-air heat. An electric generator was installed in 1938 to light the classrooms. In the 1950s, there was only one teacher who taught all the children, from kindergarten to sixth grade. After acquiring the school in the early 1960s, the Park kept it for use as part of the ski center that was dreamed of by Superintendent McManus. The ski center was never constructed, and the school was vandalized over time. It was demolished in 1984.

New Doodletown School, 1961

16. Doodletown Brook now crosses the road, and just beyond on the left is a driveway. The home of Joseph and Estelle June was on the drive under spruce trees. Remains of the cow barn, hen house, and apple and pear orchard can still be seen in the clearings behind the site of the house. The last to live there were Luther Stalter, Jr. (a grandson of John Stalter) and his wife Caroline (June).

17. Next up the road on the left is a great pine tree and a driveway which led to the home of May Brown, the school nurse, and her artist son Eugene. The last owner was Clarence June, Jr., who moved in during the 1950s. He subsequently sold this house to the Park and moved to #27.

18. A little further, just off the road on the right, is a great willow tree. There stood the 100-year-old home of Clarence and Irene June. For many years, Clarence was responsible for plowing the Doodletown roads during snowstorms.

19. Next on the right, a low concrete retaining wall is visible. It marks the site of the McLean home, built in the 1950s and sold to the Park in 1962.

20. Two hundred feet up the road, on the left, there is a stone wall high up on the hill, and a flight of concrete steps going up. A driveway just beyond led to the home of Roland and Modesta Bambino (she was a granddaughter of Caleb M. June). They sold out in 1959.

21. A driveway on the right side of the road, opposite the Bambino steps, marks the site of the home of Belding Rose and his mother Cornelia (a daughter of Caleb M. June). Belding lived there until he died in 1949. Their barn was down to the right; wild roses are there now.

22. About 500 feet further uphill, a side road, known as "The Lane," may be seen on the left. On that side road, the first house on the left was the bungalow of Frank and Dora (June) Seely, sold in 1961. Next on the left was the home of Wilbur and Violet Lauber (to 1962). To the right was the last home of Caleb A. and Ida June (to 1961). Further to the left was the home of Charles and Dorothy Lauber (to 1962). The clearings for and driveways to these homes are still visible.

23. On the hilltop, to the left of Caleb A. June's home, was the home of John and Elaine (June) DeCoteau. It was sold in 1961.

24. Go back now, down to the junction of Doodletown and Pleasant Valley Roads, and turn right onto Pleasant Valley Road. On the right, about 300 feet up the road, there is a large hemlock and a driveway that led to the house of Oscar and Minnie Herbert. Just before the hemlock, there are steps in the wall along the road. These led to the store which the Herberts kept on their lower floor. Oscar also had a blacksmith shop. A fence protected their cow and their apple trees.

25. The 1777W Trail now leaves on the right. Then, between a horse chestnut and a maple tree, was the home, around the turn of the 20th century, of Isaac "Ike" and Elizabeth (Welch) Scandell. It was the residence of Howard and Naomi (June) Urnaz Lewis from the 1940s until its acquisition by the Park in 1964.

26. About 250 feet further along, a road goes left to the Herbert Cemetery. Opposite the cemetery road, there is a stone retaining wall and a driveway which led to one of the homes of Caleb A. and Ida June, located south of a large ash tree. In later years, this was the home of Grace and Denzel Livingston and their children. Denzel is Caleb A. June's grandson.

27. In another 400 feet, on the right, is a paved driveway that led to the home of Jacob Newell. He sold it to the Park in 1928. After that, it was rented to Joseph Savignac. Also living there was his son-in-law, Art Pohl, who was a road supervisor for the Park. He paved his drive with macadam left over at the end of his day's work. Last to live there was Clarence June, Jr. His family was the last to leave Doodletown—on January 16, 1965. The house was set back rather far from the road, and it was close to the Bridle Path that was built later in 1934-35. One of Clarence's clothesline poles (with pulleys still attached) may be seen on the west side of the Bridle Path. And just east of the Path, the stone foundation of a spring house is still visible.

28. Another 125 feet up the road, on the right, a driveway leads uphill to a house near a blue spruce tree that was owned by Mr. King. After he sold it, the Park rented it to John Rose, and then to the Bowers. A small bungalow was next door.

29. The next house on the right was high on a knoll, with two foundations below on the road—one, of a garage, and the other of a shop. It belonged to Mr. Thomas, a watchmaker at the Iona Island arsenal, whose daughter worked at the Trailside Zoo. He sold out in the 1950s and moved to California. The stone foundation of the house may be seen on top of the knoll, and two iron pipes are visible along the hillside.

30. On the right side of the road, about 150 feet before the Bridle Path crossing, a highway monument is visible, surrounded by tree roots. This monument was put there by the WPA in 1933.

31. Just beyond the Bridle Path, on the right, a low stone wall and a clearing mark the site of the home of retired New York City physician Dr. W.B. Robinson. His large two-story house, which had a stone chimney, was just west of a big sugar maple. Nearby was a large barn. Dr. Robinson's son Lee, who worked for the Park, was the last owner.

32. Dr. Robinson's son George lived next door in a brick home. His wife, Millie, grew spectacular flowers, shrubs, vegetables and fruit trees. Their property was surrounded by a tall fence. A great rhododendron bush is there now.

33. Across the road from the Robinson estate (#31), a driveway next to a low stone wall goes uphill to the Howard and Anna Scandell site. Their house was one of the oldest homes in Doodletown. After their heirs sold it in 1927, it was demolished. The foundation is still there, and it is worth a visit.

34. After descending briefly, there is a row of spruce trees on the right side of the road. Here was a home once owned by Lee Robinson. He sold the house to Luther Stalter, Sr., a stone mason, who added a fieldstone veneer and porches. "Luke," who was a son of John Stalter, also built a barn by the brook, which was used for square dancing. Chauncey Pease was the last owner, holding out until 1962.

35. Pleasant Valley Road now crosses Timp Brook on a concrete bridge. Just beyond the brook crossing, on the right, was the home of James (Jim) Hurley, Sr. and his wife Edna. Jim was a Park ranger; Edna was one of the eight children of John and Elmira Stalter (they had three sons: John, Luke and Gerald). Son John was a carpenter; Gerald was the foreman at Lake Kanawauke. John and Elmira had bought the place in 1918 from Calvin Tomkins. When John, Sr. died in 1920, Elmira continued to live here with her daughter and son-in-law.

36. Just at the top of the rise, before two huge spruce trees, a driveway goes right. Here, to the right of the driveway, Nelson and Elizabeth Rose built their home on an 0.3-acre parcel purchased from Elizabeth's mother, Elmira Stalter, in 1946. In 1950, they sold the home to their nephew Gerald Stalter, Jr. (Ed) and his wife Elizabeth (Perk). For a time, Gerald, Jr. ran an auto wrecking business there. When the Stalters sold their home to the Park and left Doodletown in 1959, they dismantled their home (which they had recently remodeled) and used the salvaged materials in their subsequent homes. The stone foundation is still there, to the right of the driveway.

37. Next on the west side of the road was a large 58-acre parcel which once was the site of the home of John and Elmira Stalter. They sold to Charles Oakley in 1915 and later moved nearby to #35, which they bought in 1918. Elmira was a Bulson, born at Beechy Bottom. John was a woodcutter who came over from Verplancks about 1887. He was mentioned several times by William Thompson Howell in his diary *The Hudson Highlands*. Elmira (1862-1948) and John (1852-1920) are buried in the Herbert Cemetery. James Hurley, Jr., now retired, was one of the last Stalter family members on the Park's work force.

38. Across the road from Gerald Stalter, Jr.'s driveway was the two-story frame dwelling of Jeremiah Bailey. He raised chickens which ran around everywhere nearby. About 1940, the place was bought by Louis Salit of New York City. It was due to his persistent efforts that Rockland Light and Power Co. brought electricity to Doodletown in 1949. He sold his place to the Park in 1961.

39. 0.35 mile south of Timp Brook, at the very end of Pleasant Valley Road, another brook crosses. Here, to the left of the road, are the remains of a small bungalow and the walls of a garage (now a shelter) on 1.7 acres. The remains of a pond and dam are also visible. The bungalow had been the home of Mary Moore, who sold it to the Park in 1928. The Park rented it to a Mr. Chandler of New York City; then, about 1932, it was rented to the Riverside Church of New York City for use as a summer camp until 1953. The bungalow was demolished in 1954, and its stone chimney was knocked down by the Park in 1991 as a safety measure.

Doodletown Bridle Path

Length: 6.35 miles round trip

Miles

0.0 Tunnel under Seven Lakes Drive.

0.05 Tunnel under South Entrance Road.

0.5 Cornell Mine Trail begins, left.

0.8 1777E Trail (returning loop of Path), left.

0.95 Covered reservoir, right.

1.0 Cross Lemmon Road.

1.75 S-BM joins.

2.25 Turn right on Doodletown Road; S-BM leaves; 1777W joins.

2.8 Turn left; 1777W leaves; AT parallels Path.

3.0 Fawn Trail, right.

3.05 AT goes up, right.

3.7 S-BM joins, left.

3.85 S-BM leaves, right.

4.0 Cross Doodlekill.

4.35 Cross Pleasant Valley Road (1777 Trail).

4.65 Cross Timp Brook.

5.2 Old Turnpike goes right.

5.35 Cross bridge.

5.45 Cross Doodletown Road; go up with 1777E Trail.

5.55 Rejoin north loop.

The Bridle Path starts at the south edge of the South Parking Area at Bear Mountain, near the Administration Building. At first, it runs jointly with the 1777E Trail. It goes through a tunnel under Seven Lakes Drive, then turns right from the paved path and goes through another tunnel under the South Entrance Road. It then passes above a field where old cars are "stored." In the 1920s, that field was used for pony rides; it later became a police pistol range. After 0.5 mile, the Cornell Mine Trail (blue) begins to the left, and in another 0.3 mile the 1777E Trail (which is also the returning loop of the Bridle Path) departs to the left. Soon a large

281

covered reservoir—part of the Doodletown water system—may be seen on the right. In another 150 feet, the Bridle Path crosses Lemmon Road. The Path now swings north and parallels the Seven Lakes Drive. At 1.75 miles, the Suffern-Bear Mountain Trail (S-BM) (yellow) enters from the hillside on the right. This section of the S-BM was scouted and blazed in 1926 by Raymond Torrey. His route was later incorporated into the Bridle Path.

At 2.25 miles, the Path turns right on old Doodletown Road. Just beyond this point, as the road curves to the right, the S-BM departs to the left, while the 1777W Trail comes in from the left and joins the Path. The Path continues along the road, reaching the Appalachian Trail (AT) (white) at 2.8 miles. Here, the Path turns left, while 1777W continues straight ahead. The AT, built in 1923, used an old woods road here. The Bridle Path builders chose to avoid that rocky old road and built a parallel route to the left, but after a short distance the two trails rejoin. Soon, the Fawn Trail (red F on white) leaves to the right, and then the AT leaves to the right and goes up to West Mountain.

The Path, now at an altitude of about 650 feet, starts a mile-long descent to elevation 400 feet, where it crosses Pleasant Valley Road. On the way, it runs jointly with the S-BM for 0.15 mile, then crosses the Doodlekill. After crossing Pleasant Valley Road (the route of the 1777 Trail), the Path drops more steeply to cross Timp Brook. It then climbs again and descends to cross Doodletown Brook below the dam on a pretty stone bridge. The Path now joins Doodletown Road for a bit, then (jointly with the 1777E Trail) goes up an old road to rejoin the outgoing loop.

The Bridle Path was built during 1934-35 by workmen from New York City supplied by the Temporary Emergency Relief Administration (TERA). It was opened to the public on Sunday, May 5, 1935. It was intended for use as a ski trail as well as for horses.

On May 7, 1937, permission was granted to a Highland Falls stable to furnish and maintain riding horses at Bear Mountain State Park for rental to the public. Fourteen saddle horses were supplied and rented for $1.50 per hour.

The Bergen Evening Record of January 10, 1961 stated that 40 horses were stabled at Bear Mountain. They served 25,000 riders per year. At the end of 1961, it was determined that conditions at the stable were not fit for horses. The operation was discontinued, and the stable demolished.

Doodletown Waterworks

There are two reservoirs in Doodletown: an open pond behind the dam (1975) on Doodletown Brook, and a covered reservoir near the junction of the Bridle Path with Lemmon Road. Below the dam is a filtration plant—the source of water to the installations on Iona Island.

The covered reservoir on the Bridle Path has a capacity of 660,000 gallons. It is connected by a six-inch pipe under the Bridle Path to another reservoir on Bear Mountain above Hessian Lake. The latter has a capacity of 500,000 gallons. Those two tanks are both at 350 feet altitude and can fill one another. Normally, the water is sent by gravity from Queensboro Reservoir through the Popolopen Aqueduct to the reservoir above Hessian Lake, and from there to the Doodletown covered reservoir.

A pipe was also laid from Queensboro Lake down Doodletown Road to deliver water into Doodletown Brook, which leads to the open reservoir. If necessary, water from the water plant at the open reservoir can be pumped up to the covered reservoir on the Bridle Path, and thence to the reservoir on Bear Mountain.

Water from the reservoir on Bear Mountain is pumped to the Perkins Memorial Tower, to the Bear Mountain Inn and to the other buildings at Bear Mountain. Overlook Lodge has a separate reservoir, also supplied from Queensboro Lake.

THE
DUNDERBERG SPIRAL
RAILWAY

This railway was a project started in 1890 and abandoned, unfinished, in 1891. Only parts of the railway bed had been graded, and it is these parts that hikers see as they explore the mountain.

The easiest approach to the railway is the blue-blazed Timp-Torne Trail (T-T). About 0.2 mile from its start on Route 9W (at the road leading to Jones Point), the trail goes up stone steps and passes above a 100-foot-long masonry tunnel. The railway cars were to be drawn up by cable from the river level, over that tunnel. The final descending leg of the railway was to pass through the tunnel.

From the tunnel, the cars were to have been drawn up by cable to a loop at the 500-foot level. There the route changed to a westerly direction and continued up to the 900-foot summit. The prepared grade can be followed almost to the top of the mountain. When the obvious grade ends, hikers can climb over the top. The Ramapo-Dunderberg Trail (R-D) (red dot on white) is just beyond.

Follow the R-D west for about 0.3 mile—it will meet another level of the graded railway bed. Followed left (south), that level will arrive in 0.2 mile at the upper end of the Jones Trail, a woods road which descends to the right. Go down on the Jones Trail, which is pretty clear for a short way because until 1991 it was used to maintain an air-sensing station of Orange and Rockland Utilities. The trail gets rougher as it goes down along a brook. In 0.35 mile, the Timp-Torne Trail crosses. Turn left on the T-T and cross a brook. On the other side of the brook, to the left, is one end of another great, unfinished tunnel. Continue east on the T-T—it leads to the other end of the tunnel. On the way around, there is a beautiful view of the Haverstraw Bay to the south. You can take the T-T all the way back to the start of the hike—for 0.3 mile beyond the tunnel, it follows another grade of the railway.

One can attempt to hike the entire 10-mile route of the railway or incorporate parts of the route in a day's outing. It is always astonishing to see how much work was accomplished in that one year, only to be abandoned to Mother Nature.

The Spiral Railway project was promoted in 1889 by Henry J. Mumford of Mauch Chunk (now Jim Thorpe), Pa. In 1870, he and his brother leased from the Central Railroad of New Jersey the abandoned Mauch Chunk, Summit Hill and Switchback Railroad. It had been built in 1826 to haul coal from Summit Hill to the Lehigh River at Mauch Chunk. Mumford operated it successfully as a pleasure ride for visitors from New York City and Philadelphia. The passenger cars were pulled by cable up the mountain and returned to the base by gravity.

Mumford and his associates chose to build a spiral railway on Dunderberg Mountain, realizing that it was easily accessible from New York City by the Hudson River steamships and the recently completed West Shore Railroad. The Dunderberg Spiral Railway was incorporated on November 9, 1889. 7,500 shares of stock, worth $100 each, were issued. Mumford bought 200 shares.

Work on the mountain started in the spring of 1890. About ten gangs of laborers began in various places to create the railbed. One of the first parts to near completion was the lower tunnel—a beautiful example of stone-mason work. Bids were prepared by the Wright Steam Engine Works of Newburgh for the engines which were to haul the cars up the mountain. After a year, the enterprise faltered for lack of funds. A series of questionable deals by the Holland Trust Company—which was financing the Spiral Railway—came to light in 1890, and investors became more reluctant to risk their money. Mumford could not meet his bills or pay his workers. After about $1,000,000 had been spent, work ended in the spring of 1891, and the workers rioted. The project was completely abandoned, and soon grass and trees were growing where rails had never been laid.

The story of the Dunderberg Spiral Railway was related by George

Plan of Dunderberg Spiral Railway

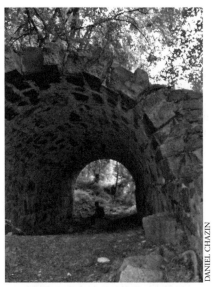

Lower tunnel of the Dunderberg Spiral Railway

E. Goldthwaite of AMC (*Appalachia*, November 1935), by Priscilla Chipman (*In the Hudson Highlands*, AMC, 1945, pp. 196-201), and by John Scott ("South of the Mountains," *Journal of the Rockland County Historical Society*, Jan. 1989). For a detailed website on the railway, by Joseph Brennan, go to www.columbia.edu/~brennan/dunderberg/.

Dunderberg Mountain itself has an interesting history. In 1791, Joshua Cholwill bought land from Caleb Seaman at the tip of Dunderberg Mountain. Cholwill (later changed to Caldwell) kept a tavern and ran a ferry across the river to Peekskill. A town named Gibraltar was laid out there in 1833. Then in 1836 Joshua T. Jones bought 100 acres of the Brad-ley/Jamison Patent on the east side of Dunderberg, including a hotel and dock on the waterfront. Eventually, the Jones family bought most of Dunderberg Mountain.

In 1883, when the West Shore Railroad was completed from Weehawken, N.J. to Albany, a station and post office were established at the foot of Dunderberg Mountain. Two years later, the Jones family managed to get the name of the locality changed from Caldwell's Landing to Jones Point, in memory of Charles H. Jones (brother of Joshua T. Jones), a major landowner on Dunderberg, who had recently died. The name change was not well received by many local residents.

The Jones family sold land on the

mountaintop to the Spiral Railway company. When the railway went bankrupt, the mountaintop became the property of Rockland County, which sold it to the Park in 1913. The rest of the railway right-of-way was acquired by the Park on December 31, 1938. Then in 1951 the remaining 640 acres of the Mary E. Jones estate were bought by the Park for $25,000—a gift of Laurance S. Rockefeller. This last purchase included most of the land on the east side of the mountain, below the railway loop at the 500-foot level, and the sand quarries where the Timp-Torne Trail now starts and where the R-D ends.

As the railway bed became increasingly hidden in new growth, hikers occasionally stumbled across it and enjoyed following the route. One such hiker was William Thompson Howell (1873-1916), son of Charles Howell of Newburgh who had prepared bids for the cable engines. William Howell was a hiker and photographer who worked for the New York Telephone Company. He often hiked with the Fresh Air Club, a branch of the New York Athletic Club. His diary, first published privately by Frederick Delano Weekes in 1933-34, was reprinted in 1982 by Walking News, Inc. (Weekes, who was one of the oldest members of the Fresh Air Club, died on May 24, 1936, aged 84 years.)

Howell's diary entry for May 30, 1906 describes a climb up the north side of Dunderberg on a woods road (our Bockberg Trail). A flume-like slide had been built along the road, down which cordwood was slid to the river level. At the top, Howell met John Stalter, the woodcutter, whom he had previously met on April 2. (Stalter, who lived in Doodletown, was given a contract in 1908 to build part of an improved State road—since abandoned—around Dunderberg to Jones Point.)

In March 1908, Howell was picking his way down another old road, now called the Jones Trail, when he discovered the "pretentious" upper tunnel and a magnificent view south to Haverstraw Bay.

THE LAKES IN BEAR MOUNTAIN/ HARRIMAN PARK

There are thirty-six lakes and ponds in the Park. Fourteen of these are natural water bodies, some of which have been enlarged by the construction of dams. The others are entirely man-made. Some information about these lakes is shown in the table that follows.

Soon after he began his duties in 1912 as General Manager and Chief Engineer, Major William A. Welch began the construction of many lakes in the Park. At first, the lakes were given numbers—Hessian Lake was Lake No. 1, Tiorati was Lake No. 2, and so on. In 1918, Major Welch sought the advice of Dr. E.H. Hall, secretary of the American Scenic and Historic Preservation Society, for assistance in naming the Park lakes. Dr. Hall made numerous suggestions, few of which were accepted by Major Welch. Instead, Welch favored names from the Mohegan Indian tongue: TIORATEE meant "blue like the sky"; KANAWAHKEE meant "place of much water"; STAHAHE meant "stones in the water." The Major's wife Camille was also interested in Indian lore, and offered suggestions.

Name of Lake	Dam Number	Date of Dam
Askoti	22	1935
Barnes		1913
Breakneck Pond		1888
Brooks		
Cohasset, Upper	9	1922
Cohasset, Lower	8	1919
Green Pond		
Hessian	1	1914
Island Pond		
Kanawauke, Upper		
Kanawauke, Middle	6	1916
Kanawauke, Lower	3	1915
Letchworth Reservoirs		
First Reservoir		1912
Second Reservoir		1927
Third Reservoir		1951
Lily Pond		
Massawippa	15	1934
Nawahunta	4	1915
Pine Meadow	13	1934
Queensboro	5	1915
Reynolds Pond		
Sebago	10	1925
Silvermine	20	1934
Skannatati	23	1938
Skenonto	18	1935
Spring Pond		1919
Spruce Pond		
Stahahe	7	1918
Summit		1873
Te Ata	11	1927
Tiorati	2	1915
Turkey Hill	14	1934
Twin, Upper		1850
Twin, Lower		1850
Wanoksink	16	1934
Welch	12	1942
Unfinished or Destroyed:		
Minsi	17	1934
Oonotookwa	21	1934
Owl	19	1934

Elevation	Size (Acres)	Shore Line (Miles)	Other Names, etc.
914	41.0	1.3	Upper Stillwater Lake
894	14.7	0.7	Acquired 8/27/21
1,083	66.0	2.0	Cranberry Reservoir
139	25.5	0.8	
901	40.0	1.5	
863	13.0	0.7	
	0.2		
156	32.8	1.2	Highland Lake
961	51.4	1.3	
828	46.0		Little Long Pond
828	62.0	5.7	
828	77.5		
690	10.0	0.5	
947	14.0	0.9	
1,076	31.4	1.2	
	3.2		
830	32.4	1.3	Brooks Hollow
781	15.2	0.7	
972	77.5	2.3	
453	35.0	1.5	
772	310.6	6.5	
715	83.9	1.7	Menomine
891	38.3	1.5	second dam built 1947
830	37.0	1.4	Big Swamp
872	2.7	0.3	old dam repaired 1934
728	4.8		
715	88.2	3.2	Car Pond
1,065	33.7	1.3	
859	31.0	1.2	
1,032	291.0	4.8	
610	58.4	1.9	
896	21.6	0.8	
861	22.7	1.1	
1,030	38.0	1.7	Christie Brook No. 1
1,015	216.0	2.9	Beaver Pond
1,070	30.0		destroyed 1984
980	70.5		Pine Meadow No. 2
712	52.0		destroyed 1987

Lake Askoti

Going south from Lake Tiorati, Seven Lakes Drive originally descended a valley called Deep Hollow and went along the edge of a swamp through which Stillwater Creek ran. In 1935, the Works Progress Administration built a dam across the creek, creating Upper Stillwater Lake. The road was rebuilt to cross the dam. By 1937, when the lake was filled with water, it had been given a new name: Askoti, which means "this side."

An old woods road goes around the south end of the lake and then climbs gradually up Rockhouse Mountain along the east side of the lake. From 1944 to 1947, that road was part of the new Red Cross Trail. The trail joined the Hasenclever Road near the mine. At present, the Red Cross Trail starts on Pine Swamp Mountain, which is west of Lake Askoti. It goes across the north end of Lake Askoti and uses a new route to the Hasenclever Road.

Another woods road, which presently carries the Long Path, goes south from the dam. From 1963 to 1981, this road was part of the Skannatati Trail to Big Hill Shelter.

Barnes Lake

Once known as Lake Miltana, Barnes Lake is on Route 293, about 0.5 mile north of the entrance to Summit Lake on Route 6. The Park acquired it in 1921 from J. Milton Barnes for $15,000. (Also included were 86 acres which extended to the top of the ridge to the east.) During that year, the lake was used for bathing and boating by children from the Central Jewish Institute of New York City. The 120 boys and girls were housed in Stockbridge's Summit Lake House at the entrance to Summit Lake (the YWCA had the use of Summit Lake).

Barnes Lake is fed by Popolopen Creek, which runs north from Summit Lake. It is a natural lake which was somewhat enlarged in 1913, during J. Milton Barnes' time, by a dam at the north end.

There still are eight private cottages near the lake, rented by the Park to the Central Valley Colony Club. Mr. Barnes stipulated in the deed that the members of the club were to have a lifetime right of occupancy. After the original club members had all died, the Park sought to acquire the cottages. But the heirs started a lawsuit, claiming that they had a right to continued occupancy. Rather than fight them in court, the Park has permitted them to remain.

The land across the highway from Barnes Lake was acquired by the Park in 1955. The Long Path is now marked through there.

Breakneck Pond

The *New York Times* reported on April 8, 1928 that Governor Smith had signed an act providing for the transfer of title to Breakneck Pond from the Rockland Finishing Company of Haverstraw to the Commissioners of the Palisades Interstate Park. The pond, it was stated, "is the source of the north branch of Minisceongo (Crooked Water) Creek."

Previously called Cranberry Pond or Cranberry Reservoir by the local residents, Breakneck Pond is a natural lake that was enlarged by a dam in 1888. Its outlet is Beaver Pond Brook, which goes into Lake Welch. The Long Path crosses that brook on a pretty wooden footbridge—where a generation of older hikers crossed on a beaver dam.

To the northwest of the pond is Cranberry Mountain, sold to the Park in 1928 by William Huffman. To the southeast is Breakneck Mountain, once called Knapp Mountain, and owned by Emma Knapp until 1917. Two unmarked trails come down from Breakneck Mountain, near the north end of the pond. Another trail goes along the eastern shore and south through laurels, to end at a cairn on Pine Meadow Road (see p. 28).

Camp Winake of the Rockland County Council, Boy Scouts of America, was opened in 1930 at Breakneck Pond. Winake, which means "a pleasant place," was the Algonquin name of the home of William P. Abbott, an active member of the Council's camp committee in 1927. Later, the camp became known as Camp Lanowa, operated by Homes for Homeless Children.

In 2005, Camp Lanowa moved from the Breakneck Pond site to its current location on Upper Twin Lake. Since then, the camp (the only camp on Breakneck Pond) has been unoccupied. As of 2010, it is being renovated by the New York State Department of Environmental Conservation, which is planning to operate another children's camp there once renovations have been completed.

The paved Park road going northeast from the Pond joins the Old Turnpike. That road comes from Willow Grove, meets the old (now abandoned) St. John's Road, and ends at Lake Welch Drive.

Brooks Lake

On the north side of Popolopen Creek, near the village of Fort Montgomery, most of the land between the brook and Mine Road is part of Bear Mountain State Park. The Park also owns a parcel of land on the north side of Mine Road, which includes Brooks Lake.

The lake and about 100 acres to the north were acquired by the Park in 1918 from the heirs of Eliza Brooks. At that time, an aerial tramway crossed above the south side of the lake. Iron ore from the Forest of Dean Mine was carried in little railway cars to a point on the eastern slope of the Popolopen Torne. There it was transferred to the tramway and carried for one mile to boats at the river edge below the town.

The West Point Aqueduct, built in 1906, goes across the hillside north of the lake. In 1925, there were five camps at Brooks Lake. The area around the lake was improved in 1934 for camping, bathing and picnicking. The Brooks Lake Trail, which circles the lake, was built in 2004.

Upper and Lower Cohasset Lakes

There are two Cohasset Lakes, both on Arden Valley Road. (The name Cohasset means "place of pines.") The lower lake, completed in 1919, was the eighth lake made by the Park. A 1923 map by Camps Director Ruby Jolliffe showed four girls' camps there (*N.Y. Post*, 5/18/23). They were used by the YWCA of the Oranges, by the Hebrew Orphan Asylum, and by the Settlement Houses. (Today, the lower lake is generally known as Lake Cohasset.)

Upper Lake Cohasset—only a short distance from the lower lake—was created in 1922. The construction of this lake required realignment of Arden Valley Road. It also cut off the junction between Surebridge Mine Road and Arden Valley Road. By 1947, five camps and a nature museum had been built on Upper Cohasset Lake. The nature museum has been closed for a number of years.

These two lakes were called "Eden without Adams," because only girls were seen there. An occasional visitor during the 1930s was Eleanor Roosevelt, wife of Governor Franklin D. Roosevelt.

Two heights familiar to hikers look down upon Upper Cohasset Lake: the northeast end of Echo Mountain (the Long Path goes up there from Surebridge Mine Road), and a rocky summit southeast of the lake, known as Paradise Rock, which can be reached by bushwhacking up from the

Long Path. A shelter was built on each of these heights, at private expense, for the use of the campers. The one on Echo Mountain is still in good condition. In 1937, Camps Director Ruby Jolliffe had pipes installed to send water to the Paradise Rock Shelter. For some reason unknown to the author, that shelter was later removed. All that remains are some pipes and a trash barrel.

Green Pond

Green Pond is familiar to hikers who walk the Dunning Trail. It lies in the hills west of Lake Stahahe and south of Island Pond, and is about 0.1 mile west of Island Pond Road. Green Pond is a tiny pond, whose shoreline is only 0.15 mile, but the marsh on its south side, which drains west into Lake Stahahe, is six or seven times as large. In 1918, during the early years of camping at Lake Stahahe, a pipeline brought fresh water down from Green Pond (*PIPC Annual Report*, 1/31/19).

Hessian Lake

The pond at the foot of Bear Mountain had been known since 1740 as Lake Sinnipink, from the Indian name of the nearby creek—Assinapink. When the British attacked Fort Clinton on October 6, 1777, there was a wall of sharpened logs between the pond and the edge of the cliff overlooking the Hudson River. After the battle, because many bodies of Hessian chasseurs had been thrown into the pond, it became known as Bloody Pond (Lossing, *Pictorial Field Book of the Revolution*). In later years, it was given more genteel names—Highland Lake, then Hessian Lake. During the nineteenth century, ice was cut from the lake by the Knickerbocker Ice Company and shipped to New York City.

In 1911, the year after Bear Mountain State Park was created, a great playground was cleared near the lake. In 1913, Boy Scouts were camping on the lakeshore, and a trail was made to the top of Bear Mountain. In 1914, the lake, which is spring-fed and 40 feet deep, was slightly enlarged by the construction of three small dams.

Island Pond

Island Pond is a natural lake with rocky shores at the north end, and extensive marshes at the south end. It has two outlets: one drains to the north into Echo Lake; the other goes south, draining into Stahahe Brook. About halfway down the pond and 500 feet from shore is the island which gives the pond its name. To the west is a ridge known as Green Pond Mountain. To the northeast is the southern peak of Echo Mountain, which hikers have always called Island Pond Mountain.

The lake and surrounding hills were part of the estate of iron maker Peter Parrott, acquired in 1885 by Edward H. Harriman. At the top of Island Pond Mountain, Harriman built a summer house (the big stones up there were the foundation) and a fire tower of wooden poles.

When Edward Harriman's widow Mary Averell Harriman gave 10,000 acres to the Palisades Interstate Park Commission in 1910, Island Pond was not part of the gift. The family retained the pond for their own use. The Park boundary on the east side of the pond was a road that came south from Echo Lake. After passing Island Pond, this "Crooked Road" turned uphill over Surebridge Mountain (its route is now used by the Dunning Trail). In 1921, the Boy Scouts' White Bar Trail came down from the Lemon Squeezer to that road. Where the road went left and started uphill, White Bar went south on a newly cut trail to Highway 416 (now Route 106). The Boy Scouts' Camp Deerslayer was located along that trail, 0.3 mile north of Route 106.

On the west side of the pond was Island Pond Road, which came up from the Harriman farm by several switchbacks, then went around the south end of the lake and continued on southward to Highway 416. Built by Edward Harriman in 1905, the road originally started at the Greenwood Furnace in Arden.

In 1927, in an exchange of land, Roland Harriman gave Island Pond to the Park. In return, he received a narrow strip of land near Echo Lake that his mother had given to the Park in 1910. When the Park became its owner, plans were made to improve Island Pond. In 1930, the road on the west side was widened to 20 feet, graded, and covered with gravel for three miles from the Harriman farm south to the state highway near Lake Stahahe. In the same year, the new Arden Valley Road, which came closer to Island Pond and avoided entering the Harriman estate, was built.

At the south end of the pond, on a point of land, the Park built a stone cabin for the Park ranger. Major Welch entertained visitors there. A young man from Johnsontown named Muzz Jones worked there as a part-time cook, caretaker and patrolman. Muzz later became a ranger on the Park

Ruins of ranger cabin at Island Pond

police force. He was the last resident of Johnsontown, where he lived until the new Sebago Beach was opened. The cabin at the south end of Island Pond was burned by vandals on January 1, 1962.

A short distance from the pond, along the northern outlet, an old unfinished stone dam can be seen. Beyond that is a more modern but also unfinished spillway made of cut stones. Near the spillway is part of a rotary gravel classifier.

About 1905, Edward Harriman started to build that stone dam. He also built a road from the dam to his Island Pond Road (*Rockland County Times*, 2/13/08). However, he abandoned the dam, which was used in later years by beavers for their own purposes. In 1930, gravel for the new Arden Valley Road was removed from the nearby hillside, by way of the convenient road to the old dam.

In 1934, with the labor force of the Civilian Conservation Corps available, the Park again planned to improve Island Pond. Plans were developed to build two dams, at the north and south ends, which would greatly enlarge the lake by extending it into the southern marshy region. Work was begun by cutting the brush along the lake shores. Also, a new level road to the lake was made from the new Arden Valley Road. It ran south along the hillside to join the older Harriman switchback road. In 1934, too, the Park began to build the northern dam, the spillway of which can still be seen. For some reason, these plans were canceled, and Raymond H.

Torrey wrote: "Those who know the beauty of Island Pond with its border of swamp vegetation will be glad to know that the plan to raise its level by heightening its dam at its north end, and by another dam at its south outlet, has been abandoned" (*N.Y. Post*, 2/8/35).

In November 1957, the Park built the William Brien Memorial Shelter on the ledge where the Appalachian Trail approached the north end of the pond. The project was funded by the bequest of William Brien, first president of the New York Ramblers, who died on October 12, 1954. A pump was also installed at the shelter.

In the spring of 1963, a new entrance was made to Island Pond from Arden Valley Road. A parking area was constructed near the shelter to accommodate fishermen's cars (they paid $1 a day for parking). In the years that followed, the easily accessible shelter became the scene of midnight parties and excessive littering. As a result, the shelter was dismantled in 1973, and Letterrock Shelter was renamed the William Brien Memorial Shelter. In 1980, the Appalachian Trail was relocated away from the north end of the pond, but the route along the north end of the pond was restored in 1993.

Lower Kanawauke Lake

This lake was created in 1915 by damming Stony Brook about 0.4 mile above Johnsontown (where Sebago Beach was later created). Boy Scout camping began there in 1917, and by 1930 there were fourteen camps around the lake.

During the construction of Lower Kanawauke Lake, old Goodspring Road was relocated. This road had run from St. John's Road, near Lily Pond, to the Monroe-Haverstraw Turnpike (now Route 106), following Stony Brook. It is now a camp road which ends at a gate on Route 106, 0.1 mile west of the Kanawauke Circle.

The Onondaga name KANAWAHKEE, which means "place of much water," was chosen in 1918 by Major Welch from a book by W.M. Beauchamp, *Indian Names in New York* (Fayetteville, N.Y., 1893).

Middle Kanawauke Lake

This lake was made in 1916 by damming Stillwater Creek where it went under the Monroe-Haverstraw Turnpike (now Route 106). The road was sent across the dam, and the big swamp on the north side became a lake. Six Boy Scout camps were opened in 1917 on Middle Kanawauke Lake. The decayed, abandoned camp in the woods north of the lake once was K-9—Camp Leeming.

Middle Kanawauke Lake was the location of the summer camping headquarters of the Brooklyn Boy Scout Council. Harvey A. Gordon was chief camp director. Beginning in 1921, the Scouts built a 35-mile system of hiking trails, known as the White Bar Trail system, with five spokes radiating from the camps on Middle Kanawauke Lake (see p. 147).

Upper Kanawauke Lake: Little Long Pond

This 43-foot-deep natural lake on Route 106 (old Route 210) drains into Middle Kanawauke Lake. At the west end of the lake, the old Johnson-town Road ends at Route 106. The old road now serves as the entrance to the Haverstraw Masons' Camp. One hundred fifty years ago, there were homes near Upper Kanawauke Lake, inhabited by the Johnsons, Conklins, Hills and Joneses.

Boy Scout camps were built at Little Long Pond in 1917. A 1930 Park map shows seven camps there. On the hillside north of the lake, on the old Crooked Road, was the Boy Scouts' Camp Matinecock (which subsequently became a Girl Scout camp, known as Camp Quid Nunc—see p. 180).

Letchworth Reservoirs

Letchworth Village State Developmental Center was a New York State custodial institution on Willow Grove Road, just east of the Palisades Interstate Parkway. It was founded in 1908 by William Pryor Letchworth, and named for him in 1909. He died on December 1, 1910 at the age of 88. Letchworth Village was closed in 1996.

In 1908, the far-sighted planners bought 640 acres in the hills drained by Horse Chock Brook, a branch of Minisceongo Creek. This was to be used for water supply (*Rockland County Times*, 2/13/08).

At present, there are three Letchworth reservoirs. The Park has acquired the land and roads around the reservoirs, but Letchworth Village retained an easement on the property, and it is not currently open to the public.

The First Reservoir was built in 1912, where the Old Turnpike comes down near Call Hollow Road. A high dam was made, and below it a water treatment plant was built.

After two years of water shortage, the Second Reservoir was built in 1927-28, using an old mill pond that belonged to the Wood family (and in 1908 was owned by the Bedford family). There once was a sawmill on the brook below the dam. The Wood home was on high ground across the road from the sawmill.

Woodtown Road, which connects the First and Second Reservoirs, continues south from the Second Reservoir. Another road goes around the west side of the Second Reservoir, upstream to the Third Reservoir, which was built in 1951-52 in the valley where the Suffern-Bear Mountain Trail comes down off Ladentown Mountain and starts up Big Hill. The trail was moved 400 feet to the west when the reservoir was filled.

For more information regarding the history of these reservoirs, see p. 212.

Lily Pond

Lily Pond is located on Lake Welch Drive, 0.5 mile east of its start near Sebago Beach. To the right of the road, High Hill is visible. Between the Parkway and High Hill is the abandoned Johnsontown Road; just south of the road is a three-acre, 0.2-mile-long natural lake known as Lily Pond.

A Park news release, dated August 29, 1934, states that this pond was the site of an old mill. The brook that drains the pond joins Whitney Brook, which runs into Lake Sebago. The High Hill that looks down on the lake was sold to the Park in 1921 by Ada Carey, who had been the caretaker of St. John's Church until 1914.

Traces of several homes can be found near the pond. Ben Jones, who was the caretaker of St. John's Cemetery, used to live here.

Lake Massawippa

This lake is located in Brooks Hollow, adjacent to Route 6. In 1918, the land for 0.8 mile east of the Barnes property—which included the site of present-day Lake Massawippa—was given to the Park by W. Averell Harriman. In the fall of 1934, Civilian Conservation Corps Camp SP-23 was set up in Brooks Hollow, and work began on Dam #15, now known as Lake Massawippa (meaning "heroine"). At one time, there were Boy Scout camps along the lake. A footpath goes along the west side of the lake, and there is a camp road (the Brooks Hollow Trail) on the east side. If the camp road is followed north in Brooks Hollow, it will intercept the Long Path, which comes down from Howell Mountain (see p. 221).

Lake Nawahunta

Lake Nawahunta was created in 1915 by the construction of a dam across Lewis Brook, a tributary of Queensboro Brook. The land did not belong to the Park then, and it was built to be a trout hatchery. It is a small lake, 7 to 10 feet deep, visible from Seven Lakes Drive just south of the Silvermine parking area. Beyond the lake is a grove of pines, planted after the lake was made.

The lake bed was formerly a farm cultivated by several generations of the Lewis family. "Scobie" Jim Lewis' grave is on the knoll across Seven Lakes Drive from the entrance to the Nawahunta Fire Road. The Park purchased the land on January 22, 1917 from Isaac Lemmon. At first, the lake was known as Lemmon Lake. The name Nawahunta is Mohegan for "place of trout."

A park fire road, built in 1954 (now the route of the yellow-blazed Menomine Trail), runs north along the east shore of the lake, on a bank above the lake. A cellar hole on that road marks the site of the Lewis farmhouse.

Seven Lakes Drive, where it passes the site of the Lewis farm, was built on the old Greenwood Turnpike. That road came over the hill from the Greenwood Furnace (now Arden), went to Queensboro, and continued on to Fort Montgomery.

Pine Meadow Lake

Pine Meadow Lake, located in the center of the Ramapo Plateau, is a hikers' favorite place. It may be reached from the west by the Pine Meadow Trail and Pine Meadow Road West, from the north by Conklin Road, from the east by the Pine Meadow and Conklins Crossing Trails, and from the south by Torne Valley Road and by the Poached Egg Trail, which leads to the Raccoon Brook Hills Trail.

The Pine Meadow Trail follows a pipeline along the north side of the lake. That pipeline, which can be followed all around the lake, ends at a never-used septic tank on Christie Brook.

About halfway along the lake, the Pine Meadow Trail passes the ruin of a stone building. It often is supposed that this was the famous Conklin's Cabin. Actually, this building was built in 1936 as a pumphouse (Palisades Interstate Park News Release, 3/11/36). The pumps there were to fill the reservoir which had been built on the hilltop, north of the lake.

Conklin's Cabin was in a clear, flat area about 0.2 mile east of the pumphouse ruin. It stood next to a black walnut tree which still is growing there, but no trace of the cabin remains. Around the base of the tree, remnants of an old wire fence can still be seen. The fence was put around the cabin in the fall of 1936, to preserve it. In spite of the fence, the cabin had been ruined by 1942 (*Walking News*, Nov. 1942). A small cow barn was behind the cabin, built against a rock. One stone wall of the barn can still be seen.

Across the lake and a little to the west was the James Conklin farm and orchard. A CCC camp was erected there in May 1933 (*N.Y. Post*, 6/23/33). On a knoll above the lake, about 0.1 mile west of the CCC campsite, is the James Conklin cemetery. It has been reported that there are eight known graves there, as well as a number of unmarked ones. Ramsey Conklin was buried there in 1952.

In the lake nearby is an island where (it has been said) there is a graveyard of the Starr family. Also in the lake, slightly to the west of Conklin's Cabin site, there was a tiny island. Nowadays, this island is visible only when the water level is low. In 1934, when the dam had been built and the lake began to fill, Ramsey Conklin protested that the water would cover the 19 graves there, including those of his mother and father. So John Tamsen, the Superintendent of the New York Division of the Park, built a pyramid of earth above the grave site, covered the sides of the mound with stone rip-rap, and planted some laurels on the top (*N.Y. Post*, 6/9/37). When the lake had filled with water, the little graveyard island could still be seen. Wind and water, however, have since lowered it to the lake level.

The history of Pine Meadow is the history of the Conklin family. The first Conklin to arrive was Nicholas (1661-1747). Cole's *History of Rockland County* shows Nicholas Conklin owning 200 acres at Pine Meadow in 1724. Those 200 acres (all of Pine Meadow) were granted by the State of New York on December 5, 1800 to Nicholas N. Conklin, by payment of $100 and the improvement of the property. The improvement was Conklin's Cabin, built there in 1779 by Nicholas' brother Matthew.

In 1895, Nicholas N. Conklin's grandson James Conklin (1866-1940) inherited 60 acres on the south side of the meadow. He eventually sold his land to Nicholas Rose for $800 in 1902. Rose in turn sold it in 1906 to Bessie Gillette, wife of a Sloatsburg doctor. (Actually, it was transferred to the doctor in payment for medical bills.) It was James Conklin who persuaded the CCC not to destroy the family cemetery on the knoll. He and his two wives are buried there.

Matthew Conklin, who had the farm on the north side of the meadow, married an American Indian woman named Phebe Jane. Their eighth child, Stephen Conklin (1815-1902), left his farm and cabin to his son Ramsey (1873-1952).

Ramsey became well known to hikers, starting in the 1920s. When the Brooklyn Boy Scouts, led by Archibald Shorey, visited the cabin in 1923, Ramsey's mother Hannah Marie was still living there, although his father had died in 1902 (Adirondack Mountain Club *Cloud Splitter,* Sept. 1973). Ramsey had three sons: Theodore (Dory), Nicholas and Stephen. In 1933, both Nick and Steve were married and had daughters, 14 and 3 years old.

So, when the Park began to build the lake, eight people were living in that two-room cabin. Like his father, Ramsey made what little money he needed by weaving baskets, called "bockeys." These baskets had been much used in times past to carry charcoal out of the hills to the iron furnaces at Greenwood (Arden). Now they were sold to tourists in New York City. Other saleable items were whittled wooden scoops for handling gunpowder in World War I, and boat bailers that floated. The mountain people brought those things down to Pincus Margulies' store in Ladentown, and Pincus sold them in New York City.

As early as 1922, Major Welch had planned a lake at Pine Meadow. A great deal of free labor became available when the Civilian Conservation Corps was formed in 1933. In May of that year, Camp SP-2 was set up in Pine Meadow on the old James Conklin farm. The construction materials were transported by trucks which went over Diamond Mountain on the western branch of Woodtown Road. That road went across the south end of a swamp on Christie Brook (later, Lake Wanoksink) and joined the north-south Woodtown Road which crossed the meadow just west of Ramsey's cabin.

Two hundred men went to work to clear trees and brush from the meadow, and to build a 650-foot core-wall dam. By September 1934, they had built 8.5 miles of roads (Pine Meadow Roads, East and West), eleven buildings, an incinerator on Diamond Mountain, a small camp on Pine Meadow Road East, and the dam.

PALISADES INTERSTATE PARK COMMISSION

Construction of the Pine Meadow Dam, 1933

Camps were also built for Lake Wanoksink (SP-20) and for Lake Minsi (SP-21), and all the crews built the water/sewer system around the three lakes as well as the two concrete reservoirs nearby. That system was to serve 35 camps which were to be built by the Works Progress Administration.

Needless to say, life was pretty hectic for Ramsey Conklin in those days. His sons joined the CCC and worked on the new dams. By 1934, when the lake began to fill with water, Ramsey knew he would have to leave. Major Welch said that he and his family could stay as long as they liked, and that their cabin would be repaired, but, of course, the lake would cover their fields and their spring. Apparently, Ramsey did not have a deed to his land. In 1931, the Park Commission paid New York City lawyer Philip Poger to search for such

a deed, but he found none.

On February 15, 1935, the Conklins left their 29 acres and moved their belongings to an abandoned schoolhouse in Ladentown, at the junction of Camp Hill and Quaker Roads. A boy who had played in that schoolyard many years before (about 1830) was Abram S. Hewitt (*N.Y. Times*, 3/24/35). He later married the daughter of industrialist Peter Cooper, became mayor of New York City, and (from 1900 to 1903) served as a Commissioner of the Palisades Interstate Park. Another of those schoolboys was Walter Gurnee, who became mayor of Chicago (in those days, Mt. Ivy was called Gurnee's Corners). The schoolhouse had been abandoned since 1923.

Ramsey and his sons were disturbed by all the traffic going by their door, so after a while they moved to a shack they built on the side of Limekiln Mountain (the remains of that shack can still be seen in a clearing on the road that services the power line, just a little west of the Tuxedo-Mt. Ivy Trail). On Monday morning, May 19, 1952, 80-year-old Ramsey left home and did not return. Policemen from the Town of Ramapo, Park rangers and Boy Scouts searched for him (*N.Y. Times*, 5/22/52). Five months later, his body was found by three Babcock boys, near the Second Reservoir (*N.Y. Times*, 10/25/52). He was buried at Pine Meadow Lake, the last one to be buried there. The Reverend Austin Conklin, who had been pastor of the Johnsontown church, officiated (*N.Y. Times*, 10/31/52). Ramsey's son Theodore continued to live in the shack on Limekiln Mountain until 1963 when the Park acquired all the land along the Ramapo Rampart and evicted the last of the mountain people.

Queensboro Lake

Queensboro Lake was created in 1915 by building a dam on Queensboro Brook, which runs north, parallel to Seven Lakes Drive, from Lake Nawahunta and Silvermine Lake. The lake, which is about 20 feet deep, is also fed by brooks from Beechy Bottom (Anthony Wayne Recreation Area) and from Turkey Hill Lake. Queensboro Lake is a reservoir that serves Bear Mountain (and, formerly, West Point). Just below the dam, on Fort Montgomery Road, is a water filtration and purification plant which was built in 1929. In 1930, an aqueduct was built along Popolopen Creek to carry water from Queensboro Lake to Bear Mountain. Another pipe was laid about 1954 to bring water to the new Anthony Wayne Recreation Area.

Near the lake is a road junction, now known as Long Mountain Circle. At the time of the American Revolution, this was Queensboro, a road center and the site of several farms. On June 2, 1774, Rivington's *New York Gazetteer* advertised for sale "2000 acres, known as Queensberry. Owner Moses Clement. There are a good frame house, large garden, meadows for 50 head of cattle, three tenant houses, landings on the river at Popolopen Kill (the road to the furnace of Dean) or on the west side of Salisbury Island [Iona Island]—a good cart road to Queensberry (the Doodletown Road)."

In 1920, there still was a little red schoolhouse at Queensboro Junction which Major Welch was trying to acquire (Memo of Major Welch to Edmund Brown, 6/15/20). Nearby was the graveyard of the Weyant and Brooks families, who owned much of the land around Queensboro. The

PALISADES INTERSTATE PARK COMMISSION

Odell cabin at Queensboro, 1925

little schoolhouse was finally acquired in 1927 (*N.Y. Times*, 11/20/27). The present road interchange was completed in September 1959.

The large home of the Brooks family stood near Long Mountain Circle, not far from the new lake. In 1919, it was made available to organizations, and was called Camp Quannacut. It was occupied in April-May 1924 by the new (1922) Adirondack Mountain Club. The new (1923) Westchester Trails Association also used Camp Quannacut in February 1924 (*N.Y. Post*, 1/14/24). To visit Camp Quannacut, take the Park work road off Long Mountain Circle. Turn right, to a work area where there are sand piles. The very first dirt road on the left goes up to a level area now used as a dump. On the hillside, in the bushes, is all that remains of the Brooks house, Camp Quannacut. In the brambles just beyond is all that remains of their latrine.

Reynolds Pond

Reynolds Pond is a small pond in the northwest region of the Park. It is just to the northeast of Summit Lake Road, about 0.1 mile before that road ends at the fence on Route 6. (It is shown as a swamp on the 2010 edition of Trail Conference Map #119.) Until 1964, a 16-acre parcel of land that started down at the highway was owned by Harold G. Reynolds, a heating oil dealer who lived in Central Valley. Sometime before 1945, Reynolds had one of his employees (a young man named Bailey, descended from the residents of Baileytown) build an earthen dam with a backhoe. Reynolds then built a summer bungalow near the lake. The remains of the bungalow can still be seen, near the stone wall above Summit Lake Road. In November 1964, the Park acquired Reynolds's land and pond for $31,500.

Lake Sebago

Lake Sebago was created by the construction of Dam #10 where Johnsontown Road crossed Stony Brook. The dam was begun in 1923 and completed in 1926. A 1,000-foot wingdam was also built at that time.

Before the lake was built, the great Emmetsfield Swamp filled the valley. Stony Brook ran south, through Johnsontown. Whitney Brook, which ran along the east side of Brundige Mountain, joined Stony Brook opposite the present American Canoe Association Camp. At the junction of the two brooks, about 200 feet from either shore of the present-day lake, there was a sawmill owned by George Blanchard. Scuba divers from the Canoe Association dock can still see that mill on the lake bottom. The bridge across Stony Brook, 1,000 feet downstream from the mill, was named the Burnt Sawmill Bridge.

When the dam was built, the old bridge was removed. At the same time, the Park improved the old Johnsontown Road from Sloatsburg and renamed it Stony Brook Drive. It crossed the top of the new dam, and went along the wingdam. In 1926, the new lake was flooded and named Sebago, which is the Algonquin word for "big water."

In 1925, Ruby Jolliffe, the Director of Park Camps, asked the new Adirondack Mountain Club (formed in November 1922) if they would like to build a camp on the lake. They were enthusiastically in favor and, under chairman Frank Oliver, chose a site on the west side of the lake. The camp was opened on April 10, 1926. About 1930, they named their camp "Nawakwa," which means "in the midst of the wilderness." The Adirondack Mountain Club still occupies Camp Nawakwa.

In 1928, the Park built a camp, not far from the dam, for the Rogers Peet Co. The camp, originally known as Camp ROPECO, was taken over in 1933 by the American Canoe Association, and is still maintained by that group.

In 1927, Baker Camp was built on Lake Sebago for the employees of four New York City banks (First National, Bankers Trust, U.S. Trust and N.Y. Trust). For this purpose, George F. Baker, Sr., President of the First

Construction of the Sebago Dam, 1926

National Bank, donated $100,000 to the Park Commission in 1925. (He had given $50,000 in 1909 and $100,000 more in both 1917 and 1920.) George F. Baker, Sr. died on May 2, 1931, at the age of 91. In 1986, Baker Camp was turned over to a concessionaire, and it is currently operated as a camp open to the public.

In 1927, New York University opened a camp on the east side of Lake Sebago. They used it until 1961. Since 1962, it has been called Sebago Cabin Camps, and cabins can be rented by interested persons.

On the east side of Brundige Mountain, not far from Baker Camp, there is a cave. In the old days, this was called Emmet's Cave, and it was believed to be the home of a witch named Auntie Emmet. She was said to be able to change herself into the form of a toad, and wayfarers were warned not to kick a toad lest it turned out to be Auntie Emmet, who could suitably punish the thoughtless one.

Around 1900, a man named Conklin who was traveling toward John-sontown was robbed and murdered. His body was hidden in Emmet's Cave. Many years later, a local farmer named Schoonover, who lay dying in the hospital, confessed to the murder. Schoonover's farm was where the present Pine Meadow Road meets the Cranberry Mountain Trail.

In 1928, facilities for motor camping were built in the flat area by Stony Brook below the dam (*N.Y. Times*, 4/15/28). By 1931, there was a comfort station there and space for 250 cars. The remains of that camp can still be seen.

In 1931, a beach area was constructed near the present hikers' parking area. Two rustic buildings were erected, and 70 concrete tables and benches were installed. That "Old Sebago Beach" served until 1952 when "New Sebago Beach" was opened at the north end of the lake, where Johnsontown had once stood. A roller rink was built there in 1957.

When the new Seven Lakes Drive was opened from Sloatsburg in 1962, the road no longer crossed the wingdam at the southern end of the lake. That section of the older road was closed to traffic, but was made available for hiker parking. From there, hikers had access to the Tuxedo-Mt. Ivy, Hillburn-Torne-Sebago and Seven Hills Trails. Unfortunately, vandalism at the Park building there led, in 1977, to the closing of that area for parking. Since then, hikers must park 0.6 mile north of the dam at the fishermen's launching area (next to Old Sebago Beach). The Seven Hills Trail was rerouted by the New York Ramblers in 1977, using the old Monitor Trail down to Old Sebago Beach.

Silvermine Lake

Silvermine Lake is on Seven Lakes Drive, 1.7 miles south of Long Mountain Circle and 2.0 miles north of Tiorati Circle. The Silvermine Ski Area (no longer operated as such) is adjacent to the lake, as are extensive picnic areas with ample room for parking. Swimming in the lake is not permitted. From the lake, hikers can start up Stockbridge, Black and Letterrock Mountains. The yellow-blazed Menomine Trail provides a convenient route north to Stockbridge Mountain or south to Letterrock Mountain. A wide path (the Silvermine Road) goes up from the dam into the notch between Black and Letterrock Mountains, crossing the Appalachian/Ramapo-Dunderberg Trail. In 1989, the Park removed the wooden walkway across the dam. Hikers must now go down and cross the brook on stepping stones, or they may use the bridge just a bit further downstream.

When the Park was first created in 1910, this basket-shaped depression in the hills was called the Bockey Swamp. Bockey—a term peculiar to this mountain region—refers to a wide-splinted woven basket used by charcoal burners. They were made and sold by mountain people, who were themselves sometimes called "bockeys."

As early as 1922, Major Welch planned to create a lake from that swamp

Skiers at the Old Silvermine Ski Area

(*N.Y. Post*, 1/2/23). In 1926, a 30-acre motor camp was built there, with a well, tables and restrooms. During these years, beavers (which had been introduced in the Park in 1920) built a dam that backed up the water in the swamp. As a result, many trees were killed. Park workers cleared the dead trees and planted rice, which they thought would attract birds. But deer ate the rice.

Then, in the spring of 1934, Civilian Conservation Corps Camp SP-27 was set up at Bockey Swamp. By September, a 600-foot dam had been built and the new reservoir began to fill. The lake was named Menomine, meaning "wild rice." More picnic tables were installed. The old picnic area extended down the road from the present parking area.

In the fall of 1936, a ski slope and rope-tow were built on the hill next to the lake. It was named the Old Silvermine Ski Area because of its proximity to the legendary Spanish silver mine on Black Mountain. R.H. Torrey related the story of the "Lone Tinker Mine" (*N.Y. Post*, 10/6/23): About 1735, a small ship visited Caldwell's Landing (now Jones Point) each year. The crew were Spanish. They made their way to Black Mountain and to a mine on its north side, near some houses of the Conklin family. They came out each time with heavy sacks. Once, in the tavern at the river, they boasted of the silver they were carrying. On their last trip, one of the crew did not return with the others. Local natives, searching for the mine, found his body in a cabin on the mountain. The crew never was seen again, and the silver mine never was found. There are two mine openings on the top of Black Mountain, but only a little iron ore came from them.

In 1934, the TERA used a section of the old Black Mountain Trail to build a fire road past Bockey Swamp up through the notch between Black Mountain and Letterrock Mountain. It was intended to be a one-way loop, but the TERA was disbanded before it was finished. In 1955, the lower end of the fire road near the lake was surfaced with gravel.

During 1942, a second ski slope was built. In 1951, the lake was re-named Silvermine Lake. A large overflow parking area was created in 1968, but the ski area has been closed since 1986.

Lake Skannatati

After Lake Askoti had been filled with water in 1937, work began on another lake across the road, already named Skannatati, which means "the other side." This second lake needed two dams. The first was finished in 1938; the second in 1947. The lake is fed by the overflow from Lake Askoti (once the Stillwater Creek, which ran into Lake Kanawauke) and by the brook, further to the west, which runs down from Pine Swamp.

There is a parking area at the lake edge, much used by fishermen and picnickers. The Arden-Surebridge Trail (red triangle on white) starts from the parking area and climbs up Pine Swamp Mountain, where there is a beautiful view of the Kanawauke Lakes to the south. The Long Path (aqua) crosses the parking area and heads west, between the lake and the mountain.

A gentle knoll projects into the north side of the lake, and just beyond is the cascade from Pine Swamp. In 1921, when the Boy Scouts built their White Bar Trail system, their Camp Forest Ranger was located on that knoll (there were six such camps on the 35-mile trail). About 1942, the Boy Scouts marked a path from Lake Skannatati to the Hogencamp Mine. This path was adopted in 1944 by the Trail Conference for their Red Cross Trail. Later it became the Skannatati Trail, and it is now part of the Long Path.

Lake Skenonto

After Lake Sebago was finished in 1926, there was still a "Big Swamp" just over the hill on the western side. This swamp became Lake Skenonto. Available records say very little about the construction of this lake—we know only that the dam was built in 1934 and that the lake was filled with water by 1936. The old Black Ash Swamp Road, marked in 1943 as the Victory Trail, passes along the west side of the lake. The Triangle Trail (yellow) comes down Parker Cabin Mountain and crosses below the south end of Lake Skenonto. Also at the south end, near a brook that comes in from a swamp, an unmarked woods road goes south for 0.5 mile to join the White Bar Trail near Dutch Doctor Shelter. There is also a trail on the east side which starts from the site of the former Boys' Athletic League camp (demolished 1993), goes over the dam and continues through the laurels to the Triangle Trail. All along the hilly west side are delightful spots for lunch stops.

Spring Pond

This little pond is 0.1 mile east of Kanawauke Circle, on the south side of Route 106. A natural pond, it was enlarged in 1919, and a pumphouse was built there to supply water to the camps on the Kanawauke Lakes. The dam was repaired in 1934.

Just across the road from the pond is a stone wall, the remains of Kiles' harness shop. On the bank above the road is a cement sidewalk—it led to the home of James and John Johnson, which had been built by B.S. Kile. Their property—a 63-acre triangular area at the junction of Seven Lakes Drive and Route 106—was bought by the Park in 1921.

Jim Johnson worked for the Park as foreman of dam construction for Lakes Nawahunta, Cohasset, Kanawauke, Sebago and Welch (PIPC News Release #207, 1/23/30). He was a direct descendant of the James Johnson who first settled Johnsontown in 1750. After he sold his home, he continued to live there, paying the Park $4.00 per month rent. Later, the Park rented the house to Paul and Essie Jones. It burned about 1960.

The county line crosses the tip of Spring Pond. Here, Orange County Route 106 ends and Rockland County Route 106 (also known as Gate Hill Road) begins.

Spruce Pond

This little pond lies in the hills west of Route 17, about 0.5 mile south of the Red Apple Rest in Southfields. A dirt road goes up from the highway, curves around the north side of 875-foot Wildcat Mountain, and leads to the east side of the pond. The pond itself is in a marshy region. There are about 15 leantos near the pond—the remains of an abandoned Boy Scout camp. In 1925, the Boy Scouts set up their Rock Oak Forest Ranger Camp here for 60 Scouts. In recent years, the camp was used for short-term camping by the Greater New York Councils of the Boy Scouts, and was known as Spruce Pond Scout Camp. It was abandoned in the early 1980s.

The region around Spruce Pond is part of the original gift of the Harriman family. The parcel starts about 0.25 mile south of the Route 106 overpass. It goes up northwest about 0.75 mile, turns northeast for 1.5 miles, and then continues southeast, coming within 235 feet of Orange Turnpike, 0.15 mile north of its junction with Route 17.

Lake Stahahe

Lake Stahahe, located on Route 106, 1.25 miles east of Route 17, is a natural lake. It is called Car Pond on old maps, but there is no record of the origin of this name. The Mohegan name STAHAHE was adopted as early as 1913 (it means "stones in the water").

Boy Scout camps were established on the lake in 1913 by Assistant Park Superintendent A.M. Herbert, who lived on the Lemmon's place in Doodletown. At that time, the area of the lake was only 17 acres—much smaller than it is now. The lake was enlarged in 1914 by the construction of three small dams (still visible below the surface). In 1918, a larger dam was completed, bringing the lake to its present size of 88 acres. A pipeline brought fresh water to the camps from Green Pond in the hills to the east (*PIPC Annual Report*, 1/31/19). In 1919, the camps on Lake Stahahe were used by social welfare organizations. Children were weighed when they entered the camp, and again when they left. The Annual Reports of the Commissioners proudly record the weight gains.

The height east of the lake is called Stahahe High Peak. It can be reached by an unmarked trail that goes up from Island Pond Road, starting 0.55 mile from Route 106.

Summit Lake

This natural lake is the source of Popolopen Creek. In 1873, when it was owned by Elisha Stockbridge, it was somewhat enlarged by a low dam. Beers's 1875 map shows Stockbridge owning 263 acres (0.4 sq. mile) in the area. Around that time, two hotels were built near the lake by Isaac Noxon of Central Valley, and they were soon sold to Stockbridge.

The first hotel, known as the Stockbridge Mountain House, was on the mountaintop northwest of the lake. It was a very large three-story building, with verandas on two levels. In 1900, the hotel was leased by New York City doctors Whitmore and Wellwood for use as a convalescent center. The rates were $20 per person per week. After Edward Harriman bought the place in 1905, it was abandoned. Local citizens helped themselves to the contents, and the building was demolished about 1908. The foundation is still visible.

The second hotel was on the main road (then known as the Dunderberg Road, now Route 6) at the road which led to the lake. In 1903, Mrs. Stockbridge still owned this 30-room hotel and 35 acres, and the hotel was operated by George Weygant as the Summit Lake House. Edward Harriman bought the hotel and the surrounding land about 1905. In 1918, Averell Harriman leased the hotel to the Park. After being used for some years as a children's camp, first by the Central Jewish Institute, and then in 1923 by the Paulist Church, it was demolished about 1930. Only its foundation can be found now, in the barberry bushes across the road from the present white Park building on Route 6. (That building was moved to this site in 1965 from another location a half mile west.)

In 1915, the YWCA of New York City operated Camp Bluefield, the old Blauvelt rifle range which had been bought by the State in 1911 and transferred to the Park in 1913. Governor Charles S. Whitman visited this YWCA camp before attending a luncheon given by George Perkins to mark the opening of the Bear Mountain Inn (*N.Y. Times*, 6/27/15). The camp director at Bluefield was Miss Ruby Jolliffe.

When the United States went to war, Camp Bluefield was requisitioned for army use, and Averell Harriman invited the YWCA to use his Summit Lake. In 1919, the Park built a camp on the lake, and it was occupied by the YWCA from 1920 to 1951. Ruby Jolliffe, who had made a very favorable impression on Major Welch, became Camps Director for the Interstate Park on December 1, 1920, replacing Edward Brown. In 1942, Averell

Harriman gave the lake and the surrounding land to the Park.

At the northeast end of the lake, there is a pumphouse that pumps water to a reservoir on the hill above. (An older concrete pumphouse, which looks like a jail cell, can be seen on the opposite side of the lake.) A road which leads up the hill behind the pumphouse goes to the reservoir, which serves both Summit Lake and Upper Twin Lake. On the way up to the reservoir, a trail diverges to Upper Twin Lake, passing along the way a corrugated metal shelter. Where the road turns north toward the reservoir, another fork leads southeast and goes down to the farm of William and Mary Bailey (abandoned in 1925).

At the south end of Summit Lake, an overgrown carriage road comes over the hill from the Harriman gate on Baileytown Road. Many camp buildings at the north end of the lake have been demolished. The entrance road has been repaved, however, and the dining hall repaired for the use of convicts from the Mid-Orange Correctional Facility who are often brought in to work in the Park during the day. For this reason, the north end of the lake may be closed to hikers.

Lake Te Ata

Near Upper and Lower Twin Lakes, a third lake was built in 1927. For want of a name, the Girl Scouts there called it "Triplet Lake." The Park authorities, however, preferred Indian names. They decided that the new lake should be called Te Ata, which in the Chickasaw language means "bearer of the morning," or "the dawn."

During the 1920s, Camps Director Ruby Jolliffe and Park Manager Major Welch became acquainted with a young Indian woman named Te Ata. In 1929, they invited her to tour the children's camps in the Park. She sang Indian songs and related Indian legends. In this way, Te Ata became acquainted with Eleanor Roosevelt, wife of the Governor, who often visited the camps in the Park.

On the evening of July 11, 1932, at Camp Paterson (LT-6), Mrs. Roosevelt dedicated Lake Te Ata with a bottle containing water from each of the lakes in the Park. Several thousand campers were present. Speakers included Major Welch; Frederick Sutro, Park Executive Director; and Miss Ruby Jolliffe, Director of Camps. Te Ata, the Chickasaw princess, came down the lake standing in the front of a canoe (*N.Y. Times*, 7/12/32).

Te Ata was born Mary Thompson in Emet, Oklahoma in 1895 and grew

Mary Thompson, Princess Te Ata, ca. 1929

up in nearby Tishomingo, the capital of the Chickasaw nation. After graduating from Oklahoma College for Women, she studied for a year at the Theater School of the Carnegie Institute in Pittsburgh. She appeared on the New York stage as Andromache in *The Trojan Women,* and became proficient at interpreting Indian songs, stories and dances. Through her work in the Harriman Park camps, she became acquainted with Governor and Mrs. Franklin D. Roosevelt, performing for them at the Governor's mansion in Albany. When President Roosevelt gave his first state dinner for British Prime Minister Ramsay McDonald in the spring of 1933, "Princess" Te Ata was on the after-dinner program.

On September 28, 1934, Te Ata married Dr. Clyde Fisher (he was 17 years older than she), who was the curator of the Hayden Planetarium. They lived together until his death on January 7, 1949. Te Ata was invited to appear before King George and Queen Elizabeth on July 1, 1939 (*N.Y. Herald Tribune,* 6/5/39). Her last performance in the Park camps was in 1946. After Dr. Fisher's death, she returned to Oklahoma, where she lived in Moore, a suburb of Oklahoma City. There she continued to lecture and perform. On Statehood Day, November 16, 1958, Te Ata was inducted into the Oklahoma Hall of Fame, and on September 18, 1987 she was proclaimed a "State Treasure" at the Governor's Arts Awards (*Sunday Oklahoman,* 9/13/87). She died on October 26, 1995 at the age of 99.

Despite its auspicious beginning, Lake Te Ata was not used by the Girl

Scouts in the years that followed, and no camps were ever built on its shores. The Twin Lakes Regional Museum is situated on the hill overlooking the lake.

Lake Tiorati

Before the Lake Tiorati dam was constructed, there were two ponds at the site of the present-day lake: Cedar Pond, half a mile long, which is the northeast end of the present lake; and Little Cedar Pond, a bog-encircled mud hole at the southwest end. When the dam was completed in May 1915, the water level was raised twenty feet, and the two ponds became one.

William Thompson Howell, in his diary *The Hudson Highlands* (Sept. 1910), described Cedar Ponds as originally one glacial lake, which gradually filled with silt and became two lakes. In 1765, when Peter Hasenclever came looking for iron ore, he journeyed up the road from Stony Point that had been made in 1760. He opened a mine not far from Cedar Ponds Brook, and bought 1,000 acres of Great Mountain Lot #3 of the Cheesecocks Patent, which included part of Cedar Ponds. To provide power for an intended furnace, he dammed the outlet of the ponds and created one large lake. After Hasenclever abandoned his project in 1769, the property passed through many hands. An iron furnace was erected on the brook in 1800.

In 1844, William Knight of Stony Point bought the lake. He broke out the dam, restoring the two ponds, and raised vegetables on the mud flats around the edges. (In 1910, the local settlers still remembered the fields of rye, buckwheat, corn and onions which grew in the flats.) Below the site of the dam, Knight built a chemical factory to produce pyroligneous acid—a mixture of acetic acid and wood alcohol, made by the destructive distillation of wood. When added to iron ore, it formed "iron liquor," a mordant used in calico printing by the textile mill in nearby Garnerville.

In 1915, the Park bought the Cedar Ponds from the Rockland County Realty Co. and built a new dam, creating what was then known as Lake No. 2. At that time, Cedar Ponds Brook (Tiorati Brook) was a source of water for the Town of Haverstraw. In 1921, after Haverstraw built a filtration plant on the brook, the Park began to move its youth camps from Hessian Lake to the Cedar Ponds area (*PIPC Annual Report*, 1/31/22).

When asked about names, the American Scenic and Historic Preservation Society favored "Cedar Lake" as the name for Lake No. 2. Nevertheless, Major Welch's Mohegan name TIORATEE, meaning "blue like the sky," was adopted by the Commissioners.

During 1915, a large double cabin was built at Cedar Ponds to house the Park engineer, forester and laborers. This cabin was made available to Trail Conference volunteers on November 27-28, 1920, when they were building the Ramapo-Dunderberg Trail. On January 1, 1923, the cabin was rented to the New York Section of the Green Mountain Club, which had been formed in 1915. They named their camp "THENDARA," said to mean "Mountain of the Gods." Camp Thendara is still used by this group, now known as the Thendara Mountain Club.

In 1922, another camp was built for the New York Life Insurance Co. on a knoll on the west side of the lake. The company contributed $25,000 for the construction of their Camp NYLIC. In 1932, they gave it up, and it became Camp TERA for unemployed women (Temporary Emergency Relief Administration), sponsored by Eleanor Roosevelt. During 1936-37, the National Youth Administration used the camp; from 1938 to 1944 it was used by the Metropolitan Jewish Center. It was then demolished.

In 1935, the beach and a refreshment stand were built near Tiorati Circle. At present, Lake Tiorati is extensively used for group camping and public recreation.

Turkey Hill Lake

Turkey Hill Lake nestles in a valley bounded by Long Mountain on the west, Summer Hill on the south, and Turkey Hill on the east. The valley was once called Curtis Hollow, and there was a Curtis Hollow Trail which went north from Route 6, passing to the west of Summer Hill and along the west side of the swamp in the hollow. That trail is now part of the Anthony Wayne Trail. The Popolopen Gorge Trail (red square on white) goes along the southern side of the present lake.

In April 1933, Civilian Conservation Corps Camp SP-1 was set up on the Van Wart farm, near the Mica Mine on the Beechy Bottom East Road. Those 200 young men were assigned to build a new reservoir at Turkey Hill. First they built the Summer Hill Road around the east side of Summer Hill to the dam site and beyond, a total of 1.4 miles. By April 1934, they had cleared the swamp and finished the road and the dam.

At first, the new lake was called Curtis Lake (*Paterson Morning Call*,

Turkey Hill Lake

7/10/36). R.H. Torrey proposed the name "Shikenumpak," which is Lenape for Turkey Hollow (*N.Y. Post*, 4/4/36). The name "Turkey Hill Lake" first appeared on the Park's 1937 trail map.

The water which goes over the dam continues down the brook into the Queensboro Lake reservoir. The pipes that are seen hanging over the dam were installed during a period of low water, to enable water to be siphoned over into the brook.

Upper and Lower Twin Lakes

Upper and Lower Twin Lakes are natural bodies of water that were somewhat enlarged by dams built about 1850. They are the headwaters of Popolopen Creek, and drain northward through Brooks Hollow to Mine Lake, a pretty lake visible from Route 293 on the way to West Point.

In 1918, the Park acquired Lower (North) Twin Lake, with two camp buildings and a tenant house. In 1919, the Park purchased Upper (South) Twin Lake and the 30 acres around its shore from William Weygant. That sale included a house and five furnished cottages. In 1924, Charles Bailey sold to the Park 100 acres on the hillside west of Upper Twin Lake, and 73 acres south of that (an old farm, now covered by barberry bushes) was sold to the Park in 1925 by Mary Bailey. In 1930, the Park bought 170 acres on the southwest side of Baileytown Road (adjacent to Stockbridge Mountain) from Samuel Bailey. That parcel included the family cemetery.

The Dunderberg Lodge, owned by Mrs. R.H. Green in 1903, was located where Baileytown Road reached the road from Central Valley (Route 6, then known as the Dunderberg Road). The lodge and the surrounding 250 acres were acquired by Averell Harriman in 1918 and leased by him to the Park.

The region around Upper Twin Lake was called Baileytown. In 1930, when the Park acquired the last Bailey properties, the family was permitted to remain in their homes for the rest of their lives. In 1942, Lester Bailey died while hunting raccoons nearby (*N.Y. Times*, 11/2/42). He was 72 years old. The last surviving member of the family was Lester's cousin Irving Bailey, a recluse. On Christmas Day 1947, he died alone in his home, aged 59.

When the Commission bought the Bailey properties, a search was made of the titles to lands in the area. It was then discovered that the area had once been owned by Peter Hasenclever, the engineer for an English mining company. The first conveyance is entitled: "The Colony of New York, to Peter Hasenclever, Letters Patent, Dated March 25, 1767, Recorded in the Office of the Secretary of State, Book No. 14 of Patents, page 201." This patent covered 1,000 acres lying between the Ludlow patent northwest of Baileytown, toward Popolopen Pond, and 4,000 acres granted to the children of Richard Bradley (who was formerly Attorney General of New York) (Park News Release #261A, 2/9/31).

In the summer of 1924, the recently organized Adirondack Mountain Club rented a two-story farmhouse on Upper Twin Lake—one of the Weygant buildings. They named it Camp Bluebird (UT-10). To get to their camp, those members who didn't have cars had to walk four miles up from Central Valley. They used that camp for two years until the spring of 1926, when they opened Camp Nawakwa on Lake Sebago.

The camps on Upper and Lower Twin Lakes have been in continuous use since 1918. At present, they are used by various Girl Scout councils, by the YMCA and by "Homes for the Homeless."

Lake Wanoksink

Lake Wanoksink is on the Ramapo Plateau, 0.2 mile north of Pine Meadow Lake. Wanoksink, and unfinished Lakes Minsi and Oonotookwa, were built on Christie Brook, a tributary of Pine Meadow Brook. Christie Brook is named for the Christie family who had a sawmill in 1850 on the headwaters of the brook, at the junction of Woodtown Road and Pine Meadow Road East.

Before 1933, the brook there ran through a swamp. A wagon road came through the notch between Conklin and Diamond Mountains, turned south down the valley, crossed Christie Brook, and then went across the south end of the swamp. There it met a north-south road called Woodtown Road. From that junction, Woodtown Road went south across Pine Meadow, through the old James Conklin farm, and on down Torne Valley to Ramapo.

In the fall of 1933, Civilian Conservation Corps Camp SP-20 was built where the road came down from Diamond Mountain. Its foundations still can be seen there, in the laurels just east of the road. Two hundred young men started to build an 850-foot dam across the east end of the swamp. At the same time, the men from Camp SP-2 at Pine Meadow built a 300-foot dam across the notch that had carried the Woodtown Road. Camp SP-21 also built a 113,000-cubic-foot concrete reservoir on a hilltop east of the new lake and north of Pine Meadow.

The lake called Christie Brook No. 1 was finished in 1934 and named Lake Wanoksink. According to Major Welch, this meant "place of sassafras" in the Mohegan language. The mile-long section of Woodtown Road north of the new dam was renamed Conklin Road by Bill Hoeferlin in 1945.

As with Pine Meadow Lake to the south and Lake Minsi to the north, pipelines and reservoirs were installed around the lake to serve the children's camps that were never built. Once the Great Depression ended and World War II had been won, there was no longer a need for more children's camps in Harriman.

Lake Welch

Lake Welch was started in 1928, on a large swampy area which had been dammed by beavers long before. It was then known as Beaver Pond. State Route 210 (now County Route 106) crossed the region over a slightly higher area where there were five homes. The community of Sandyfield, where there were about 25 more homes, was located on high ground to the north and west of the swamp. Sandyfield had been founded about 1760 when the first road through the hills had been built from Stony Point to Central Valley. Hikers now know this road as the Hasenclever Road.

Soon after the Park was created in 1910, the Commissioners notified residents of Sandyfield that the Park wished to acquire their homes. The residents resisted. They had an early supporter in the Reverend Mytton Maury, rector of St. John's Church (*N.Y. Times*, 8/16/14). In 1927, the Park began to plan a lake for the Beaver Pond site. The dam was completed in 1929. Apparently, it was not high enough, because a new dam was started in 1934 using workers from CCC Camp SP-26. Sandyfield residents, who opposed the construction of the dams, petitioned Governor Lehman and President Roosevelt to abolish the Park Commission (*N.Y. Times*, 11/22/34).

In 1939, the Park ordered residents Fred Odell, Albert and Aaron Baisley, and Sarah Benson to move out. The residents finally moved out in 1942. The new road around the lake was completed on October 11, 1942, and the lake began to fill with water. There was a cemetery (about where the beach is now) which would be flooded by the lake. The graves and gravestones were all removed to a cemetery in Stony Point.

On October 6, 1947, the new lake was dedicated in memory of Major William A. Welch, General Manager of the Park, who had died in 1941. In 1953, family camping began on the site of the earlier CCC camp. And on June 15, 1962, a new beach and bathhouses were opened to the public.

Where St. John's Road meets Gate Hill Road (old Route 210), an unused road leads down to the lake. Along that road there is a memorial to Major Welch. From the memorial, a gravel road goes along a hillside above the lake. Near the start of this road, there is a plaque which marks the site of the Sandyfield school. Further along the road, near a refreshment building, is the Odell cemetery. (The Odell home was flooded by the lake.) The road continues past picnic areas to the north end of the lake.

THE UNFINISHED LAKES

Lake Minsi

For many years, hikers visited an unfinished lake, northeast of Lake Wanoksink and near Conklin Road. This was Lake Minsi, called Christie Brook No. 2 when work on it was started in 1934. Civilian Conservation Corps Camp SP-21 was built on the high ground just north of a swamp on Christie Brook. The CCC boys cleared the swamp and built a 500-foot dam, but the dam was never finished by filling both sides with rocks and earth. On a low hill west of the lake, a 141,000-cubic-foot concrete reservoir was built. Around the lake went the water and sewer pipes that were to serve the camps that never were built.

In fact, the men of the three CCC camps built a water and sewage system all around Pine Meadow, Wanoksink and Minsi Lakes. The water was to come from the reservoirs; the sewage was to go to a great septic tank on Christie Brook just above its junction with Pine Meadow Brook.

A letter from Park Manager W.A. Welch, dated March 9, 1935, to Conrad L. Wirth, Assistant Director of the National Park Service, explained why the work was not finished. Major Welch requested the withdrawal of CCC workers from Bear Mountain/Harriman State Park because the State could not supply the funds that would be needed to maintain the camps which were to be built. (Although work here was suspended, some other Park CCC camps were continued until 1942.)

Sometime after the work was suspended, the drainage pipe at the dam became clogged, and the lake actually was partly filled. The dam, however, was always a hazard. In 1984, it was destroyed, and the lake was drained. At the north end of what was formerly the lake, the old road which the CCC boys took to their camp is once again visible.

The name Minsi means "stones piled together." It is also the name of the Indian tribe that inhabited this area until they were driven away by the Dutch, and later by the English.

Lake Oonotookwa

A third lake on Christie Brook was also begun in 1934. At first called Pine Meadow No. 2, it later was named Lake Oonotookwa, meaning "place of cattails." The lake was to be downstream from Lake Wanoksink, in the swamp between Diamond Mountain and Pine Meadow Mountain. An office was built at the foot of Diamond Mountain, where the Pine Meadow Trail meets the Diamond Mountain-Tower Trail. The foundation of the building can still be seen there. A flat region was created below the camp office, bounded by a wall—perhaps for a parking area. The dam which was begun just upstream from that place was left unfinished. The great septic tank was finished but never used.

Owl Lake

In 1934, the Civilian Conservation Corps set up their Camp SP-22 in lower Beechy Bottom. Their task was to transform Owl Swamp into a lake. A concrete dam was built but, like the one at Lake Minsi, it was left unfinished when the CCC camps were withdrawn in 1935 (*N.Y. Post*, 7/12/35). For about 50 years, hikers often sat on the end of the dam and ate their lunches. Then in 1987 the Park opened the dam, and in 1988 the concrete was broken into pieces. Had it been finished, Owl Swamp was to have been named Ookwae ("bear").

Another task assigned to those CCC boys by Major Welch was to build a pair of scenic roads through the Beechy Bottom valley, approaching each other at the two ends of Owl Lake dam. They would connect Tiorati Brook Road in the south with Seven Lakes Drive and Long Mountain Parkway at Queensboro. Some work was done on these roads, but they were never completed. (For a discussion of these roads and the extent to which they were actually built, see pp. 172-73.)

THE ROADS
IN AND AROUND
THE PARK

Route 6 (Long Mountain Parkway)

As we know it today, Route 6 in the Park starts from the Bear Mountain Circle and runs west 8.3 miles to Route 17 at Harriman. Since it was first built, the road has had many changes.

In 1809, the Dunderberg and Clove Turnpike Company was chartered by Orange County, with a capital of $20,000. It built a road from Joshua Caldwell's ferry at the point of Dunderberg Mountain (now Jones Point), around the foot of the mountain and up through Doodletown. That old road can still be seen where it is cut by modern Route 9W, 0.1 mile south of the gate that blocks the 1907 road. The 1809 road is up on the bank, 15 feet above the present-day paved road. Still further south, it can be seen on the hillside below Route 9W. Hikers on the Cornell Mine Trail will step across the old road as they approach Bald Mountain. It joined Doodletown Road (where a reservoir was built in 1974), and used that road to Long Mountain Circle (Queensboro). From there, it went west to Smith's Clove (now Central Valley).

The road was improved in 1919, when Major Welch made it a 16-foot-wide gravel-surfaced road from Queensboro to Summit Lake. The line of the road was changed, too. It followed a sweeping arc up along the side of Cranberry Hill, went around a knob (where our present hikers' pull-out is now), and then made another sweeping arc south of a swamp (this arc is visible from the Long Path).

The road still was not very good, as evidenced by a letter, dated August 8, 1926, from George C. Myer, Postmaster at Highland Falls, to Major Welch: "Sir: It is my duty to report to you that the condition of the Long Mountain Highway makes it unsafe to travel in safety with the United States mails." The postmaster mentioned stretches of bare rock, 31 ditches, and visibility obscured by high brush.

In 1930, the road was designated as U.S. Route 6, and in 1936 it was made 30 feet wide. The 1919 line can be compared with the 1936 line on the sweeping arc west of the Long Mountain pull-out. The older route uses a little bridge at the southern edge of that wide curve, where it crosses a brook.

As one starts up towards Long Mountain from the Queensboro Circle, a Park road departs to the right. That was the old Route 6 until 1967. A quarter-mile up that road there is an abandoned motor camp on the left. Beyond there, the 1919 and 1936 roads made a big arc, crossing the present highway and rejoining it higher up.

Near the old motor camp, a woods road comes in from the right. That woods road was the original 1809 Dunderberg-Clove Turnpike. It comes down from the hikers' pull-out on Long Mountain. From there, the old road went west, approximately on the line of the present road.

The present route was built in 1965-67, and was opened to traffic on September 24, 1967. It goes up toward Long Mountain on a less sweeping curve, and cuts through a knob at the top of the rise, leaving for us that convenient pull-out.

After passing Lakes Massawippa and Te Ata, Route 6 meets Baileytown Road, which comes from Twin Lakes, on the left. There, in 1903, was the Dunderberg Lodge and a school operated by Mrs. R.H. Green. In 1851, the home of W. Van Tassel was on the north side of the road. His grandson worked for the Park in 1919, and was the last one to live in the Brooks house at Queensboro. His great-grandson Norman Van Tassel became a Park electrician and lived in the stone house at Arden Valley Road and Route 17.

A little further west, at the junction with Summit Lake Road, there is a home which is presently occupied by a Park employee. When construction of new Route 6 to the Thruway was begun on September 10, 1965, there were several houses and a service station 0.5 mile west of Summit Lake Road. All of these buildings, except one, were demolished. That one house was moved to the junction with Summit Lake Road, where it remains today. Opposite this house is a parcel of land, once owned by Elisha Stockbridge, on which a hotel was formerly located (see p. 316).

Until 1967, Route 6 turned right, 0.7 mile past Summit Lake Road, and continued downhill to Central Valley. The present-day 1967 road goes straight ahead and, after crossing the Thruway just south of Exit 16, reaches Route 17 just north of Harriman. The abandoned road now carries the Long Path down into the valley toward Schunemunk Mountain.

Route 9W

Hikers are well acquainted with the highway that passes the Bear Mountain Inn and Bridge, and crosses the Popolopen Viaduct on its way to Albany.

PALISADES INTERSTATE PARK COMMISSION

Popolopen Viaduct, July 15, 1916

There was no such road in 1777, when Sir Henry Clinton's troops marched from Stony Point to Bear Mountain. Their road, then known as the King's Road, went up over the Dunderberg and down through Doodletown. The 1777 Trail now follows this route. From Doodletown, the road went down to the river level, and then continued up to Highland Lake (now known as Hessian Lake). In 1809, another road was built through Doodletown to Caldwell's Landing (Jones Point), where it met a road coming north from Tomkins Cove.

In 1907, the State built a new road around Dunderberg Mountain at Jones Point. When the new road was opened, the older 1809 road was abandoned. The *Rockland County Times* of September 23, 1909 said: "People who have never driven over the new Tomkins Cove-Highland Lake Road, and observed what a charming view of the river the new road affords, now have the opportunity." (In 1912, the road was continued down to Haverstraw.)

One man engaged in building the road around Dunderberg Mountain was John Stalter, a woodcutter who lived in Doodletown. To supply water for the construction workers, he installed a pipe from a spring (the "Stalter Spring") near the top of the mountain (see pp. 175-76).

After twenty years, it became apparent that the 12-foot-wide river-level road was too narrow to carry the growing volume of traffic. Rather than widening that road, which would have meant closing it to traffic during construction, Major Welch in 1928 planned a southbound road higher up the slope of Dunderberg. While this new 18-foot-wide road, which rises to about 300 feet above the Hudson, was being built, Federal funds became available, and the "bench" was widened to 30 feet for the 2.4 miles from Iona Island to Jones Point (*N.Y. Times*, 6/29/30). The new road was opened to traffic in September 1931 (*N.Y. Times*, 9/7/31). Sometime later, the river-level road was closed (the river-level road is now part of the Hudson River Greenway Trail.)

When the Park was formed in 1910, the road north of Highland Lake "straggled down to a little iron bridge over Hell Hole" (*N.Y. Post*, 1/4/29). The abutments of that bridge are still there, on the Popolopen Gorge Trail. The Report of the Commissioners for 1914 said: "The present road (Route 3) north from Bear Mountain is one of the most dangerous in the state: coming down into the gorge of the Popolopen Creek at a steep grade, crossing the canyon in a very bad turn, and climbing up the other side of the gorge on steep grades." The report recommended that a steel bridge be built over the gorge.

One of Major Welch's first engineering projects was the construction of a new bridge across Popolopen Gorge. He started in 1915 to build the 140-foot-high steel arch, which opened to traffic on July 15, 1916 as part of State Highway Route 3 (it was renumbered 9W in 1930). In 1936, the width of the Popolopen Viaduct was doubled by building a second bridge of similar design on the west side of the 1916 bridge. In the same year, Route 9W into Fort Montgomery was straightened by the construction of still another 491-foot span over the gully just north of the Popolopen Gorge bridge.

When the Popolopen Viaduct was opened, those who strolled across the bridge could see Henry Hudson's ship, the *Half-Moon*, at anchor in the mouth of the brook below.

The ship, a full-size replica of the ship that carried Henry Hudson up the river in 1609, was a gift of the government of the Netherlands. It was presented in time for the 1909 Hudson-Fulton Celebration, held in New York harbor. A replica of Robert Fulton's *Clermont* was also built, and both ships sailed up the river to Albany. On October 11, 1909, the *Half-Moon* arrived at Cohoes, just north of Albany.

After the Celebration was over, the

PALISADES INTERSTATE PARK COMMISSION

Hell Hole Bridge

Half-Moon was given to the Palisades Interstate Park Commission. In July 1910, it was moored at the Englewood Boat Basin. In May 1911, it was taken to Nyack, and in 1912 it was moved to the new dock at Bear Mountain. When regular steamboat service from New York City to Bear Mountain began in 1913, the little *Half-Moon* was often found to be in the way at the dock, so it was moved to the mouth of Popolopen Creek, where Henry Hudson had anchored in 1609.

There it stayed, under the care of Park employee Captain Augustus Allen. After a few years, it began to leak, and Major Welch proposed to encase it in concrete. Then, in 1923, Daniel J. Cosgro, Mayor of Cohoes, suggested that the *Half-Moon* would be better cared for in Cohoes. He persuaded Governor Alfred E. Smith,

and in April 1924 the *Half-Moon* was legally transferred to the City of Cohoes. The partly sunken ship was refloated. Its ballast was removed, and it was eased up over the West Shore Railroad tracks by two horses operating a windlass.

Before going to Cohoes, the *Half-Moon* was once again taken down the river to the Spuyten Duyvil inlet by the tugboat *Libbie Barker*. There, on September 28, 1924, a crew of ten boys from DeWitt Clinton High School, dressed as sailors, manned the ship in commemoration of the 315th anniversary of Hudson's landing at 215th Street and Inwood Hill Park.

After ten days, the *Half-Moon* was towed to Cohoes. It came to rest on Van Schaick Island, where it was surrounded by a fence. For a few years

PALISADES INTERSTATE PARK COMMISSION

The Half-Moon *at the mouth of the Popolopen Creek*

the town took pride in their historic ship. But Mayor Cosgro retired in December 1929, and he died soon afterward. The fence was broken. Teen gangs overran the ship. Hoboes slept below decks. Finally, on July 22, 1934, the *Half-Moon* was destroyed by fire.

An interesting epilogue to the *Half-Moon* saga occurred in March 1946. At that time, the Palisades Interstate Park Commission received a bill in the amount of $10,552.50 for duty and internal revenue on the *Half-Moon* as of July 23, 1909 (the date

the ship was received in the Brooklyn Navy Yard). At that time, the ship had been accepted "on condition of bond." The bond, on file in the Custom House, apparently had been broken, so that the duty was therefore payable (Commission Minutes, 3/13/46). Exactly what happened then has not been recorded, but the minutes of the Commission meeting of October 11, 1946 state that "the Treasury Department has cancelled the bond."

In order to make the Park more accessible to the population of the surrounding region, the Commissioners also built bridges outside of the Park boundaries. In 1923, the Park built a 400-foot steel-arch bridge across Tiorati Brook in Stony Point. That bridge was commemorated on May 30, 1988 by a plaque which named it the James A. Farley Memorial Bridge. Farley had been Town Supervisor of Stony Point from 1920 to 1923; National Chairman of the Democratic Party from 1922 to 1940;

and Postmaster General, under President Franklin D. Roosevelt, from 1933 to 1940. In 1926, the Park built a 1,200-foot span over Sparkill Creek in Piermont, N.Y.

Another section of State Route 3 was the road around Storm King Mountain. In 1903, the State appropriated funds to build this road. But a group of financiers, disguised as a quarry company, bought the land at the river level, thus frustrating the State's plans. In 1913, under the direction of Major Welch, a new route was surveyed 400 feet above the river. Construction of the Storm King Highway began in July 1915. This highly scenic but narrow (20 feet) road was completed in September 1922. Immediately afterward, Dr. Ernest G. Stillman gave to the Park 800 acres on the south side of Storm King Mountain.

By 1937, it was realized that the Storm King Highway was inadequate, and Major Welch planned a Storm King Bypass. Construction was started in the spring of 1939, with much apprehension in the ranks of organized hikers who feared that beautiful Crow's Nest above West Point would be defaced. The present Route 9W around Storm King was opened to traffic on September 26, 1940 (*N.Y. Times*, 9/27/40).

Route 17

A road most familiar to those who hike in Harriman Park is New York State Route 17, which runs from Suffern through Arden to Harriman, N.Y.

In 1778, Robert Erskine prepared a map for General Washington which showed this road along the Ramapough River, then known as the Albany Road. A mile and a half north of Suffran's tavern, the road crossed the river (this portion of the road is now designated as Route 59), then passed Sidman's Tavern (still standing, just south of Sloatsburg—a name on the tree there is "Mapes"). It passed through Slott's (Sloatsburg), where the Eagle Valley Road went west to Ringwood. Before the Revolution, Erskine had been master of the Ringwood Iron Works.

The Albany Road crossed to the east side of the river at Greenwood (Arden). It went past June's Tavern in Smith's Clove (the site of this tavern is in the cloverleaf approach to the northbound lanes of the New York Thruway at Harriman) and Smith's Tavern in Highland Mills (on Route 32, just south of St. Patrick's Church), and continued past Schunemunk Mountain to New Windsor. Washington's troops made many trips through this valley from their headquarters at New Windsor.

Since it was the road the stagecoach took to Albany, the Albany Road was an especially significant route in the winter, when the Hudson River was closed to ships. From Suffern to Southfields, it also was the road to Goshen, the county seat of Orange County. The road to Goshen, known as the Orange Turnpike, departed from the Albany Road at Southfields, and went west, through Monroe, to Goshen.

To keep the road to Goshen in repair, the Orange Turnpike Company was chartered on April 4, 1800. Among the 67 original stockholders were Aaron Burr, J.A. Pierson and John Suffern. In 1859, there were tollgates on the Albany Road in Sloatsburg at Eagle Valley Road, at Greenwood (Arden) and at the Houghton Farm at the foot of Schunemunk Mountain. The toll for a wagon and two horses was 6 1/4 cents.

The appearance of the valley was much changed by the building of the New York and Lake Erie Railroad. Construction began in the Ramapo Pass in 1836, and the line was opened to Goshen in September 1841.

Much of the ore used at the Greenwood Furnace (built at Arden in 1811) came from the O'Neil and Forshee Mines in the hills west of the Pass. A road from the furnace crossed to the west side of the river and turned north along the hillside. After 0.5 mile, the road went up left over the ridge to what later was named Harriman Heights Road. It reached Harriman Heights Road 0.5 mile north of its intersection with Orange Turnpike. To find the O'Neil Mine, continue north on Orange Turnpike for 0.3 mile past its intersection with Harriman Heights Road. At a turnout where the road bends, an old road goes left to the O'Neil Mine.

In 1906, when Edward Harriman began to build his new mansion, the Arden House, he wanted the Albany Road moved to the west side of the Ramapo River, so that it would be further away from his home. In August 1909, he bought from the Town of Woodbury three miles of the Albany Road, from Arden to Central Valley. In return, he gave the town part of the O'Neil Mine Road on the western hillside and two more miles of right-of-way for a new road along the west side of the river to Turner's Junction (now Harriman) (*N.Y. Times*, 8/5/09).

This newer road—which was paved in 1911—ran parallel to and slightly above the present-day Route 17. It continued to Central Valley, where it joined the older route north. Hikers who follow it today, on the hillside west of Route 17, will note that the pavement is surprisingly good in many places. The present Route 17 was built about 1928.

When the New Jersey state roads were given numbers, sometime before 1930, our present-day Route 17 was designated as Route 2. North of Ramsey it was known as the Franklin Turnpike. It went through Mahwah and followed the Erie tracks through Suffern and Hillburn. In 1932, a new highway was built, roughly parallel to the Franklin Turnpike. This road crossed to the west side of the Ramapo River near Mahwah, and continued through Hillburn to Ramapo, where it met the old road (now known as Route 59). In the early 1990s, Route 17 was relocated to follow the New York Thruway from the state line to just north of Route 59, and the road through Hillburn now serves local traffic only.

New York State Thruway

The Thruway is the modern Albany Turnpike through the Ramapo Pass. Construction of the 14-mile section from Suffern to Harriman was begun in the spring of 1953, and it was opened to traffic on May 27, 1955. Needless to say, the Thruway brought many changes to the hikers' familiar trails.

In Sloatsburg, the northern branch of Johnsontown Road to Dater's Crossing (now known as Washington Avenue) was cut off, and the road was relocated to pass under the Thruway. In Tuxedo, the Kakiat Trail had crossed the Ramapo River on a footbridge south of the railroad station, and had gone directly uphill, south of the Italian Village. After May 1955, the approach to the Ramapo-Dunderberg, Tuxedo-Mt. Ivy, Kakiat and Triangle Trails was through the underpass on East Village Road.

At Southfields, the old footbridge which carried the Nurian Trail over the Ramapo River had been washed away in 1946. In 1950, the Park built a steel bridge across the river, only to have the trail cut again in 1953 by the Thruway. Through the efforts of the Trail Conference, a footbridge was finally built, and was opened on July 15, 1956 (see p. 69).

At Arden, the new highway remedied a long-existing deficiency of Arden Valley Road, which carried the Appalachian Trail. When first built in 1930, the road followed a roundabout route which went under the Erie tracks and through the river on a concrete-paved ford (see pp. 340-41). The overpass, built in 1954, remedied that situation. Also, until 1953 the Arden-Surebridge Trail (A-SB) had come south from the Arden station, using Harriman's Arden Road. That road was cut by the new Thruway, so

A-SB was rerouted along the west side of the tracks, and up the old road to the new overpass. (That route was abandoned in 1970.)

Route 106 (Old Route 210)

The road which crosses the middle of Harriman Park, now known as Route 106, was chartered in 1824 as a "New Turnpike" from Monroe to Haverstraw (in those days, Southfields was called Monroe). The New Turnpike started at Roger Parmelee's slitting mill (nail factory), and it crossed the Ramapo River on a wooden bridge. (The site of this bridge is just north of the present Nurian Trail bridge over the Ramapo River— the old abutments are still visible.) The road went south about a mile, around the end of the ridge, and passed Car Pond (now Lake Stahahe). This road from Southfields is still used by hikers, who sometimes think that it was built by Edward Harriman. In fact, Harriman's Level Road (the Arden Road), which was built in 1894, went north from Southfields (see pp. 165-66).

The New Turnpike passed Little Long Pond, then went through the village of Sandyfield (Beaver Pond). Until 1870, there was a tollgate where the road started downhill (near the crossing of Minisceongo Creek) and, heading east from there, the road was known as Gate Hill Road. Downstream from the tollgate, the road divided: the right fork (now known as Willow Grove Road) went down to Willow Grove, where it joined the Old Turnpike to Haverstraw. The left fork, which later became Route 106, joined the road from Cedar Ponds (Lake Tiorati) and went to Stony Point (King's Ferry).

In the early part of this century, the New Turnpike was a gravel road which was known as County Highway 416. When the Park was formed in 1910, the part of the New Turnpike leading to Southfields was called the Southfields Road. In 1913, it became part of the road to Bear Mountain which was later named the Seven Lakes Drive. The western section of the road was rerouted by the County in 1915 to its present end at the Wildcat Bridge. The older route, around the mountain to the railroad station at Southfields, was abandoned. The girder bridge at Southfields was disassembled and re-erected at its present location.

In 1923, a new road was built west to Greenwood Lake Village, replacing the older Warwick Turnpike. Now known as Route 17A, it was opened in May 1926. About this time, responsibility for the road through the Park was transferred from the counties to the State of New York, and it was designated New York State Route 210. In 1982, the state turned responsibility for maintaining the road back to the counties, and it is now known as County Route 106.

In the spring of 2007, Rockland County discovered that two historic stone-arch culverts under Route 106 near the Kanawauke Circle on Seven Lakes Drive had deteriorated. The County wanted to replace them with concrete pipes, but the Park and the state Office of Parks, Recreation and Historic Preservation were not pleased with this solution. As a result, the County imposed a five-ton weight limit on one culvert and closed the second. Access to a camp located between the two culverts was thus severely limited.

As a result of negotiations between the Park and the County, an agreement was reached providing that the County would rehabilitate the entire Route 106 through the Park, after which the Park would take over the road from the County. As of January 2010, the two culverts had been rehabilitated and the road reopened, but additional work remains to be completed before the Park will accept responsibility for maintaining the road. When control of the road is assumed by the Park, it will probably be given a new name. The Park has also reserved the right to close the road (or portions of it) in the winter.

Route 202

Route 202 is often used by hikers to reach the Kakiat and Tuxedo-Mt. Ivy Trails and the Long Path. The modern road goes northeast from Suffern to Ladentown, and then continues on a more easterly course to Mt. Ivy and Haverstraw. On old maps, it was called the Suffern-Haverstraw Highway.

General Robert Erskine's 1779 map shows a military road going northeast from "Suffran's," but after crossing the Mahwah River (near Viola) it turned east (on the present Grandview Avenue) to the hamlet of Kakiat (settlers from Long Island later changed the name of Kakiat to New Hempstead). From there the road (our Route 45/202) went north to Mt. Ivy and east to Haverstraw and King's Ferry (Stony Point).

A country road ran parallel to the Mahwah River from Viola to a crossroads where Michael Laden opened a store and tavern in 1816. That store was acquired in 1902 by Pincus Margulies of Brooklyn. In the years that followed, Margulies held various offices in the town, and bought the baskets and woodenware made by the folks who lived in the nearby hills. He died on November 15, 1952, but his daughter Hazel continued to live in the old building until she died in 1993.

In 1820, an improved road was built from "Suffran's" through Ladentown to Mt. Ivy, where it joined the older military road to Haverstraw. When roads were first given numbers, that road became N.Y. State Route 61. In 1934, it became Route 122, and in 1936 it became Route 202.

Arden Valley Road

This two-lane road runs for 4.8 miles between Tiorati Circle and Route 17 at Arden. At 0.35 mile from the Circle, the joint Appalachian/Ramapo-Dunderberg Trail crosses, and at 0.5 mile, at a sharp left turn, the Long Path crosses. The woods road which leaves to the right at the Long Path crossing was the route of Arden Valley Road until 1917. At this turn, too, an even older road once went north to Central Valley.

At 0.9 mile, a rocky path on the right leads to the large Bradley Mine. Further downhill, Upper and Lower Cohasset Lakes are passed. Then, at 1.85 miles, the road turns sharp left. Here, on the right side, a dirt road, blocked off by a gate, leads into the Harriman Estate. Until 1930, this estate road was the public road from the Erie Railroad station at Arden. After Roland Harriman gave Island Pond to the Park in 1927, a new Park road was planned. This road, opened in 1934, goes along the southern boundary of the lands retained by the Harriman family. It passes the entrance to Island Pond and further down goes by the Elk Pen hikers' parking area.

Things looked different in 1934. The road had to cross the Erie Railroad and the Ramapo River. That problem was solved by making an underpass under the Erie tracks, at the point where Arden Brook joins the Ramapo River. A ford was built there, paved with concrete. The tracks above were supported by a bridge built of steel beams which had been removed from the Tallman Mountain quarry. Stepping stones were provided for walkers.

One can still follow that 1934 road: From Route 17, go to the stone cabin near the Thruway bridge. Across from the cabin, a grassy old road goes downhill to the river level, where it turns under the culvert. The concrete pavement in the river is still visible. Now the Thruway is on the other side of the ford, but before it was built in 1953 the road turned south for

0.5 mile, went up a bank and swung north again to the present line. The area there now used for hikers' parking was part of the old 1930 road. The wire fence of the Elk Pen can still be seen there.

Toward the end of 1919, Major Welch received from Yellowstone Park a herd of 75 elk, male and female. Actually, many had died en route, and more died soon after arrival. The surviving elk were kept in a great wire pen, between Arden and Southfields, built by Park Forester Raymond Adolph. Despite considerable efforts to care for them, the elk did not thrive. Their numbers gradually dwindled. Some could still be seen in 1935, but by 1942 they were all gone.

Johnsontown Road

Johnsontown Road starts in Sloatsburg at the first left turn after Seven Lakes Drive passes under the New York Thruway. It goes northeast from there for 1.6 miles, parallel to the Seven Lakes Drive but on the west side of Stony Brook. The paved road presently ends at a circle (where there is ample parking), just beyond the Park boundary. The Blue Disc Trail goes up to the left just before the end of the road, following the right-of-way of the Columbia Gas Transmission Company.

Johnsontown Road once was a main Park drive which continued past the site of the present New Sebago Beach to end at old Route 210 near Little Long Pond. From the 1920s to 1962, the road was shown on Park maps as Stony Brook Drive. On November 10, 1962, after the new Seven Lakes Drive had been opened, the road was closed beyond the circle. We will describe the old road, which still is walkable.

Proceeding northeast from the circle, the road is now marked with the white blazes of the White Bar Trail. After 0.3 mile, the Kakiat Trail comes in from the left, runs along the road for 300 feet, then leaves to the right. Just beyond this point, a stone wall begins to run along the right side of the road. Here, the Matthew Waldron family once had their home and blacksmith shop. At 0.5 mile, the old road forks. The left fork, followed by the White Bar Trail, goes to the Dutch Doctor Shelter and beyond. The right fork is Johnsontown Road. It is necessary to cross Seven Lakes Drive here and follow the old road on the other side. A path on the west side of the Drive, carrying a buried telephone cable, once was the camp road which led to the American Canoe Association (ACA) Camp and the ADK Camp Nawakwa on Lake Sebago. A quarter mile up the camp road, on the right, was the home of the William Lewis Becraft family.

Now the old Johnsontown Road is on the east side of Seven Lakes Drive. 0.5 mile north of the Kakiat Trail crossing, the old road approaches the new Drive, but immediately swings east again. At this point, on the right, there is a wide path that leads up to the ridge above Stony Brook. In a clearing on the ridge is the cellar of a home that was built there in 1935 by Fred Koerber. In 1960, when the Park condemned his land, he had his house moved down the road and re-erected at its present location—125 Johnsontown Road.

The old Johnsontown Road goes around a small hill and again crosses Seven Lakes Drive. 0.4 mile further on, it crosses the road to the ACA camp and follows the shoreline to the Drive, where it crosses over the dam. Before the dam was completed in 1926, the road crossed the brook on the Burnt Sawmill Bridge.

After the dam was built, the road ran along the top of the dam, then went through an area where Old Sebago Beach was built in 1932. At the same time, a car-camping area, which included a comfort station and picnic tables, was built near the brook below Sebago Dam. Today, the old road goes along the top of the hikers'/fishermen's parking area. North of the parking area, a red-blazed ski trail uses the old road. The road continues across the entrance to the Sebago Cabin Camps (formerly, the NYU Camp) through a grove of young trees, and crosses the Drive 250 feet south of the gate on Pine Meadow Road. The old road crosses Pine Meadow Road, and 0.2 mile farther re-crosses the Drive and continues along the Park road leading to Baker Camp.

The old Johnsontown Road follows the Baker Camp Road for 0.3 mile, until the road makes a sharp left turn. Here, the old road continues straight ahead, past a boulder barrier. It is now a wide, grass-covered high-way which ends above a cut of the modern Seven Lakes Drive. A woods road, known as the High Hill Trail, once started here. Its beginning is now marked by a cairn atop a large boulder on the east bank (see p. 241).

Scramble down now, and follow the new road around to the entrance to Sebago Beach (opened on May 24, 1952). We now are approaching old Johnsontown, where the new beach is now. But first, walk along the Drive for about 0.1 mile beyond the road leading to the beach. There, down left, in a grove of pines, is one of the Johnsontown cemeteries. There are perhaps 150 graves, many marked with plain fieldstones. Only a few have

Johnsontown Cemetery

inscriptions, the most recent being the gravestone of Mary Johnson, who died on February 11, 1884, aged 75 years.

Go back and make a right turn onto the beach road, then take the first left turn. This road passes the other Johnsontown cemetery. Most of the stones here have inscriptions, the latest being Louise Johnson, 1858-1957. Now, go back to the beach road, and follow it to the parking area beyond the beach. There are several picnic tables on the hillside on the right edge of the large parking area; these tables are sitting on the old Johnsontown Road. Just north of those picnic tables, there is a short stone staircase on the right, and beyond that is a driveway that leads around to a cellar hole near a great hemlock on a knoll. This was once the home of Fred Johnson, who sold it to the Park in 1918. It was not demolished until the 1940s.

Up the road 0.25 mile from the parking area, a camp road from Lake Skenonto joins on the left. To make a circular hike of about nine miles, take this road to the Victory Trail, turn left onto the Victory Trail and follow it to its end at Black Ash Swamp, and then return to Johnsontown Circle via the Blue Disc Trail. Beyond the road to Lake Skenonto, old Johnsontown Road continues northerly for another 0.8 mile. It ends at a gate on Route 106, just west of Little Long Pond.

In 1907, the County Superintendent of Roads reported: "One new section of road was taken on during last year, that leading from Johnsontown to the Burnt Sawmill Bridge, which is known as the Diamond Valley Road. This is one of the most picturesque drives in our county, although it is little used, owing to the condition of the road. This was nothing but a poor wood road, but since it became a county road the bad places have been stoned in, and it has been widened out in many places" (Rockland County Board of Supervisors Proceedings, 4/25/07).

Johnsontown Road was described in 1923 in the first *New York Walk Book* as "a good dirt road through farming country." On the first Park trail map in 1920, the Park boundary crossed Johnsontown Road 0.3 mile south of the present Sebago Dam.

In the valley along Stony Brook close to Sloatsburg were two large farms, owned by Robert Reeves and by George Grant Mason. The Reeves' farm line started on the north side of Stony Brook, opposite the point where Reeves Brook joins Stony Brook. From there the property line went northwest to Johnsontown Road where the circle is at present. Taking in land for 0.1 mile west of the road, Reeves' line proceeded southwest for 0.55 mile, then crossed back to the brook. All of Reeves' land was north and west of Stony Brook.

The meadow on the southeast side of the present-day Seven Lakes Drive, where the Reeves Meadow Visitor Center is now located, was once part of a farm owned by George Grant Mason. (What is nowadays called Reeves' Meadow actually was Mason's Meadow!) Mason was a wealthy man who lived in Tuxedo Park. Born in 1868 of Scottish parents, he married Marion Peak in 1897. In 1907, Mason, who then lived in Mason City, Iowa and was superintendent of the Jim River Division of the Chicago, Milwaukee and St. Paul Railroad, learned of the death of his uncle James Henry Smith (Silent Smith). Smith had inherited $56,000,000 from his uncle George Smith. The fortune included a large holding in the Milwaukee Road (as the railroad was commonly known). Silent Smith who, about 1890, had built a mansion in the new (1886) Tuxedo Park, was on his wedding trip when he died in Kyoto, Japan (*N.Y. Times*, 3/28/07). In his will, he left $12,000,000 to his nephew George Grant Mason, and $6,000,000 to George's brother William Smith Mason (*N.Y. Times*, 5/8/07). George got the Tuxedo Park home, and William got a farm in Sloatsburg which Silent Smith had bought in 1903 from a local man named Nicholas Rose. Rose had owned it since 1865. For reasons unknown, in 1908 George Mason bought his brother's farm, and used it to raise pedigreed cattle, and also fish. When his farm superintendent became ill in 1919, he decided to give his farm to the Park if they would dam the brook and create a lake for children's camps. He did give the 125-acre farm to the Park in 1921, and it was valued at $25,000 (Commission Minutes, 4/26/21).

The plan to build a lake was opposed by his neighbor Robert Reeves who, in 1915, helped form the Ramapo Mountains Water Supply and Service Co., which acquired the land north to Lake Sebago and east up to Pine Meadow. Their plan to draw water from their property collapsed when the Park began proceedings to condemn the land east of Johnsontown Road. However, because of Reeves' opposition, the Park never did build a lake on the former Mason property.

Before his death on April 30, 1955 at age 86, George Grant Mason, together with banker George Baker, endowed a new Tuxedo Park High School. Their portraits hang in the school auditorium. Mason had a daughter, Margaret Peabody, and a son, George, Jr. (1904-1970), who was a founder of Pan American Airways.

During the years after 1922, the Mason farmhouse was occupied by Chief Park Ranger Bill Gee, who had joined the force in 1914. He continued to operate a fish hatchery there for the Park. He retired in 1941 and died in 1943, aged 74 years. After that, the farmhouse was home to John and Grace Snyder until it was demolished in 1953. The cement bridge over Stony Brook leading to the farm was demolished in 1993.

The old Reeves' farmhouse is still at 115 Johnsontown Road. It was first built about 1760 by Heinrich Bosch, a native of Leyden, Holland. Before

1917, it had belonged to Thomas Donovan. Robert Reeves bought it at auction, and eventually sold it in 1946. Since then, the 110-acre farm has passed through several owners, and is now much smaller in area.

Going north along the old road, one passes several more farm sites: the Waldron blacksmith shop (at the circle where the paved road now ends); the Becraft place (where the camp road starts); and two Waldron farms (near the entrance to Pine Meadow Road). To the left of the ski trail as it goes through a hemlock grove is the tombstone of Abram Waldron (1819-1897). In 1917, Mary Waldron sold both family farms to the Park. Her home, which was demolished in the early 1930s, stood on the old road overlooking the present Sebago Cabin Camps. Her granddaughter Alpha and grandsons Avery and Grant are buried in the Sloatsburg Cemetery.

In 1962, the old Johnsontown Road was cut, where it turned westward, by the new Seven Lakes Drive. At the intersection where Lake Welch Drive now starts, the Johnsontown Methodist Church (built in 1872) formerly stood. The church was razed in 1950. Its last minister was Reverend Austin W. Conklin.

The village of Johnsontown was located where the beach is now, on the edge of a great swamp. In 1870, there were 30 homes, some up towards Little Long Pond, others east towards St. John's Church. (The road leading east to St. John's Church was also called Johnsontown Road.) There were also

PALISADES INTERSTATE PARK COMMISSION

James Johnson house

three stores and a school. Many residents sold out to the Park in 1913; others stayed until the lake was built in 1924. Two residents who left then were Henry and Sherman Youmans. They moved to Garnerville. A story was told about Sherman, that he once agreed to "rassle" a performing bear. After a while, Sherm was heard to say, "Get this damned bear off me, or I'll kill him." The family of Muzz Jones, the last to live in Johnsontown, finally sold out in 1952.

Johnsontown was first settled about 1750 by James Johnson, of English/French descent, whose family came to New York about 1700. They made a living by cutting tall trees for ship masts. In the years that followed, the eldest son always was named James. In 1930, Jim Johnson was the construction foreman for the Park. He lived across the road from Spring Pond, just east of the Kanawauke Circle. In 1917, his daughter Mary Bessie married John Tamsen who later became Park Superintendent. They are buried in St. John's Cemetery.

Lake Welch Drive

Lake Welch Drive is a 5.6-mile road which starts from Seven Lakes Drive near the entrance to Sebago Beach, and ends at Exit 16 of the Palisades Interstate Parkway. It was opened to traffic on June 26, 1971.

At 1.0 mile from Seven Lakes Drive, a paved road on the right goes to Camp Lanowa at Breakneck Pond. That road once was part of the Old Turnpike (pre-1824) from Haverstraw to Southfields. On its way west, the Old Turnpike joined the road from St. John's Church (known as Johnsontown Road), then passed through Johnsontown (now Sebago Beach). The older road, still visible, was abandoned after Lake Welch Drive was built in 1967. At 1.45 miles, St. John's Road, which passes St. John's Church and ends at Route 106, goes off to the right. Lake Welch Drive then goes over Route 106, passes picnic areas on the right, above the lake, and, at 3.3 miles, reaches the entrances to the beach. Before the new Drive was built, the beach was reached by a road which turned off Route 106 just west of St. John's Road (that road is still open to traffic, and it provides an alternate route to the lake).

Continuing northwest from the lake, Grape Swamp is visible on the left, and the road descends a mile-long valley. The road here obliterated the Suffern-Bear Mountain Trail which once went around Grape Swamp and down this valley to Tiorati Brook. Tiorati Brook Road joins from the left, and then Lake Welch Drive ends at the Palisades Interstate Parkway.

Palisades Interstate Parkway

The Commissioners of the Palisades Interstate Park, led by George W. Perkins, were determined to make it possible for large numbers of people to reach and enjoy the Park—first in New Jersey, and later in the Hudson Highlands. In 1909, they proposed a scenic drive along the top of the Palisades. In 1914, they planned a road from Fort Lee to Storm King Mountain (*N.Y. Times*, 4/5/14). Because most of the land along the top of the Palisades was still privately owned, these plans could not immediately be implemented. In 1916, though, the Park built the eight-mile Henry Hudson Drive between the ferry landings at Edgewater, Englewood and Alpine.

In 1933, Major Welch gave the Civilian Conservation Corps the task of building a pair of roads from Queensboro south through the Beechy Bottom valley between Black Mountain and West Mountain. The north/south lanes were to join at Tiorati Brook Road and go down to Route 9W at Stony Point. Parts of those roads (which roughly parallel the present-day Parkway) were built, and are occasionally used by hikers (see pp. 172-73). Before they could be finished, however, the Corps was disbanded and the project suspended.

When John D. Rockefeller in 1935 gave the Commission 700 acres on top of the Palisades, it was possible once again to plan a highway from the George Washington Bridge to Bear Mountain (*N.Y. Times*, 2/17/41).

By 1946, the surveys had been completed. Both New York and New Jersey appropriated funds, and construction began in 1947. In 1951, the first southern mile was opened, and on November 30, 1953 the section from Mount Ivy to the Bear Mountain Bridge was opened. (From the Queensboro Circle to the Bear Mountain Bridge, the new Parkway incorporated the route of the older Popolopen Drive.) On June 22, 1957, with the help of Governors W. Averell Harriman and Robert B. Meyner, the New York and New Jersey sections were joined. The final 5.2 miles, from Orangeburg to the New York Thruway, were opened on August 28, 1958. The 38-mile road had cost $47,000,000.

During those years, hikers followed the construction of the road with mixed feelings. Indeed, hikers all through the years had protested the building of roads in the Park because the construction created such scenes of destruction, and changed the familiar course of the hiking trails. For example, in 1960, as a result of the construction of the Parkway, the Timp-Torne Trail was rerouted entirely away from Bear Mountain.

As part of the Parkway project, the Anthony Wayne Recreation Area was created in 1951. The original 35 acres for bathing, picnicking and playfields were opened by Governor Harriman on Saturday, June 18, 1955. The area was expanded in 1958, but the swimming pools have been closed for the last several years.

The New York section of the Parkway is patrolled by state troopers; the New Jersey section by the Palisades Interstate Park police.

Perkins Memorial Drive

The Perkins Memorial Drive is popular with Park visitors because it enables them, with little effort, to reach the top of Bear Mountain and enjoy its views and picnic areas.

The road starts from the Seven Lakes Drive, 1.0 mile east of the Palisades Interstate Parkway. In 2.0 miles the road climbs 650 feet to the elevation 1,280 feet, where it circles the Perkins Tower (the actual summit, elevation 1,305 feet, is 600 feet north of the Tower). Just east of the Tower, a side road, now known as the Scenic Drive, descends gradually for 1.0 mile to a dead-end viewpoint. That side road once was a part of Perkins Drive, when it was a one-way loop extending from the Seven Lakes Drive to Popolopen Drive on the north side of the mountain (see below).

On the way up the road, the Appalachian Trail (white) crosses at 0.35

mile. Here, on the east side, the abandoned route of the Drive extends for 0.6 mile to the turnaround where the Scenic Drive presently ends. The Appalachian Trail now follows a portion of this route (from 1976 to 2010, it continued up the Drive for another 0.5 mile and then headed east towards the summit of Bear Mountain). On the west side of Perkins Drive, the abandoned road continues 0.7 mile down to Popolopen Drive.

At 1.4 miles, the Major Welch Trail crosses the Drive. Near the trail at this point is a stone marker which shows the 1910 boundary of the new Bear Mountain State Park. At that time, the West Point Military Academy owned a pie-shaped 50-acre piece of the north side of the mountain, across Popolopen Creek from the Torne. In 1942, the Park acquired that piece and the Torne, in exchange for land on Long Mountain and Turkey Hill which they had bought in 1928 from the Fort Montgomery Iron Corporation (see pp. 63-64).

Perkins Drive was built as a memorial to George Walbridge Perkins, Sr., the first chairman of the Palisades Interstate Park Commission (he served in that capacity from 1900 until his death in 1920). The initial survey was made in 1923 (*N.Y. Post*, 11/5/23). The plans were drawn up by Major Welch, and the construction was directed by John J. Tamsen, Superintendent of the New York Division of the Park. The work did not actually begin until November 21, 1932, when Temporary Emergency Relief Administration workers from New York City and Orange and Rockland Counties became available. During the first year, 1,520 men worked on the project, and 764 men worked for another 18 months. The work was 95% hand labor, and the men were paid an average of $12 per week.

The 4.5-mile-long road was dedicated on October 31, 1934 by two grandsons of George W. Perkins, Sr.: George Edward Freeman and George W. Perkins 3rd (*N.Y. Times*, 11/1/34). The entrance then was on Popolopen Drive, about 0.25 mile west of the crossing of the Timp-Torne Trail (which had been blazed in 1921). The exit was on Seven Lakes Drive (as it is today).

At the same time that the road was built, a memorial Tower was constructed on the summit—a gift of George W. Perkins' widow and son. A steel fire tower which had been on that spot was removed and re-erected on Diamond Mountain in 1935. For nineteen years, until it was closed on May 23, 1953, Perkins Tower was used as a weather station and fire lookout.

In 1990, George W. Perkins' daughter-in-law and other members of the Perkins family donated $100,000 to defray the costs of producing new exhibits for installation in the Tower, and also agreed to donate $650,000 over a period of years to provide an endowment for maintaining the Tower and its exhibits (Commission Minutes, 9/24/90, pp. 16-20). The new exhibits visually relate the visitor to the surrounding topography, and also graphically recount the history of the Park and the role played by its founders. The renovated Tower was rededicated on September 18, 1992.

In 1950, Perkins Drive was closed by rock slides. In rebuilding the road, the Park engineers took into consideration the effect of the new Palisades Interstate Parkway, which was started in 1951. They rebuilt Perkins Drive as a two-way road, with a single entrance on Seven Lakes Drive. It was reopened to the public in the spring of 1952.

Popolopen Drive

Popolopen Drive is now part of the Palisades Interstate Parkway (1953) and of U.S. Route 6.

When Bear Mountain State Park was opened to the public on July 5, 1913, there was an old woods road which went around the north side of Bear Mountain, high above Popolopen Creek. The Park's first trail map in 1920 called this the Queensboro Trail. In 1923, the new Appalachian Trail went up this road for 0.5 mile from the bridge approach (the bridge was opened on November 27, 1924), then turned up the mountain on the route now called the Major Welch Trail.

Early in 1925, the Park Commission decided to build an entirely new road around the north side of Bear Mountain to meet the Seven Lakes Drive and the Long Mountain Parkway at Queensboro (*N.Y. Times*, 2/8/25). The 18-foot-wide road opened to traffic in 1927. During 1933-34, it was widened to 30 feet (3 lanes), with the help of the Works Progress Administration.

On November 30, 1953, Popolopen Drive, having been widened to four lanes, became part of the new Palisades Interstate Parkway.

Seven Lakes Drive

In 1912, after Major Welch joined the Palisades Interstate Park, he made plans to build a road west from Bear Mountain through the recent-

PALISADES INTERSTATE PARK COMMISSION

Popolopen Drive construction, 1926

ly acquired Harriman lands to Southfields. Construction of the "South-fields Road" was started in September 1913, and the road was opened in August 1915. Ten and one-half miles of 10-foot-wide gravel road had been built from Bear Mountain to County Route 416 (now Route 106), where Lake Kanawauke was created in 1916. From there, the Southfields Road (which was soon renamed Seven Lakes Drive) continued west along County Route 416. The lakes it passed at that time were: Hessian, Queens-boro, Nawahunta, Tiorati, Kanawauke, Little Long Pond and Stahahe. Un-til 1915, when the present route and the Wildcat Bridge over the Ramapo River/Erie Railroad were built, the Seven Lakes Drive turned north after Lake Stahahe, and went around the mountain to Southfields. In 1933, the Drive was widened to 30 feet.

In October 1961, bulldozers began clearing a new 75-foot-wide road north from Sloatsburg, parallel to the older Johnsontown Road (known as Stony Brook Drive from the Park boundary near Sloatsburg to the Ka-nawauke Circle), and crossing it in several places. When this new road was opened in September 1962, it was named Seven Lakes Drive (today, it passes nine lakes). Stony Brook Drive was closed at the Park boundary, two miles from Route 17. The remaining part of this road is now, once again, known as Johnsontown Road.

St. John's Road

Presently, St. John's Road branches from Lake Welch Drive 1.4 miles east of Seven Lakes Drive, and goes 0.75 mile to a junction with Route 106.

At the junction with Lake Welch Drive, the Long Path crosses. Further along St. John's Road, on the left, is St. John's Cemetery, and just beyond is St. John's Episcopal Church (known since the 1920s as St. John's-in-the-Wilderness). This is a mission church of the Protestant Episcopal Diocese of New York.

In 1870, an orphanage known as the House of the Good Shepherd was built in Tomkins Cove. Soon afterward, Ada Bessie Carey came to the orphanage from Guernsey, Channel Isles. She was a teacher who, in her spare time, rode a white horse into the nearby mountains to gather botany specimens. She found that there were many mountain children who could not get to a school. By 1874, Ada Carey had started a school in a log cabin for the mountain children.

This touching story was seen in a New York City newspaper by Margaret Zimmerman. She invited Ada Carey to New York City to talk about possibly building a church and school in the mountains as a memorial to her husband, who had died in Palestine in 1876. Advised by Ada Carey, Mrs. Zimmerman purchased land, and on June 23, 1880, a cornerstone was laid. Ada Carey taught in the school and was caretaker of the church until she returned to Guernsey in 1914. Mrs. Zimmerman died in 1921; Ada Carey died in Guernsey in 1925.

The first rector (who served from 1878 to 1918) was Dr. Mytton Maury, who was editor of the well-known Maury's geography textbook.

Reverend Dr. Mytton Maury was born in Wales on January 18, 1839, and was brought to New York City at the age of ten. He took his M.A. at Columbia University in 1860. Rev. Maury became a Hebrew scholar and teacher, and served as curate of St. Thomas Church in New York City for ten years. He married Virginia Draper, daughter of John Draper, the historian. They had three children: Carlotta (1878-1938), who became a paleontologist for the government of Brazil, and a geologist for oil companies; Antonia (1867-1952), who was a research astronomer at the Harvard Observatory from 1889 to 1935; and a son, Dr. John William Draper Maury.

The next rector was Reverend Burton Lee, who served from 1918 to

DANIEL CHAZIN

St. John's Church

1928. He also served churches in other places, such as Willow Grove and Doodletown. Reverend Lee was followed by Reverend Walter Frederick Hoffman, who served from 1928 until he died at the age of 58 on February 5, 1950. In 1952, the New York-New Jersey Trail Conference solicited contributions for a Hoffman memorial window for the church. It was during Reverend Hoffman's tenure that the hikers' Palm Sunday service was started by Frank Place of the Tramp and Trail Club (*Trail Walker*, Sept./Oct. 1971). After a lapse of several years, the Palm Sunday service was started again in 1935 by Walter Shannon of the Adirondack Mountain Club.

Several rectors came after Reverend Hoffman. At present the rector is Reverend William Dearman of Peekskill.

In the nearby cemetery, some of the names on the gravestones are: Reverend Walter Hoffman (1891-1950); Ruby Jolliffe (1882-1968) (she was Park Camps Director); John Tamsen (1892-1973) (was Park Superintendent, 1915-1940); and Frank Ballard (1918-1977) (was Police Chief of Sloatsburg, 1950-1977).

Across the road from the church are a social hall and the home of the church caretaker. Fifty yards up the road, on the right, is a path which will take hikers to the Long Path.

Before Lake Kanawauke was built in 1915, St. John's Road went west from the church, past Lily Pond, where it branched. Parts of that old road can still be walked. The right branch, known as Goodspring Road, went north along Stony Brook (which later became Lake Kanawauke) and ended at the Monroe-Haverstraw Turnpike (now Route 106). In 1917, after the lake had been built, Goodspring Road was rebuilt for 1.25 miles along the shore. In 1929, when the new Stony Brook Drive was built south from the Kanawauke Circle, that lakeside piece of Goodspring Road became a camp road. The left branch of St. John's Road was known as Johnsontown Road; it went to Johnsontown (now Sebago Beach). This left branch (as well as St. John's Road itself, west of the junction with the Camp Lanowa Road) had been part of the Old Turnpike, built before 1824 from Monroe (i.e., Southfields) to Haverstraw. These roads are clearly shown on R.F. O'Connor's 1854 map of Rockland County. In 1907, the County Superintendent of Roads reported that "the road heading from Beaver Pond at the Stony Point line, through to Johnsontown, by way of the St. John's Church was widened and graveled, and is now the best gravel road, excepting none, in our county" (Rockland County Board of Supervisors Proceedings, 4/25/07).

Tiorati Brook Road

Tiorati Brook Road was once called the Cedar Ponds Road, and extended from Cedar Ponds (Lake Tiorati) to Stony Point. Presently, it runs 4.0 miles from the Tiorati Circle to a junction with Lake Welch Drive, just before Exit 16 of the Palisades Interstate Parkway. Going southeast from Tiorati Circle, the Ramapo-Dunderberg Trail goes off to the left at 0.35 mile, the Lake Tiorati dam is crossed at 1.15 miles, and the Red Cross Trail crosses at 1.5 miles. After entering Rockland County at 1.8 miles, the Beech Trail comes in from the right at 2.35 miles (parking is available here), and Tiorati Brook crosses (and the Beech Trail leaves to the left) at 2.5 miles. Tiorati Brook Road ends at Lake Welch Drive, 4.0 miles from the start. The road is closed to traffic during the winter months.

Robert Erskine, Surveyor General for George Washington, did not show Cedar Ponds Road on his 1778 map, but it is shown on David Barr's 1839 map of Rockland County. The road in those days was not a good one. One correspondent remembered that in 1900, the only way to get to Cedar Ponds was on foot, or by side-bar buggy over the old road from Stony Point (*N.Y. Post*, 1/4/29). In 1907, Calvin T. Allison, Superintendent of Roads, reported to the Rockland County Board of Supervisors: "The road from Pingyp to Cedar Pond is in poor condition for a county road. This is one of the most neglected roads in the town [of Stony Point]. It became a county road in 1899" (Rockland County Board of Supervisors Proceedings, 4/25/07).

In May 1915, the new Interstate Park rebuilt the Cedar Ponds dam, and in 1916 it began improving the road along the eastern shore, widening it to 26 feet and surfacing it with gravel. About 1931, the road was paved from Tiorati Circle to its junction with Route 210.

In 1953, the new Palisades Interstate Parkway was built through this area. On its way north, the Parkway joined Tiorati Brook Road at the foot of the Pingyp. (Coming from the southeast, Tiorati Brook Road still joins the northbound lanes of the Parkway at this point.) After about half a mile, the Parkway departs north, following Stillwater Brook.

Then, in 1971, Lake Welch Drive was opened. The Drive "borrowed" another half-mile of Tiorati Brook Road, and the two roads now run jointly for this distance.

THE MINES
IN BEAR MOUNTAIN/
HARRIMAN PARK

There are over 20 known mines in the Park—always interesting places to go for a hike. Several of these are really only prospector holes, and more such holes without names will be seen along the trails. Much of the following information on the iron mines in the Park comes from James M. Ransom's Vanishing Ironworks of the Ramapos *(Rutgers University Press, 1966).*

For more detailed material on the various iron mines described in this chapter, see Iron Mine Trails: A History and Hiker's Guide to the Historic Mines of the New Jersey and New York Highlands, *by Edward J. Lenik (New York-New Jersey Trail Conference, 1999).*

Barnes Mine

The Barnes Mine can be easily seen on the hillside north of Lake Welch Drive, 0.2 mile east of its intersection with St. John's Road. A pile of tailings shows its location. The mine can be approached by a road going uphill from the Drive, 0.1 mile further east. An old, overgrown road goes left along the hillside to the mine, which is a rather large cavity in the hillside.

The mine is on a 17-acre parcel bought in 1846 by Isaac Barnes. It probably was he who first opened a mine there, and the place was known as the "mine lot." By 1864, it belonged to John Charleston. In 1871, he leased the mine to the Rockland Nickel Company, which operated the Nickel Mine on nearby Grape Swamp Mountain. It appears that mining operations at the Barnes Mine were suspended in 1884.

The land remained with the Charleston family and was sold to the Park by Jerome Charleston in 1938. His farm was located about where Lake Welch Drive now passes. The mine was approached through his farm yard (and that of his son Russell) from St. John's Road. That farm lane is now a private driveway just a short distance east of St. John's Church. This driveway led to a house which was owned by the Park and leased to a Park employee. Unfortunately, this house—the last remnant of the community of Sandyfield—was destroyed by fire in February 1999. Its last occupant was Dalton Stalter.

The Barnes Mine is mentioned in a book by Cornelia F. Bedell, *Now and Then and Long Ago in Rockland County* (1941).

Boston Mine

The Boston Mine is located on the Dunning Trail (yellow) just east of Island Pond Road. It is 0.85 mile north of Route 106 or 0.3 mile south of the junction of the Arden-Surebridge Trail (red triangle on white) with Island Pond Road.

There is a large opening in the side of a low hill, leading to a water-filled shaft. The mine was last worked in 1880, and from the size of the dump it appears not to have been very deep. The ore was sent to the Clove (anthracite) Furnace at Greenwood (Arden) (Ransom, p. 231).

DANIEL CHAZIN

Entrance to the Boston Mine

One of the "Wednesday Hikers" in 1987 told of visiting the library at Oxford University, where he asked for a book on Peter Hasenclever. There he read that ore from one mine in the Ramapo Mountains was sent to Boston, where it was made into iron products, which was then against the law.

Bradley Mine

Bradley Mine is on the north side of Arden Valley Road, about 0.9 mile west of Tiorati Circle. An eroded path goes steeply up to the mine entrance. There is no marker at the road to show the way. A vein about 10 feet wide ran for 150 feet into the hillside, then became a "pod" of rich ore about 200 feet long and 75 feet wide. The main chamber, which is at least 200 feet deep, is now filled with water.

There is a hole in the roof of the main chamber, through which light comes from above. Agile hikers can climb up there and, when they do, they discover another chamber—a limestone cave in the rock above the mine.

From 1922 to 1949, the Fingerboard-Storm King Trail went up the hillside past the mine opening and over the two summits of Bradley Mountain.

It has often been supposed that this mine and mountain were named after Richard Bradley who, in 1722, was appointed Attorney General of the Province of New York. King George II made several grants of land to Bradley and his children. These grants, however, were in the vicinity of Bear Mountain, and did not extend to Bradley Mountain.

Further study now reveals that, during the period of the American Revolution, a man named Bradley first opened iron mines on the land which in 1885 was bought by Edward Harriman (*Middletown Times Herald*, 2/24/40). Later, the land was bought at a sheriff's sale by James Cunningham of Warwick, N.Y. (Orange County Deeds, Liber N, Page 402, 9/1/1810). It was he who, in 1811, built the charcoal blast furnace which he named Greenwood Furnace.

After several further changes of ownership, the land, mines and furnace became the property of Robert P. Parrott in 1837. The Bradley Mine was worked until 1874.

Christie Mine

This mine is located on the eastern side of Horse Chock Mountain—the mountain to the east of Horse Chock Brook, which drains the Letchworth Reservoirs.

To reach the Christie Mine, follow the gas pipeline on the east side of the mountain for 0.75 mile north of File Factory Brook. Here, another brook comes down the hill, and the Christie Mine will be found in that gully, about 0.2 mile up from the gas line. A map of Haverstraw Township in the *New Historical Atlas of Rockland County* (1876) shows a mine on Horse Chock Mountain, belonging to the Christie Mining Company. The mine does not appear to have been extensively worked.

In the early 1800s, the Christie family owned much land in the eastern Ramapo Mountains. They were descended from James Christie, born 1672 in Scotland, and living in Schraalenburgh, New Jersey about 1720.

Cornell Mine

The Cornell Mine consists of a group of mine openings at the top and on the north side of Bald Mountain. It may be reached by the Cornell Mine Trail (blue) and by the Ramapo-Dunderberg Trail (R-D) (red dot on white). At the 980-foot level, where these two trails meet, a large depression in the earth marks the site of one of the old mine workings. Higher up, to the left of the R-D, almost at the top of the mountain, is a larger opening.

A third, much larger opening is slightly northeast of the summit of Bald Mountain, and about 80 feet down. The characteristic pile of tailings shows its location. This hole is about 15 by 20 feet in area.

The fourth opening is directly downhill from the third one, about 50 feet lower. (It is at about the same level as the junction of the Cornell Mine and R-D Trails, and may also be reached by bushwhacking a short distance west from the trail junction.) It, too, has its pile of tailings. This opening is worth a visit—it is a real tunnel, with water at least five inches deep, that goes horizontally into the hillside for about 50 feet. Bring a good flashlight!

In 1874, Minerva Herbert inherited from a previous husband a 175-acre parcel which went uphill from Pleasant Valley Road, over the top of Bald Mountain, to the cliff above the Jones Trail. This had once been a part of the 3,000-acre tract granted by King George III in 1769 to William Kempe, James Lamb and John Crum. (Minerva Herbert's grave may be found in one of the Doodletown cemeteries.)

In 1880, Minerva leased her property for twenty years to Alexander Phyfe of New York City, for the purpose of mining iron ore. In 1885, the lease was transferred to Thomas Cornell of Kingston, New York. Thomas Cornell was an affluent businessman who had been a New York State Senator in 1867-69 and 1881-83, and was president of the Ulster and Delaware Railroad. Hikers will recognize that as the railroad (now largely abandoned) that parallels Route 28 in the Catskills, from Kingston to Phoenicia, Belleayre, Arkville and beyond. In 1879, Cornell's name was given to one of the Catskill peaks by Princeton geology professor Arnold Guyot.

Cornell was also president of the Cornell Steamboat Company, which operated two dayliners and a fleet of tugboats which towed barges down the Hudson River from the Delaware and Hudson Canal (of which Cornell was a director). No doubt, Cornell wanted to carry iron ore in his barges, too.

Cornell hired a local man named Baldwin to operate the mine on Bald Mountain. Baldwin lost his eyesight in a premature explosion (this story was related by Oscar Herbert, a nephew of Minerva Herbert, who thought that the name Bald Mountain was a shortened form of Baldwin Mountain; *N.Y. Post*, 5/26/38).

Like the Doodletown Mine and the Herbert Mine, the upper two openings on Bald Mountain were probably made before 1859. The lower openings were probably made between 1885 and 1890. There is no record of how much iron ore this mine produced. It seems likely that all activity there ended in 1890, when both Minerva Herbert and Thomas Cornell died.

Cranberry Mine

On Seven Lakes Drive, 0.3 mile west of Long Mountain Circle, there is an abandoned comfort station on the north side of the road. Behind the building, a trail goes up, west, about 0.8 mile to the Cranberry Mine. To follow the trail, it is necessary to go around a gravel pit which interrupts it. The mine will be recognized by its steel door, which nowadays is open. It is a dry mine, which extends about 100 feet into the hillside.

In the early days of the Interstate Park, the mine on Cranberry Mountain was used for the storage of dynamite. Major Welch's letter to John Pratt White (then president of the New York Commission), dated April 16, 1924, described the mine: "A magazine was constructed there several years ago with a capacity of 100,000 pounds—entirely underground, dry, ventilated. The entrance is sheet iron-faced, doors of steel plate. Nearby is a corrugated steel building with a capacity of 2000 pounds." As of March 31, 1934, there were 99,500 pounds of TNT in the Cranberry Mine. In recent years, the Park's dynamite has been stored elsewhere.

Daters Mine

About 1.35 miles south of its start in Tuxedo, the Kakiat Trail (white) turns sharply right as it goes around the southern end of Dater Mountain. A path there goes uphill from the trail, almost to Daters Mine. Climb a bit higher, and you will see a fairly large mine.

It is not known just when the mine was worked. In 1800, Abram Dater built two forges on the Ramapo River, north of Sloatsburg. The site of these forges was where the present-day Washington Avenue crosses the Ramapo River. Here, the remains of a dam, foundations and slag are visible. This bridge was once known as Dater's Crossing.

In 1812, Abram Dater was the second largest taxpayer in the Township of Ramapo (he paid $17.50 in taxes per year). He had another forge on Stony Brook, about where the Thruway now crosses the brook, and owned 2,600 acres between Stony Brook and the Ramapo River, in Rockland and Orange Counties. Abram Dater died in 1831. His grandson, George Washington Dater, operated a hardware store in 1884 across the highway from Dater's Crossing. The building is still there, occupied now by an antique shop.

Doodletown Mine

Going southeast across Doodletown Valley, the Suffern-Bear Mountain Trail (yellow) leaves the Bridle Path at the foot of West Mountain. The Doodlekill is crossed 0.15 mile further southeast along the Bridle Path. About 200 feet beyond the brook, a vague old road, marked with cairns, goes uphill 0.25 mile to the Doodletown Mine. At the end of the road, a pile of tailings may be seen on the hillside to the left. Climb this pile to reach the mine, a water-filled shaft.

Little is known about the mine. Oscar Herbert, who worked there, is mentioned in the *New York Evening Post* of May 26, 1938.

Greenwood Mine

The Greenwood Mine is located where the Appalachian Trail (white) comes down from Fingerboard Mountain and runs along the Surebridge Mine Road. There are extensive dumps of broken stone and a large opening in the hillside. Remains of the foundation of a pumphouse can be seen near the shaft, as well as a piece of large pipe. A second pit may be seen a bit higher on the hillside.

Also called the Patterson Mine, the Greenwood Mine was worked as early as 1838, a year after Peter Parrott bought the furnace at Echo Lake (the Greenwood Furnace). The ore was used during the Civil War in both the Greenwood and Clove Furnaces. Unused from 1870 to 1879, the mine was last worked in 1880.

Harris Mine

The main complex of the Harris Mine is located on the northwest side of Arden Valley Road, 0.6 mile northeast of the gravel road that leads to

Hasenclever Mine

Island Pond. There are two large mine openings, with piles of tailings nearby, both on private property, less than 100 feet from Arden Valley Road.

Older (pre-1995) editions of the Conference map showed this mine as being located southeast of Arden Valley Road, on the southern slope of Echo Mountain. Old mining roads do lead to several shallow exploratory pits in this area, but according to Ed Lenik, the main operations of the mine were north of Arden Valley Road, which was constructed long after the mine was abandoned. Lenik believes that the Harris Mine was most likely operated by the Parrott brothers to supply ore to their furnaces at present-day Arden, New York.

A column by Raymond Torrey (*N.Y. Post*, 12/29/23) was entitled, "Where Is the Harris Mine?" He confessed that he had not found it, although he did find two other mine shafts higher up on Echo Mountain.

Hasenclever Mine

The Hasenclever Mine is on the Red Cross Trail, 0.55 mile south of Tiorati Brook Road. The trail here follows the old Hasenclever Road. Peter Hasenclever traveled along that road in 1765 and discovered a deposit of iron ore. He immediately bought 1,000 acres there, including most of Cedar Ponds (Lake Tiorati). It seems likely that he had the ore transported across the Hudson to a furnace he had bought in Cortlandt, near Peekskill. In 1767, he built a dam on the brook that drained Cedar Ponds. That made one pond where there had been two, to provide power for a furnace he intended to build. Hasenclever was recalled to England before he could build the furnace.

During the Revolution and for some time afterward, the mine was operated by Samuel Brewster under lease. On June 1, 1799, Hasenclever's thousand-acre tract was bought by Jonas Brewster of Stony Point, and about 1800 he erected a furnace on Hasenclever's site. Its remains can still be seen on Tiorati Brook, above the crossing of the Red Cross Trail.

The mine changed owners many times. In 1854, it belonged to the Haverstraw Iron and Mining Company. They began to build a railroad from the mine to Stony Point. It was to run in a trench, across the road from the mine. The cars were to be loaded from the banks of the trench. The railroad was never finished, but the trench can still be seen.

The long history of the Hasenclever Mine is recited in James M. Ransom's *Vanishing Ironworks of the Ramapos* and in Edward J. Lenik's *Iron Mine Trails*. The mine, which is said to be 100 feet deep, is now filled with water.

Herbert Mine

The Herbert Mine is a sizeable pit, opened before 1859 and named for the local Herbert family. To reach it, follow Timp Pass Road up from the 1777 Trail, as shown on Trail Conference Map #119. About 0.2 mile from the start, a cairn will be seen on a rock to the right. From here, a road crosses Timp Brook and goes up 0.2 mile to a fork. Follow the right fork, which leads in 0.5 mile to the mine, at the 980-foot contour. Two openings can be seen above piles of tailings. The Suffern-Bear Mountain Trail is 200 feet higher on the mountain. (The left fork of the road goes through an interesting region and leads in 0.5 mile to Timp Pass.)

Hogencamp Mine

The Hogencamp Mine is on the Dunning Trail, about 0.2 mile south of its junction with the Long Path, and 0.2 mile north of a junction with the woods road coming up through the abandoned camp at Little Long

Pond. The largest openings are fairly narrow cuts on the mountainside. There are at least six openings, all in the line of one vein of ore. One opening is a vertical shaft about 12 feet across. Another shaft near the trail is filled with water. A six-inch pipe rises from the water. Across the trail, iron bars are fixed in a rock, and nearby is a concrete base with more bars. These were probably used to anchor machinery for pumping and hoisting.

Ore from the mine was put into buckets and hoisted over the cliff above the mine. The buckets were carried on a tramway which took them up a valley (the Long Path runs along the hill on the side of that valley) to a point on a mine road where they could be unloaded into horse-drawn carts. The stone supports of the old tramway can still be seen on the cliff above the mine, and in the valley up to the point where the Long Path joins the old mine road. Sharp-eyed hikers may also see up there pieces of the cables and pulleys that carried the buckets.

As at the Pine Swamp Mine, there was a small village near the mine. A well can be seen near the road, which was called the Pine Swamp Trail before 1943 when Joe Bartha made it part of the Dunning Trail.

The mine was worked steadily from 1865 to 1885 (Ransom, p. 237).

A piece of rail from the line used to carry ore from the Hogencamp Mine

Lewis Mine

This rather small opening is located 25 yards east of the Nawahunta Fire Road, 0.3 mile from the Seven Lakes Drive. There is a hole and a short shaft in the hillside.

One summer day in 1973, Tom Dunn of the Westchester Trails Association was hiking in Harriman Park with his young nephew. After lunch, while Tom was trying to rest, the boy was anxious to go. Tom said: "Go find a mine or something." Not long afterward, the boy came running back, shouting: "Uncle Tom, I found one!" When that story was heard by cartographer Don Derr, the Dunn Mine appeared for the first time on the 1982 edition of the Conference map. In his *Iron Mine Trails* book, Ed Lenik calls this mine the "Lewis Mine," after the Lewis family who formerly resided on this property, and that is how it is designated on Trail Conference Map #119.

Mica Mine

The Mica Mine is about 50 feet west of the Beechy Bottom East Road, 0.4 mile south of the start of the Fawn Trail. It can be reached from the southernmost parking lot of the Anthony Wayne Recreation Area. From the north end of that lot, a path goes uphill toward West Mountain. Go up that path until it reaches Beechy Bottom East Road. Go south about 300 feet, then down from the trail about 50 feet. The opening is at the foot of a steep bank, just above a marshy area. Pieces of mica may be found lying about.

The mineral found around this mine is a biotite, a silicate of potassium, magnesium, iron and aluminum. It occurs in dark shining plates, often as triangular-shaped crystals.

The mine was opened in 1893. Large sheets of "isinglass" were obtained. A vein of graphite was also found there (*News of the Highlands*, 12/16/1893, 1/27/1894).

In 1920, when the Ramapo-Dunderberg Trail was being blazed, there still was a farmhouse near the Mica Mine, the home of Park employee Paul Stout. Trail blazers E. Cecil Earle and A.B. Malcolmson boarded at the Stout farmhouse. That farmhouse had been built in 1877 by John Wesley Van Wart, who lived there until his death in 1892.

Nickel Mine

This mine is on the north side of Grape Swamp Mountain, near the crest of the ridge. It may be reached from Tiorati Brook Road by following the unmarked Grape Swamp Mountain Trail (see pp. 224-25). The mine is fairly large, and there are two openings, separated by about 500 feet. The east opening is larger than the west opening.

For many years, it was believed that this mine really was an iron mine owned by a man named Nichol. That was the opinion of Raymond Torrey (*N.Y. Post*, 5/26/38). The facts are different.

Before the Park was formed in 1910, both Grape Swamp Mountain and Pound Swamp Mountain belonged to Brewster J. Allison, a resident of Stony Point. In 1871, a mine was opened on Grape Swamp Mountain on land of B.J. Allison, leased to John Sneviley of New York City. He sold his rights in 1875 to the Rockland Nickel Company. For ten years, nickel ore was taken from the mine. It was abandoned in 1884 (Cole, *History of Rockland County*, 1884, p. 330).

Pine Swamp Mine

The Pine Swamp Mine is located in the area surrounding the junction of the Dunning Trail (yellow) and Arden-Surebridge Trail (A-SB) (red triangle on white). There are eight openings to the mine, the largest being the one farthest south. This opening is on the Dunning Trail, about 0.15 mile south of its junction with the A-SB Trail, or 0.5 mile north of its

Opening of Pine Swamp Mine along the A-SB Trail

intersection with the Long Path (aqua). A large mine dump of rock tailings rises about 60 feet on the hillside near the trail. By climbing over the dump, one comes to a large cut, about 25 feet wide, with high walls on each side. In the cut, there is a perpendicular shaft, now filled with water. The cut leads into a 30-foot-high passageway tunneled into the hillside, which runs uphill for about 125 feet. A skylight overhead lets some light into the passageway. Other openings may be found a little further north along the Dunning Trail, and on the A-SB Trail, just east of its junction with the Dunning Trail.

When this mine was active, there was a small village nearby, with homes, barns, stores and a saloon. The foundations of some of these structures can still be seen along the A-SB Trail, east of its junction with the Dnnning Trail (about 500 feet southeast from where it leaves the old mine road).

The mine was probably first worked in 1830 by Gouverneur Kemble, owner of the West Point Foundry at Cold Spring, New York (Ransom, pp. 141, 238).

Spanish Mine

On the summit of Black Mountain, just a bit north of the Appalachian/Ramapo-Dunderberg Trail, are two mine openings. They were first shown on the Park's December 1930 trail map, and then again on the Park's 1937 map. Bill Hoeferlin named this mine the "Spanish Mine" on his June 1943 Hikers Region Map #16. Through the years, it has been mistakenly called the Silver Mine, a name given in 1936 to the nearby ski hill. The legend about the Spanish seamen said that they carried out sacks of silver coins from a mine on Black Mountain (see pp. 91-92).

Surebridge Mine

The Surebridge Mine is located on Surebridge Mine Road, 0.5 mile north of "Times Square" and 0.1 mile south of the Bottle Cap Trail.

In a fairly level, tree-covered region just east of the Surebridge Mine Road there are several fairly large water-filled shafts. One is visible from the road; others are further up on the hillside. They were worked during the Civil War for the two Greenwood Furnaces. A total of 458 tons of ore was raised in 1880 (Ransom, p. 239).

THE STORY OF
BEAR MOUNTAIN

On September 15, 1609, Henry Hudson's ship, the *Half-Moon*, rode at anchor in the mouth of Popolopen Creek. His crew had to defend themselves from hostile natives—the Haverstroo Indians. After the Dutch founded New Amsterdam and Albany in 1624, Hudson's River was the route for their commerce. They named the mountains Dunderberg, Pingyp, Timp, Anthony's Nose and Bear Hill (now known as Bear Mountain).

After driving the Dutch away in 1664-67, the English began to acquire title to the lands along the Hudson. In 1683, during the reign of Charles II, Sakaghkemerk, sachem of the Haverstroos, sold for "the sum of six shillings, silver money" all of Bear Mountain, Hessian Lake and Iona Island to Stephanus van Cortlandt, the Mayor of New York City. The same Indians sold the same land in 1685 to New York Governor Dongan and his friends. It was under Governor Dongan that a representative assembly in October 1683 passed a law providing for representation and for religious liberty.

In 1743, King George II granted the 800-acre Bear Hill tract to Richard Bradley who was, at the time, Attorney General of the Colony of New York. He soon sold the tract to Theodorus Snedeker of Hempstead, Long Island. During the following years, Snedeker acquired much of the land between Haverstraw and Bear Mountain. Because he was a Tory during the Revolution, Snedeker's land was confiscated by the State of New York.

The State transferred the land on the north side of Bear Mountain to the Military Academy at West Point. The rest of the mountain was sold to Samuel Brewster on May 15, 1790. In 1849, Brewster's land at Bear Mountain became the property of the Knickerbocker Ice Company, which cut ice on Highland Lake (now Hessian Lake) and sold it in New York City. Their land passed to Alfred C. Cheny in 1874, and then to Charles E. Lambert of Perth Amboy, New Jersey.

The Formation of Palisades Interstate Park

The Hudson Highlands and the Palisades of the Hudson were a much admired feature of American landscape, popularized by the artists of the Hudson River School. They were also much admired by quarrymen who, after 1875, used Alfred Nobel's dynamite to destroy the cliffs. Between Fort Lee and the state line there were 17 quarries.

George W. Perkins

Public agitation developed in the 1890s to stop the quarrying. In 1894, New Jersey and New York passed bills which ceded 16 miles of the face and base of the Palisades to the Federal Government as a military reservation. This measure was rejected by Congress in 1895 and again in 1898. Meanwhile, the quarrymen, seeing the handwriting on the cliff, demolished more and more landmarks. In March 1898, 7,000 pounds of dynamite reduced Washington Head and Indian Head at Fort Lee to 2.5 million cubic yards of traprock.

Then in 1899 the New Jersey Federation of Women's Clubs secured passage of a bill empowering the Governor to appoint a commission which would suggest a method of preservation. A similar bill was passed in New York State with the backing of Governor Theodore Roosevelt. In March 1900, the commissioners recommended that a permanent Interstate Park Commission be given power to acquire Palisades land for recreational purposes. This proposal was voted into law by both legislatures and signed by Theodore Roosevelt for New York and by Governor Voorhees for New Jersey. The jurisdiction of the Commission extended from Fort Lee, New Jersey to Piermont, New York. In 1906, it was extended to Stony Point, including Hook Mountain.

Governor Roosevelt appointed George W. Perkins, a vice-president of New York Life Insurance Company, as President of the new Commission. When Roosevelt telephoned Perkins, the latter tried to decline, but Roosevelt said he hadn't called to ask Perkins, but to tell him the appointment had already been made.

George Walbridge Perkins, Sr., a resident of Riverdale, New York, was born in Chicago on January 31, 1862. With only a public school education, he began work as an office boy in the Chicago office of New York Life Insurance Company. After many promotions, he became a vice-president of the company in 1898. When Perkins became President of the Interstate Park Commission, the two states had provided only $10,000 to stop the quarrying. He soon learned that about $125,000 was needed. He approached J.P. Morgan, Sr. for help. Morgan replied that he would put up the whole sum, provided that Perkins would agree to become a Morgan partner. Perkins agreed, and the Carpenter Bros. quarry at Fort Lee was bought for $132,500. On Christmas Eve 1900, the blasting was stopped forever.

The Fight to Save the Highlands

In 1908, the Commission on New Prisons which had been appointed by New York Governor Higgins made known plans to build a new Sing Sing Prison at Bear Mountain. One reason for the choice of that 500-acre site was that it would yield a great deal of traprock for building new highways (*Rockland County Journal*, 2/1/08). By mid-summer, hundreds of convicts were living on the terrace above the river. On January 9, 1909, the State purchased the 740-acre Bear Mountain tract from Charles Lambert's widow.

To conservationists and lovers of the Hudson Highlands, this scheme to build a prison at Highland Lake seemed like sacrilege. They were inspired by the success of the Interstate Park in stopping the defacement of the Palisades. Foremost among those who fought for the preservation of the Hudson Highlands was Dr. Edward Lasell Partridge, a New York City physician and medical teacher who had a summer home on Storm King Mountain.[1] In a lengthy article in *The Outlook* magazine for November 9,

---

[1] Partridge's summer "cottage," known as the Spy Rock House, was on a saddle between Storm King and Whitehorse Mountain. Hikers following the present-day Butter Hill Trail from the parking area on Route 9W up Storm King will encounter the ruin of that cottage on West Rocks. In 1936, the Interstate Hiking Club described that two-story house as "deserted" (*Paterson Morning Call*, 5/1/36).

Averell Harriman presenting a check to George Perkins

1907, Dr. Partridge had advocated the formation of a national preserve, to include 65 square miles between Peekskill and Breakneck Mountain, and 57 square miles between Jones Point and Storm King.

The public interest in the upcoming Hudson-Fulton Celebration of 1909 created much opinion in favor of the Partridge proposals. A *New York Times* feature article on Sunday, September 20, 1908 urged a "Fight to Save Beauties of the Hudson" and decried the State's decision to build a prison at Bear Mountain.

After long discussions, the New York State Legislature in 1909 created the "Highlands of the Hudson Forest Preserve." A state forester was appointed to oversee the preserve, and Dr. Partridge was made secretary of a commission to administer it.[2] The prison, however, was not cancelled.

Mary Averell Harriman

Fortunately for the generations to come, one of those upset by the plan to construct the prison was Mary Averell Harriman, whose husband, Ed-

---

[2] In 1913, Dr. Edward L. Partridge was appointed to the Palisades Interstate Park Commission. He served the Commission for many years as its treasurer and as a member of various committees until his death on May 2, 1930, at the age of 77.

ward H. Harriman, had died on September 9, 1909. The Harriman estate included over 30,000 acres in the Highlands west of the Hudson, which had been assembled over a period of twenty years. Edward and Mary Harriman had long wanted to preserve the woodlands from exploitation, and to make part of their land available to the public as a park. They were personally acquainted with like-minded persons such as James Stillman and Dr. Edward Partridge.

On December 15, 1909, Mrs. Harriman wrote to Governor Charles Evans Hughes that she would convey to New York State 10,000 acres of land in Orange and Rockland Counties for a state park, and give $1,000,000 in cash to administer the park, provided that the State of New York appropriate $2,500,000 for the Park Commission to acquire lands and build roads; that the State discontinue construction of a prison at Bear Mountain; that by January 1, 1910 a further $1,500,000 be raised by private subscription; and that the State of New Jersey appropriate such amount as the Park Commissioners deemed to be its fair share.

Before Mrs. Harriman sent her letter, George W. Perkins had begun negotiations to ensure that the desired private contributions would be forthcoming. By December 31, 1909, Mr. Perkins informed Governor Hughes that $1,625,000 had been subscribed. Among the contributors were John D. Rockefeller, Sr. and J. Pierpont Morgan, Sr., who gave $500,000 each; and Mrs. Margaret Sage, William K. Vanderbilt, George F. Baker, Sr., James Stillman, John D. Archbold, William Rockefeller, Frank A. Munsey, Henry Phipps, E.T. Stotesbury, Elbert H. Gary and George W. Perkins, Sr., who contributed $50,000 each.

In March 1910, the New York Legislature passed the necessary measures, and the New Jersey Legislature appropriated $500,000 to build the Henry Hudson Drive along the river in the New Jersey section of the Park. On October 29, 1910, on behalf of his mother, 18-year-old W. Averell Harriman presented to the Palisades Interstate Park Commission $1,000,000 and 10,000 acres of land.

The Life of Edward H. Harriman

Edward Henry Harriman, whose love of the woods and mountains made possible our great State Park, was born on February 25, 1848 in the Episcopal rectory in Hempstead, Long Island. His father was the Rev. Orlando Harriman. While a young boy, Edward spent a summer as a timekeeper at the Greenwood Furnace owned by the Parrott family. It was then that he became acquainted with the hills and lakes in the Ramapo Mountains.

At the age of 14, he left school and started as an office boy in Wall Street. When he was 22, he opened his own broker's office, and became very successful. After his marriage in 1879 to Mary Williamson Averell, Harriman became a director of his father-in-law's Ogdensburg and Lake Champlain Railroad Co. In 1883, he was made a director of the Illinois Central Railroad. He later became chairman of the executive committee of the Union Pacific Railroad (1898), and president of the Southern Pacific Railroad (1901).

Edward and Mary Harriman had three sons: Henry Neilson (1883), William Averell (1891) and Edward Roland (1895). They also had three daughters: Mary (1881), Cornelia (1884) and Carol (1889).

In 1885, Harriman learned that the Parrotts had put up their estate for sale. He learned, too, that certain land speculators intended to divide it, and to sell the lumber that still grew there. To thwart those plans, Harriman bid at the auction for the entire 7,863 acres. His bid of $52,500 was accepted, to the disappointment of the Parrotts, who believed they would have received more money if the land had been sold in pieces.

The Harrimans, who had a Manhattan home at 22 East 51st Street, took possession of the Parrott farm in the summer of 1888. They gave the estate the name Arden, which had been Mrs. Parrott's maiden name. In the next two years, Edward Harriman bought about 40 different farms and tracts— an additional 20,000 acres. To make all parts of his estate accessible, he built 40 miles of bridle paths.

Bear Mountain/Harriman Parks: 1910-1920

Although they adjoin each other and both are part of the Palisades Interstate Park system, Bear Mountain and Harriman State Parks are technically separate entities. For historical reasons, Bear Mountain State Park extends south from Brooks Lake in Fort Montgomery, and includes Popolopen Torne, Bear Mountain, West Mountain, Iona Island and Dunderberg Mountain. It contains 5,067 acres. In November 1923, the Palisades Interstate Park Commission decided that "all of the Park lying west of Bear Mountain [later, west of West Mountain] shall be designated Harriman State Park." That park now contains 47,106 acres.

In 1901, the Commission retained as consultant the eminent landscape

PALISADES INTERSTATE PARK COMMISSION

Major William A. Welch

engineer Charles W. Leavitt, Jr. (*N.Y. Times*, 10/23/01). Leavitt served as Chief Engineer from 1901 to 1912, and was responsible for the development of the park along the Palisades. In 1912, he was succeeded as Chief Engineer by Major William. A. Welch.

William Addams Welch was born in Cynthiana, Kentucky on August 20, 1868. He was educated at Colorado Springs (1882) and at the University of Virginia (1886), where he received a Master of Engineering degree. For six years, he worked for the U.S. Government in Alaska, where he assembled the first iron steamship to be built in the territory. Later he worked in the western states, in Mexico and in Bolivia (1906).[3] He returned to the United States in 1907, and was working for the Olmstead Brothers when he met George Perkins in 1912. Perkins persuaded him to become General Manager and Chief Engineer of the Palisades Interstate Park.

Major Welch's work for the Park won him fame as father of the state park movement. Together with Stephen Mather and Horace Albright, he

---

[3] The legendary 228-mile Madeira-Mamoré Railway in Bolivia that Welch helped build was described in a *New York Times* feature article on November 26, 1989.

PALISADES INTERSTATE PARK COMMISSION

Construction of the Bear Mountain Inn, 1914

was also a pioneer in the national park movement. In the years that followed, he built 23 lakes, 100 miles of roads and 103 children's camps. He helped found the Palisades Interstate Park Trail Conference, and later served as chairman of the newly organized Appalachian Trail Conference.

Work began at Bear Mountain in 1910 with the demolition of the prison and the building of a dock for steamboat excursion traffic. In 1911, the West Shore Railroad built a new station near the dock, and in 1912 a replica of Henry Hudson's *Half-Moon* was moored at the new dock. A comfort station was built at Hessian Lake, and a reservoir and water mains were constructed. Spring water was provided in ice-filled green barrels, with free cups. A park office was built from parts of the prison barracks. The Park was first opened to public use by Commissioner Perkins on July 5, 1913. Regular steamboat service from New York City was begun in the summer of 1913 by the McAllister Steamboat Company, and 22,590 passengers were carried by the boats that season. Camping was begun around Hessian Lake, and in 1913 the first Boy Scout camps were built at Car Pond (later named Lake Stahahe).

Bear Mountain Inn was completed in 1915, built of great boulders and chestnut logs. The stones for the fireplace came from old stone walls.

Some hikers may remember the sections of a great 350-year-old chestnut tree which were made into chairs, a settee, a cigar case, and a cashier's cage for the upstairs dining room. The tree came from the western border of the Harriman estate, where it died about 1912 of the chestnut blight. The Inn was opened on June 27, 1915 by George W. Perkins, who gave a luncheon for the Governor of New York, Charles S. Whitman. Rooms at the Inn were $4.50 per day, which included lodging and three meals. In December 1927, two bronze bears were purchased to adorn the entrance to the Inn. They are still there, painted black.

In September 1913, construction was begun on a road to link Bear Mountain with the Harriman lands to the west. This road, originally called the Southfields Road and later renamed Seven Lakes Drive, was opened in August 1915. (At that time, it did not extend to Sloatsburg.) As soon as the Southfields Road was underway, Major Welch began planning a new bridge across Popolopen Gorge. In 1916, the Popolopen Viaduct to Fort Montgomery was opened. That bridge and similar ones at Stony Point (1923) and Sparkill (1926), the highway around Storm King Mountain, and the dock and railroad station at Bear Mountain, were all constructed in order to make the Park more accessible to the population of the surrounding region.

The year 1919 saw the acquisition of the steamboats *Clermont* and *Onteora*.[4] Both ships had been built in Newburgh, the *Onteora* in 1898, and the *Clermont* in 1911. The round trip from New York City on weekends was 85 cents for adults and 45 cents for children.

The Growth of the Parks: 1920-1936

On June 18, 1920, friends of the Park were saddened by the death of George W. Perkins, Sr., who had been President of the Park Commission for twenty years. In his memory, the Commission declared at its meeting of June 25, 1920:

> The Palisades Interstate Park as it now exists was the conception of Mr. Perkins, and it was he and he alone who raised the money for its acquisition and development. As the Park grew in size and useful-

---

[4] Actually, these two boats were initially acquired by George Perkins in the fall of 1919, since the Commission then lacked funds to purchase them. After Perkins died in June 1920, the boats were acquired by the Commission with funds from the Laura Spelman Rockefeller Memorial Fund.

ness, his ideas and enthusiasm grew with it, until in the latter years of his life he conceived a playground large enough and complete enough to afford rest and recreation to all the people of New York and New Jersey who lived near enough to enjoy it, and where all the facilities for such enjoyment should be furnished at cost, without profit to concessionaires or others.

In 1921, the Commission decided that a proper memorial to George Perkins would be a scenic road to the top of Bear Mountain.

Winter sports began at Bear Mountain in the 1922-23 season. 1923 saw the completion of the first 16-mile section of the Appalachian Trail, from the Hudson River to Arden. The Bear Mountain Hudson River Bridge Co. was incorporated in 1922, with E. Roland Harriman as president. Opened on Thanksgiving Day 1924, the Bear Mountain Bridge was the longest span in the world at that time. The bridge became the property of the New York State Bridge Authority at midnight, September 25, 1940. The construction of Dam No. 10 for Lake Sebago was begun in 1923.

In 1925, the War Department (which owned the land) gave permission to build Hell Hole Drive around the north side of Bear Mountain. When opened in 1927, this 18-foot-wide road was christened Popolopen Drive. It was widened to three lanes in 1933-34.

In 1926, the Commission authorized Major Welch to construct three trail shelters, including the ones at Big Hill and at Tom Jones Mountain.

The Trailside Nature Museum and the Bear Mountain ski jump were opened in 1927. In 1929, a 12-inch pipe was laid along Popolopen Gorge to supply water from Queensboro Lake to Bear Mountain.

Roland Harriman gave Island Pond to the Park in 1927. In exchange, the Park built a new Arden Valley Road past the Elk Pen, so that traffic would no longer go through Harriman land, and Roland would no longer be surprised by hikers peering through his windows.

The period of the Great Depression which began in 1929 saw increased construction activity in Bear Mountain/Harriman Parks. Under Governor Franklin D. Roosevelt, New York State set up the Temporary Emergency Relief Administration (TERA), which sent unemployed workers each day to Bear Mountain on the West Shore Railroad. The TERA workers built the Perkins Memorial Drive and the Doodletown Bridle Path. When Roosevelt became President of the United States, other agencies were created to put unemployed men to work on public works projects. Men from the Works Progress Administration (WPA) built the new Administration Building

(1937)[5] and a number of bridges in the Park. Between 1933 and 1942, the Civilian Conservation Corps (CCC) established nine camps in the Park (other camps were at Storm King, Blauvelt and the Palisades). Each camp employed 200 young men who stayed for 18 months. The CCC men built ten lakes: Pine Meadow, Wanoksink, Massawippa, Minsi, Owl, Welch, Silvermine, Turkey Hill, Skenonto and Skannatati. They also built many roads, such as the Beechy Bottom Road, Owl Lake Road, Summer Hill Road and Deep Hollow Road, and several ski trails.

Unfortunately, the State could not provide funds for the construction and maintenance of the children's camps which were proposed to be built on the lakes being constructed by the CCC. In a letter dated March 9, 1935 to Conrad L. Wirth, Assistant Director of the National Park Service,[6] Major Welch requested the withdrawal of the CCC workers. Despite this request, the CCC camps in the Park were not immediately disbanded. However, the workers were gradually withdrawn during the next several years, and all camps were closed in 1942.

In 1936, the first ski tow, known as the Old Silvermine Ski Tow, was built on the slopes at Lake Menomine. (In 1951, the name of the lake was changed to Silvermine Lake.)

The Growth of the Parks: 1937–2010

Since its formation in 1900, the Interstate Park had been governed by ten commissioners: five appointed by the Governor of New York and five appointed by the Governor of New Jersey. Legally, there were two commissions—the New Jersey commission owned the park lands in New Jersey, and the New York commission owned the park lands in New York. Although they legally formed two separate commissions, in practice all ten commissioners functioned as one body. This arrangement continued until 1937, when a compact was entered into by both state legislatures and approved by a joint resolution of the United States Congress. It provided for one commission, with five members appointed by the Governor of New York and five by the Governor of New Jersey. Title to all Interstate Park property in both states now resides in the ten-member Commission. The Compact assured the permanence of the Park as an interstate undertaking.

---

[5] This building replaced an earlier one, built in 1920.

[6] In 1964, Conrad Wirth became a Commissioner of the Interstate Park.

At their meeting of August 17, 1938, the Commissioners noted that Raymond H. Torrey, for many years in charge of publicity for the Commission, had died on July 15, 1938.

In the fall of 1938, the residents of Beaver Pond (now Lake Welch) lost their last court appeal to block the Park's acquisition of their land. Their claims were finally settled, and the lake was filled with water in 1942.

In 1939, Harry Keevil of Cornwall was authorized to operate a riding academy at Bear Mountain. Riding horses were available until December 1961, when conditions in the stables were found to be unfit for the horses.

Major Welch, who had been General Manager since 1912, retired on February 1, 1940, and was followed by A. Kenneth Morgan. Morgan had worked for the Long Island State Park Commission, and most recently had been responsible for the design and operation of the 1939 New York World's Fair.

One of Morgan's first tasks was to prepare plans for a Palisades Interstate Parkway, which was to extend from the George Washington Bridge to the Bear Mountain Bridge. In February 1943, he requested $7,000,000 for the construction of the Parkway, but construction was delayed by the entry of the nation into the Second World War. During the war, the Army used the Pine Meadow and Beaver Pond areas (on weekdays only) for training personnel in ground photography. In 1945, the Navy built a water line from Doodletown Brook to Iona Island to supply the naval base there. On September 3, 1947, a contract was signed to build the first section of the Palisades Interstate Parkway, from Bear Mountain to Mt. Ivy. That section was opened to traffic on November 30, 1953. The Parkway was completed on August 28, 1958—at a cost of $47 million. As part of the highway project, the Anthony Wayne Recreation Area was begun in 1951 and opened to the public on June 18, 1955 by Governor W. Averell Harriman.

On January 10, 1960, George W. Perkins died. He had been a commissioner since 1922 and President of the Commission since 1945, and also served as the permanent U.S. representative to NATO. Like his father, he devoted much of his life and fortune to the welfare of the Interstate Park. Perkins was succeeded on the Commission by his wife. When she resigned in 1973, Governor Rockefeller appointed her son, George W. Perkins, Jr., to the Commission. He resigned in 1988 and was succeeded in 1990 by his sister Anne Perkins Cabot, who served until 2007.

In 1962, Lake Welch Beach was opened to 1,100 guests (it rained). In 1965, the last residents left Doodletown, and the new Long Mountain Parkway was begun. In the same year, the entire Park was declared to be a National Historic Landmark. The Navy gave up Iona Island in 1965 and transferred its title to the Park. The buildings on the island are now used for storage and other administrative purposes.

On August 28, 1969, after 29 years of service, A.K. Morgan retired as General Manager of the Park. He died shortly afterward. In his memory, the lodge (near the Bear Mountain Inn) that Morgan had recently built was designated by the Commission as the A.K. Morgan Overlook Lodge.

Taking Morgan's place on September 1, 1969 was Nash Castro. Born on January 14, 1920, he was educated at St. Thomas Aquinas College in New York and at George Washington University. In 1939, he began a career with the National Park Service, which culminated in his service as Director of the Capital Region (Washington, D.C.) from 1961 to 1969. Castro's service with the Commission marked a period of important growth, including the acquisition by the Commission of Minnewaska State Park.

In February 1974, construction was begun on the Doodletown Reservoir, which was designed to supply drinking water to Iona Island and to serve as a backup to the Bear Mountain supply.

On October 7, 1978, "Sammy" the bald eagle, a resident of the Bear Mountain Zoo since 1954, succumbed in an encounter with a raccoon.

In 1979, an anonymous donor gave $200,000 to pay for a youth corps for trail improvements. It was later learned that the donor was DeWitt Wallace, the founder of Reader's Digest. In the years that followed, the DeWitt Wallace Fund gave the Park over $1.5 million for summer youth work programs. Other donors, including the commissioners themselves, have also given gifts to the Park over the years. The Mary W. Harriman Fund makes an annual gift to bring inner-city children to the Tiorati Workshop for Environmental Learning.

The 60th anniversary of the Appalachian Trail was celebrated in June 1983 at the Bear Mountain Inn. Three hundred people heard Commissioner Mary Fisk speak about the many years of cooperation between the Commission and the Trail Conference. She then cut a six-foot-long birthday cake, with the help of her grandson.

Hikers and all friends of the Park were saddened to learn of the death of W. Averell Harriman on July 26, 1986. Born on November 15, 1891, he was an 18-year-old Yale student in 1910 when he presented to Governor Charles Evans Hughes, on behalf of his mother, a deed for 10,000 acres and a gift of $1,000,000, which led to the formation of Bear Mountain State Park. He was appointed a commissioner of the Park in 1915, when he was 24 years old (he was already a vice president of the Union Pacific Railroad). He remained a commissioner for the next 59 years (except for the period from 1955 to 1959, when he was Governor of the state). When he resigned in 1974, his daughter Mary Fisk took his place (she served as a commissioner until her death in January 1996). Averell Harriman's concern for the welfare of the Park was never failing; he often made gifts of land and money to the Commission. He was survived by his wife, two daughters, six grandchildren and six great-grandchildren. The Harriman family is currently represented on the Commission by David Mortimer.

The year 1990 brought the retirement of Executive Director Nash Castro.[7] On April 15, 1990, he was succeeded by Robert O. Binnewies, who came to the Park from the New York State Department of Environmental Conservation, where he served as Deputy Commissioner for Natural Resources. Binnewies began his career in 1960 as a ranger in Yellowstone National Park.

During Bob Binnewies' tenure as Executive Director, in February 1998, the Commission acquired nearly 14,000 acres of Sterling Forest—the culmination of many years of efforts to protect this land by a consortium of public and private organizations. Although this land is entirely in the State of New York, the State of New Jersey contributed $10 million towards the purchase of this property, much of which serves as a watershed for the State of New Jersey. (Interestingly, in 1900, when the Commission was first created, the State of New York contributed $400,000 towards the purchase of the Palisades along the Hudson River in New Jersey, which was part of the viewshed of New York City residents across the river.)

In 1995, the jurisdiction of the PIPC in New Jersey was expanded to include Passaic, Morris, Warren, Hunterdon and Somerset Counties, in addition to Bergen County. This broadening of the PIPC's jurisdiction makes it possible for the Commission to expand its efforts in preserving environmentally sensitive lands in the New Jersey Highlands.

Bob Binnewies retired as PIPC Executive Director in February 1999,

---

[7] During Castro's tenure, the position of General Manager was renamed Executive Director.

DANIEL CHAZIN

Bear Mountain Merry-Go-Round

and was succeeded by Carol Ash, who previously served as the director of The Nature Conservancy of New York State.

On April 29, 2001, the Bear Mountain Merry-Go-Round was dedicated. As early as 1916, consideration had been given to the construction of a "carousel" at Bear Mountain, to complement the newly-constructed Bear Mountain Inn, but, at the time, the Commission did not have sufficient funds to pursue this idea. In 1998, the idea to build a merry-go-round at Bear Mountain resurfaced, and this time, the Perkins family generously provided the necessary funds in memory of their parents, former Commissioners George W. and Linn Perkins. The merry-go-round building is beautifully constructed of stone and wood in a traditional style that complements the adjacent historic Administration Building and Bear Mountain Inn. It includes 38 carved animals that are native to the Hudson River Valley, as well as two chariots for accessible seating.

In January 2007, Carol Ash became the Commissioner of the New York State Office of Parks, Recreation and Historic Preservation. She was succeeded as Executive Director of the Commission by James F. Hall. Prior to coming to the Commission, Jim Hall worked for the New Jersey Department of Environmental Protection, serving for 10 years as Assistant Commissioner for Natural and Historic Resources. He became Superintendent of the New Jersey Section of the Park in December 1999 and was named Deputy Executive Director in December 2004.

Now in its second century of service to the people of New York and

New Jersey, the Commission can count on the hearty cooperation of the organized hikers of the metropolitan area, represented by the New York-New Jersey Trail Conference, as it faces the challenging times ahead.

The Trailside Museum

In 1920, a new scoutmaster, Benjamin Talbot Babbitt Hyde, came to the Boy Scout camps on Lake Kanawauke. Fondly known as "Uncle Benny," he was a Patron of the Museum of Natural History. In the huge Scout headquarters building, he established the first museum in the Park, and filled it with snakes, flowers, rocks and tree specimens. By 1925, three more such museums had been created in the camps at Twin Lakes, Cohasset and Tiorati. Uncle Benny's work ended when the Scout camps left the Park in 1929.

In 1925, Dr. Frank E. Lutz, Curator of Entomology at the American Museum of Natural History, established a Station for the Study of Insects. The Park allotted him 40 acres on Wildcat Brook, on the west side of Route 17. His nature trail, which included informative signs, was soon imitated in twenty camps around the Park.

In 1926, with the assistance of a $7,500 grant from the Laura Spelman Rockefeller Memorial Foundation, plans were made for a museum and zoo at Bear Mountain, on the site of old Fort Clinton. William H. Carr, who had been Uncle Benny's assistant in 1922, was appointed the Museum's first director. Construction of the first building was completed in September 1927, and by 1934, three more buildings had been added. The museum thrived through the following years. In 1942, Daniel Carter Beard, a founder of the Boy Scouts of America, gave much of his personal memorabilia for an exhibit at the Trailside Museum.

The Trailside Museum has had seven directors:

William H. Carr	1927-1944
John C. Orth	1946-1955
John J. Kenney	1955-1970
John H. Mead	1972-1987
John Yurus	1987-1988
John Focht	1988-2005
Edwin McGowan	2005-

THE NEW YORK-
NEW JERSEY
TRAIL CONFERENCE

During the early years of the twentieth century, a number of organized groups actively promoted hiking. These groups (and the dates they were founded) were:

Torrey Botanical Club - 1868
Fresh Air Club (New York Athletic Club) - 1877
Paterson Rambling Club - September 15, 1904
Appalachian Mountain Club (N.Y. Chapter) - 1911
Tramp and Trail Club - September 11, 1914
Green Mountain Club (N.Y. Section) - 1915
Inkowa Club for Women - 1915
Nature Friends -
Boy Scouts and Girl Scouts -

Newspapers, such as the *New York Evening Post* and the *New York Times*, devoted much space to walking and hiking, especially after the formation in 1910 of the Bear Mountain-Harriman State Parks. Already by 1913 the Boy Scouts were camping at Car Pond (Lake Stahahe), and in 1917 they made their headquarters at Lake Kanawauke. By the time Major Welch published his first trail map in 1920, all those clubs had developed leaders who were quite familiar with hiking routes in the Highlands and Ramapos.

In the *New York Evening Post* for Friday, August 27, 1920, Meade C. Dobson of the Fresh Air Club described the new Park map and proposed to the walking clubs that they cooperate with the Park Commission to develop new hiking trails. Dobson was an engineer and Boy Scout executive who later chaired the New York Chapter of the Adirondack Mountain Club.

With the cooperation of Major William A. Welch, General Manager of the Park, a meeting was held at 8:15 p.m. on October 5, 1920, in the log cabin atop the Abercrombie and Fitch building in Manhattan. The object of the meeting was to organize a Palisades Interstate Park Trail Conference. Those present included: Major W.A. Welch; Edward F. Brown, Superintendent of Camps; Albert Britt of Outdoor Publishing Co.; Meade C. Dobson of the Boy Scouts; and Raymond H. Torrey, Editor of the *New York Evening Post* Outings Page.

Also present were representatives of the various hiking clubs and other interested parties: Appalachian Mountain Club (William W. Bell, James D. Merriman, Sidney E. Morse and Dr. Mary Goddard Potter); Fresh Air Club (Mortimer Bishop, James T. Horn, Frederick D. Ilgen and Benjamin F. Seaver); Green Mountain Club (J. Ashton Allis, Major William D. Ennis, Prof. Will S. Monroe and George F. Parmelee); Tramp and Trail Club (Elizabeth G. Baldwin, E. Cecil Earle, Frank Place, Jr. and A.B. Malcolmson); Associated Mountain Clubs (LeRoy Jeffers); League of Walkers (Dr. George J. Fisher) and New York State College of Forestry (Dean F.F. Moon).

Albert Britt was asked to act as chairman of the meeting. He spoke briefly on the need for new trails, and then appointed Meade C. Dobson as secretary. After much discussion of the need for trails, and suggestions for trail requirements, Dr. George Fisher moved that the chairman appoint a committee to study the problems and report back with definite proposals. The committee later appointed by Mr. Britt included J. Ashton Allis, William W. Bell, Albert Britt, Meade C. Dobson, Dr. George J. Fisher, Frederick Ilgen, LeRoy Jeffers, Dean F.F. Moon and Edgar D. Stone.

The chairman was empowered to appoint a chairman of a Committee on Camps and Shelters. Dr. Monroe was later appointed to this post. It also was decided to have a Committee on Ways and Means.

Because the fall was the best time for scouting and blazing trails, the new Conference got busy immediately. They elected Major Welch as their permanent chairman and Raymond H. Torrey as secretary. The first trail to be tackled, proposed by Major Welch, was the one from Tuxedo to Jones Point, later called the Ramapo-Dunderberg Trail (R-D). On May 6, 1921, Torrey reported that the trail was practically complete. A second trail, from Mt. Ivy to Tuxedo, was proposed for the summer of 1921 (it was started in 1923). Actually, the next Conference trail was the Timp-Torne Trail (built in the fall/winter of 1921-22), which was regarded as a branch of the R-D. Another branch, started in the summer of 1922, was the Fingerboard-Storm King Trail.

During the years 1920-23, the Boy Scouts, under Chief H.A. Gordon, and led by Archibald T. Shorey of Brooklyn, were building their 35-mile White Bar trail system.

The next big event in Trail Conference history was the proposal by Benton MacKaye to build a trail from Maine to Georgia along the Appalachian ridges. His plan was described by Torrey in the *New York Evening Post* of April 7, 1922. It was quickly adopted by the Palisades Interstate Park Trail Conference as their main project.

Because the new trail would go through two states from the Connecti-
cut line to the Delaware River, the Conference was reorganized on April
25, 1922 as the New York-New Jersey Trail Conference (*N.Y. Post*, 4/28/22).
Twenty organizations became members. The officers of the new Confer-
ence were: W.A. Welch, Chairman; W.W. Bell (AMC), Vice-Chairman for
New York; C.P. Wilbur (State Fire Warden), Vice-Chairman for New Jersey;
J. Ashton Allis (ADK), Trails Committee; Frank Place (Tramp and Trail
Club), Publicity; and Raymond H. Torrey (GMC), Secretary.

There was great enthusiasm for the new task. J.A. Allis and his Trail
Committee immediately started scouting a route for the Appalachian
Trail (AT). By October 7, 1923, the AT had been completed through Bear
Mountain-Harriman Park (the Bear Mountain Bridge was opened on November 27, 1924), and the trail makers concentrated on extending the
route north and south. During this period, the Tuxedo-Mt. Ivy Trail was
marked (1923) and the Suffern-Bear Mountain Trail (1924-27) was begun.

On March 2-3, 1925, the Appalachian Trail Conference (ATC) was
formed in Washington, D.C. Major W.A. Welch was elected Chairman;
Raymond Torrey became Treasurer. During this period, Welch and Torrey
became active in the national park movement as members of a commission to study extensions of the national parks. Because of his increasing
commitments, Welch relinquished his active ATC role in 1927 to Judge
Arthur Perkins. In 1928, Welch became Honorary Chairman and J.A. Allis
became Treasurer of ATC.

Back in Harriman Park, hikers were becoming concerned over the lack
of maintenance on the trails they had made. In 1928, Jack Spivack of the
New York Ramblers (organized on October 25, 1923) suggested that trails
should be assigned to hiking clubs for maintenance. Some clubs began
to volunteer: the Green Mountain Club asked for the Arden-Surebridge
Trail; the New York Ramblers took the Seven Hills Trail; and the Catskill
Mountain Club took the Fingerboard-Storm King Trail.

On April 21, 1931, Bill Burton of the Green Mountain Club called a
meeting of metropolitan hiking clubs to discuss uniform standards of
trail marking. This meeting turned out to be a reorganization of the New
York-New Jersey Trail Conference, which since 1925 had in effect been a
branch of the Appalachian Trail Conference. Raymond Torrey was chosen
as Chairman; Angelique Rivolier of the Inkowa Outdoor Club became Secretary. A committee on methods of trail marking was led by Bill Burton;
another committee on allocation of trail work among the hiking clubs

was chaired by Frank Place.

In June 1931, the new Conference issued its first handbook on trail building and maintenance. The color system in use by the New York State Conservation Department was adopted: red for east-west trails, blue for north-south trails, and yellow for diagonal trails.

In 1938, the Trail Conference was stunned by the death of their leader, Raymond Torrey. In that year, Frank Place became Chairman; J. Ashton Allis, Treasurer; and Richmond Barton, Secretary. Bill Hoeferlin, who became Conference Secretary in 1939, began publishing a monthly subscription newsletter, "Walking News," to replace Torrey's *New York Evening Post* column, "The Long Brown Path."

A new constitution for the Conference was adopted on February 4, 1942. On December 6, 1944, Joseph Bartha was named head of the Trail Patrol (which had been formed under J.A. Allis in 1940). He continued that activity until December 5, 1951, when he became 80 years old. He was replaced by Bill Burton, who was then 70.

In April 1958, the Conference became incorporated in New York State. In November 1963, it began publishing a newsletter for its members, which in 1965 was named the *Trail Walker*. Rosa Gottfried, who proposed this newsletter, was its first editor. Harry Nees was then the President of the Conference. The lead article in 1965 blasted Consolidated Edison's plan to build a pumped storage power plant at Storm King Mountain. That issue also announced the first Litter Day, organized by Elizabeth Levers. In 1976, the Trail Walker adopted the present newspaper format.

The Conference had 35 member clubs in 1969, maintaining 600 miles of trails. In that year, new by-laws provided for individual memberships (Class C members). In January 1973, the Conference took an office at 15 East 40th Street, New York City, and the following year hired Bob Parnes as part-time Executive Director. In November 1975, Jim Robinson became the first full-time Executive Director. Subsequent Executive Directors include Albert "Cap" Field, Madeline Dennis and JoAnn Dolan. Since 2001, Edward Goodell has served the Conference as Executive Director.

An early contribution to the hiking community was the *New York Walk Book* by Torrey, Place and Dickinson, first published in 1923. Revised editions appeared in 1934, 1936, 1951, 1971, 1984, 2001 and 2005. Beginning with the 1998 edition, a separate *New Jersey Walk Book*, which covers trails in New Jersey, has been published.

PRESIDENTS AND CHAIRS OF
NEW YORK-NEW JERSEY TRAIL CONFERENCE

1. 1920-1931 Major William A. Welch (1868-1941)
2. 1931-1938 Raymond Torrey (1880-1938)
3. 1938-1941 Frank Place (1881-1959)
4. 1941-1945 William Burton (1881-1966)
5. 1945-1947 Murray H. Stevens
6. 1947-1950 Ridsdale Ellis (1887-1955)
7. 1950-1951 Mortimer Bloom
8. 1951-1953 Ridsdale Ellis (1887-1955)
9. 1953-1955 John Coggeshall (d. 1960)
10. 1955-1956 Carl Geiser
11. 1956-1961 Samuel Wilkinson (d. 1973)
12. 1961-1964 Harry Nees (d. 1989)
13. 1964-1970 George Zoebelein (d. 2001)
14. 1970-1972 Elizabeth Levers (d. 1998)
15. 1972-1974 John Danielsen (d. 1998)
16. 1974-1975 George Zoebelein (d. 2001)
17. 1975-1976 Arthur J. Paul (d. 1988)
18. 1976-1978 Walter D. Houck
19. 1978-1984 Donald B. Derr
20. 1984-1987 Richard J. Kavalek
21. 1987-1999 H. Neil Zimmerman
22. 1999-2001 Gary Haugland
23. 2001-2007 Jane Daniels
24. 2007-2010 Robert Boysen

At present, the office of the Trail Conference is at 156 Ramapo Valley Road, Mahwah, N.J. 07430. The Conference, which now includes over 100 outdoors and hiking clubs and over 10,000 individual members, maintains over 1,700 miles of marked trails extending from the Connecticut border to the Delaware Water Gap. Conference activities are largely carried out by volunteers who work together

- to build and maintain trails and trail shelters in New York and New Jersey
- to promote the public interest in hiking and conservation
- to protect wild lands, wildlife and places of natural beauty.

Current projects of the Conference include extending and relocating the Highlands Trail in New York and New Jersey and the Long Path in New York, local management planning for the Appalachian Trail in New York and New Jersey, and the construction of a new route for the Appalachian Trail on Bear Mountain. The Conference has also been active in the relocation of portions of the Appalachian Trail off roads and onto a protected trail corridor, and in the preservation of Sterling Forest.

Conference publications include the *New York Walk Book*, the *New Jersey Walk Book*, the *Appalachian Trail Guide for New York-New Jersey*, *Hiking Long Island*, *Kittatinny Trails*, *Scenes and Walks in the Northern Shawangunks*, and *Walkable Westchester*, and maps for Harriman/Bear Mountain Trails, North Jersey Trails, East Hudson Trails, West Hudson Trails, Kittatinny Trails, South Taconic Trails, the Shawangunks, the Catskills, Sterling Forest and the Hudson Palisades. It also publishes the *Trail Walker*, a bimonthly newspaper for members.

About Measuring Trails

NOTE: The introduction to the "About Measuring Trails" chapter was written by Bill Myles and, for historical reasons, is retained in this edition exactly as it appeared in the 1999 edition of the book. The list of measured trails and the names of those who measured them is also unchanged from the 1999 edition. Most relocations of marked trails made since then have been measured by Daniel Chazin with a wheel. For many of the unmarked trails, GPS measurements by John Timm have been used as the basis of the measurements given in this edition of the book.

Back in 1943, the Trail Conference made plans to measure by surveyor's wheel all the unmeasured marked trails in Bear Mountain/Harriman Park (*Walking News*, Nov. 1943). The measurements were made on 25 day trips between March and June 1944 by Bill Hoeferlin, Joseph Bartha, Paul Schubert and others. The result of their efforts was Bill Hoeferlin's *Harriman Park Trail Guide*, published in October 1944. Seven editions of Bill's guide were issued through 1976. It served Harriman hikers well.

When the present author first planned a book on Harriman trails, it was clear that many changes had taken place in the trails, and that the measurements in Bill Hoeferlin's guide could no longer be relied upon. To avoid all the work of remeasuring the trails, the author simply measured the trails on the Conference's Harriman-Bear Mountain Trails maps (then designated Maps #3 and #4).

When Dan Chazin, the editor, received the text of the book, the trail lengths set forth in the manuscript had been computed by map measurements. Now the editor (bless him!) is a man who places great importance on precision. He himself had previously measured the Appalachian Trail with a wheel, and my map-measure was over 2.5 miles less than his wheel figure. So, as part of the editorial process, Dan Chazin, together with other volunteers he recruited, have measured many of the trails, using surveying measuring wheels. All of the marked trails were measured, as have many of the unmarked trails. The following table sets forth the names of those who measured each trail:

Anthony Wayne Trail—Bill and Mary Ann Pruehsner; Robert and Lois Pruehsner

Appalachian Trail–Daniel Chazin
Arden-Surebridge Trail–Daniel Chazin
Beech Trail–Bill and Mary Ann Pruehsner
Blue Disc Trail–Dianne Philipps and Duane Nealon
Bottle Cap Trail–Daniel Chazin; Bill and Mary Ann Pruehsner
Breakneck Mountain Trail–Daniel Chazin
Conklins Crossing Trail–Bill and Mary Ann Pruehsner
Cornell Mine Trail–Bill and Mary Ann Pruehsner
Diamond Mountain-Tower Trail–Daniel Chazin; Bill and Mary Ann Pruehsner
Dunning Trail–Daniel Chazin
Fawn Trail–Bill and Robert Pruehsner
Hillburn-Torne-Sebago Trail–Daniel Chazin
Hurst Trail–Daniel Chazin
Kakiat Trail–Dianne Philipps and Duane Nealon
Lichen Trail–Bill and Mary Ann Pruehsner
Long Path–Wayne Richter, Daniel Chazin and Doug Broadbent
Major Welch Trail–Bill Pruehsner
Menomine Trail–Daniel Chazin
Nurian Trail–Daniel Chazin and Torey Adler
Pine Meadow Trail–Torey Adler
Popolopen Gorge Trail–Bill and Mary Ann Pruehsner
Raccoon Brook Hills Trail–Daniel Chazin
Ramapo-Dunderberg Trail–Bill and Mary Ann Pruehsner
Red Arrow Trail–Daniel Chazin
Red Cross Trail–Daniel Chazin
Red Timp Trail–Daniel Chazin
Reeves Brook Trail–Daniel Chazin
Seven Hills Trail–Dianne Philipps and Duane Nealon
Suffern-Bear Mountain Trail–Daniel Chazin; Bill and Mary Ann Pruehsner
Timp-Torne Trail–Daniel Chazin; Bill and Mary Ann Pruehsner
Triangle Trail–Daniel Chazin; Dianne Philipps and Duane Nealon
Tuxedo-Mt. Ivy Trail–Daniel Chazin and Torey Adler
Victory Trail–Torey Adler; Bill and Mary Ann Pruehsner
White Bar Trail–Daniel Chazin; Bill and Mary Ann Pruehsner
White Cross Trail–Torey Adler
1777 Trail–Bill and Mary Ann Pruehsner

1777E Trail–Bill and Mary Ann Pruehsner
1777W Trail–Bill and Mary Ann Pruehsner
1779 Trail–Bill and Mary Ann Pruehsner
Arden Road–Bill Pruehsner
Beechy Bottom East Road–Bill and Mary Ann Pruehsner
Bockberg Trail (part)–Daniel Chazin
Bockey Swamp Trail–Daniel Chazin and Jonathan Goldstein
Buck Trail (part)–Daniel Chazin
Crooked Road–Daniel Chazin; Bill and Mary Ann Pruehsner
Dean Trail–Daniel Chazin
Hasenclever Road–Torey Adler
Iron Mountain Trail (part)–Torey Adler
Island Pond Road–Daniel Chazin
Jones Trail–Daniel Chazin
Pine Meadow Road (part)–Daniel Chazin
Sherwood Path–Daniel Chazin
Sloatsburg Trail–Dianne Philipps and Duane Nealon
Stony Brook Trail–Torey Adler
Surebridge Mine Road–Daniel Chazin
Woodtown Road–Daniel Chazin
Cranberry Mountain Trail–Daniel Chazin
Hasenclever Mountain Trail–Daniel Chazin
Rockhouse Mountain Trail–Daniel Chazin
North "Ski" Trail–Daniel Chazin
North-South Connector–Daniel Chazin
South "Ski" Trail–Daniel Chazin
Timp Pass Road–Daniel Chazin
Doodletown Bridle Path–Bill and Mary Ann Pruehsner

INDEX

Page numbers in **bold** refer to the primary description of the trail or other feature.

We invite you to join

the organization of hikers, environmentalists, and volunteers whose skilled efforts have produced this edition of *Harriman Trails: A Guide and History*.

The **New York-New Jersey Trail Conference**, founded in 1920, is a federation of member clubs and individuals dedicated to providing recreational hiking opportunities in the New York-New Jersey region, and to representing the interests and concerns of the hiking community. The Trail Conference is a volunteer-directed public service organization committed to:

- Developing, building, and maintaining hiking trails.
- Protecting hiking trail lands through support and advocacy.
- Educating the public in the responsible use of trails and the natural environment.

Join now and as a member:

- You will receive the *Trail Walker*, a bi-monthly source of news, information, and events concerning area trails and hiking. The *Trail Walker* lists many hikes in the New York-New Jersey metropolitan area, led by some of our more than 100 member hiking clubs.
- You are entitled to purchase our authoritative maps and books at significant discounts. These highly accurate, up-to-date trail maps, printed on durable Tyvek, and our informative guidebooks enable you to hike with assurance throughout the region.
- You are also entitled to discounts of 10% (and sometimes more!) at most local outdoor stores and at many mountain inns and lodges.
- Most importantly, you will become part of a community of volunteer activists with similar passions and ideas.

Your membership helps give us the clout to protect and maintain more trails. As a member of the **New York-New Jersey Trail Conference**, you will be helping to ensure that public access to nature will continue to expand.

New York-New Jersey Trail Conference
156 Ramapo Valley Road ♦ Mahwah, NJ 07430 ♦ (201) 512-9348
www.nynjtc.org ♦ info@nynjtc.org

Other Hiking Books Available From the Trail Conference!

Authoritative Hiking Maps and Books by the Volunteers Who Maintain the Trails

WALKABLE WESTCHESTER

First Edition (2009), Jane and Walt Daniels

A comprehensive guide to trails throughout Westchester County, this book covers over 180 parks and preserves, with almost 600 miles of trails. It includes historical information and sketch maps for most parks, and it indicates which parks are suitable for the handicapped, bikes, horses, dogs and cross-country skiing. The parks are arranged by size, and a locator map is provided. Information on public transportation is also included.

sc. 428 p. 6 x 9, B&W photos and maps

NEW YORK WALK BOOK

Seventh Edition, Revised (2005), Edited by Daniel Chazin

The hikers' "bible" since 1923, it is still the same indispensable regional reference book. Full trail descriptions with maps, sections on geology, history, hiking tips, and much more. The magnificent sketches include many new ones by Jack Fagan. This last printing has updated trail descriptions and completely revised chapters for Black Rock Forest, Storm King, and Sterling Forest.

sc. 484 p. 5 3/8 x 8 1/8, B&W illustrations, full color maps

HIKING THE JERSEY HIGHLANDS

First Edition (2007), George Petty

A new illustrated guide to 35 hikes in the Highlands of New Jersey. There are introductory chapters on the Highlands' history and preservation, its geology, plants, and wildlife, with a special 16-page insert of color photos of wildflowers seen along the trails. The hikes are graded from starter hikes for beginners, to challenges for experienced hikers, with a trail map for each.

sc. 420 p. 5 3/8 x 8 1/8, B&W photos and full color wildflower section

Visit www.nynjtc.org—for more information and newest products!